THE ROUGH GUIDE TO

The Beatles

Third edition

by
Chris Ingham

www.roughguides.com

Credits

The Rough Guide to The Beatles

Editor: Matthew Milton
Layout: Michelle Bhatia
Proofreading: Diane Margolis
Production: Rebecca Short, Vicky Baldwin

Rough Guides Reference

Director: Andrew Lockett
Editors: Kate Berens, Peter Buckley, Tracy Hopkins, Matthew Milton, Joe Staines, Ruth Tidball

Picture Credits
Alamy: 3, 61, 64, 175
Corbis: inside cover, 129, 149, 153, 154, 159, 180, 225, 231, 234, 239, 241, 248, 251, 292, 301, 310
Getty Images: 6, 9, 12, 15, 22, 38, 44, 45, 56, 68, 92, 108, 110, 163, 217, 275, 298
Mersey Partnership (TMP): 253, 261, 265
Moviestore Collection: 87, 141

Publishing information

This third edition published November 2009 by
Rough Guides Ltd, 80 Strand, London WC2R 0RL
375 Hudson St, New York 10014, USA
Email: mail@roughguides.com

Distributed by the Penguin Group:
Penguin Books Ltd, 80 Strand, London WC2R 0RL
Penguin Putnam, Inc., 375 Hudson Street, New York 10014, USA
Penguin Group (Australia), 250 Camberwell Road, Camberwell, Victoria 3124, Australia
Penguin Books Canada Ltd, 90 Eglinton Avenue East, Suite 700, Toronto, Ontario, Canada M4P 2Y3
Penguin Group (New Zealand), Cnr Rosedale and Airborne Roads, Albany, Auckland, New Zealand

Printed in Singapore

336 pages; includes index

A catalogue record for this book is available from the British Library

ISBN: 978-1-84836-525-4

1 3 5 7 9 8 6 4 2

Contents

Introduction

What is it with the world and The Beatles? The passion of what Derek Taylor once called "the world's greatest romance" shows no signs of fading. Thirty-one years after they ceased to exist, their *1* greatest hits album made the group the biggest selling recording act of 2000; Cirque Du Soleil's *Beatlemusic* and dance show *Love* has done standing-room-only business in Las Vegas since 2006; and in 2009, the long-delayed appearance of the remastered albums and the Beatles *Rockband* video game has made the 40th anniversary of the Beatles' split another amazing year for the Fab Four.

Nostalgia is obviously part of it. The 1960s – the decade in which The Beatles spearheaded so much of consequence in popular music and culture – was undoubtedly a time filled with possibility for the young, classless and free. Now, hearing Paul McCartney give *Sgt Pepper's* "Fixing A Hole" its first ever live airing on his 2005 US tour, and likewise "A Day In The Life" in 2008 in Liverpool (with Yoko Ono and Olivia Harrison singing along), it's all someone who grew up with their music can do not to burst into tears.

But it's the endurance of the music too. From the early-days appeal of a good tune, an upbeat sentiment and a dash of genius to the emotionally complex, musically mature work of their middle and late period, The Beatles represent one of the few times in musical history when the most popular was also the best. That much of what they achieved amounts to the best pop has had to offer is now a rarely disputed given.

However, there is a bit of a love-hate thing going on. Generation after generation of pop group, guitar band and singer-songwriter remain in thrall and indebted to The Beatles' achievements, while very few even approach their ingenuity, stylistic dexterity and – this is sometimes overlooked – their instinctive musical technique. Then, even if they do, they're often accused of being Beatles-esque, as if that were a bad thing. Truth is, after 1970 pop music didn't get much better and for the most part it got considerably worse. So anyone who cares about how good pop music can be *has* to care about The Beatles. What musicians have to do to get out from under their shadow is one of the artistic challenges of the age.

The Rough Guide To The Beatles is your one-stop shop for the remarkable story of the group and beyond, the essential songs, the films they made, the places they played, the people who were nearly Beatles but not quite, some trivial but fascinating bits and bobs and a few tips on where to go next. That'll do for a start.

Chris Ingham

Acknowledgements

Condensing the lure and lore of The Beatles into a Rough Guide would have been impossible without the research and insights of the myriad writers who have blazed their own particular trail of Beatle info: Mark Lewisohn, Keith Badman, Bill Harry, Alan Clayson, Ian Macdonald, Paul Du Noyer, Hunter Davies, Ian Peel, Geoffrey Guiliano, Alenn J. Wiener, Barry Miles, Philip Norman, Joe Cushley, Ray Coleman, Albert Goldman, Walter Everett, Tim Riley, Roy Carr, Tony Tyler, Steve Turner, Jon Savage, Charles Shaar Murray, Michael Braun, Derek Taylor, Johnny Black, Mat Snow, Jim Irvin, David Fricke, Bill DeMain, Ray Connelly and Mark Hertsgaard. There are more but hey, you know...

I once spoke to Paul McCartney on the phone for half an hour and chatted with Yoko Ono in the Dakota for a morning. They seemed nice. Among the commissioning editors who have encouraged my aspirations to journalistic adequacy over the years are Paul Du Noyer, Barney Hoskyns, Mat Snow, Pat Gilbert, Paul Trynka, Sylvie Simmons, Keith Cameron, Jenny Bulley, Paul Lester, Chris Hunt, Jon Bennett, David Pesheck and Jim Irvin. Bless you all. For CDs and books, thanks to Shoshanna Gilbert and Jon Bills at Parlophone and Jane Richardson at Music Sales.

Of my family and friends: between them, my parents and Auntie Doris and Uncle Ken had several key records, so for that, among other things, I love them; Tracy wonders whether The Beatles were actually "very nice people", Polly thinks they're "overrated" and Al has got a bit of Ringo's drag about him; Andy Brown (bass), implausibly, loves The Beatles and Anthony Braxton equally; Kevin Flanagan (sax) remains sceptical, though thinks Junk is a nice tune; Russell Morgan (drums) does a reasonable, if puzzled, facsimile of Ringo's drum-fill entrance on "Hey Jude"; Mike Harris (bass) once asked what the "fucking awful' music was playing at a party (it was *Sgt Pepper*); Joe Cushley (harmonica) has recently learned to enjoy the post-Quarrymen output and lent his peculiar expertise to the bizarre covers list.

Thanks to editor Matt Milton for careful, clever work and his astute suggestion that the clause count for any given sentence should be kept down to single figures. Special thanks to Jim Irvin for being too busy to do this himself, but not too busy to share it with me, supplying several chunks of text and 90% of the encouragement. Special thanks also to my live-in family who – now that I have emerged from the distracted, irritable netherworld of full-time authordom – don't quite know what to do with me. I hope they know how much I love them.

The Rough Guide to

The Beatles

by Chris Ingham

Part 1: The Life

The early years: 1957–62

When Ivan Vaughan suggested to his 15-year-old school friend Paul McCartney that he might want to come to St Peter's Church fete in Woolton, on Saturday, July 6, 1957 to see his mate John Lennon play in his skiffle group, The Quarry Men, he added as further inducement not that the event would be the pivotal moment in shaping the direction of popular music for the remainder of the twentieth century and beyond, but that it might be a good place to pick up girls.

It may well have been, but that afternoon McCartney was more interested in the group playing in the field behind the church, enthusiastically slapping and scratching their way through the Del-Vikings' tune "Come Go With Me". The 16-year-old Lennon was clearly the leader of the bedraggled combo (Colin Hanton on drums, Pete Shotton on washboard, Rod Davis on banjo, Eric Griffiths on guitar and Len Garry on tea-chest bass). Playing rough-house guitar and singing, his energetic vocals were impressively unencumbered by his sketchy knowledge of the lyrics – he just made up his own.

Vaughan introduced Paul to the group in the church hall, where they were also to play for the evening dance. They had a few beers while McCartney demonstrated his comparatively adept upside-down (left-handed) guitar playing, sang Gene Vincent's **Be Bop A Lula** (one of Lennon's favourites) and surprised them all by knowing all the words to Eddie Cochran's **Twenty Flight Rock**. Most impressive of all, he not only knew how to tune a guitar – Lennon's gang had been paying a neighbour to tune theirs – but he also knew some proper guitar chord shapes (whereas Lennon had been struggling by on the banjo chords his mother had taught him).

While John was aware that this talented youngster, who could also play a bit of piano and **When The Saints Come Marching In** on trumpet, was an obvious threat to his leadership, he was also convinced McCartney could strengthen the group. Paul also had an advocate in Eric Griffiths, who enthused to John: "Paul's so good. He'll contribute a lot to the group. We need him with us." Two weeks later, Pete Shotton bumped into Paul whilst out riding his bike and, as all had agreed, invited McCartney to join The Quarry Men. Paul accepted.

Lennon, like most musicians of his generation, had been inspired by the UK skiffle craze but

The not-yet-Fab three, outside the McCartneys' house on Forthlin Road, c.1960

was increasingly enamoured of the rock'n'roll of **Elvis Presley**. At **The Cavern** – a Liverpool jazz club based in the dank music cellar on Mathew Street – skiffle was just about tolerated, but rock'n'roll was another matter. During The Quarry Men's Cavern debut in August 1957, Lennon insisted on subjecting a sceptical audience (and even band – Rod Davis hated rock'n'roll and unfortunately McCartney was on holiday at the time) to his versions of **Hound Dog** and **Blue Suede Shoes**. The owner sent an angry note to the stage – "Cut out the bloody rock" – and apart from one more engagement in January 1958 the boys didn't play the venue again for over three years.

The arrival of McCartney in The Quarry Men coincided with and assisted the band's natural evolution into a rock'n'roll outfit. They skiffled on for a few months but by March 1958 McCartney's chum George Harrison had been recruited into the band and their repertoire soon expanded to include Carl Perkins and Buddy Holly numbers. Lennon had a few "anti-kid" reservations (George was only 14) but, as Paul pointed out, "By God he can play Raunchy well". Harrison's ability to play Bill Justis' twangy guitar hit had won John over. Shortly afterwards, in mid-1958, The Quarry Men recorded a demonstration disc of Holly's **That'll Be The Day** and **In Spite Of All The Danger**, an early McCartney composition.

Meanwhile Lennon and McCartney had taken to skipping classes (Liverpool Institute in Paul's case, Liverpool Art College in John's) to set up in Paul's front room for the afternoon while Paul's father Jim was at work, smoke tea leaves in a pipe (McCartney: "We'd think we were right little rebels") and write songs. Sitting opposite one another and armed with acoustic guitars, right-handed Lennon mirrored left-handed McCartney and, mutually inspired, they hammered out their juvenilia. They scribbled the lyrics and occasional musical reminder in a school notebook, but the unspoken rule was that if they couldn't remember the tune the next day,

The skiffle explosion

The word "skiffle" – a slang term loosely translatable as "makeshift"– was coined to describe the impromptu jazz heard at black American house parties in the 1920s. Skiffle music was mostly spirituals, folk blues and nineteenth-century pop songs, played on whatever was to hand – usually acoustic guitar or banjo – with the rhythm kept on such items as a **washboard** (a corrugated zinc surface usually struck with thimbled fingers) and a crude double bass made from string and a broom handle pushed into a tea chest. This was the form seized upon by British jazz bands looking for ways to make themselves sound more "authentic". Skiffle sets were a useful way of keeping dancehall punters amused while the main band took a break, and they were common in the late 1940s and early 1950s. Chris Barber's band, with British star **Ken Colyer**, featured a skiffle interlude fronted by the band's hyperactive, reedy-voiced banjo player, Lonnie Donegan. A Donegan track from Barber's album, *New Orleans Joys*, called **Rock Island Line**, was an enormous hit when released as a single in 1956 and kick-started a huge craze for skiffle among postwar adolescents spurred by the music's energy and accessibility, qualities echoed in the punk boom 21 years later. It was this spirit, that anyone could pick up such instruments, learn a few simple songs and start bashing them out, that moved John Lennon to form The Quarry Men and begin performing within weeks.

it couldn't have been any good. The (self-perpetuated) myth told of over a hundred formative Lennon/McCartney compositions written in this early period. However, while unheard songs such as **That's My Woman**, **Just Fun** and **Thinking Of Linking** have become part of the mythical "lost Beatles canon", McCartney later admitted the number of early songs was considerably fewer than the legend.

Lennon suffered an almighty personal tragedy in July 1958 when his mother died after being knocked down by a car outside his Aunt Mimi's house. Though brought up by his aunt, John's relations with his free-spirited mother had recently begun to improve, and he was deeply hurt. Though it was years before he was able to properly express his grief, the bereavement engendered a curious bond between John and Paul, who had lost his own mother to cancer in October 1956.

The Quarry Men were now down to a nucleus of Lennon, McCartney and Harrison. "The rhythm's in the guitars," they explained, when queried about the lack of bassist or drummer. Their next eighteen months were erratic, including a residency at the **Casbah**, a new coffee house and teenage hang-out, and several unsuccessful auditions for talent contests, but there were several long stretches with no bookings at all.

That'll Be The Day/In Spite Of All The Danger

The Quarry Men

Private demo recorded mid-1958; compiled on *Anthology 1*

Recorded direct to disc at a cost of 17 shillings and

sixpence (to have a tape and a disc would have cost £1, which the group baulked at). The only copy was passed around Paul, John, George and Colin Hanton before ending up, forgotten, in the possession of John "Duff" Lowe, sometime piano player with The Quarry Men. His attempt to sell it at Sotheby's in the 1980s was halted when Paul McCartney stepped in and did a deal for an undisclosed figure (Lowe allows that "it was more than £5000", the sum expected at auction). With a misty audio fidelity closer to a 1908 recording than a 1958 one, it's nevertheless an interesting document. **That'll Be The Day** features a spirited quasi-impersonation of Buddy Holly from Lennon and, already, some typically detailed harmony work from McCartney – as does **In Spite Of All The Danger**, which Lennon also sings. "Danger" was a McCartney-penned doo-wop ballad (clearly inspired by Elvis's **Trying To Get To You**) but was credited on the handwritten label (and, curiously, on *Anthology 1*) as McCartney/Harrison: an ingenuous acknowledgement of 16-year-old George's keen but not inappropriate guitar solo.

1960: Don't fear the Reeperbahn

"Where are we going, boys?"
"To the top."
"Where's that?"
"To the toppermost of the poppermost!"

Beatle battle cry of the early 1960s

By 1960 the group had acquired a bassist, **Stuart Sutcliffe**, who was John's best friend from art college and a talented painter. With John in agreement, they renamed the group The Beatals in homage to Buddy Holly's Crickets. Lacking any particular musical ability, Sutcliffe would turn his back to the audience to hide his fretboard fumblings. Despite this, local promoter Allan Williams showed an interest in the band, got them a drummer (Tommy Moore, an older player) and although it was suggested they change their name to Long John and the Silver Beetles, it was shortened at John's insistence to just The Silver Beetles.

They failed a Williams-arranged audition for London promotion giant Larry Parnes to be the backing band for Billy Fury. Instead they were booked backing Liverpudlian singer **Johnny Gentle** on a seven-date Scottish tour during May 1960. It was a dispiriting, badly organized affair and on their return to Liverpool Tommy Moore left the band in the middle of a string of June dates (including residencies at the Jacaranda Coffee Bar and the Grosvenor Ballroom, Wallasey) for the security of a job at the Garston bottle works.

By a combination of promotional tenacity and good luck, Williams had got to know Bruno Koschmider, a German club owner. Williams had provided Merseyside group **Derry and the Seniors** for a successful residency at the smart Kaiserkeller in Hamburg, and Koschmider had been so encouraged that he asked Williams for another combo to revamp his failing strip joint, the Indra, as a new rock'n'roll club. After ascertaining that neither Rory Storm and the Hurricanes, nor Cass and the Cassanovas, nor **Gerry and the Pacemakers** were available, Williams offered it to The Silver Beatles (as they were now spelled) on condition that they found themselves a drummer.

At a loose end one Saturday night in August 1960 due to a cancelled gig, the four boys chanced upon a handsome eighteen-year-old pounding a brand new kit for resident band The Blackjacks in the Casbah Coffee Club. The drummer was Pete Best, son of the Casbah's owner, Mona Best. With a perfunctory audition, Pete was in. The "Silver" tag was dropped from the name and, on August 16, The Beatles piled into Alan Williams' van and went to Hamburg.

When Derry and the Seniors heard that it was The Beatles coming to Hamburg to capitalize on the scene they had created, they were disappointed. "I just didn't think they'd be suitable," remembered saxophonist Howie Casey. "[But] when they did turn up they were brilliant, they'd come on in leaps and bounds ... they were really doing it, they were great, no two ways about it."

While staying on the **Reeperbahn**, Hamburg's notorious red-light district, The Beatles had to put up with grim living conditions, bunking up behind the projection screen at the Koschmider-owned Bambi-Filmkunsttheatre. They discovered alcohol, drugs and sex. Spurred on by Koschmider's cries of "Mach schau!" ("Make a show of it!"), they performed gruelling sets of four and a half hours on week days, six hours at the weekend. They found within themselves a riotous rock band which could mach one hell of a schau for the excitement-hungry Hamburg audiences. Playing old standards, huge lists of Little Richard, Fats Domino and Everly Brothers material, and an endless version of Ray Charles's **What'd I Say**, they were getting tougher and tighter by the week. As Lennon would later say, they didn't grow up in

The Fab Five *"mach shau"* in Hamburg

Liverpool, they grew up in Hamburg.

Although they were popular with the drunken sailors, good-time girls and tough-guy bouncers of the late-night rock clubs, The Beatles also appealed to a group of students and artists known as The Exis, clad in black and intellectually and existentially inclined. Three of them – Klaus Voorman, his girlfriend **Astrid Kirchherr** and friend Jürgen Vollmer – were regular, entranced observers of The Beatles' show. They soon became friends. Astrid supplied the boys with Preludin, a slimming pill and an "upper" (Astrid: "My mummy knew someone at the chemist") which could get them through their long, chaotic sets. She also took some early, iconic photos of the band, and fell in love with Stuart.

The Indra engagement was cut short by noise complaints, and the Beatles relocated to the Kaiserkeller on October 4, where they alternated sets with Rory Storm and the Hurricanes, whose drummer was one Ringo Starr. They also took to jamming with Tony Sheridan and the Jets, who were appearing at a new Hamburg club, The Top Ten. Furious at The Beatles' appearances for a rival, which he considered a betrayal, Koschmider gave the group notice. Then, in November, George Harrison was deported for performing underage, followed closely by Paul and Pete, who were reported to the police by Koschmider after setting fire to some wall tapestry (and in some reports, some condoms) to see their way around the Bambi cinema in the dark. John returned on his own in December 1960, leaving Stuart behind with Astrid.

Back in Liverpool, ex-Blackjack **Chas Newby** stood in on bass for a couple of weeks and Mona booked them into a couple of Casbah gigs. On December 27 at Litherland Town Hall the Hamburg-toughened Beatles delivered a scorching set, and the local buzz about the "Fabulous Beatles" began.

Hallelujah, I Love Her So/You'll Be Mine/ Cayenne

Private rehearsal; recorded 1960; currently available on *Anthology 1*

With four guitars and no drummer, The Beatles' rehearsal of Eddie Cochran's version of Ray Charles's **Hallelujah** is certainly enthusiastic, but suffers perhaps from a certain rhythmic indiscipline. **You'll Be Mine** is a spoof of an Ink Spots style breast-beater with the zany results comparable to *The Goon Show*, an anarchic UK radio comedy programme that particularly appealed to Lennon. Clearly recorded for the group's own amusement, there's just about enough compositional detail amongst the hammy vocals to convince, and it anticipates the oddball satirical sensibility they would return to on "You Know My Name (Look Up The Number")" seven years later. **Cayenne** is an undeveloped, vaguely Shadows-esque minor blues by McCartney, featuring some decent juvenile guitar jamming.

1961: Merseybeat and moptops

"There was an air about them that seemed to say, if you didn't like them, too bad, they couldn't care less."

Paddy Delaney, Cavern bouncer

By early 1961, Paul had moved to bass – George wanted the band to be a four-piece but refused to play bass, as did John – and gigs had started rolling in. Sometimes billed on posters as "direct from Hamburg" (leading audiences to believe, for a while, that they were German) they were now compelled to employ a road manager, and **Neil Aspinall**, a close friend of Pete's, shuttled them from ballroom to town hall to coffee club. Clad in black leather, they served up the same combination of casual stagecraft (eating, smoking and swearing on stage) and wild musical excitement they had perfected in Hamburg. The Beatles began to take their home town by storm, not least by regular appearances at the now beat-friendly **Cavern.**

During a second, band-negotiated stint at the Top Ten Club in Hamburg between April and July 1961 (for which they were threatened with spurious legal action by a hurt Allan Williams), The Beatles backed singer Tony Sheridan on a recording session for the producer and bandleader Bert Kaempfert. "My Bonnie" c/w "The Saints" was released as a single in Germany on Deutsche Gramophon/Polydor. Billed as "by **Tony Sheridan and the Beat Brothers**" ("Beatles" was considered too close to *peedles*, meaning "small penises" in German), the single did well on the local chart.

Soon after they returned to Liverpool, a friend from art college, Bill Harry, began the fortnightly paper **Mersey Beat,** which captured the excitement and added to the vibrancy of the burgeoning Liverpool music scene. When the paper car-

The Beatle haircut

Stuart Sutcliffe, influenced by his girlfriend **Astrid Kirchherr**, had already started styling his hair similarly to the German **Exi** clique, flopping it forward over his forehead instead of greasing it back like a rocker.

Unimpressed at the time, John and Paul changed their minds during a French holiday. When John received £100 from a relative for his 21st birthday in October 1961 he and Paul went to Paris to celebrate, where they met up with **Jürgen Vollmer**, another friend from the artistic, intellectual crowd The Beatles had befriended in Hamburg.

In the mood for a change of look, they persuaded Jürgen to style their hair similarly to his, but leaving it long at the back. The rocker/Exi hybrid became the Beatle haircut. Asked when they got home why they did it, McCartney remembers reasoning, "Well, you know ... hey!" George adopted it. Pete didn't.

Hamburg-tough Lennon with Rickenbacker 325, the Cavern, December 1961

"I can't think why I didn't walk out of the Cavern within a few minutes ... these four ill-presented youths and their untidy hair."

Brian Epstein, 1963

ried the story "Beatles sign recording contract", along with Cavern MC and DJ Bob Wooler's recommendation that the group were "rhythmic revolutionaries", the band's local fame went up a notch. Merseyside fans soon began asking for "My Bonnie" at local record shop N.E.M.S. which, alongside the *Mersey Beat* coverage, piqued the curiosity of the shop's manager, **Brian Epstein.**

Venturing to the Cavern one lunchtime in November 1961, Epstein caught The Beatles in all their leather-clad unruly glory, and was spellbound. After several meetings, he persuaded the cautious but highly flattered group to let him manage them, promising to negotiate better-paid gigs and find them a British record contract. He even convinced the group to adopt smarter stage clothes, firstly sleeveless black jumpers and ties and, before long, suits. By mid-December, he had managed to arrange a rare visit up north by a London A&R man – Mike Smith of **Decca Records** – to the Cavern. Smith was impressed enough to invite the group to London for a test recording.

Studio recordings 1961

AIN'T SHE SWEET/CRY FOR A SHADOW/WHEN THE SAINTS GO MARCHING IN/WHY/IF YOU LOVE ME BABY/SWEET GEORGIA BROWN/MY BONNIE/NOBODY'S CHILD

Recorded June 1961 (and possibly April 1962); "My Bonnie" and "The Saints" released summer 1961; currently available on *The Beatles First! Featuring Tony Sheridan* (Mercury); "My Bonnie", "Ain't She Sweet" and "Cry For A Shadow" also available on *Anthology 1*

There is some confusion over which of these surprisingly well-recorded tracks sung by Tony Sheridan (veteran of the family TV music show *Oh Boy*) actually feature The Beatles.

This certainly hasn't done Polydor Records any harm. Although the group were originally billed as The Beat Brothers on the "My Bonnie" single, several of Sheridan's other backing groups were given the same name on later recordings well into the mid-60s.

Beyond question is the single itself – two unsubtle, rocking arrangements of ancient standards – and also the two tracks The Beatles were allowed to tape sans Sheridan. They had toughened up **Ain't She Sweet** from its easier-going 1958 Gene Vincent version for the Hamburg clubs, and it has a genuine swagger about it, particularly when Lennon's singing. He's already in a different vocal class to the capable but erratic Sheridan, whose musical personality is Elvis one minute, Jerry Lee the next but mostly catch-all rock'n'roll fool.

Cry For A Shadow, credited to Harrison/Lennon, is one of only three instrumentals The Beatles ever recorded (the others being 1965's **Twelve Bar Original**, unreleased until 1995's *Anthology 2*, and 1967's **Flying**, on *Magical Mystery Tour*). It's also a nifty pastiche of The Shadows who, led by Hank Marvin, dominated the UK charts in the early 1960s with their exotic, twangy guitar instrumentals.

The boys do a reasonable job of the doo-wop backing vocals on Sheridan's self-penned **Why** and it could be them on **Sweet Georgia Brown**, although Sheridan's vocal – clearly overdubbed after The

Beatles became famous – muddies the waters. On Jimmy Reed's **If You Love Me Baby** and the traditional **Nobody's Child** only Sheridan's guitar and voice (and, arguably, McCartney's bass and Pete Best's drums) are audible but, as Lennon said of the whole encounter, "it could be anyone".

1962: The Fab Four

"Good God, what've we got 'ere?"

EMI engineer Norman Smith,
upon the arrival of The Beatles at Abbey Road, June 1962

On New Year's Day 1962, The Beatles arrived at Decca Records to record their audition. The fifteen songs The Beatles recorded were selected by Brian Epstein to show off the group's versatility, and ranged from special arrangements of standards (**September In The Rain, The Sheik Of Araby**) to show tunes (**'Til There Was You**) to rockers (**Money**) to Lennon/McCartney originals (**Love Of The Loved, Like Dreamers Do, Hello Little Girl**). After an agonizing four-week wait, Decca eventually rejected The Beatles on the grounds that "guitar groups are on the way out".

Stung but resolute, Brian hawked the Decca tapes elsewhere. He was turned down by Pye and Oriole but, in February 1962, the tapes reached **George Martin**, head of A&R at the EMI label, Parlophone. Martin, while hardly bowled over, could hear some potential – he liked Harrison's guitar playing and McCartney's singing – and agreed to meet them.

In April, The Beatles flew to Germany to fulfil a seven-week engagement at Hamburg's Star Club. They were met at the airport by Astrid Kirchherr, who told them that their old bassist and John's closest friend, Stuart Sutcliffe, had died the previous day of a brain haemorrhage, aged just 21. It was a shock to everyone to lose a friend and contemporary, but for the brash-sensitive John it was another personal tragedy that he could barely make sense of.

Meanwhile, for several weeks George Martin had been "in a meeting", much to Brian Epstein's frustration. One story tells of Epstein threatening to boycott all EMI product at his N.E.M.S. music store unless progress was made with The Beatles. Eventually, on June 6, 1962, The Beatles arrived at EMI Studios on London's **Abbey Road** for what they and Epstein probably assumed was the first session of their new recording contract. In fact it was yet another audition, this time for George Martin. Luckily, Martin was charmed – not so much by their music, which he found a little rough, but by their personal charisma and humour. Feeling he had little to lose, he offered them a paltry deal and authorized their signing as Parlophone recording artists.

Martin had one reservation, however – the "quiet, almost sullen" **Pete Best**. Though his playing was respected in Liverpool, the producer didn't consider Pete's drumming quite good enough to record. This apparently confirmed what the group themselves felt about Pete, whose natural reticence rather excluded him from the witty, exuberant Beatles gang, despite everything they'd been through together in the previous two years. Pete had also, supposedly, refused to restyle his hair to the iconic Beatle **moptop**. Pete claims he was never asked. When, on August 16, 1962, Brian Epstein – acting on behalf of the group – told him that he was out, his response was an understandably devastated "Why? What have I done wrong?" A member of the group for two years almost to the day, from that moment Pete had no personal contact with Lennon, McCartney or Harrison again. "We were cowards," Lennon later admitted.

In 1962, Pete Best was "The Handsome Beatle". Not for long...

George Martin:

"Tell me if there's anything you don't like."

George Harrison:

"I don't like your tie for a start."

The Beatles' first recording session, June 1962

His replacement was the drummer who at the time was playing on a Butlins summer season with Rory Storm and the Hurricanes: Richard Starkey, professionally known as **Ringo Starr**. The Beatles had known him since the Kaiserkeller double bill almost two years previously and had got on well. He had occasionally deputized for Pete in The Beatles, and George Harrison in particular was convinced he was the right man for the job. After he had shaved his beard, Ringo played his first gig as an official Beatle on August 18 at Birkenhead.

On August 23, 1962, John married a pregnant **Cynthia Powell**, his art-school sweetheart, at Liverpool registry office. It was a low-key affair which was kept from public knowledge for the time being. Ringo was not even told, let alone invited. Noisy roadworks drowned out the registrar, the wedding was followed by a chicken lunch in the pub over the road, and John spent his wedding night playing with The Beatles in Chester. Brian Epstein gave the couple the use of his Liverpool flat as a wedding present.

Riding out a wave of "Pete forever, Ringo never!" controversy from the local fans (not to say Pete's mate, roadie Neil Aspinall, who Ringo recalls refusing to set up his drum kit for a while), the group gigged on. They returned to EMI in September to record **Love Me Do**, an early Lennon/McCartney song, and Mitch Murray tune George Martin had selected, **How Do You Do It**. But Martin was not especially convinced by Ringo's drumming either. For the follow-up recording date a week later, he booked session drummer Andy White for, among other tracks, a re-recording of Love Me Do, much to the new Beatle's frustration. "I was devastated that George Martin had his doubts about me," remembered Ringo.

Their debut single, "Love Me Do" appeared in October 1962 and peaked at #17 in December thanks to big sales in the north-west (there were rumours of Epstein-arranged bulk-buying). As the new year approached, The Beatles found themselves having to fulfil long-held bookings (including two reluctant stints back at the Star Club Hamburg, the first of which they shared with **Little Richard**) among a rush of promotional radio and local TV appearances and a quietly escalating national reputation.

Decca Audition

SEARCHIN'/THREE COOL CATS/THE SHEIK OF ARABY/LIKE DREAMERS DO/HELLO LITTLE GIRL

Recorded January 1, 1962; currently available on *Anthology 1*

Five of the fifteen titles recorded for Decca Records and, presumably, a fair representation of the kind of rocking showbiz hokum The Beatles were purveying at the time: all are cheekily and cockily done to a tee, complete with funny voices and comic asides. A pair of Leiber/Stoller novelty songs, a clunky 1940 Tin Pan Alley item delivered Joe Brown style and a couple of early Lennon/McCartney originals. And yet there's an attention to detail – the elaborate chord cycle introducing McCartney's rockin' rhumba **Like Dreamers Do** (later a top-twenty hit for fellow Liverpudlians The Fourmost), the carefully conceived harmonies and coda for Lennon's first ever song **Hello Little Girl** (later a top-ten hit for The Applejacks) – that shows off a precocious musical rigour.

Parlophone Audition

BESAME MUCHO/LOVE ME DO

Recorded June 6, 1962; currently available on *Anthology 1*

Five months later and a palpably nervous group (McCartney's pitching is hopeless) attempt to impress important Mr Martin at EMI Studios, Abbey Road. Interestingly, the star of **Besame Mucho** is Pete Best who explodes from the floor-tom rumble of the verse to the splashing hi-hats of the refrain with genuine panache. An unusual early version of **Love Me Do** features a harmonica solo in straight rock time, in fetching contrast to the lopey swing of the rest of the song, an awkward idea that was subsequently dropped.

Parlophone Session

HOW DO YOU DO IT

Recorded September 4, 1962; currently available on *Anthology 1*

Even though it was an obvious potential hit, The Beatles hated Mitch Murray's tune. However, at George Martin's request they turned out a professional arrangement (Harrison's guitar fills are particularly tidy), an effort that was later virtually duplicated by **Gerry and the Pacemakers** for their first #1 single in April 1963. Just supplanted as their debut by **Love Me Do**, Martin nevertheless intended it as the follow-up single, until he was convinced by The Beatles' reworking of **Please Please Me**.

Love Me Do/P.S. I Love You

Parlophone single; recorded September 4/11, 1962; released October 5, 1962; Ringo on drums version currently available on *Past Masters Volume 1*

The original red label single release of **Love Me Do** featured Ringo on drums, although subsequent pressings (and the "Please Please Me" album track) used the Andy White version with Ringo on sulky but adept tambourine. #17 in *Record Retailer*, #27 in *NME*. "The best of the bunch. It was John's harmonica that gave it its appeal" (George Martin).

Live! At The Star Club In Hamburg, 1962

I SAW HER STANDING THERE/ROLL OVER BEETHOVEN/HIPPY HIPPY SHAKE/SWEET LITTLE SIXTEEN/LEND ME YOUR COMB/YOUR FEET'S TOO BIG/TWIST AND SHOUT/MR MOONLIGHT/A TASTE OF HONEY/BESAME MUCHO/REMINISCING/KANSAS CITY/AIN'T NOTHING SHAKIN'/TO KNOW HER IS TO LOVE HER/LITTLE QUEENIE/FALLING IN LOVE AGAIN/ASK ME WHY/BE-BOP-A-LULA/HALLELUJAH I LOVE HER SO/RED SAILS IN THE SUNSET/EVERYBODY'S TRYING TO BE MY BABY/MATCHBOX/TALKIN' 'BOUT YOU/SHIMMY SHAKE/LONG TALL SALLY/I REMEMBER YOU

Lingasong; recorded December 31, 1962; released May 1977; highlights currently available on import as *1962 Live At The Star Club Hamburg* (Walters)

Recorded by Adrian Barber – founder member of **Cass and the Cassanovas** (later The Big Three) and who in 1962 was the stage manager of the Star Club – to test his newly designed sound system. Later acquired by Ted Taylor (leader of **Kingsize Taylor and the**

Dominoes) who said John Lennon gave him "permission" to record the performance in exchange for a drink, the recordings eventually found their way onto the market in 1977 and have appeared in myriad shoddy forms over the years. The Beatles eventually got a court injunction against the recordings in 1998 (thanks to an effective court appearance by George Harrison in which he argued that a drunken agreement between Taylor and Lennon hardly constituted a recording contract) but a "remastered" CD of dubious legality appeared in 2000. It's a fascinating glimpse into the infamous, chaotic Hamburg nights (a waiter even gets to sing a couple of songs) for those who can take the appalling recording quality.

Beatlemania!: 1963–64

"You can be big-headed and say, 'Yeah, we're gonna last ten years.' But as soon as you've said that you think, 'We're lucky if we last three months!'"

John Lennon, 1963

The Beatles kick-started 1963 with their second single, **Please Please Me**, which entered the charts in January and, thanks in part to their appearance on *Thank Your Lucky Stars*, their national TV debut, hit the heights of #1 in the *New Musical Express* charts in February. The group were in the middle of their first package tour of the UK (headlined by Helen Shapiro) when the news of their chart triumph broke, and they worked their way up from bottom of the bill to closing the first half of the show. Their swift, intense rise saw them depose American chart stars Tommy Roe (of "Sheila" fame), Chris Montez ("Let's Dance") and even one of their all-time heroes **Roy Orbison** from the top of the bill on subsequent UK tours later in the year.

Pursuing a gruelling schedule of concerts, recording sessions, radio and TV appearances, The Beatles pounded up and down the A6 motorway, developing an astonishing level of collective good humour and professionalism as England gradually went Beatles mad. Their third single **From Me To You** appeared in April, followed by their debut album *Please Please Me* in May, both of which reached the #1 spot. By the summer, The Beatles were appearing in their own BBC radio series, *Pop Go The Beatles* and had a fan magazine, *The Beatles Monthly Book*. Brian Epstein was now only booking The Beatles into theatres (as opposed to clubs or ballrooms) and by the time their fourth single **She Loves You** appeared in August, the group had made their 274th and last ever appearance at the Cavern.

Paul's 21st birthday bash at his auntie's house brought The Beatles their first piece of negative publicity. Newspapers in June reported that Lennon had beaten up **Bob Wooler**, the Cavern's MC. Wooler had apparently teased John about having an affair with Brian Epstein (the Beatle and his manager had just returned from a holiday in Spain) and a drunken John lashed out. Wooler was persuaded by Brian (and £200) not to press charges. It wouldn't be the last time Lennon would rock the boat.

Their in-person appearances had begun to spark off frenzied behaviour, particularly from the female members of the audience, with their often hysterical screaming utterly drowning out the band. While parents and sociologists scratched their heads, The Beatles began to fear for their physical safety and eventually had to hire an assistant roadie-cum-bodyguard – Liverpool telephone engineer **Mal Evans** – so Neil Aspinall could concentrate on getting the group in and out of the gig without anyone getting hurt.

Though the national press gave the teenage hysteria a name – **Beatlemania** – the group's appeal wasn't exclusive to the kids (as Paul McCartney said in 1964, "Don't for heaven's sake say we're the new youth, because that's a load of old rubbish"). Everyone loved them. Only a few months earlier they had been delivering the raucous musical goods to rock-crazed Germans in the seediest side of Hamburg. Now, in October 1963, they were delighting the UK's living rooms from the cosiest entertainment show on TV, Val Parnell's *Sunday Night At The London Palladium*.

It was but a short step to full acceptance into the entertainment establishment via the Royal Command Performance, which they performed in November 1963 at the Prince of Wales Theatre in front of Princess Margaret and the Queen Mother. The beautifully judged irreverence – Lennon famously introduced **Twist And Shout** by suggesting "Those in the cheaper seats, clap your hands, and the rest of you, if you'll just rattle your jewellery" – only endeared the lovable moptops to the nation even more. "It's one of the best shows I've seen," endorsed the Queen Mother. "The Beatles are most intriguing."

By late 1963, it was clear from the time spent on the motorway and money spent

The charts

In the 1960s, there was no nationally recognized record chart. The *Record Retailer* (later *Music Week*) trade paper chart was not considered standard until 1969, when the BBC started using it. Most music papers had their own chart and though the *Melody Maker* placings were always of interest, the *New Musical Express* chart was considered more important because pop radio station *Radio Luxemburg* used it, and it was printed in the *Daily Mail*. This only becomes a problem for The Beatles fan when trying to work out which position the few records that *didn't* make #1 actually peaked at. However, most generally accepted retrospective statistics are based on the *Record Retailer* chart.

on hotels that The Beatles had to relocate to London. For a while, all four shared a "Beatles pad" on Green Street, Park Lane. But when, inevitably, John's marriage to Cynthia became common knowledge, the couple (and baby son Julian) took a flat in Kensington, leaving Ringo and George in Park Lane. Paul had been dating seventeen-year-old actress Jane Asher since meeting her at the Royal Albert Hall in April (where she was asked to write an article and pose as a screaming Beatles fan by the *Radio Times*) and was offered a room at the top of her parents' house on Wimpole Street. Never really comfortable in the Green Street flat, he gratefully took it and stayed for nearly two years.

The release of their second album, *With The Beatles*, had been delayed until sales of *Please Please Me* showed signs of slowing, and it eventually appeared in November 1963, selling 500,000 copies in its first week of release. **She Loves You** had been #1 all through autumn and was only knocked off by the next single, **I Want To Hold Your Hand**, in December. The group settled into the Astoria Cinema, Finsbury Park, for a three-week run of their Epstein-conceived **Beatles Christmas Show**, a variety evening of music and sketches. That straight-backed bastion of British respectability *The Times* newspaper named them "the outstanding English composers of 1963". It was clear that Britain had completely succumbed. Now it was the rest of the world's turn.

1963 Singles

Please Please Me/Ask Me Why

Parlophone; recorded November 26, 1962; released January 12, 1963; "Please Please Me" currently available on *Please Please Me*, *1962–1966* and *1*; "Ask Me Why" on *Please Please Me*

Record Retailer #2, *Melody Maker* #1 (along with most other charts). "A really enjoyable platter, full of beat, vigour and vitality" (*NME*).

From Me To You/Thank You Girl

Parlophone; recorded March 5, 1963; released April 11, 1963; UK #1, US #116; "From Me To You" currently available on *1* and *1962–1966*; "Thank You Girl" on *Past Masters Volume 1* and *Capitol Albums Volume 1*

Seven weeks at #1. "In defiance of the tiresome trend towards weepie lost-love wailers, **From Me To You** is a rip-roarin' uptempo ballad which has a happy-go-lucky romantic story line" (EMI press release).

She Loves You/I'll Get You

Parlophone; recorded July 1, 1963; released August 23, 1963; "She Loves You" currently available on *1* and *1962–1966*; "I'll Get You" on *Past Masters Volume 1*; and both songs are on *Capitol Albums Volume 1*

Four weeks at #1 and The Beatles' first million-seller. "At first I thought it was a little banal … but it grows on you!" (Brian Matthew, BBC disc jockey).

I Want To Hold Your Hand/This Boy

Parlophone; recorded October 17, 1963; released November 29, 1963; "I Want To Hold Your Hand" currently available on *1* and *1962–1966*, "This Boy" on *Past Masters Volume 1*; and both songs are on *Capitol Albums Volume 1*

Five weeks at #1, and over fifteen million copies sold worldwide. "It's repetitious almost to the point of hypnosis, has an easily memorised melody, and some built-in hand-clapping to help along the infectious broken beat" (*NME*).

1963 EPs

All EPs (and singles) are currently still available in collected box sets.

The Beatles' Hits

FROM ME TO YOU/THANK YOU GIRL/PLEASE PLEASE ME/LOVE ME DO

Parlophone; recorded September 1962–March 1963; released September 1963

Twist And Shout

TWIST AND SHOUT/A TASTE OF HONEY/DO YOU WANT TO KNOW A SECRET/THERE'S A PLACE

Parlophone; recorded February 11, 1963; released September 1963

The Beatles No. 1

I SAW HER STANDING THERE/MISERY/ANNA/CHAINS

Parlophone; recorded February 11, 1963; released November 1963

1963 Albums

Please Please Me

I SAW HER STANDING THERE/MISERY/ANNA/CHAINS/BOYS/ASK ME WHY/PLEASE PLEASE ME/LOVE ME DO/P.S. I LOVE YOU/BABY IT'S YOU/DO YOU WANT TO KNOW A SECRET?/A TASTE OF HONEY/THERE'S A PLACE/TWIST AND SHOUT

Parlophone; recorded September 11, 1962–February 11, 1963; released April 1963; currently available on CD

"One-two-three-four!" Paul counts them off and The Beatles swing, unknowingly, into musical history, opening their debut album with a bravura, brilliant original song and condensing everything they'd learnt in the Kaiser Club and Cavern into thirty thrilling minutes. The ten tracks that weren't already recorded for singles were caught in a single twelve-hour session. Some of the scruffier performances betray EMI's intention that **Please Please Me** would be a cursory (and customary for the time) hits 'n' filler affair. However, between McCartney's count-in for **I Saw Her Standing There** (the song which introduced those exuberant, head-shaking "woooh"s) to his gleeful shout at the end of the raw, Lennon-led throat-tearing excitement of the Isley Brothers' **Twist And Shout** (famously recorded in one go-for-broke take at the end of their exhausting day), there is a palpable magic and passion here, which still can be felt over forty years on. **Please Please Me** immediately set The Beatles apart from the prevailing norm. From this point on they'd be setting all the benchmarks.

Note the songs' insistent details and emergent characterful traits. Arthur Alexander's **Anna** features Lennon's emotive catch-in-the-throat "oh-oh-oh-oh"s; Ringo's propulsive fills are striking throughout; and even the straight-ahead rocking cover of The Shirelles' **Boys** contains a McCartney bass line full of careful staccato and a thoughtful, surprising Harrison guitar solo.

The group's propensity for fulsome harmony (Lennon's lovely **Ask Me Why** and his old-fashioned **Do You Want To Know A Secret?** utilize similarly schmaltzy chords) and corny exotica (McCartney's **P.S. I Love You** aspires to be a rumba, whilst their po-faced cover of **A Taste Of Honey** clunks from waltz to swing time and wearily back again) is on cheery display. But the songwriting highlight, Lennon/McCartney's **There's A Place**, is a subtle and elusive piece of work that, at least in retrospect, precociously points beyond their contemporary standing as a cheeky showbiz beat group.

With The Beatles

IT WON'T BE LONG/ALL I'VE GOT TO DO/ALL MY LOVING/ DON'T BOTHER ME/LITTLE CHILD/TILL THERE WAS YOU/ PLEASE MR POSTMAN/ROLL OVER BEETHOVEN/HOLD ME TIGHT/YOU REALLY GOT A HOLD ON ME/I WANT TO BE YOUR MAN/DEVIL IN HER HEART/NOT A SECOND TIME/ MONEY

Parlophone; recorded July–October 1963; released November 22, 1963; currently available on CD

Only one record could dislodge **Please Please Me** from #1 and that was its follow-up, which became the obligatory Christmas gift for British teenagers in 1963. Though following a similar pattern of originals and covers as their debut, *With The Beatles* contained none of that year's hit singles and as such was a fascinating (and admirably good value) parallel to their central commercial output of the time. Afforded a generous half-dozen Abbey Road recording sessions in late summer and early autumn 1963 – squeezed between tour dates – the musical and technical improvement over its predecessor is, for the most part, obvious. It contains three of The Beatles' best-ever cover ver-

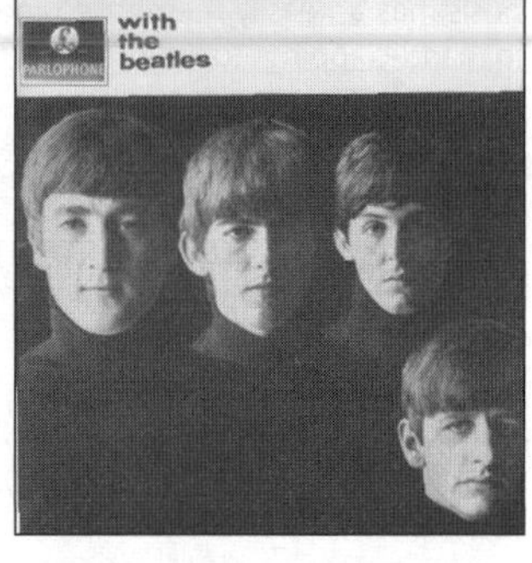

Busy busy busy in 1964

sions: Harrison and Lennon carefully harmonize their way through Smokey Robinson's intricate **You Really Got A Hold On Me**; Lennon avariciously tears into Barrett Strong's **Money**; and a delicious, elastic groove supports a dense curtain of guitars and harmonies on the Marvelettes' **Please Mr Postman**. However, there remains a pair of quaint, mildly embarrassing efforts to further showcase their much-touted "versatility" as all-round entertainers: Paul's doe-eyed take on the Broadway hit **Till There Was You**, perfect for – and subsequently performed at – the Royal Command Performance, and George's slick version of an obscure doo-wop horror **Devil In Her Heart**.

Lennon continues to assert his authority (and his perceived musical leadership) with some superb lead vocals on seven of the fourteen tracks, although his songwriting is no less striking. He was largely responsible for **It Won't Be Long**, the powerful lead track. Its explosive call-and-response vocals slyly exploit **She Loves You**'s "yeah yeah yeah" signature and it is memorable enough to be a single, but was never even performed live by the group. A pair of intriguingly halting major-to-minor-key compositions (**All I've Got To Do** and **Not A Second Time**) are the work of an already distinctive songwriter with an identifiable lyrical style (much "crying", some punning, and a general downbeat tone) and an instinctive ear for a harmonic twist. **Don't Bother Me**, by George Harrison, displays a similar if exaggerated attraction to the bittersweet but, being the younger man's songwriting debut, is comparatively naive.

Little Child is a fair-to-middling original rocker that idly reprises "Please Please Me"s and "Twist And Shout"s "c'mon c'mon"s. **Hold Me Tight** probably didn't merit the muscular delivery it receives from the group, and also suffers from the single worst McCartney vocal ever recorded. The biggie from the album, however, was McCartney's rollickingly optimistic **All My Loving**, a recording of almost absurd musical sunniness and confidence, which was largely instrumental in McCartney being perceived as being an equal partner with Lennon in the group.

1964: Conquest of America

"What do you think of the criticism that you're not very good?"
"We're not."

George Harrison, 1964

The Beatles' first major engagement of 1964 was a three-week residency at L'Olympia, Paris. The band struggled to impress the Parisians (who were rather more taken with Trini Lopez, who was also on the bill) but they consoled themselves in the luxury of the Hotel George V by constantly listening to *The Freewheelin' Bob Dylan* album. Further occupied in Pathe Marconi Studios by dubbing German vocals onto **She Loves You** and **I Want To Hold Your Hand**, and recording **Can't Buy Me Love**, they were also impatiently anticipating their first trip to the USA.

Until 1964, the USA had mostly been a closed shop to British pop performers. Cliff Richard had made little impact with middle-of-the-bill touring, yet The Beatles, with magnificent arrogance, stated they wouldn't tour America until they had a #1 record. George Martin had sent copies of "Please Please Me", "From Me To You" and "She Loves You" to his American EMI/Capitol colleagues, enthusing about the group's UK popularity. But, convinced The Beatles had nothing to offer the US market, Capitol had passed and the records were fumbled by the smaller labels **Vee Jay** and **Swan**.

However, in a stroke of luck, Ed Sullivan, one of the biggest stars of US TV, had become aware of the group in October 1963 when he witnessed London's Heathrow Airport besieged by fans. Impressed by The Beatles phenomenon, but conscious he was taking a risk with a group unknown in America, he booked them onto three of his shows in February 1964 at a reduced fee.

With the arrival of **I Want To Hold Your Hand** and the imminent *Ed Sullivan Show* appearances, Capitol agreed to take the group on, although Brian Epstein shrewdly had them guarantee to spend an unheard-of $40,000 on promotion. So it was that Capitol went into campaign overdrive in December 1963, proclaiming in whichever way they could – buttons, T-shirts, stickers, even moptop wigs – that "The Beatles Are Coming!"

In a country ready for some jolly distraction in the wake of President Kennedy's shocking assassination in November 1963, it worked. In

The clean-cut Fabs cram in a quick pre-show shave, April 1964

January 1964, the news came through to the group in Paris that **I Want To Hold Your Hand** had bounded to #1 in the **Cashbox** charts with sales of over one million in two weeks. Epstein now confidently booked them into the only two shows they could squeeze in – New York's Carnegie Hall and Washington Coliseum – and when they touched down at JFK Airport on February 7, 1964, America was already theirs.

Fans besieged the airport and a charmed, agog media reported every kooky utterance of the group's press conferences – virtuoso displays of The Beatles' natural, unruffled wit. Their first appearance on *The Ed Sullivan Show* was watched by a record 73 million people; in March the single **Can't Buy Me Love** sealed the deal; and at one point in April The Beatles held all top five slots in the US singles charts. America had never seen anything like it.

Back in the UK, the boys spent most of March and April shooting their first feature film, **A Hard Day's Night**, though they still found time to headline the *NME* Poll Winner's concert at Empire Pool, Wembley, and appear in a TV variety special, *Around The Beatles*. In March, Lennon even had his first book published, **In His Own Write**, a collection of surreal poetry, short stories and drawings of the sort he had been doing since he was a teenager. Foyles held a literary lunch in his honour in April, much to John's discomfort, at which his embarrassed acceptance speech was heard to consist of "Thank you very much, you've got a lucky face."

By June, the indefatigable Beatles had just about managed to squeeze in a much-needed two-week holiday. John, Cynthia, George and his girlfriend Patti went to Tahiti, where John wrote much of his second book, **Spaniard In The Works**, whilst Paul, Jane, Ringo and his girlfriend Maureen went to the Virgin Islands. Then it was back to work, recording enough material for both an all-original album to accompany their forthcoming movie, plus

The Beatles' unbreakable record

Due to the proliferation of independent American labels with the rights to early material, on the week ending April 4, 1964, The Beatles held all five of the top five positions on the *Cashbox* charts – at that time the most influential pop-singles ranking in America. It was an unprecedented, and to this day, unique achievement, made all the more remarkable by the presence of a further seven Beatles singles in the Top 100.

They were: 1. "Twist And Shout" (Tollie); 2. "Can't Buy Me Love" (Capitol, leaping up from #21 in its second chart week); 3. "She Loves You" (Swan, and previously #1 for two weeks); 4. "I Want To Hold Your Hand" (Capitol, and another former chart-topper) and 5. "Please Please Me" (Vee-Jay). The Vee-Jay label had also released "Do You Want To Know A Secret" (which was up from #75 to #28 the same week), "From Me To You" (#41) and "Thank You Girl" (#86). Capitol of Canada was importing copies of "Roll Over Beethoven", which had reached #33, "All My Loving" (#61) and "Love Me Do" (#77). "Can't Buy Me Love"'s B-side, "You Can't Do That", was also listed at #97.

Long Tall Sally, a four-track EP. Due to tour Australasia via Denmark, the Netherlands and Hong Kong, Ringo missed the first five dates of the 27-day foreign tour due to tonsillitis. He was replaced, despite George's objections, by The Shubdubs' tub-thumper **Jimmy Nicol** for ten performances, but Ringo rejoined The Beatles in Australia in mid-June just in time to witness scenes as manic, if not more so, as those in America. In Adelaide and Melbourne the band waved at crowds of up to three hundred thousand from their hotel windows.

There were similar scenes back in the UK in July for the premieres of *A Hard Day's Night*: first in Piccadilly, London, where entire streets were cordoned off, and then again for the northern premiere, in Liverpool. The band had heard that the folks back home had resented The Beatles going national, particularly when they had left to live in London, so it was a specially warming homecoming to find their childhood streets lined with over two hundred thousand proud well-wishers. At the Town Hall civic reception, Lennon's nervy irreverence went as far as giving an extremely ill-judged Nazi salute on the balcony in front of the gathered hordes – his "Hitler bit", as Neil Aspinall called it. The gesture, while probably just a tasteless joke to relieve the tension at the time, retrospectively serves as an ironic comment on how unquestioning the world's devotion to The Beatles had become. The single and album of ***A Hard Day's Night*** appeared concurrently with the well-received film in July. In August, The Beatles returned to the USA for their first tour, a punishing 32 shows in 24 cities over 34 days. For a good while now The Beatles' concerts had been played out to a constant backdrop of high-pitched screams from the audience, but in the huge American auditoria like the **Hollywood Bowl**, the experience had become bizarre and disorientating. Ringo could barely hear any music at all and relied on the body language of the rest of the group to keep his place.

The Beatles, for their own safety, existed for the most part in a vacuum-packed world of limousines, hotel rooms, dressing rooms and aeroplanes while the world outside – the frenzied fans, frothing reporters, harried authorities or businessmen selling used Beatle bed linen at $10 a square – fretted and buzzed. Then, when not gigging or at a press conference, there was a constant round of celebrities and local dignitaries and their families to charm – not to mention a stream of physically and mentally disadvantaged children whom promoters and parents saw fit to usher into The Beatles' presence so the group could "bless" them with their attention. The Beatles soon found their compassion wearing thin. Also, the unpredictability of people's behaviour around them – at a party at the British Embassy in Washington in 1964, Ringo had to contend with someone trying to cut off a lock of his hair – had made them very wary of any situation outside their inner circle. "Their life was merciless, actually," George Martin observed. The Beatles had already begun to feel trapped by their peculiar fame.

"Would you like to walk down the street without being recognized?" "We used to do this with no money in our pockets. There's no point to it."

John Lennon, 1964

Yet their worldwide celebrity did have its perks. In America they got to meet their heroes **Chuck Berry, Carl Perkins** and **Fats Domino**. Whilst in New York they met up with a new hero of theirs, **Bob Dylan**, whose *Freewheelin' Bob Dylan* album had dazzled them with its wit, poetry and literary attitude. It was at this meeting that Dylan famously introduced them to marijuana. Dylan had misheard "I can't hide ...", in **I Want To Hold Your Hand**, as "I get high ..." and had assumed that they were regular users. The Beatles had indeed tried it before in Liverpool, but alcohol and "uppers" were The Beatles' drugs of choice. When they shared the grass Dylan had brought with him and giggled the night away, they acquired a taste for it. McCartney got particularly high that night and, convinced he was experiencing some kind of profound insight into the meaning of life, instructed **Mal Evans** to write down his thoughts. The following day McCartney's words of cryptic wisdom were found to be merely "There are seven levels."

Back in the UK the group made the usual round of recording sessions and live appearances through October and November. Their next single, **I Feel Fine**, and album, *Beatles For Sale*, appeared in time for the Christmas market, and ***Another Beatles Christmas Show*** took up a three-week residency at Hammersmith Odeon in December.

1964 Singles

Can't Buy Me Love/You Can't Do That

Parlophone; recorded January 29/February 25, 1964; released March 20, 1964; "Can't Buy Me Love" currently available on *A Hard Day's Night*, *1962–1966* and *1*; "You Can't Do That" on *A Hard Day's Night*

Four weeks at #1, with advance orders of over a million in the UK and over two million in the US. "A pounding, vibrating, fast-medium twist in the r-and-b mould, with a fascinating trembling effect in the middle eight" (*NME*).

A Hard Day's Night/Things We Said Today

Parlophone; recorded April 16/June 2, 1964; released July 10, 1964; "A Hard Day's Night" currently available on *A Hard Day's Night*, *1962–1966* and *1*; "Things We Said Today" on *A Hard Day's Night* and *Capital Albums Volume 2*

Three weeks at #1. "Just to go through the motions, let me tell you that it's a bouncy finger-snapper, with a pounding beat and a catchy melody" (*NME*).

I Feel Fine/She's A Woman

Parlophone; recorded October 18/November 8, 1964; released November 27 1964; "I Feel Fine" currently available on *1962–1966* and *1*, "She's A Woman" on *Past Masters Volume 1*; both on *Capitol Albums Volume 1*

Five weeks at #1. "After a startling, reverberating opening, it develops into a happy-go-lucky mid-tempo swinger" (*NME*).

1964 EPs

All My Loving

ALL MY LOVING/ASK ME WHY/MONEY/P.S. I LOVE YOU
Parlophone; recorded September 1962–July 1963; released February 7, 1964

Long Tall Sally

I CALL YOUR NAME/SLOW DOWN/LONG TALL SALLY/ MATCHBOX
Parlophone; recorded March 1–June 4, 1964; released June 19, 1964; currently available on *Past Masters Volume 1* and *Capitol Albums Volume 1*

One of only two EPs (*Magical Mystery Tour* is the other) released in the UK to exclusively feature non-album tracks.

A Hard Day's Night 1

I SHOULD HAVE KNOWN BETTER/IF I FELL/TELL ME WHY/ AND I LOVE HER
Parlophone; recorded February 25–27, 1964; released November 4, 1964

A Hard Day's Night 2

ANY TIME AT ALL/I'LL CRY INSTEAD/THINGS WE SAID TODAY/WHEN I GET HOME
Parlophone; recorded June 1–2, 1964; released November 6, 1964

1964 Albums

A Hard Day's Night

A HARD DAY'S NIGHT/I SHOULD HAVE KNOWN BETTER/IF I FELL/I'M HAPPY JUST TO DANCE WITH YOU/AND I LOVE HER/TELL ME WHY/CAN'T BUY ME LOVE/ANY TIME AT ALL/ I'LL CRY INSTEAD/THINGS WE SAID TODAY/WHEN I GET HOME/YOU CAN'T DO THAT/I'LL BE BACK
Parlophone; recorded January 29–June 2, 1964; released July 10, 1964; currently available on CD

A remarkable and virtually unheard-of all-original set, ***A Hard Day's Night*** – The Beatles' third album and partly the soundtrack to their first movie – was not only a significant advance for the group, but the best of it represents the pinnacle of what rock-era pop music had yet achieved. Gone are the rock, soul and showbiz covers, replaced by thirteen new compositions that express the group's range more profoundly than their earlier attempts at conventional stylistic versatility.

There was the driving, bluesy title track with its unforgettable opening chord (chosen specifically to be a startling musical curtain-raiser to the movie). There were two mature ballads – Lennon's touching **If I Fell** and McCartney's glorious **And I Love Her** (see p.179) – which were instantly seized upon by the adult pop world as new standards, and covered by tuxedoed balladeers accordingly. There was the zesty swing rock of **Tell Me Why** and **Can't Buy Me Love** (the latter almost immediately covered by jazz singer Ella Fitzgerald), and the deep, grinding grooves of **You Can't Do That** (see p.178) and **When I Get Home**. Also, courtesy of George Harrison's new Rickenbacker 12-string, there were some exotic new textures, notably on the jangling fade of **A Hard Day's Night** and the plangent chord work in the bridge of **I Should Have Known Better**.

McCartney's skilful, haunting **Things We Said Today** wallows in the minor–major ambivalence that also intrigues Lennon on his evocative **I'll Be Back**. Though the songs, as ever, were attributed to Lennon/McCartney, it's Lennon's compositional and vocal presence that dominates. With a recent single A-side having been taken by McCartney's **Can't Buy Me Love**, Lennon appears to reassert his governance of the band (possibly

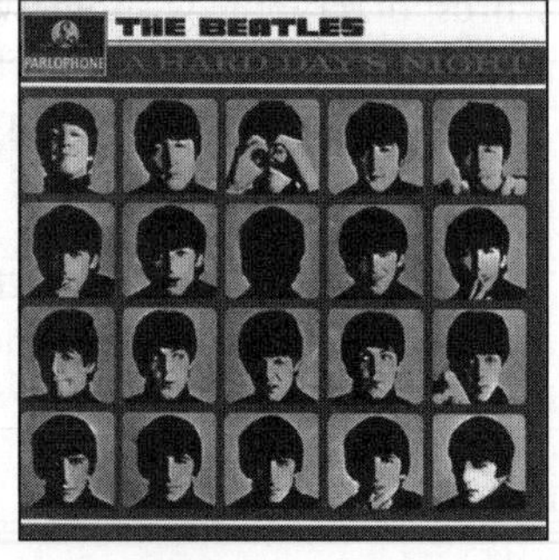

taking advantage of Paul being distracted by his romance with Jane Asher and London culture) by lead composing or lead singing on ten of the thirteen tracks.

There is evidence, however, that he may have over-stretched himself. Inevitably, with the writing done in the bubble of Beatlemania, the songs – however uniformly spirited the performances – occasionally sounded formulaic. **Any Time At All** is a lumbering rewrite of **All I've Got To Do, I Should Have Known Better** is catchy but slight, **When I Get Home** is perhaps one bluesy holler too many. That said, the UK release (the inferior US version had George Martin's incidental movie instrumentals on side two) was simply years ahead of anything in British pop at the time.

Beatles For Sale

NO REPLY/I'M A LOSER/BABY'S IN BLACK/ROCK AND ROLL MUSIC/I'LL FOLLOW THE SUN/MR MOONLIGHT/MEDLEY: KANSAS CITY-HEY, HEY, HEY, HEY/EIGHT DAYS A WEEK/ WORDS OF LOVE/HONEY DON'T/EVERY LITTLE THING/I DON'T WANT TO SPOIL THE PARTY/WHAT YOU'RE DOING/ EVERYBODY'S TRYING TO BE MY BABY

Parlophone; recorded August 11–October 26, 1964; released November 27, 1964; currently available on CD

George Martin noted that the boys were "rather war weary" when they arrived at Abbey Road to bash out another album in time for Christmas 1964. The cynical title and the tired-looking faces on the cover betray their mood. And the return of some Cavern-era covers was generally considered a retrograde step following the all-original triumph of *A Hard Day's Night*. While fans undoubtedly adored it at the time, with hindsight *Beatles For Sale* is an interesting but relatively unimportant item in the group's catalogue.

Once more dominated by Lennon (he sings lead on five of the first six cuts), ***Beatles For Sale*** is notable for a pessimistic folksy and country flavour on tracks like **No Reply**, **I'm A Loser**, **Baby's In Black** (see p.181) and **I Don't Want To Spoil The Party**. He allows a Bob Dylan influence to permeate his writing for the first time (in tone that is, rather than style or substance), there is much earnest acoustic strumming (with George Harrison contributing arch Chet Atkins and Carl Perkins-style fills) and the lyrics are discernibly moodier: tales of girls who lie, girls who love other guys, girls who don't turn up, girls who don't answer the phone and tears "falling like rain". None of these songs would figure in a Lennon Top Ten, but you wouldn't want to be without them either.

McCartney's originals – the slight but carefully recorded **What You're Doing** and the quietly dramatic **Every Little Thing**, with John on vocal (a rare occasion where the main composer didn't sing the lead) – hardly approach his best work but are absorbing examples of a huge talent drawing from a not-quite-dry well. The upbeat swing of **Eight Days A Week** has a ring of classic Beatles about it, but was pipped to the post for the choice of single toward the end of the sessions by John's **I Feel Fine**, which wins by a nose.

Happily, the album contains two of The Beatles' best ever straight-rock covers, which are thrilling, genuine tributes to their rock'n'roll heroes: Lennon's lustrous version of Chuck Berry's **Rock And Roll Music** and McCartney's delirious revamp of Little Richard's **Kansas City/Hey, Hey, Hey, Hey**. To hear them is to marvel at how two of the greatest British rock singers ended up in the same band. Another hero of the Fabs, Carl Perkins, is saluted on Ringo's hopeful, rather hopeless **Honey Don't** and George's **Everybody's Trying To Be My Baby**. These two tributes fare less well, though the latter generates some stylish rockabilly rhythms.

It's probably the least essential of The Beatles' albums; needless to say everyone should still have it.

Middle period: 1965–66

"We were smoking marijuana for breakfast ... nobody could communicate with us, because we were just all glazed eyes, giggling all the time. In our own world."

John Lennon, 1980

It may have been a year of broken box-office records and official honours but, in terms of most of The Beatles' activities, 1965 was a slightly less exciting rerun of 1964. Another film (not so good as the first), another Lennon book (not so good as the first), more tours and airports and records, but marginally thinner hordes to see them off and welcome them back – even a few not-quite-sold-out shows here and there. However, at a time when it would have been easy to rest on their laurels, 1965 was also the year when The Beatles somehow arrested the temporary dip in their musical standards and began to transform themselves from mop-tops into true artists of pop.

After completing *Another Beatles Christmas Show*, and after John had appeared reading from his *In His Own Write* on the BBC2 Peter Cook and Dudley Moore TV show ***Not Only ... But Also***, The Beatles began 1965 with a holiday. John and Cynthia went to St Moritz with George Martin and his wife, Paul and Jane went to Tunisia, and in February Ringo married Maureen Cox, his long-time girlfriend from the Cavern days.

Later that month, The Beatles began filming their second movie, provisionally entitled ***Eight Arms To Hold You*** (later named *Help!*), in the Bahamas before relocating the shoot to Austria and Twickenham in March. The Beatles were not creatively involved in the movie (beyond providing the songs) and relieved their boredom by getting regularly stoned on the marijuana provided by the actor

Yesterday: the most covered song of all time

First offered to British rocker Chris Farlowe, who turned it down (though he sang it eventually) and first covered as a single by crooner Matt Munro in 1965, "Yesterday" – McCartney's song that came to him in a dream – has been covered by hundreds of artists of all kinds: Cilla Black, Ray Charles, Alma Cogen, Perry Como, Placido Domingo, Bob Dylan (recorded but not released), En Vogue, Marvin Gaye, Benny Goodman, Jan and Dean, Tom Jones, Gladys Knight & the Pips, Brenda Lee, Liberace, Vera Lynn, Willie Nelson, Elvis Presley, Nelson Riddle, Smokey Robinson and the Miracles, Frank Sinatra, The Smothers Brothers, The Supremes, The Temptations, Sarah Vaughan and Wet Wet Wet.

and Beatles fan Brandon De Wilde, child star of the 1950s Western *Shane*.

Since they started taking The Beatles seriously in 1964, the American label **Capitol** had gone its own cavalier way with record releases, ignoring the British albums and compiling shorter-length LPs (at a lesser royalty rate) from various periods, with different names from the UK releases. Capitol eventually ceased this practice after *Revolver* in 1966, but still managed to produce nineteen albums during The Beatles' lifetime compared to the UK's thirteen (see p.312). They even chose which singles to release out of the official 45s. For instance, in August 64, **Matchbox** was released with Ringo on vocals to exploit the drummer's stateside popularity and ensure a steady stream of product. In April **Eight Days A Week** (a ***Beatles For Sale*** album track not considered strong enough for a single release in the UK) topped the US charts followed closely by the new single and trailer for the forthcoming *Help!* movie **Ticket To Ride**, in May. McCartney's solo piece **Yesterday** was also a huge US #1 single in 1965 and, though it went on to be the most covered song in the history of popular music, it remained just an album track on ***Help!*** in the UK until 1976.

In June, The Beatles heard they were to be awarded **MBEs** in the Queen's birthday honours list. Though they were fully aware of the political agenda (Prime Minister **Harold Wilson** had courted The Beatles in pursuit of the youth vote since 1963, when he was still Leader of the Opposition), they accepted with their usual amused sense of the absurd. As a gesture to their undecorated manager, George said he thought MBE stood for "Mr Brian Epstein". Some medal holders, particularly war veterans, saw it as a debasement of the award and returned theirs in disgust. Officially honoured for "services to export" (in the absence, perhaps, of an honour for "making people feel really good"), John's controversial response to the irate ex-military was, "We deserve ours for not killing people".

In July ***Spaniard in the Works***, Lennon's second book, was published, followed later in the month by the single **Help!** and in August the album and movie of the same name, though the Beatle episode of the summer of 1965 was a now legendary record-breaking concert. The first date of their third US visit in August was at a baseball arena in New York, **Shea Stadium**, in front of 55,000 people. It was a momentous event and the TV film shows The Beatles, and John in particular, responding in a slightly crazed manner, as if the adrenalin were just too much to handle. Two thousand security men and high wire fences were employed to keep the audience in check, and though **Vox** had made 100-watt amplifiers especially for the tour, the house PA system was barely up to the job and the group was hardly heard. All things considered, The Beatles performed well, although not so faultlessly that the TV film could be broadcast without overdubbed tweaking of the soundtrack.

On August 27, another historical event took place, though witnessed by rather fewer people: the band met their all-time musical

"We'll never get to that stage of releasing rubbish because we know people will buy it."

Paul McCartney, 1965

hero, **Elvis Presley**. The Beatles had been wanting to meet him for a while, and Paul had even managed to chat to him on the phone in 1964. This time, however, *NME* journalist Chris Hutchins had arranged for them to visit Elvis at his Beverly Hills house. Stoned and star-struck, the group and their entourage managed to get through an awkward three hours with a strangely "disconnected" King and his entourage.

They sang a few songs (including Chuck Berry's **Johnny B. Goode** and Cilla Black's recent hit, **You're My World**), strummed guitars (with Elvis on bass), played pool, talked movies and music, and Lennon did a Peter Sellers impersonation for Elvis's benefit. Elvis's wife Priscilla was introduced and removed within the space of five minutes. Elvis didn't take The Beatles up on the invitation for a return visit to their pad the following day. "Odd," said Paul later. "Total anti-climax," John told Pete Shotton. No pictures were taken.

By the end of 1965, The Beatles were changing. Bob Dylan had opened their ears to taking their lyrics seriously. Lennon had started exploring the various authors that critics had attributed as an influence on him (such as **James Joyce**) and Harrison had begun what was to be a life-long interest in Indian music and religion.

Whilst the others had bought houses in the suburban stockbroker belt, McCartney had bought one in St John's Wood and was very much the culturally alert Beatle-about-town. He absorbed a great deal of contemporary artistic activities, some of which were filtering subtly through into the group's approach to writing and recording.

And the drugs were making an impact. The pills they had taken since the Hamburg days to keep them going had been largely replaced by pot, which, when not making them snigger incoherently, encouraged a certain sensory awareness, introspection and amicability. **LSD**, on the other hand, utterly blew their minds. John and George, along with Cynthia and Patti Boyd, George's girlfriend, had been slipped some acid early in 1965 at a dinner party which resulted in a "terrifying, fantastic" evening tripping around London. John, though disturbed by his first experience, took it again in August 1965 when at a party in LA with **The Byrds**, while George described being on acid as "a very concentrated version of the best feeling I'd ever had in my whole life". Paul avoided it for the time being.

They could still knock out the moptop stuff (as they did on their final UK tour in December) but the music they recorded in October and November, which emerged in December as the album *Rubber Soul* and a double A-sided single **We Can Work It Out/Day Tripper**, had a weightier tone than followers of the Fab Four were used to. The Beatles had already gone far beyond what was expected of a pop group in 1965. This was music made by thoughtful men, and the world was about to get thoughtful with them.

1965 Singles

Ticket To Ride/Yes It Is

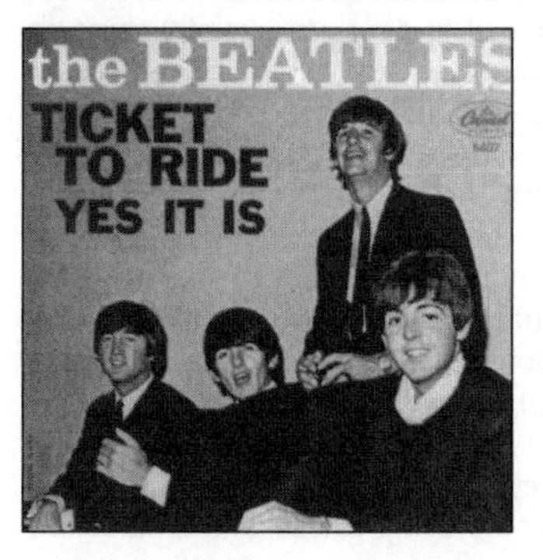

Parlophone; recorded February 15 and 16, 1965; released April 9, 1965; "Ticket To Ride" currently available on *Help*, *1962–1966* and *1*. "Yes It Is" on *Past Masters Volume 1*

Three weeks at #1. "It's not that unusual though, it's still us. It's no more unusual than we are. Does that make it unusual?" (John Lennon).

Help!/I'm Down

Parlophone; recorded April 13–June 14, 1965; released July 23 1965; "Help" currently available on *Help*, *1962–1966* and *1*; "I'm Down" on *Past Masters Volume 1*

Three weeks at #1. "It's a bit more involved than the others we've done because it has a counter melody going as well as the main melody" (George Harrison).

We Can Work It Out/Day Tripper

Parlophone; recorded October 16–29, 1965; released December 3, 1965; both currently available on *1962–1966* and *1*

Five weeks at #1 and the first Beatles double A-side. "Startling in conception … a sort of mid-tempo shuffle rhythm, except where the pace suddenly slackens in a fascinating way" (*NME* on **We Can Work It Out**). "A very 'Groupy' sort of record … there's a funny middle which stays on one chord" (George Harrison on **Day Tripper**).

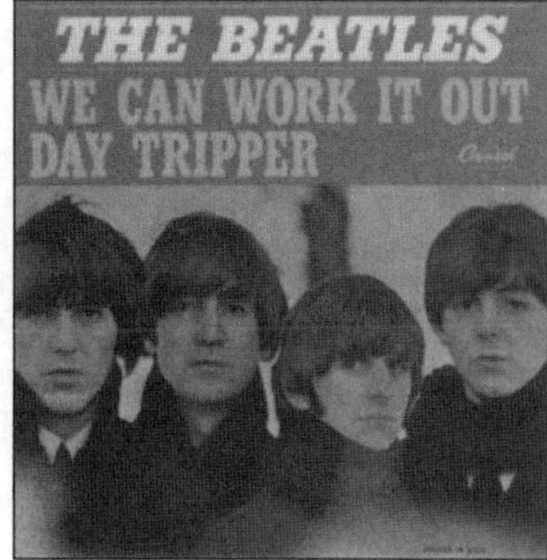

1965 EPs

Beatles For Sale No. 1

NO REPLY/I'M A LOSER/ROCK AND ROLL MUSIC/EIGHT DAYS A WEEK

Parlophone; recorded August 14–October 18, 1964; released April 6, 1965

Beatles For Sale No. 2

I'LL FOLLOW THE SUN/BABY'S IN BLACK/WORDS OF LOVE/I DON'T WANT TO SPOIL THE PARTY

Parlophone; recorded August 11–October 18, 1964; released June 4, 1965

Beatles' Million Sellers

SHE LOVES YOU/I WANT TO HOLD YOUR HAND/CAN'T BUY ME LOVE/I FEEL FINE

Parlophone; recorded July 1, 1963–October 18, 1964; released December 5, 1965

1965 Albums

Help!

HELP!/THE NIGHT BEFORE/YOU'VE GOT TO HIDE YOUR LOVE AWAY/I NEED YOU/ANOTHER GIRL/YOU'RE GOING TO LOSE THAT GIRL/TICKET TO RIDE/ACT NATURALLY/IT'S ONLY LOVE/YOU LIKE ME TOO MUCH/TELL ME WHAT YOU SEE/I'VE JUST SEEN A FACE/YESTERDAY/DIZZY MISS LIZZY

Parlophone; recorded February 15–June 17, 1965; released August 6, 1965; currently available on CD

The Beatles' schizophrenic fifth album was a tie-in release with their second film and represents – following the relative underachievement of *Beatles For Sale* – a return to musical form in the shape of four key moments.

The title track was Lennon's most autobiographical song to date (see p.183) – and in the space of two minutes twenty seconds it contained more Beatles ensemble magic than all 90 minutes of the movie. Lennon/McCartney's magnificently brooding **Ticket To Ride** (see p.182) was the most intense music The Beatles had yet recorded. McCartney's much-covered and oft-discussed **Yesterday** (the first Beatles record to spotlight a single Beatle, and the first to feature strings) became an instant classic, and perhaps the ultimate Beatles "standard". **You've Got To Hide Your Love Away** was the most overt, and probably the most effective, example of Lennon's downbeat Bob Dylan style, being finer-hewn than any of his similarly toned songs on ***Beatles For Sale***.

Elsewhere there were several originals that are, by comparison, rather ordinary. Lennon/McCartney's banal **It's Only Love** is only partially redeemed by a spirited chorus and an arresting revolving-speaker effect on Harrison's guitar. The professional jobs done to McCartney's **The Night Before** and his rather smug **Another Girl** only go some way to disguising the mediocrity of the material, while the diffident, folksy arrangement of **Tell Me What You See** exposes it as the slight, simple throwaway number it is.

In this company, Harrison's callow originals **I Need You** and **You Like Me Too Much** made the cut. But despite a striking use of the guitar **volume pedal** on the former track, there's still a compositional awkwardness to the pair that betrays George's ingénue songwriter status when compared to what John and Paul were capable of.

The group continued to dally with country styles on McCartney's tumbling, ingenious **I've Just Seen A Face** (preceded, apropos of nothing, by a gorgeous eleven-second guitar-picking duet) and Ringo's amiable turn, a cover of Buck Owens' **Act Naturally**. To close, Lennon delivers a typically committed rock vocal, a cover of Larry Williams' **Dizzy Miss Lizzy**. But the almost comically inept double-tracking of its insistent whining guitar riff (which keeps coming around every two bars like a disorientated wasp) encapsulates the sense that mid-success complacency and a hectic schedule caught The Beatles with their eye off the ball. As an album, *Help!* spreads itself a little too thinly; it would have made one hell of an EP.

Rubber Soul

DRIVE MY CAR/NORWEGIAN WOOD (THIS BIRD HAS FLOWN)/YOU WON'T SEE ME/NOWHERE MAN/THINK FOR YOURSELF/THE WORD/MICHELLE/WHAT GOES ON/GIRL/I'M LOOKING THROUGH YOU/IN MY LIFE/WAIT/IF I NEEDED SOMEONE/RUN FOR YOUR LIFE

Parlophone; recorded October 12–November 11, 1965; released December 3, 1965; currently available on CD

From the slightly disappointing to the largely sublime in the space of a few months, the appearance of the majestic *Rubber Soul* marked an emphatic end to The Beatles' mid-career artistic dip. Everything was better: the arrangements, the playing, the sound, and the songs.

The Beatles had not only tightened up their own quality control over the previous fifteen months or so, but had made a record that upped the ante for pop music all over the world. *Rubber Soul*'s virtues were so self-evident that capable contemporaries were spurred on to their best work (notably Brian Wilson of The Beach Boys on his 1966 masterwork, *Pet Sounds*), and the listening world re-acknowledged The Beatles as the leaders in their field.

The sound is full and sparkly (thanks to McCartney's new Rickenbacker bass and the liberties taken with the studio's high frequencies) and the plentiful three-part vocal harmonies are nothing short of resplendent. As its punning title suggests, the album's key influence is American soul music, and the group groove as never before on tracks like **The Word**.

With evolved arrangements often featuring intricate unison passages, the propulsive opener **Drive My Car** (see p.185) is their tautest, most focused ensemble performance to date. The Starr/McCartney rhythm section conjures up some of their all-time finest moments and, with Harrison on particularly strident form throughout, a second-division Lennon/McCartney song like **Wait** is expertly transformed into something thrilling. Prudently selected and skilfully applied new textures (sitar, harmonium and fuzz bass) conjure whole new worlds of expression. Harrison's compositions – **If I Needed Someone** and **Think For Yourself** – are for the first time afforded deserved, careful attention, and the meticulously stacked harmonies on the former are particularly impressive.

Many of Lennon and McCartney's songs here were among their best yet, and several of them offer tantalising glimpses into the state of their private lives at the time. Lennon's **Norwegian Wood** (see p.184) is a barely disguised story about a secret affair; the lyric of **Nowhere Man** (see p.189) is a heavy-hearted expression of the directionlessness of his private life and marriage.

On the other hand, **In My Life** (see p.187) pays touching tribute to "friends and lovers" of the past while (in a rush of tenderness, guilt or craftsmanship) affirming commitment to a present love. McCartney too – in **I'm Looking Through You** and **You Won't See Me** — doesn't flinch from detailing bitter disappointment with the progress of his relationship with Jane Asher.

Even what they might have called their "work songs" had the advantage of being devised by craftsmen at the top of their game. **Drive My Car** was their wittiest tale to date. **Michelle** (see p.189) and **Girl** are surprisingly novel odes to imaginary females: the former setting a simple lyric of Gallic cuddle and cooing to a detailed, delicate harmonic structure, the latter being an alluring description of a vaguely sadistic relationship featuring startling German two-step interludes.

It's not perfect. **What Goes On** is a rather dreary country showcase for Ringo, which has, arguably, the gawkiest Harrison guitar-playing on a Beatles record. Lennon's vitriolic **Run For Your Life** is old-style Beatles-by-numbers, not to mention anachronistically misogynistic for a group who elsewhere on the album is telling us, through a haze of marijuana, that "the word is love".

Often placed somewhere below the next four Beatles LPs in all-time-great album polls, it's undoubtedly their pre-acid, pre-antagonism masterpiece: beat music as high art.

1966: Tours and 'taches

"The Beatles are just a small part of my life now, and I want to keep it that way. Musically we're only just starting."

George Harrison, 1966

"We've all of us grown up in a way that hasn't turned into a manly way. It's a childish way ... Now we're ready to go our own ways. We'll work together only if we miss each other."

Paul McCartney, early 1967

Apart from an early January session to repair the soundtrack to the Shea Stadium TV film, the Fab Four took the first quarter of 1966 off from "Planet Beatle". On January 21 George married Patti Boyd in Epsom, with Paul as his best man. Honeymoons and holidays were taken, and private lives were lived. The Beatles seemed to be enjoying soaking up all that 1960s London had to offer. They took in plays (David Halliwell's cult classic *Little Malcolm And His Struggle Against The Eunuchs*), concerts (**Stevie Wonder** at the Scotch of St James nightclub, and **Luciano Berio** at the Italian Institute) and films (the premiere of *Alfie*, which starred Jane Asher), and hung out in clubs like the Ad Lib and the Bag O' Nails.

The first 1966 Beatles event of consequence was not a concert or a record, but a photo session. Robert Whitaker was an Australian photographer with a surrealist bent whom Brian Epstein had hired to shoot the cover of yet another US compilation album, *Yesterday And Today*. In a coarse satire of pop art, Whitaker put The Beatles in white butcher's coats and adorned them with the dismembered body parts of plastic dolls and slabs of raw meat. Capitol objected but the band, especially John and Paul (keen to subvert the group's cosy image), insisted. The album was manufactured but quickly withdrawn after complaints from dealers and a bland, inoffensive photo was glued over the top. Although it made the original sleeve an instant collector's item, it was a significant lapse of judgement in a year that was to be blighted by PR disasters.

For most of April and much of May, The Beatles hunkered down at Abbey Road studios to record the album to be known as ***Revolver***. Early Beatles recording sessions had been efficient, conventional

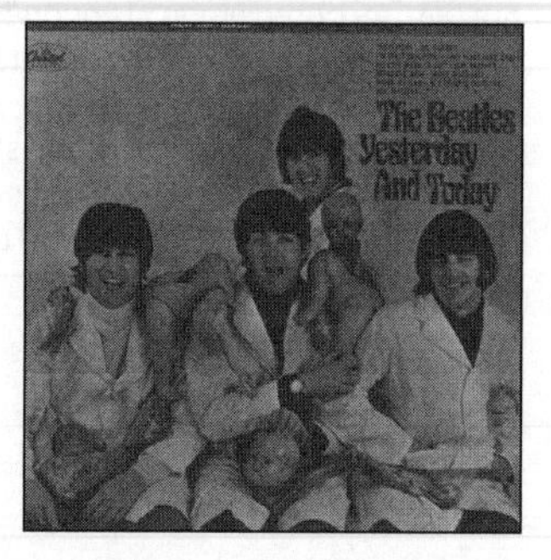

"One cannot say that our basic music approach has changed, but there is one thing about our new LP, there won't be many people copying our ideas. The sound is harder to emulate, although we still have the same lousy voices!"

John Lennon, 1966

affairs with the group's live playing being tidied up by producer George Martin and quickly recorded, usually over two three-hour sessions per day. By *Revolver*, the band's artistic imagination and ambitious sonic demands meant sessions would often extend into the early hours, a practice previously unheard of in the EMI studios. They were taking more interest in the **mixing process** – something they had previously left to George Martin – and would encourage engineer Geoff Emerick to "break the rules" in their quest to "create magic", as McCartney put it at the time.

They made no attempt to play any of the then-unreleased *Revolver* songs live at the *NME* poll-winners concert in May, but then neither did they at their live concerts through the summer. The *Revolver* tracks were studio creations, full of electronic nuance and subtle effects, and there was no way a four-piece rock'n'roll group could do them justice, particularly through the desensitizing wall of the fans' screams. "Live Beatles" and "Studio Beatles" had become entirely different beasts.

In June, with *Revolver* complete and a new single, **Paperback Writer**, in the charts (which they did attempt live a few times, with uneven results), the band returned to Hamburg for the first time in three years as part of the German leg of their 1966 world tour and met up with old friends Astrid Kirchherr and Bert Kaempfert. (Another old Hamburg friend, Klaus Voormann, had designed the cover of *Revolver*.) From there it was to Tokyo where the promoter had booked them to play the **Budokan**, a centre for the traditional sport of **sumo**, which prompted massive nationalist protests. Police escorts, an eight-foot-high stage and a round-the-clock confinement to their hotel room were employed as safety measures. Traders and even geisha girls (who were, apparently, refused entry) were sent to their room, and The Beatles ended up killing time by doing a collaborative, four-way painting.

But the furore of Japan was a picnic compared to the Philippines, their next stop. First, they were virtually kidnapped at the airport by a **militia gang** who wanted the kudos of having The Beatles stay on their boat. Second, a Manila newspaper had spuriously announced that The Beatles were to pay a "courtesy call" to **President Marcos** and his family. When they didn't, headlines reading "Imelda Stood Up" heralded what Ringo would call "the most frightening thing that's ever happened to me". Drivers refused to chauffeur them, the promoter refused to pay them (for two concerts

Off on tour in 1966

before a total of 80,000 people), armed policemen tried to punch them and crowds shouting "Beatles Go Home" jostled them as they struggled with their own luggage at the airport, where the escalators had been shut down. On their return to England, even the peace-loving George was moved to snarl something about bombing the place.

Distraught with nerves, Brian Epstein went on a rest-and-recuperation holiday to Wales but had to return early to deal with another scandal. A remark made by John Lennon during an interview with *Evening Standard* journalist and friend Maureen Cleave back in March 1966 (and inspired by Lennon's reading of Hugh J. Schonfield's *The Passover Plot*) had been discovered and reprinted in American teen magazine *Datebook* on the eve of The Beatles' US tour. The headline quoted John saying "I don't know which will go first – rock'n'roll or Christianity." In the same article, John had observed that for today's generation "we're [The Beatles] more popular than Jesus" and that "Jesus was alright, but his disciples were thick and ordinary." In the face of Bible-belt fury, organized Beatles-record burnings and **Ku Klux Klan** death threats, Brian flew to America to read an apology and considered cancelling the tour.

The tour went ahead but it was no fun. At a tense Chicago press conference before the first date in August, a nervous, clearly rattled John delivered his version of an apology-cum-explanation. In Memphis the nervy Beatles jumped when a firecracker went off, convinced they had been shot at. Though the noise from the audience was as intense as ever there were fewer fans turning out (including 11,000 unsold seats at their return to **Shea Stadium**) and the disheartened, disinterested Beatles played badly.

Discontent about The Beatles' unfulfilling concert routines had been brewing in the group for a while, with George and John being the main objectors. Paul had been the one who had held out longest for The Beatles to remain a live act but, with the Philippines debacle and the death threats in the US, even he agreed that, at least for the time being, The Beatles should retire from the stage. By the time they played Candlestick Park, San Francisco, on August 29, everyone in The Beatles camp knew their touring days were over.

For a few months, in autumn 1966, The Beatles went their different ways. John acted in Richard Lester's film ***How I Won The War*** (Lennon: "pretty damn boring"), cropping his hair and adopting National Health "granny" glasses for the role, which he retained afterwards as part of his quirky image. Ringo holidayed, decorated his house and joined John on set for a while. Paul continued to keep himself up to date on cutting-edge culture and, with George Martin's help, he scored the soundtrack to the British movie ***The Family Way***. Perhaps most significantly, George took an extended break in India to absorb the culture and philosophy and to study sitar with **Ravi Shankar**, growing a moustache (at Ravi's suggestion) to disguise himself. Coincidentally, Paul grew one to hide a split lip caused by a moped accident and later John and Ringo followed suit (as did many men of the Western world).

> ***"That's it, I don't have to pretend to be a Beatle anymore."***
>
> George Harrison, on the plane out of The Beatles' final live concert, August 1966

In November 1966, John attended Yoko Ono's exhibition **Unfinished Paintings and Objects** at the Indica gallery and was intrigued and amused by the Japanese avant-garde artist's cryptic, witty exhibits: an all-white chess set, an apple on a perspex stand (priced at £200) and on the ceiling in tiny lettering, visible only after ascending a stepladder and looking through a magnifying glass, the word "yes". Though it would be a while before the Beatle and the artist got together, it was here that they would say they first "connected".

The group reconvened in late November 1966 to begin work on the album that would be known as ***Sgt Pepper's Lonely Hearts Club Band***. As the sessions (that lasted until mid-April 1967) progressed, it became clear to those on the inside that, while rumours were circulating throughout the media that The

Beatles were finished, the boys in Abbey Road studios were hitting an artistic peak.

1966 Singles

Paperback Writer/Rain

Parlophone; recorded April 13–16, 1966; released June 10, 1966; "Paperback Writer" currently available on *1962–1966* and *1*; "Rain" on *Past Masters Volume 2*

Two weeks at #1. "It's not one of our best songs, but it was the only one we had ready for the record release date" (John Lennon).

Eleanor Rigby/Yellow Submarine

Recorded April 28–June 6, 1966; released August 8, 1966; both tracks currently available on *Revolver*, *1962–66* and *1*

Four weeks at #1. "If Jesus were alive today in a physical form, not a metaphysical one, he would find **Eleanor Rigby** a very religious song, a song of concern with human experience and need" (US reporter).

1966 EPs

Yesterday

ACT NATURALLY/YOU LIKE ME TOO MUCH/YESTERDAY/IT'S ONLY LOVE

Parlophone; recorded February 17–June 17, 1965; released March 4, 1966

Nowhere Man

NOWHERE MAN/DRIVE MY CAR/MICHELLE/YOU WON'T SEE ME

Parlophone; recorded October 13–November 11, 1965; released July 8, 1966

1966 Albums

Revolver

TAXMAN/ELEANOR RIGBY/I'M ONLY SLEEPING/LOVE YOU TO/HERE THERE AND EVERYWHERE/YELLOW SUBMARINE/SHE SAID SHE SAID/GOOD DAY SUNSHINE/AND YOUR BIRD CAN SING/FOR NO ONE/DOCTOR ROBERT/I WANT TO TELL YOU/GOT TO GET YOU INTO MY LIFE/TOMORROW NEVER KNOWS

Parlophone; recorded April 7–June 21, 1966; released August 5, 1966; currently available on CD

Revolver is the album in which the "versatility" of The Beatles (for so long touted as a marketable "showbiz" asset by Brian Epstein) turned into a swaggering, surreal eclecticism. There were kids' songs, **acid rock**, hard soul protest rants, soothing ballads, Indian classical-style music, and arrangements for double string quartet. There were paeans to lovers, paeans to mind expansion, and even a sardonic paean to a drug dealer.

Hallucinatory dissonance met melodious beauty, and each disparate element was as convincing and intoxicating as the other. The group's interest in new sonic colours and textures, mirroring their drug-enhanced perceptions, was manifest on *Revolver* by a myriad of technical effects like Artificial Double Tracking (invented by the engineers of Abbey Road especially for The Beatles), varispeed, **reversed tape loops**, severe compression and tonal equalization), making for a record unlike anything anyone had heard before.

The most extreme example of the Fabs' new musical experimentation is the closing track, Lennon's remarkable **Tomorrow Never Knows**. It is a heady brew of thundering drums, incantational drones and apparently random electronic sound painting, with Lennon's voice

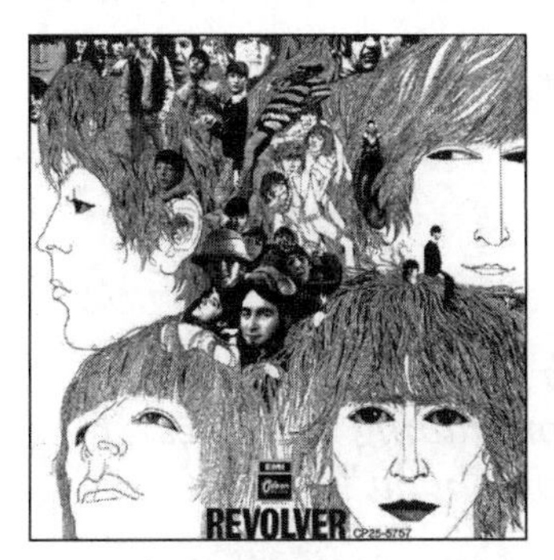

at the centre of the sonic storm, a distorted Dalai Lama (or so he had hoped) singing a psychedelic, philosophical lyric he adapted from the Tibetan **Book Of The Dead** (see p.190).

If it were all that radical and intense, ***Revolver*** may have been easier for The Beatles' mainstream audience to dismiss as simply strange, but the album eases the listener toward that shattering finale via a series of quieter but no less enthralling revolutions. **Taxman** (see p.192), George's tough whinge about 95 percent of his money disappearing to the government, is a scything opener.

Eleanor Rigby (see p.192) is a chilly, almost shockingly haunting tale sung by a spookily blank Paul McCartney to the sound of sawing cellos. **I'm Only Sleeping** makes the idea of a lie-in sound like the grooviest thing to do (thanks to varispeed and a backwards guitar solo), while **Love You To** is scarcely The Beatles at all – it's George doing Hindustani-esque classical music with some musicians from the North London Asian Music Circle. What's going on?

McCartney almost outdoes "Yesterday" for unadulterated melody with the straightforwardly romantic **Here There And Everywhere**, although his **For No One**, with its unusual, almost Pinter-esque vignette of a couple's emotional drift, has an intriguing, disconnected allure. **Good Day Sunshine** is one of the great feelgood summer songs, and still manages to pack in more time and key changes than most groups would bother with on an entire album.

Got To Get You Into My Life – all fat horns and drum fills – thumps along like a metronomic Motown number (although The Supremes were usually singing about love, whereas McCartney was singing about drugs). After largely acoustic instrumental contributions to the previous three albums, Lennon rediscovers his electric guitar and contributes three sinister, chiming rockers: **She Said She Said** (see p.193) is a stupendous group performance and has the biggest conventional rock sound on the album; **And Your Bird Can Sing** combines sneering put-down, compassionate loyalty and a defiant snarl of individuality in a tour de force of lead guitar double-tracking; and **Dr Robert** is an acrid, acid-country piece about an American drug contact for celebrities. Ringo singing one of the greatest kids' songs ever in **Yellow Submarine** is a reassuringly dopey moment but then those peculiar piano notes on Harrison's **I Want To Tell You** (nasty flat ninths, courtesy of that nice Paul McCartney) are, frankly, a bit disturbing.

There's an edge to the sound and a danger in the air on ***Revolver*** that makes listening to it an uncomfortable trip. It's easy to admire, even to be awed by, but some listeners find *Revolver* a little harder to love. It is, however, clearly brilliant, and for many it is the richest Beatles feast of all, vying regularly with The Beach Boys' *Pet Sounds* and The Beatles' own *Sgt Pepper* for top spot in Greatest Album Of All Time connoisseur polls.

A Collection Of Oldies... But Goldies

SHE LOVES YOU/FROM ME TO YOU/WE CAN WORK IT OUT/HELP/MICHELLE/YESTERDAY/I FEEL FINE/YELLOW SUBMARINE/CAN'T BUY ME LOVE/BAD BOY/DAY TRIPPER/A HARD DAY'S NIGHT/TICKET TO RIDE/PAPERBACK WRITER/ELEANOR RIGBY/I WANT TO HOLD YOUR HAND

Parlophone; recorded March 1963–June 1966; released November 9, 1966; original collection unavailable; all tracks currently available on *1962–1966* and *1* (except "Michelle" available only on *1962–1966* and *Rubber Soul* and "Bad Boy" available on *Past Masters Volume 1*)

A fair, if safe, mid-career compendium. For years it was the only place UK fans could purchase The Beatles' cover of Larry Williams' **Bad Boy**. Appearing briefly on EMI's budget label MFP, it was ultimately rendered redundant by subsequent collections and never made it to CD.

The studio years: 1967–68

"Everything we've done so far has been rubbish as I see it today. Other people may like what we've done but we're not kidding ourselves. It doesn't mean a thing to what we want to do now."

George Harrison, November 1966

The majority of early 1967 was spent on the sprawling recording sessions for the *Sgt Pepper* album, though the band found a few days at the end of January to make a pair of suitably strange promo films for the February-released double A-sided single, **Strawberry Fields Forever** and **Penny Lane** (see p.193). The last new Beatles music had appeared six months earlier, a relatively long gap for the band and, although the more experimental tracks on *Revolver* had clearly signalled a new direction, these two new tracks were something else entirely and the world didn't seem quite ready. Paul's "Penny Lane" was remarkable in its own right, and catchy enough to hit #1 in the US, but John's "Strawberry Fields Forever", splitting the airplay, was perhaps too rich a brew for the UK, and the single missed the top spot – The Beatles' first to do so for years.

But it would take more than a less-than-optimum UK chart position to knock Paul McCartney's confidence. With the extraordinary new album virtually complete, he knew The Beatles were on to something. When visiting friendly rivals The Beach Boys in April he even suggested Brian Wilson would need to "hurry up" with the Californians' response to *Revolver*. Indeed, Paul was feeling so inspired, he began to draft out a new project idea that started forming on the plane home: ***Magical Mystery Tour***.

Sgt Pepper's Lonely Hearts Club Band was rush-released on May 24, brought forward from the official release date of June 1. For millions it was the kaleidoscopic soundtrack to summer 1967, soon to be christened the **Summer Of Love**. Even the cover was special: an explosively colourful collage by Peter Blake. It depicted the moustachioed band dressed in dayglo military uniforms and holding wind instruments. They stand in a flowerbed next to rather forlorn-looking Madame Tussauds-style waxworks of their former selves (in moptops and suits) and they are haloed by dozens of famous and obscure personalities, from Oscar Wilde to Lenny Bruce, Stuart Sutcliffe to Stan Laurel. For the first time on a rock album the lyrics were printed on the back, inviting close

"Oh, I get it. You don't want to be cute anymore."

Bob Dylan, upon hearing *Sgt Pepper's Lonely Hearts Club Band*, May 1967

scrutiny and vivid interpretation. The gatefold sleeve opened up to reveal the four in close-up, looking dreamily into the camera. A cardboard insert featured five Sgt Pepper cut-outs including, indispensably, a **brown moustache**.

Musically, the album was a triumph and was received accordingly. The Beatles' artistic capabilities had exploded in response to their new tour-free existence, the influence of the avant-garde and, in George's case, a heightened sense of the spiritual. The Beatles had outdone themselves with a fantastical visual and aural overload of signs and signifiers that was not only a fabulous musical entertainment, it was one that sounded like it might actually mean something.

This was fabulous for the tuned-in generation, but parts of the British establishment were perturbed. The BBC banned the album's closing track **A Day In The Life** from airplay for supposed drug references – the presence of the phrases "I'd love to turn you on" and "Made my way upstairs and had a smoke" and the general air of hallucinatory wooziness suggest they may have had a point. Then Paul caused quite a scandal when, buttonholed by a news camera team, he admitted he'd taken LSD. The press had a field day and the other Beatles were annoyed. "Once Paul said it," remembered Ringo, reflecting on the interdependency of the group's reputation, "we all had to deal with it."

Later in June, The Beatles were given the opportunity to sing to the whole planet via the BBC's *Our World*, the first satellite broadcast to reach around 400 million people in 24 countries. Choosing John's casual message of hope, **All You Need Is Love** – "a subtle bit of PR for God" adjudged Harrison – The Beatles somehow managed to be both dangerous drug-takers and avatars of love. Such were the times.

After an aborted, substance-fuelled Greek holiday in July, having predictably decided against buying an island for the four of them to live on, The Beatles began to move away from drugs following George's August walkabout in **Haight-Ashbury**, San Francisco's hippy central. Expecting to find "groovy gypsy people making works of art", instead he found hordes of stoned, star-struck 'spotty youths' trying to give him drugs. In his tripping, fish-out-of-water paranoia, George quickly realised that "this was not it".

What *was* it, he decided, was transcendental meditation. In August John and Paul accompanied George to a lecture at the Hilton hotel given by **Maharishi Mahesh Yogi**, a mystical Indian advocate of meditation as a way of healing the world. Inspired by Maharishi's words of wisdom ("The flower of life blooms in love and radiates love all around," among others), they immediately signed up to his weekend course at Bangor, excited by the idea of a drug-free route to enlightenment.

While in Bangor, the shattering news came on August 27, 1967 that Brian Epstein had died of

Filming *Our World*

them from the NEMS contract. Eventually, the group decided to expand **Apple** – the publishing arm of a holding company within NEMS that Brian had set up for The Beatles before he died – and began managing themselves. With barely a pause for breath, The Beatles spent much of September and October recording the music and shooting the TV film of ***Magical Mystery Tour***, an improvised "happening" of a movie with no director, no script and a busload of whimsy. Paul did much of the organizing, John went along with it, George was, to use his phrase, "in another world", whilst Ringo thought it was "a lot of fun".

an apparently accidental overdose of pills in his flat in London. Comforted by the Maharishi's words that there was no such thing as death, and that Brian had merely "passed on", The Beatles were nevertheless numb with shock.

Quite apart from the devastating personal loss, there were The Beatles' business affairs to consider. Brian's brother Clive inherited NEMS, but wasn't interested in managing The Beatles. **The Bee Gees**' manager Robert Stigwood – to whom Brian had sold a majority share of NEMS – was very interested, only The Beatles weren't very interested in him. They even threatened never to record anything but "God Save The Queen" again if Stigwood refused to release

Paul, getting the taste for pointing a camera, directed the promo film for **Hello Goodbye**, the November single. It was unrelated to the forthcoming ***Magical Mystery Tour*** and commercial enough to have the *NME* pronouncing it "the complete answer for those who think The Beatles are going too way out". George, who had felt less than fully involved in the preceding few Beatles projects, began recording the soundtrack to the animated film ***Wonderwall*** while Ringo went to Rome to act in the movie *Candy*.

Six songs from *Magical Mystery Tour* appeared as a double EP in mid-December, and the colour was shown on black-and-white BBC1 at peak viewing time (8.35pm) on Boxing Day to a bemused, bored Britain. Critics were merciless. "It's colossal, the conceit of The Beatles," said the *Daily Mail*. "Blatant rubbish,“ said the *Daily Mirror*. "We will get over it," said Paul McCartney.

1967 Singles

Penny Lane/Strawberry Fields Forever

Parlophone; recorded November 24, 1966–January 17, 1967; released February 17, 1967; both tracks currently available on *1967–1970* and *Magical Mystery Tour*; "Penny Lane" also available on *1*

#2, kept off #1 by Engelbert Humperdink's **Please Release Me**. "Certainly the most unusual and way-out single The Beatles have yet produced … quite honestly, I don't really know what to make of it" (*NME*) (see p.193–195).

Shellshocked in Bangor, having learned of Brian's death

All You Need Is Love/Baby You're A Rich Man

Parlophone; recorded May 11–June 24, 1967; released July 7, 1967; both tracks currently available on *Magical Mystery Tour*; "All You Need Is Love" also on *1967–1970* and *1*

Three weeks at #1. "They wrote it because they really wanted to give the world a message. It is a wonderful, beautiful, spine-chilling record" (Brian Epstein).

Hello Goodbye/I Am The Walrus

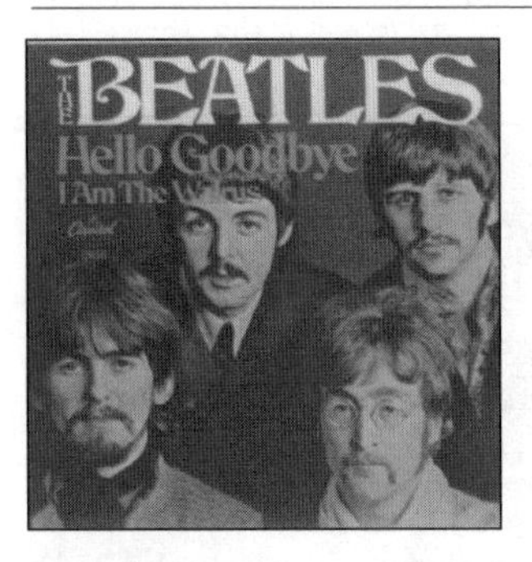

Parlophone; recorded September 5–November 7, 1967; released November 24, 1967; both tracks currently available on *1967–1970* and *Magical Mystery Tour*, "Hello Goodbye" also on *1*

Seven weeks at #1. **Bill Turner**, an old friend of The Beatles from Liverpool, on **Hello Goodbye**: "Well to be honest with you, I thought it was bit repetitious really, and not one of your best records". The *NME* on **I Am The Walrus**: "You need to hear it a few times before you can absorb it".

1967 EPs

Magical Mystery Tour

MAGICAL MYSTERY TOUR/YOUR MOTHER SHOULD KNOW/I AM THE WALRUS/FOOL ON THE HILL/FLYING/BLUE JAY WAY
Parlophone; recorded April 25–October 20, 1967; released December 8, 1967; all tracks currently available on *Magical Mystery Tour*; "Magical Mystery Tour", "I Am The Walrus" and "Fool On The Hill" also available on *1967–1970*

This double EP set reached #2 in the singles chart, kept off the top spot by **Hello Goodbye**. Lavishly presented with a 24-page full-colour booklet featuring photographs from the film and drawings by Bob Gibson, the artwork was an integral part of the *Magical Mystery* **Tour** experience at the time. Unfortunately some 12" and album CD issues omitted the booklet, though it was complete in the EP Box Set.

1967 Albums

Sgt Pepper's Lonely Hearts Club Band

SGT PEPPER'S LONELY HEARTS CLUB BAND/WITH A LITTLE HELP FROM MY FRIENDS/LUCY IN THE SKY WITH DIAMONDS/GETTING BETTER/SHE'S LEAVING HOME/BEING FOR THE BENEFIT OF MR KITE/WITHIN YOU WITHOUT YOU/ WHEN I'M SIXTY FOUR/LOVELY RITA/GOOD MORNING GOOD MORNING/SGT PEPPER'S LONELY HEARTS CLUB BAND (REPRISE)/A DAY IN THE LIFE
Parlophone; recorded December 6, 1966–April 4 1967; released June 1, 1967; currently available on CD

700 hours in the making, the trippy invention of this imaginative and musical record blew the world's mind in 1967. The most famous and discussed rock record of all time, it remains forty minutes of astounding popular art. Produced at a time when Paul McCartney was perhaps the most creative, adept and confident man in pop, Lennon could still be sufficiently inspired and intimidated into producing major work for The Beatles, and the group (not to mention their remarkably supportive producer and engineer) were prepared to spend as long as it took to make it extraordinary, ***Sgt Pepper*** can

still have the listening world shaking its head in wonder.

Paul's loosely applied concept of openly disguising The Beatles' identity behind a fictional band gave the group a licence to be as diverse and wilful as they chose. Given that LSD was at the time the recreational drug of choice for the band, this could have resulted in self-indulgent chaos. But these "divine messiahs, the wisest, holiest, most effective avatars the human race has yet produced" (as LSD guru **Timothy Leary** would put it in 1968) were still pop craftsmen at heart and the marshalled results from their freed imaginations were dazzling.

Set up as if it were an imaginary, continuous concert (complete with ambient audience noise, an orchestra tuning up, a welcoming theme, and the first two tracks famously segued together), the album actually soon settles into a more conventional unrelated sequence of tracks, albeit bound together by a reprise of the opening theme. However, the richness of the material, Peter Blake's enigmatic sleeve and the lyrics printed on the back cover encouraged all sorts of interpretations, meanings and a sense of continuity to be gleaned. Or, as Lennon would say later, "It worked because we said it worked".

Held together by George Martin's washy sonics and McCartney's inventive bass playing, it's a dizzying assortment of mood and manner. The opening number **Sgt Pepper** manages to cram spitting rock and a cheerful brass band into the same song (see p.197). Then there's the amiable pop of Ringo's slyly self-effacing turn, **With A Little Help From My Friends**, and Paul's whimsical daydreaming on **Fixing A Hole**; there's the "Lennon-in-Wonderland" of the effortlessly otherworldly **Lucy In The Sky With Diamonds** (see p.197); the sinister circus fantasy **Being For The Benefit Of Mr Kite!**; and depiction of the drudgery of an inappropriate marriage in Lennon's **Good Morning Good Morning**. George Harrison's philosophical meditation on life and love beyond self, **Within You Without You** (beautifully put together with Indian musicians and complemented by a superb George Martin string arrangement – see p.199), is perhaps the most outré five minutes of the album but, once surrendered to, is a central part of the *Pepper* experience.

It may be that many of the songs work best heard in the context of the album, but a couple of them stand out as masterpieces in their own right. McCartney's exquisite **She's Leaving Home** (see p.198) is a tale of genuine poignancy and empathetic wisdom, while Lennon/McCartney's **A Day In The Life** (see p.196) literally stands outside the LP's "virtual band" concept, fading in after the **Sgt Pepper** reprise as if the real Beatles have crept back onto their own album to tell it how it is. However, like **Tomorrow Never Knows** on *Revolver*, it is the climax which the album has been building up to. A track of startling dynamic range and seductive, apparently profound detail, it is The Beatles' greatest "stoned" moment.

It was inevitable that some of the critical assessment of subsequent generations would grumble. Some have griped about the archness of the band-within-a-band concept, the elaborate studio artifice, the dominance of McCartney's songs (routinely but unfairly considered as lightweight and bourgeois), the virtual freezing-out of George Harrison (McCartney played most of the telling lead-guitar lines himself) and the only episodic interest of a perpetually tripping Lennon. However, as long as there are pairs of ears willing to disappear under headphones for forty minutes, curious to find out what the fuss was all about, *Sgt Pepper* will continue to cast its considerable spell.

Magical Mystery Tour

MAGICAL MYSTERY TOUR/THE FOOL ON THE HILL/FLYING/ BLUE JAY WAY/YOUR MOTHER SHOULD KNOW/I AM THE WALRUS/HELLO GOODBYE/STRAWBERRY FIELDS FOREVER/ PENNY LANE/BABY YOU'RE A RICH MAN/ALL YOU NEED IS LOVE

Parlophone; recorded November 1966–November 1967; released USA November 1967, UK November 1976; currently available on CD

The reputation of the music of ***Magical Mystery Tour*** suffers somewhat from being related to the ill-received film that spoiled so many grown-ups' Boxing Day evening in 1967. Granted, the title track (some hope-

ful huckstering in the lyrics, the bare bones of a song accompanied by faintly tired brassy parping), the dreamy, functional twelve-bar instrumental **Flying** and McCartney's ho-hum kitsch **Your Mother Should Know** wouldn't be on anyone's Desert Island Beatles list, but the other three tunes are essential Beatlemusic.

McCartney's **Fool On The Hill** (see p.200) conjures obscure, cloudy magic while being catchy enough to inspire many a clueless cabaret version through the late 1960s. Harrison's **Blue Jay Way** is (after **Within You Without You**) his most haunting and convincing musical contribution of the period and possibly the most unnerving of all Beatles tracks. Lennon's mighty **I Am The Walrus** (see p.200) is among his own, his group's and his producer's greatest achievements, a snarling grab-bag of stream of consciousness imagery set to a suitably confusing chord sequence and a thunderous arrangement of "organised chaos", as George Martin put it.

"**Hello Goodbye**" is McCartney's harmless, facile word and chord-play that kept the far more challenging "Walrus" from being the A-side of the first post-Epstein single (much to Lennon's chagrin). It would have made a striking double-A side, even more magnificently polarised than the January 1967 tour-de-force that coupled Lennon's "Strawberry Fields Forever" (see p.193) to McCartney's "Penny Lane" (see p.195), tracks that also feature on the ***Magical Mystery Tour*** album. On that single, two of the most original pop writers of the century paraded their distinct musical personalities as if they were different ways of walking – in Lennon's case a halting, overwhelmed exploratory stumble, in McCartney's a bouncing, wide-eyed-with-wonder march – and it is routinely cited as the greatest single of all time. Interestingly, probably neither is as vivid in current popular consciousness as **All You Need Is Love**, Lennon's nonchalantly positivist anthem which is wheeled out whenever the troubled world needs some there-there reassurance.

1968: First bite of the Apple

"Although it was very beautiful and I was meditating about eight hours a day, I was writing the most miserable songs on earth."

John Lennon on Rishikesh, 1970

Contracted to film four Beatles movies for United Artists, the band allowed their third to be developed by an American animation company, King, who devised a cartoon based around Beatles' songs, "Yellow Submarine", without the band's direct involvement. They were persuaded, however, to make a swift in-person appearance at the end of the movie (filmed in January 1968) and to contribute four original songs. Three were semi-rejects from mid-1967 and the fourth, **Hey Bulldog,** was knocked off in a single recording session in February, which doubled as a promo shoot for **Lady Madonna,** their March-released single.

By mid-February, all four Beatles with wives, girlfriends and various friends in tow, had arrived in **Rishikesh**, India, for an extended drug-free meditation sojourn with the **Maharishi** at his Himalayan meditation centre. There were too many flies for Ringo and Maureen, who returned to England after two weeks. Paul lasted a month, while George and John, amid rumours of less than chaste behaviour by the Maharishi with a female member of the party, came home after two months.

The Beatles' Apple business venture had begun in December 1967 with the opening of the **Apple Boutique** on Baker Street, and in May 1968 John and Paul flew to New York to announce their extended plans for The Beatles' company. Apple was to be a non profit organization dedicated to artistic endeavour in the fields of music, film and electronics. Anyone with a good idea was invited to approach Apple and it was promised they wouldn't have to "go down on their knees".

Over the next year or so, with varying degrees of interest, "a high quotient of sincerity ... as well as a bit of madness", as Apple press director Derek Taylor observed, The Beatles dabbled at being hippy businessmen. The Apple office was located on **Savile Row** in London and housed Apple Records, Apple Films, Apple Electronics and associated employees, freaks and fools, conscientiously finding ways of spending The Beatles' money.

The most active arm of the company was Apple Records, and for their initial single releases, along with The Beatles' **Hey Jude** (see p.203) in August 1968, Paul produced **Those Were The Days** for 18-year-old winner of TV talent contest *Opportunity Knocks* Mary Hopkin. McCartney also wrote for and produced the Black Dyke Mills Brass Band, while George did the same for Liverpool singer Jackie Lomax. Both "Hey Jude" and "Those Were The Days" made #1, whilst the other two failed to chart. Future releases (often "under-promoted", the artists would complain) would feature James Taylor, Badfinger, The Modern Jazz Quartet, Billy Preston and the classical composer **John Tavener**, but were only sporadically successful.

Meanwhile, it was time for a new Beatles album. The weeks at Rishikesh had produced many new songs and with the individual composers reluctant to shelve any (perhaps with a view to quickly fulfil recording quotas), it was decided to record a double LP. The group convened at Abbey Road on May 30, 1968 to begin, but it soon became clear that the

> ***"We're in the happy position of not needing any more money. So for the first time, the bosses aren't in it for profit. We've already bought all our dreams. We want to share that possibility with others."***
>
> Paul McCartney on Apple, 1968

sessions were not going to go smoothly. Many things had changed within The Beatles camp, not least of which was John's obsessive affair with Yoko Ono.

Lennon's attraction to Yoko developed from artistic collaboration to a sexual relationship and, before long, total fixation. Back on the night of May 19, 1968, with Cynthia on holiday, John had invited Yoko to **Kenwood**, his Weybridge home, where they improvised some experimental tape recordings. They ended the evening in each other's arms. From pretty much that moment on – and for several years to come – neither his wife Cynthia, The Beatles nor anyone else would get the chance to deal with John without having to deal with Yoko by his side.

The Beatles' recording sessions ground on through the late spring and summer of 1968, often in a strained atmosphere. The other Beatles were unnerved by the constant presence of John's new love and a sense of **paranoia** began to pervade the group. John was only half-interested, particularly in songs that weren't his, and he was getting tenser by the day at the hostility – both perceived and real – towards himself and Yoko. George, as ever, was having to fight to get his songs seriously considered. Ringo felt so unwanted that he went as far as leaving the group for two weeks, until persuaded back by the others (he returned to find flowers adorning his drums). Trusted engineer **Geoff Emerick**, sickened by the atmosphere, also left and didn't return until mid-1969.

During breaks in the recording period, John and Yoko began to cut an exotic dash for the media, staging a series of art events (see p.222). And in July 1968 two events occurred that all in all seemed to firmly put a lid on The Beatles' psychedelic phase. ***Yellow Submarine***, the animated psychedelic fantasy, finally opened, both waving goodbye and sealing in celluloid forever the cartoon images of Pepper-era Beatles. And the **Apple Boutique** – once adorned with a trippy mural, now whitewashed into anonymity – closed due to lack of interest among both the public and the proprietors. The colourful clothes were given away.

The Beatles' image had become a lot more radical, largely due to Lennon's recent public profile and his song **Revolution** – an articulate refutation of violent upheaval that nonetheless still sounded dangerous – which was the B-side of the new single. But people still loved their music. **Hey Jude**, released in late August 1968, was a huge worldwide hit and it became their biggest-selling American single ever.

In September, Paul invited New Yorker Linda Eastman to move into his St John's Wood house with him. Paul and Jane Asher had split several months previously, after she had caught him with another woman, and Linda had been an occasional date of his since mid-1967. A photographer and former society girl, her innate rebelliousness, freedom of spirit and earthiness appealed to Paul and they soon developed an understanding that led to a life partnership of almost thirty years.

In a rush to complete the album, the final weeks of recording saw The Beatles putting in sixteen-hour days and taking over several studios at once in Abbey Road, recording what, in part at least, amounted to a series of solo tracks with group backing. Between October 16 and 17, 1968, John, Paul and George Martin spent 24 straight hours to sequence the 30 songs they had recorded into an album called *The Beatles* which, owing to the pure white cover designed by Richard Hamilton, quickly became known as ***The White Album***.

A day after the sequencing session, on October 18, John and Yoko were arrested for drug possession at their temporary home at Ringo's London apartment in **Montagu Square**. Tipped off by a journalist, they had cleaned the apartment days before, but arresting officer Detective Sgt Pilcher nevertheless managed to find some marijuana (Pilcher was jailed, much later, for planting evidence while investigating a different case). Lennon pleaded guilty in order to spare a pregnant Yoko, who was absolved of charge, and he received a mere £150 fine, but the mark on his record led to years of legal wrangling and personal anxiety when he tried to obtain a green card to reside in the United States in the Seventies.

November 22 saw the release of *The White Album*. It made it into the *Guinness Book of Records* as the fastest-selling album ever – almost two million in one week. Earlier in the month, there had been the little-heralded issue of ***Wonderwall***, the soundtrack to an Indian-made film, which featured Indian-inspired music by George Harrison. The next solo Beatle album, however, released on November 29, received rather more attention. Not only had John and Yoko decided to release the tapes they had made at Kenwood in May 1968, under the title *Unfinished Music No. 1: Two Virgins*, they also appeared completely nude on the sleeve. EMI refused to distribute it. "Why didn't you use Paul instead?" asked its chairman, Joseph Lockwood. "He's much better looking." **The Who**'s label Track distributed it in a brown paper cover, whilst many shops wouldn't handle it at all. "I didn't think there'd be such a fuss," said John. "The picture was to prove that we are not a couple of demented freaks, that we are not deformed in any way, and that our minds are healthy." Paul McCartney, himself quietly shocked, supplied the cryptically supportive sleeve note: "When two great saints meet, it is a humbling experience." The world looked on, wondering what on earth had happened to the Fab Four.

1968 Singles

Lady Madonna/The Inner Light

Parlophone; recorded January 12–February 8, 1968; released March 15, 1968; both currently available on *Past Masters Volume 2*; "Lady Madonna" also available on *1* and *1967–1970*

Two weeks at #1. "We've been trying to make a decent rock'n'roll record ever since we started and, as far as I know, we haven't done a decent one yet. This is another bash; it's pretty near it" (Ringo Starr) (see p.201).

Hey Jude/Revolution

Recorded July 9–August 1, 1968; released August 30, 1968; both currently available on *1967–1970* and *Past Masters Volume 2*; "Hey Jude" also available on *1*

Only two weeks at #1 in the UK, but nine weeks at the top in the US. "I wasn't sure if it was any good. I can never tell" (Paul McCartney) (see p.203).

1968 Albums

The Beatles (aka The White Album)

BACK IN THE USSR/DEAR PRUDENCE/GLASS ONION/OB-LA-DI, OB-LA-DA/WILD HONEY PIE/THE CONTINUING STORY OF BUNGALOW BILL/WHILE MY GUITAR GENTLY WEEPS/ MARTHA MY DEAR/I'M SO TIRED/BLACKBIRD/PIGGIES/ROCKY RACCOON/DON'T PASS ME BY/WHY DON'T WE DO IT IN THE ROAD/I WILL/BIRTHDAY/YER BLUES/EVERYBODY'S GOT SOMETHING TO HIDE EXCEPT ME AND MY MONKEY/SEXY SADIE/HELTER SKELTER/LONG LONG LONG/REVOLUTION 1/HONEY PIE/SAVOY TRUFFLE/CRY BABY CRY/REVOLUTION 9/GOOD NIGHT

Recorded May 10–October 14, 1968; released November 22, 1968; currently available on CD

The most opulent of Beatles albums, this seesaw of a record encompasses such a wide stylistic range that listening to it is like spinning the dial around a dozen different radio stations. Austerely packaged and grittily performed, it makes the technicolour psychedelic stew of ***Magical Mystery Tour*** seem an age away.

The famously tortuous recording sessions produced the most vivid manifestation yet of strong musical personalities threatening to overshadow the group's identity. There is no more Lennon-esque moment in the Fab canon than the bitter admonishment of his last guru **Sexy Sadie** (originally entitled **Maharishi, Maharishi What Have You Done**). There is no more McCartney-esque moment than the "fruity" (to use Harrison's word for McCartney's comic story songs) ska of **Ob-la-di, Ob-la-da**. Yet elsewhere on the record each man defies his caricature. **Goodnight**, John's lullaby for Julian, out-schmaltzes anything Paul would dare offer the group ("possibly over-lush", Lennon would later concede), while McCartney's sex-and-drugs-rush-number **Helter Skelter** (see p.205) is the most unruly shock rock the group ever committed to tape. Harrison meanwhile took a break from Indian music and composed his first major rock song for The Beatles, **While My Guitar Gently Weeps**, on which Eric Clapton guested on guitar (see p.202). He also contributed to one of his most overlooked songs, the almost not-there but quite lovely **Long Long Long**. Even Ringo got his first composition on there, **Don't Pass Me By**, a song he'd been talking about since 1963.

This has led many to suggest that *The White Album* is barely a Beatles album at all, but rather a series of solo tracks with the rest of the band acting as session musicians. While this is true to a point – neither Lennon nor McCartney was interested in songwriting collaboration at the time – the album's ensemble performances are nonetheless magnificent. As supporting musicians, the respective composers could hardly have wished for more sympathetic, expressive interpreters. Who else could have drilled Lennon's hazy maze of metric shifts into the brilliant, surreal whole that is **Happiness Is A Warm Gun** (see p.204)? And the group is as taut as a punch to the throat on his sarcastic **Glass Onion**, a contemptuous sneer at over-zealous lyric interpreters. Unfortunately, one such interpreter of this LP was the psychopathic Charles Manson, who claimed to have heard "messages" on *The White Album* which he used as justification for ordering members of his cult to commit murder in 1969.

From the compellingly visceral (**Yer Blues** and **Birthday**) to the comically whimsical (**Honey Pie** or **Martha My Dear**); from obscure confessionals (**Julia** and **Everybody's Got Something To Hide**) to wily political commentary (**Revolution** and **Blackbird**), some claim *The White Album* is the pinnacle of The Beatles' genius, others a disappointingly slack and indulgently incongruent effort. George Martin tried to persuade the band to trim the fat and make it a "really super" single album, starting a debate that continues to this day. But what would you leave off? **Savoy Truffle** (George's tough soul song about a box of chocolates)? **Wild Honey Pie** (Paul's semi-improvised exercise in descending diminished chords)? **Revolution 9** (John and Yoko's outrageous avant-garde tape-loop tone poem)? As McCartney said years later, "It's the bloody Beatles *White Album* – shut up!"

The end: 1969–70

"I took Paul home and I ended up in the garden crying my eyes out."

Mal Evans

Paul McCartney thought it was time to get The Beatles back to basics. His idea was to learn some songs, record them without frills, play them at a concert and film the whole thing. The Beatles convened on January 2, 1969 on a cold film stage at **Twickenham Studios** for what John would remember as "the most miserable session on earth". With relationships within the band already strained and further inhibited by the presence of the cameras, the only member with any real enthusiasm for the project was Paul. Harrison grew tired of McCartney's cajoling, and became irritated by Yoko's ubiquity and Lennon's unwillingness to engage. Feeling he was being musically bullied, he walked out after eight days.

An emergency meeting decided against filming any rehearsals, against Twickenham and against a concert, but decided in favour of recording a back-to-basics album and continuing to shoot an accompanying film. The project was moved into the basement of Apple at Savile Row, where the head of Apple Electronics, John's friend and current quasi-guru Alex Mardas (aka **Magic Alex**), had botched the installation of a promised 72-track studio (EMI had only just graduated to eight-track) so new equipment had to be borrowed. The adapted venture, named ***Get Back*** for the time being, recommenced on January 22.

A marginally happier mood prevailed, helped by the presence of keyboardist **Billy Preston**, whom The Beatles knew from their Hamburg days back when he was a 16-year-old organist in Little Richard's band. George bumped into Preston on the steps of the Apple office and, remembering how Eric Clapton's cameo on **While My Guitar Gently Weeps** had improved the atmosphere, invited him along to play. The project and film climaxed with a hastily arranged but well-played thirty-minute live set on the roof of Apple on January 30, before the police stopped the show after complaints about all the noise.

Though the album was always intended to present The Beatles' sound unadorned, the band were disheartened by the quality of the tapes and, apart from getting the songs **Get**

Back (see p.207) and **Don't Let Me Down** (see p.206) into a releasable state for their next single, they left engineer Glyn Johns to compile the best album he could on his own. Unimpressed by the results, The Beatles shelved *Get Back* for the time being.

Apple Corps, meanwhile, was spiralling out of control. "If we carry on like this," John said at the time, "all of us will be broke in six months." Long since bored by the idea of being businessmen, it was agreed that someone had to do something. John, George and Ringo wanted the legendarily tough New York negotiator and missing-royalty "discoverer" **Allen Klein** to sort out the group's affairs and Paul didn't, favouring instead Linda's father and brother, New York attorneys Lee and John Eastman. After a series of catastrophic meetings which descended into personal slanging matches between Klein and the Eastmans, Klein was appointed despite Paul's objections and took over Apple, firing most of the staff. "It wasn't just slimming down," remembered Neil Aspinall, "it was end of story."

The Apple rooftop gig: the last live Beatles performance

"I am not signed with Allen Klein because I don't like him."

Paul McCartney, 1969

In March 1969 Paul and Linda were married (the tenacious police sergeant **Norman Pilcher** chose that day to bust George and Patti Harrison at home for drug possession). John and Yoko, divorces from respective ex-spouses complete, were married in Gibraltar later in the same month, deciding to use the publicity as a platform to campaign for world peace. They staged a "bed-in", settling down in a room at the **Amsterdam Hilton** where they entertained the world's press from the comfort of their bed for several days, quite prepared to "be the world's clowns", as John put it, to promote the cause.

Although none of The Beatles were invited to either wedding, in April John and Paul got together at Abbey Road to record **The Ballad of John and Yoko** (see p.208), which became the next "Beatles" single, released in May, while **Get Back** was still #1 in the UK charts. John and Yoko flew to Canada for further "bed-in" events and recorded **Give Peace A Chance** in their hotel room in Montreal.

There had been sporadic Beatles' recordings since the aborted ***Get Back*** project, but there had been no particular purpose in mind. It was decided to invite George Martin – whose traditional role had rather faded during the *Get Back* sessions – back to record and produce an album in July and August. The sessions began without John, who had been in a car crash in Scotland, but when he returned to the studio – complete with an injured Yoko in a Harrods-provided bed – The Beatles put aside personal and business differences for a few weeks to make the album that would be their final record together, *Abbey Road*.

The album complete, John flew to Toronto to play in a rock'n'roll revival show on September 13, rehearsing the hurriedly assembled **Plastic Ono Band** of Eric Clapton (guitar), Klaus Voormann (bass) and Alan White (drums) as best he could on the plane journey. At a meeting back in London, John informed the stunned Beatles that he was leaving the group but was persuaded by Allen Klein not to make an announcement for business reasons. From autumn 1969, just as ***Abbey Road*** was released and Harrison's **Something** was selected by Allen Klein as the single, the four Beatles went about their own separate lives.

"Like anybody when you say 'divorce', their face goes all sorts of colours. It's like he [Paul] knew really that this was the final thing."

John Lennon, 1970

Over the following months, John Lennon was the most visibly active Beatle and continued to grab the headlines. His solo single **Cold Turkey**, a song offered to and declined by The Beatles, was a harrowing musical description of Lennon's withdrawal from heroin, something he and Yoko had been sporadically strung out on for a year. It charted in October 1969, while the elaborately packaged ***Wedding Album***, John and Yoko's third and final avant-garde release, didn't. In November the increasingly politicised and congenitally irreverent Lennon returned his MBE to the Prime Minister in protest against Britain's involvement in Biafra and Vietnam, and "against "Cold Turkey" slipping down the charts". December saw John and Yoko endorse the "Hanratty Is Innocent" protest (a controversial campaign to clear the name of Michael Hanratty, a young man convicted and hanged for murder in 1962); launch a **War Is Over If You Want It** poster campaign; and release *Live Peace In Toronto* in time for Christmas.

Ringo began recording an album of standards. George quietly joined the country-rock duo **Delaney and Bonnie** on their European tour. Paul retreated with his new family to his farm in Scotland to suffer what he would later describe as "almost a nervous breakdown".

1969 Singles

Get Back/Don't Let Me Down

Apple; recorded January 22–February 5, 1969; released April 15, 1969; both tracks currently available on *Past Masters Volume 2* and *1967–1970*

Six weeks at #1. "A song to roller-coast by" (Paul McCartney) (see p.207).

Ballad Of John And Yoko/Old Brown Shoe

Apple; recorded April 14–18, 1969; released May 30, 1969; both tracks currently available on *1967–1970* and *Past Masters Volume 2*; "Ballad Of John And Yoko" also available on *1*

Three weeks at #1. "It's 'Johnny B. Paperback Writer'" (John Lennon) (see p.208).

Something/Come Together

Apple; recorded April–July 1969; released October 31, 1969; both tracks currently available on *Abbey Road*, *1967–1970* and *1*

Only #4 in the UK. "A real quality hunk of pop" (*NME*) (see p.210–211).

1969 Albums

Yellow Submarine

YELLOW SUBMARINE/ONLY A NORTHERN SONG/ALL TOGETHER NOW/HEY, BULLDOG/IT'S ALL TOO MUCH/ALL YOU NEED IS LOVE/PEPPERLAND/SEA OF TIME*/SEA OF HOLES*/SEA OF MONSTERS*/MARCH OF THE MEANIES*/ PEPPERLAND LAID WASTE*/YELLOW SUBMARINE IN PEPPERLAND* (*GEORGE MARTIN ORCHESTRA)*

Apple; recorded May 26, 1966–February 11 1968; released January 17, 1969; currently available on CD

A tie-in "half-Beatles album" for the animated film of the same name, having only four "new" Beatles tracks made it a purchase of questionable value. Of the four, only Lennon's peculiarly menacing **Hey Bulldog** approaches blue-chip Beatles work. Harrison's *Sgt Pepper* reject **Only A Northern Song** features some possessed Starr drumming but little else of interest. McCartney's **All Together Now** only connects with pre-school kids who can manage to sit through the film, which was probably its intention. Though it starts invitingly enough, Harrison's **It's All Too Much** soon descends into lazily random, atonal fragments over a trippy drone: the dribbling nadir of The Beatles' psychedelic phase, at six and a half minutes it is indeed all too much.

Abbey Road

COME TOGETHER/SOMETHING/MAXWELL'S SILVER HAMMER/ OH! DARLING/OCTOPUS'S GARDEN/I WANT YOU (SHE'S SO HEAVY)/HERE COMES THE SUN/BECAUSE/YOU NEVER GIVE ME YOUR MONEY/SUN KING/MEAN MR MUSTARD/ POLYTHENE PAM/SHE CAME IN THROUGH THE BATHROOM WINDOW/GOLDEN SLUMBERS/CARRY THAT WEIGHT/THE END/HER MAJESTY

Apple; recorded February 22–August 18, 1969; released September 26, 1969; currently available on CD

Following the rancorous *Get Back* sessions and the bitter business feuding, against all odds the old teenage gang, who had somehow become the greatest pop group of all time, managed to keep the inevitable at bay for a precious few months, pull it all together and record a glorious swansong.

Unlike the comparatively raw *White Album*, ***Abbey Road*** has a proud, George Martin polish. It's the most luxurious-sounding Beatles record of all. Yet it retains *The White Album*'s astoundingly good group performances of involved, thought-through arrangements: The Beatles sound like a better band than they had ever been.

The ensemble coherence is especially involving on **Come Together** (see p.211), Lennon's semi-nonsensical Chuck Berry meets Timothy Leary in New Orleans number, and on the lusty heavy rock of **I Want You (She's So Heavy)** (see p.209). George, Paul and John even trade sets of four-bar guitar licks on **The End** (see p.212), the collaborative musical equivalent of tossing a ball around.

Throughout the album, quality control hardly seems to falter despite its giddy mix of styles and moods. There's a grotesquely light-hearted tale of homicide (McCartney's **Maxwell's Silver Hammer**), throwaway R&B (**Oh! Darling**), gossamer-delicate ballads (Harrison's beautiful **Something** – see p.210), Lennon's harmony-fest **Because**). Even Ringo's **Octopus's Garden** (another nautical-but-nice kids' song) is treated to a glossy, jazzy introduction and comically hammy backing harmonies.

As the final document of two musical giants attempting to share the same artistic space, it's fascinating. Though Lennon would later talk of himself and Paul "cutting each other down to size" being the reason The Beatles could no longer function as a group, it's also the reason why *Abbey Road* is such a success.

Individual excesses (a current taste for the "pure" and visceral on Lennon's part, a certain glibness on McCartney's) are by and large curbed while individual strengths, inspired by healthy but fierce competition, are built upon and lent generous artistic support, particularly McCartney's magnificent playing on Lennon's songs.

The cosmic pop-opera aspirations of side two's long medley is slickly presented but despite moments of obvious solemnity (such as McCartney's sighing comment on business squabbles **You Never Give Me Your Money**; see p.212), it never takes itself too seriously.

Moments of beauty (**Sun King**) give way to brutal humour (**Mean Mr Mustard**), the lullaby of **Golden Slumbers** segues into the apparently carefree barroom sing-song of **Carry That Weight** and even the earnest, moving maxim of **The End** – "the love you take is equal to the love you make" – has the rug pulled from it by the bathetic, irreverent sign-off of **Her Majesty**. *Abbey Road* remains a heartbreakingly fitting epitaph, perfectly summing up what The Beatles were: consummate artists with a light touch. Get a certain kind of music fan of a certain age in a certain mood and he'll tell you that pop music went downhill from here.

1970: Curtains

"We can't stop being Beatles, whatever we do. Besides, we're contracted to each other until 1977. I've only just found that out."

George Harrison, 1970

In the rough cuts of the *Get Back* film, George could be seen strumming what he calls "a heavy waltz" to Ringo at Twickenham entitled **I Me Mine**. The Beatles hadn't returned to the song at Apple so in order that it appear on the soundtrack album, on January 3 and 4, 1970, George, Paul and Ringo (John was out of the country) gathered at Abbey Road to record it and add some overdubs to **Let It Be**.

Though this was the last-ever Beatles recording session, it still wasn't the end of the *Get Back* project. Glyn Johns's second attempt to compile an album was turned down and in March, impressed with his work in helping record the Plastic Ono Band's single "Instant Karma" in late January, John and George invited Phil Spector to try to salvage a releasable album from the *Get Back* tapes. For seven days in March and April, Spector mixed, overdubbed choirs and orchestras and got Ringo to re-record his drums.

Paul had felt aggrieved enough (to the point of throwing Ringo out of his house) at having the release of his *McCartney* album postponed to make way for the new Beatles album, now pointedly renamed by Lennon *Let It Be*. McCartney managed to retrieve his original release date but, when he heard what Spector had done to The Beatles' music, he hit the roof.

When the album *McCartney* was released, to avoid having to face the press, but wanting something to promote his record, Paul wrote a "self-interview" and had it inserted into the sleeve of the record. Among the questions was "Do you foresee a time when Lennon/McCartney becomes an active songwriting partnership again?" to which he answered "No". It was all the press needed to announce to the world that Paul had left The Beatles.

Derek Taylor issued a hopeful press release in April 1970: "The World is still spinning, and so are we and so are you. When the spinning stops, that'll be the time to worry, not before. Until then, The Beatles are alive and well and the beat goes on, the beat goes on." In spite of Taylor's optimism, when the film and album of *Let It Be* were finally released a month later, in May 1970, it was almost in the atmosphere of a wake. The Fab Four were no more.

1970 Singles

Let It Be/You Know My Name (Look Up The Number)

Apple single; recorded May 1967–January 1970; released March 6, 1970; both currently available on *Past Masters Volume 2*; "Let It Be" on *Let It Be*, *1967–1970* and *1*

Peaked at #2. "Nothing to do with The Beatles" (John Lennon) (see p.208).

1970 Albums

Let It Be

TWO OF US/DIG A PONY/ACROSS THE UNIVERSE/I ME MINE/ DIG IT/LET IT BE/MAGGIE MAE/I'VE GOT A FEELING/ONE AFTER 909/THE LONG AND WINDING ROAD/FOR YOU BLUE/ GET BACK

Apple; recorded January 1969–April 1970; released May 8 1970; currently available on CD

"The wrong goodbye", "The black album": *Let It Be* has been called many things and, while none of them may be exactly right, they all concur that the last Beatles album amounted to a second-class send-off.

Recorded six months before ***Abbey Road*** but released nine months later, while it never approaches the heights of The Beatles' best work, Phil Spector's clever salvage job on the ragged ***Get Back*** tapes is a smooth if occasionally glutinous listen.

His much-maligned arrangement and production on McCartney's **Long And Winding Road** remains of questionable taste but his judicious pruning (trimming the lugubrious chromatic approach to the verse and chorus of **Dig A Pony**, for example), pertinent editing (extending Harrison's **I Me Mine** into a decent length) and gleaming sound, make a pretty decent record out of what Lennon would describe as the "shittiest load of badly recorded shit".

There's even the illusion of a group happily going about the collaborative business of expressing themselves. John and Paul sing joyously together on **Two Of Us** and **One After 909** (their first vocal harmony duets since **Day Tripper**) and cheerfully collide on **I've Got A Feeling**, featuring a McCartney verse and bridge bolted onto a Lennon interlude. The ensemble feel of the group as a whole is tidily businesslike throughout – the silky canter of **Get Back** is one of The Beatles' great grooves, and the addition of Billy Preston's electric piano on several cuts produces some welcome rootsy musical input and texture.

Though it was Lennon's energy that at long last got the album finished, his contributions – the riffily convoluted gobbledegook of **Dig A Pony** and the benignly hallucinatory **Across The Universe** (remixed from a February 1968 session) – are rather outshone by his erstwhile partner's.

McCartney's yearning **The Long And Winding Road**, despite Spector's dubious harps and heavenly choirs, quickly became a standard, as **Yesterday**, **Michelle** and **Here, There And Everywhere** had before it. His calming ballad **Let It Be** (see p.208) had an affecting sense of posthumous closure to it, despite having been written about eighteen months before The Beatles finally split.

Initially released in a box with a lavish, full-colour booklet (which was still named ***Get Back***), within a few weeks of the announcement of the split, the album was badly received. From today's perspective, however, ***Let It Be*** is clearly neither a "new phase Beatles album", as **Derek Taylor**'s back-cover blurb hyped it, nor indeed a "cheapskate epitaph, a cardboard tombstone", as *New Musical Express* seemed to think. The truth, as ever, lies somewhere in between.

Part 2: Afterlife

Don't believe in Beatles: 1970–80

For many who had grown up with the group, living through the break-up of The Beatles was a saddening experience. To see the beloved band that had represented such an explosion of artistic, social and spiritual possibilities in the 60s begin the 70s as bitter, feuding businessmen seemed to suggest that all the good feeling and optimism of the previous decade was an illusion to be somehow grown out of, especially when The Beatles played out much of their rancorous split in the public arena during 1970 and 1971.

There were the relatively restrained artistic statements. The cover of George's solo debut album proper **All Things Must Pass** pictured four garden gnomes symbolically insignificant next to a newly-risen earth father, the magnificently bearded Harrison in their centre. Lennon announced on his solo debut that among the things he didn't believe in (Buddah, kings, Kennedy) was "Beatles". Ringo meanwhile accentuated the human aspect of losing the old gang on **Early 1970**, the B-side to his 1971 single, "It Don't Come Easy", where he devoted an affectionate, comic verse to each of his old pals.

And then there was the musical sniping. From George toward Paul on *All Things Must Pass* (**Wah Wah**); from Paul towards John on his 1971 album *Ram* (**Too Many People**) and in a blistering climax to it all, from John to Paul on his 1971 album *Imagine* (**How Do You Sleep?**).

But then there was also the unthinkable court case in which Paul was forced to sue John, George and Ringo to dissolve The Beatles' partnership and rid himself of Allen Klein. Getting little joy from personal and legal letters or meetings with The Beatles through 1970, he served notice on his bandmates on December 31, 1970. Advised by Klein to resist McCartney's attempts to break up the partnership (for tax reasons), John, George and Ringo sent carefully worded affidavits to the February 1971 High Court hearing which, while admitting personal and business tension, amounted to a puzzled shrug as to why Paul would want The Beatles to end. Given it was Lennon himself who had pushed for "divorce" in the first place, his legal statement was particularly disingenuous, claiming

Paul and Linda leave the High Court, February 1971

that he couldn't understand why Paul would want to break up their partnership for any reason beyond their Klein and Eastman bickering.

And there was also the sour discourse conducted through the pages of the music press. The responses of John, George and Ringo, when asked about Paul's solo work, ranged from the "disappointed" (Harrison) to the scathing "rubbish" (Lennon). John gave a widely quoted, militant anti-Beatles interview to *Rolling Stone* in late 1970 in which he asserted that The Beatles were the "biggest bastards on earth".

Having succeeded in getting a receiver appointed to handle Apple in March 1971 and to freeze the individual Beatles' earnings until the mess was sorted out (after which the defeated three Beatles reputedly drove to McCartney's Cavendish Avenue house and put a brick through his window), Paul gave an interview to *Melody Maker* in November expressing the wish that the four Beatles could just get together and "sign a piece of paper saying it's all over". This prompted John to fire a vicious letter to the same paper which, despite being trimmed by *Melody Maker* for potentially libellous content, was no less scurrilous than "How Do You Sleep?", accusing McCartney of having politics akin to Mary Whitehouse. "What about the tax?" raved Lennon. "It's all very well playing simple honest ole human Paul in the MM but you know damn well we can't just sign a piece of paper."

Relations eventually improved between John and Paul from 1972 onwards when they sat down to dinner in New York and agreed to stop "slagging each other off in the press". In 1974, they even jammed together in Los Angeles with, among others, **Stevie Wonder**. Businesswise, The Beatles' partnership was officially dissolved in April 1975 although, ironically, John, George and Ringo had fired Allen Klein as their business manager by 1973. "Let's say possibly Paul's suspicions were right," said John at the time.

For the whole of the 1970s, despite pursuing their separate careers and doing their best to avoid meeting in public, the four Beatles constantly had to field the big question about a possible **reunion**, and their answers varied hugely. John said in 1973 "The chances are practically nil". Then, later that year, the promising "There's always a chance. As far as I can gather from talking to them all, nobody would mind doing some work together again." In 1974, he backtracked: "No, what for? We did it all. Christ, we can't even get the four of us together for a meeting, let alone play." And backtracked again later that year: "You never know, you never know. I mean, it's always in the wind." George admitted in 1974 that he'd "join a band with John Lennon any day", but that he "couldn't join a band with Paul McCartney". Paul, two years into his new band Wings seemed doubtful in 1974: "I just don't think it'll work actually, it might not be as good." John was more upbeat in the following year: "I've lost all negativity about the past … I'd do **Hey Jude** and the whole damn show, and I think George will eventually see that."

> ***"I think I'm happier than I've ever been."***
>
> Paul McCartney, 1974

American promoters started publicly inviting The Beatles to re-form. In 1976 LA promoter **Bill Sargent** offered $50 million for a one-off televised concert and, when he received no response, doubled the offer to $100 million. John was reportedly keen, although Paul revealed, "I spoke to the bugger [John] and he didn't even mention it. Where do you go from there?" The same year Sid Bernstein, The Beatles' original US promoter, took out a full-page ad in the **New York Herald Tribune** suggesting The Beatles reunite for a charity concert. "It's trying to put the responsibility of making the world a wonderful world again onto The Beatles," George pointed out, "I think that's unfair." Lorne Michaels, host of the TV show *Saturday Night Live*, offered a tongue-in-cheek $3000 for a Beatles reunion on air. As it happened, John and Paul were actually watching the programme during one of their rare evenings together at John's New York apartment, and went as far as booking a taxi to the show. "We almost went down to the studio, just as a gag," John later recalled, "but we were actually too tired."

EMI meanwhile explored a range of repackaging schemes to exploit their Beatles catalogue in the 1970s. In 1973, the double album collections *1962–1966* (the "Red" album) and *1967–1970* (the "Blue" album) appeared and sold remarkably well. For fans who already had everything, the only really interesting release of the period was *The Beatles Live At The Hollywood Bowl*. This was closely followed in October by another EMI/Capitol double album compilation, *Love Songs*, which prompted Ringo to complain. "Please let us know what you're doing with the records we made," he asked of EMI in an interview at the time. "We'd like it done, how do I say … nicely!" With the reissue programme, the silly money offers and the fact that Paul's hugely successful **Wings Over America** tour was featuring Beatles songs in his live set for the first time, it's little wonder reunion speculation reached fever pitch in the mid-1970s.

But ultimately, the only four-way reunion The Beatles could be persuaded to endorse was a legal one to prevent unofficial Fab-related product they were unhappy about. Through the 1970s, there were various Beatle-connected items that had nothing to do with the group and which they could do little about. They didn't sue the producer (Robert Stigwood) of Willie Russell's 1974 stage play *John, Paul, George, Ringo and Bert*, but they didn't think much of it either; George left at the interval, Paul objected to being portrayed as the spoilsport villain and denied Stigwood the film rights. However, The Beatles' failure to prevent the 1977 album release of a 1962 live performance from Hamburg's **Star Club**, and their inability to influence or prevent the artistic fiasco of Stigwood's 1978 movie ***Sgt Pepper's Lonely Hearts Club Band***, resolved them to get organized. "We've just got together a group of people to go and sue them all," announced George in an unguarded moment in 1979. The first targets were the producers of a hugely successful stage show called ***Beatlemania*** that had

> ***"Well, if it's money you want, there's no problem here … You know the words. It'll be easy. Like I said, this [cheque] is made out to 'The Beatles' – you divide it up any way you want. If you want to give Ringo less, it's up to you. I'd rather not get involved. I'm sincere about this …"***
>
> Lorne Michaels, *Saturday Night Live*, April 24, 1976

been running since April 1977 and which had spawned five other productions showing all over the US. Settling for several million dollars in "actual and punitive damages", the group's new tough attitude was represented by George Harrison's statement at the time: "People were just thinking The Beatles were like public domain," he said. "You can't just go round pilfering The Beatles' material."

Lennon and McCartney's briefly renewed friendship came to an abrupt end when an annoyed John told Paul off in 1976 for arriving unannounced, guitar in hand, at John's New York apartment in the **Dakota** (a huge nineteenth-century building near Central Park) once too often. "It's not 1956 and turning up at the door isn't the same anymore," John recalled telling him. "That upset him."

They were never to meet again. In the memoirs of former employees of John and Yoko's that would later emerge, it was alleged that Yoko would intercept Paul's calls to John, with one in particular being rather controversial. In January 1980 Paul suggested visiting the Dakota before flying from New York to Japan for a tour, mentioning he had some particularly potent marijuana on him to share. Yoko said no. Two days later, McCartney was arrested at **Tokyo airport** for possession of illegal substances and spent ten days in jail. It was hinted at that the Japanese authorities might have received a tip-off from someone with insider information – someone who would have known exactly what Paul was carrying.

Paul did try to contact John again in mid-1980, having heard that he was back in the

The death of John Lennon

By autumn of 1980, Mark David Chapman – a 25-year-old Beatles fan with deep psychological problems – had become obsessed with the idea that John Lennon was a "phoney". He quit his job as a security guard in Honolulu, travelled to New York and telephoned his Japanese wife to tell her he was planning to "murder John Lennon". Stalking the street outside the Dakota building, Chapman waited for a sight of Lennon for weeks. He finally got lucky at 4pm on Monday, December 8, when John was leaving the Dakota for a recording session and stopped to sign a copy of *Double Fantasy*, his new album, for Chapman. Later that evening, at 10.52pm New York time, John and Yoko returned from a recording session and stepped from their limousine onto the near-deserted street outside the Dakota. From the shadows, Chapman called out "Mr Lennon" and fired five bullets into John. Lennon staggered into the lobby of the Dakota, losing a great deal of blood. Rushed to St Luke's Roosevelt Hospital by ambulance, efforts to revive him failed and he was pronounced dead at 11.07. Lingering at the scene of the crime, Chapman was arrested while calmly reading a copy of J.D. Salinger's novel of teenage alienation, ***Catcher in the Rye***. "I've got a big man inside of me and I've got a little man inside of me," he was heard to say. "The little man is the man who pulled the trigger."

studio after five years of being a house husband but, allegedly, Yoko once more refused to put him through to John. Recalling the occasional phone conversation he and John had in the 1970s about babies and bread-baking, McCartney talks of how relieved he is that he and John "made it up" before Lennon was killed. Yoko, however, has intimated that Paul promotes the "friends again" scenario because "it suits him".

John Lennon's tragic death in New York at the hands of a deranged fan on December 8, 1980, shocked the world. The public's expression of grief took the form of vigils in New York and Liverpool and was testament to how meaningful Lennon, The Beatles and their songs still were to people, ten years after the group's demise.

Mourners gather outside the Dakota, its flag at half-mast, the day after Lennon's murder

"The Red Album" 1962–1966

LOVE ME DO/PLEASE PLEASE ME/FROM ME TO YOU/SHE LOVES YOU/I WANT TO HOLD YOUR HAND/ALL MY LOVING/ CAN'T BUY ME LOVE/A HARD DAY'S NIGHT/AND I LOVE HER/EIGHT DAYS A WEEK/I FEEL FINE/TICKET TO RIDE/ YESTERDAY/HELP!/YOU'VE GOT TO HIDE YOUR LOVE AWAY/WE CAN WORK IT OUT/DAY TRIPPER/DRIVE MY CAR/ NORWEGIAN WOOD/NOWHERE MAN/MICHELLE/IN MY LIFE/GIRL/PAPERBACK WRITER/ELEANOR RIGBY/YELLOW SUBMARINE

Apple; recorded June 1962–August 1966; released May 1973; currently available on CD

"The Blue Album" 1967–1970

STRAWBERRY FIELDS FOREVER/PENNY LANE/SGT PEPPER'S LONELY HEARTS CLUB BAND/WITH A LITTLE HELP FROM MY FRIENDS/LUCY IN THE SKY WITH DIAMONDS/A DAY IN THE LIFE/ALL YOU NEED IS LOVE/I AM THE WALRUS/HELLO GOODBYE/THE FOOL ON THE HILL/MAGICAL MYSTERY TOUR/LADY MADONNA/HEY JUDE/REVOLUTION/BACK IN THE USSR/WHILE MY GUITAR GENTLY WEEPS/OB-LA-DI, OB-LA-DA/GET BACK/DON'T LET ME DOWN/THE BALLAD OF JOHN AND YOKO/OLD BROWN SHOE/HERE COMES THE SUN/ COME TOGETHER/SOMETHING/OCTOPUS'S GARDEN/LET IT BE/ACROSS THE UNIVERSE/THE LONG AND WINDING ROAD

Apple; recorded December 1966–January 1970; released May 1973; currently available on CD

The Allen Klein-compiled, career-spanning-Beatles double-album collections were released (despite Paul's objections) to combat the blatant marketing of the **Alpha Omega** bootleg compilations in America. Some strange weighting (six cuts from *Rubber Soul*, only two – the singles – from *Revolver*, only three from the thirty-track *White Album*) and odd, possibly partisan choices on Klein's part (George's idiosyncratic B-side **Old Brown Shoe**) notwithstanding, these were enjoyable and very popular collections. Though packaged as rather unwieldy, not to say poor-value double-CD sets, they remain the only compact singles-and-beyond overviews available and are decent starting-places for Beatle rookies and sceptics.

Live At The Hollywood Bowl

TWIST AND SHOUT/SHE'S A WOMAN/DIZZY MISS LIZZY/ TICKET TO RIDE/CAN'T BUY ME LOVE/THINGS WE SAID TODAY/ROLL OVER BEETHOVEN/BOYS/A HARD DAY'S NIGHT/ HELP!/ALL MY LOVING/SHE LOVES YOU/LONG TALL SALLY

Parlophone; recorded August 1964 and August 1965; released May 1977; currently unavailable

Recorded by Capitol producer Voyle Gilmore for possible release at the height of Beatlemania, the band thought the tapes weren't releasable at the time, although John did hand them to Phil Spector after his ***Let It Be*** duties, who reportedly got the tapes to acetate stage ready for release on Apple in 1971. In 1977 EMI asked a sceptical George Martin, who remembered the shows as unsatisfactory, to do what he could. Martin and Geoff Emerick transferred the three track recordings to 24-track and edited the best material from two shows a year apart into a seamless "single concert". The end result has a palpable sense of excitement. There's a musical exuberance and commitment that belies the tiredness and growing cynicism the band later admitted to feeling about their shows of the period. That they played anything of musical value at all given the inadequate amplification and the wall of teenage hysteria that faced them (and, on the record, us) is miraculous. Unfortunately, the record never made it onto CD and was deleted from the catalogue in the mid-1990s so as not to distract from the live tracks on the **Anthology** releases, although there has been talk of a reissue. Meanwhile, the vinyl is well worth tracking down in the secondhand bins.

We were worlds apart: 1981–90

In the aftermath of John's death, the remaining three Beatles briefly relaxed their guard about being seen together in any situation that may have been misconstrued as a reunion. Paul sang backing vocals and Ringo drummed on George's tribute single to John **All Those Years Ago** in 1981 – their first recording together since 1970's "I Me Mine". They were photographed together, along with their wives, at Ringo's wedding to actress **Barbara Bach** in April 1981. Ringo continued to get on well with both the other Beatles (and ended up drumming on McCartney's next album, ***Tug of War***) but George remained wary of Paul. "The thing with Paul is one minute he says one thing and he's really charming," pondered George in the 1980s, "and the next minute, you know, he's all uptight."

On the anniversary of John's death in December 1981 EMI announced the release of all The Beatles' original EPs in a box set (a singles box appeared a year later). They also declared that, in the year since Lennon was killed, an incredible **75 million Beatles records** had been sold around the world. From October 1982, the company embarked on a decade-long twentieth-anniversary release schedule of all The Beatles' singles, mirroring the original release dates of twenty years earlier, along with the rather feebly packaged **The Beatles 20 Greatest Hits**.

Neil Aspinall had already completed a version of the long-mooted official history of The Beatles, *The Long And Winding Road*, as far back as 1971 but prevarication and disinterest from the band meant that in November 1982 they were beaten to the punch by the independently produced two-hour video rockumentary *The Compleat Beatles*. However, Apple Corps' recently strengthened legal muscle ensured that The Beatles received substantial royalties from the video sales. Another litigation target was Apple Computers over use of the name and logo, resulting in a large settlement in favour of Apple Corps. Even EMI itself was taken to court, for alleged royalty discrepancies. This dispute was resolved in The Beatles' favour in time for the long-awaited release of The Beatles albums on CD over the course of 1987, centring on a twentieth-anniversary release of *Sgt Pepper* in June 1987, an occasion the album's opening line was made for.

From the mid-1980s, Ringo, George and Yoko were involved in a legal battle with Paul and EMI. In the 1970s McCartney had re-signed to Capitol/EMI in a substantial solo deal in which he negotiated himself a bigger cut of royalties from existing Beatles records. The remaining three Apple partners, when they found out, decided to challenge the legality of the deal. This alienated Paul to such an extent, he cited the "still-existing business differences" as the reason not to attend The Beatles' induction into the third **Rock and Roll Hall of Fame** in New York in 1988. George, Ringo and Yoko (with John's sons Julian and Sean) showed up, with Yoko announcing, pointedly, that "John would have been here." "We all loved him so much," said George of John in his speech, before adding, "and we all love Paul so much."

> ***"For about ten years I didn't really know Paul... but more recently we've been hanging out, getting to know each other, going for dinner, meeting, having a laugh."***
>
> George Harrison, 1988

Thankfully, by November 1989 a deal that suited all parties had been reached – one "that no one would be permitted to make any comment on", according to the EMI spokesman. McCartney, clearly relieved, even announced that he had been discussing "a lot of exciting possibilities with George and Ringo".

A meticulously compiled pair of albums of rarities – *Past Masters Volumes 1 & 2* – appeared in March 1988, ensuring that everything The Beatles released on EMI between 1962 and 1970 was now available over a total of fifteen CD albums. An agreement reached with EMI/Capitol in 1989 also gave The Beatles control of future use of all their EMI recordings. This meant that any shoddy repackaging ideas (like 1983's pointless *Reel Music*, deleted after two years, and the ignominious relegation of the Rock 'N' Roll Music collection to EMI's budget label, Music For Pleasure) could now be nipped in the bud by Apple.

Past Masters Volume One

LOVE ME DO/FROM ME TO YOU/THANK YOU GIRL/SHE LOVES YOU/I'LL GET YOU/I WANT TO HOLD YOUR HAND/ THIS BOY/KOMM, GIB MIR DEINE HAND/SIE LIEBT DICH/ LONG TALL SALLY/I CALL YOUR NAME/SLOW DOWN/ MATCHBOX/I FEEL FINE/SHE'S A WOMAN/ BAD BOY/YES IT IS/I'M DOWN

Parlophone; recorded September 1962–June 1965; released March 1988

Past Masters Volume Two

DAY TRIPPER/WE CAN WORK IT OUT/PAPERBACK WRITER/ RAIN/LADY MADONNA/THE INNER LIGHT/HEY JUDE/ REVOLUTION/GET BACK/DON'T LET ME DOWN/THE BALLAD OF JOHN AND YOKO/OLD BROWN SHOE/ACROSS THE UNIVERSE/LET IT BE/YOU KNOW MY NAME (LOOK UP THE NUMBER)

Parlophone; recorded October 1965–January 1970; released March 1988; currently available on CD

Mopping up the remaining singles, B-sides and EP tracks not already on CD, the *Past Masters* releases built on the earlier, short-lived and incomplete 1979 vinyl collection *Rarities*. For the generation of Beatles fans that grew up in the 1970s or later, with only the albums to go on, they were revelatory. Compiled with typical thoroughness by Beatles authority Mark Lewisohn, *Past Masters* remains the only place you can hear Ringo playing **Love Me Do** from September 4, 1962 (sounds alright to me, Mr Martin) and various B-sides from the Beatlemania era that may be throwaway but have plenty to recommend them. **Thank You Girl** has some excitable fills from Ringo on the outro, **I'll Get You** is amusingly barefaced formula writing and **This Boy** features some delightful early-Fabs vocal harmonies.

The entire "Long Tall Sally" EP, recorded during the sessions for *A Hard Day's Night*, is here, although the music is clearly less accomplished than that which made the album. Lennon's **I Call Your Name** is an ersatz **You Can't Do That**, with a clumsy ska middle section, and **Slow Down** is all over the place. On the other hand, McCartney's take on Little Richard's **Long Tall Sally** is positively ecstatic.

McCartney's 1964 perky pop-blues **She's A Woman** and Lennon's lush **Yes It Is** remain two of the best Beatles B-sides, while the sonorous clang of Lennon's 1966 song **Rain** (featuring career-high performances from Starr and McCartney; see p.191) was so persuasive that later neo-psychedelic groups based a large part of their musical style on it.

The Inner Light is the final and perhaps the loveliest of Harrison's Indian-influenced tracks, the **Revolution** you'll find here is the faster, fuzzed-up version from "Hey Jude"'s B-side, and Lennon's heartfelt **Don't Let Me Down** (see p.206) which, though rightfully now part of 2003's *Let It Be ... Naked*, was originally only available as the B-side to "Get Back".

1969's **Old Brown Shoe** is perhaps the densest, sharpest Harrison song to make it onto a Beatles record, while 1969's **You Know My Name** (released in March 1970 as the B-side of "Let It Be") is a goofy ramble into Goons territory that had been hanging around half-finished since 1967.

The ***Past Masters*** albums' blend of the ephemeral with the essential, the over familiar with the dusty and obscure, makes for an uneven listen. But, for the handful of key tracks unavailable elsewhere, without which the picture of The Beatles' music would be incomplete, they continue to be essential.

It's the next best thing: 1991–2009

In the early 1990s the three Beatles, through Apple Corps, sued Apple Macintosh again. Nine years earlier, they had allowed the computer company to trade with the name and logo Apple on the understanding that Apple computers would not be used to make music. The fact that from the late 1980s Apple computers had been widely used for musical purposes cost Apple Mac an undisclosed but substantial sum in 1991.

In the same year, EMI ran foul of Apple Corps once more (by trying to release the **"Red"** and **"Blue"** albums on CD without asking The Beatles first) as did Sony, who tried issuing their own version of live recordings from the **Star Club** in Hamburg.

But it wasn't all sue-me-sue-you blues in the 1990s. The Beatles' settlement with EMI had given them the authority to exploit their released and unreleased recorded legacy howsoever they chose. Excerpts from The Beatles' BBC sessions recorded between 1962 and 1965 had appeared on bootlegs since the 1970s and on various radio series in the 1980s, but in 1994 the official release of the 56-track CD ***Beatles Live At The BBC*** appeared. Featuring versions of thirty songs unavailable on any officially released Beatles record, it was hugely popular, eventually selling upwards of an astonishing nine million copies worldwide.

However, this was nothing compared to the media frenzy that accompanied The Beatles events of 1995. There had been increasingly enthusiastic talk within The Beatles' camp of picking up the abandoned *Long And Winding Road* documentary film project and even George, the least sentimental of The Beatles, agreed that it was time to tell the story their way. There were even hints that the remaining Beatles were thinking of composing some new background music for the project.

Then George and Neil Aspinall decided to approach Yoko to find out if she had any undeveloped demo tapes of John Lennon's that they could work with, with a view to the remaining three Beatles finishing them off to create "new" Beatles music. Things went well enough to convince Paul to attend the 1994 **Rock and Roll Hall of Fame** to induct John Lennon. Paul and Yoko gave each other a public hug and Yoko handed over private tapes of four of John's songs with her good wishes. "Give the three of them a chance!" she implored at a press conference.

In previous discussions about the documentary, George had vetoed using a McCartney song as the title of the project. This, and the appointment of Harrison's pal Jeff Lynne (leader of the **Electric Light Orchestra**, producer of Harrison's 1987 album *Cloud Nine* and fellow Traveling Wilbury) as producer, suggested that he might well have been reluctant to face the McCartney/Martin consortium so dominant on the later Beatles sessions.

The official line was that George Martin's failing hearing meant he didn't trust himself for the job – although he did manage to oversee all three of the CDs that would accompany ***Anthology*** perfectly well. Jeff Lynne cleaned up the Lennon demos while McCartney managed to take the heat out of the emotionally charged sessions by suggesting that the remaining Beatles imagine John had gone on holiday with the instruction to "finish up" the tracks in his absence. Paul and George disagreed about lyrics and arrangements (Paul later conceded that George "was right") but the "Threetles" managed to grind out two tracks during a handful of sessions over fifteen months before George decided enough was enough, leaving a third track incomplete.

Though undoubtedly a triumph from a marketing and financial perspective, the ***Anthology*** project produced mixed results – both the documentary and the accompanying music. After all the hype surrounding the "new Beatles single", **Free As A Bird**, it was ultimately rather upstaged by Joe Pytka's remarkable collage video made to accompany it when it was eventually released in December 1995. The ***Anthology*** documentary was turned into a six-part TV series, and was sold to 110 countries. The second new single, **Real Love**, released in March 1996, suffered the indignity of not even being playlisted by BBC Radio One, Britain's national pop radio station, which had been proud to premiere **Free As A Bird** only months earlier.

And the three ***Anthology*** double CDs featuring Beatles outtakes and previously unreleased rarities were generally thought to be, even by Beatles enthusiasts, rather more than was entirely necessary. Yet that didn't stop them selling over twenty million copies and, along with knock-on sales of other Beatles albums in the wake of all the publicity, 1996 became the biggest year ever for Beatles album sales.

Relationships amongst The Beatles in the late 1990s were characterized by fresh frost. "He's not been that easy to get on with," said Paul of George in 1997. "I've rung him and maybe he hasn't rung back." Yoko, in response to Paul's self-aggrandizing in his official biography **Many Years From Now** in 1997, claimed John to be the "spiritual leader" of the group: "He [John] was the visionary and that's why The Beatles happened." When Linda McCartney died in 1998, Yoko was not invited to the memorial service in New York.

The ***Yellow Submarine Songtrack*** was released in 1999, in tandem with the remastered DVD release of the 1968 cartoon movie, and caused a bit of a stir among purists due to its being remixed, but the ***Anthology*** book was to grab more headlines that year. Its eventual appearance (four years after the TV series) saw midnight launch parties in bookshops in 1999 and healthy business. Putting even that event in the shade, however, was the clamorous arrival in late 2000 of *1* (a 27-track collection of #1 hit singles) which meant – based on only five weeks of sales – that the group ended up as the bestselling musical act of 2000, thirty years after they split up.

For a while through 2002, following George's tragic death from cancer in November 2001, once more Beatlemusic was heavy with poignancy. For all the vulgar, awkward spectacle of most of the Queen's Jubilee Concert in June 2002, the sights and sounds of Paul (along with Eric Clapton, reprising his guitar role on the original) singing **While My Guitar Gently Weeps** in tribute to George was undeniably moving. And when Paul sang "Something" and "All Things Must Pass" at the Concert For George at the Royal Albert Hall in November 2002, grown men wept.

That event also marked the first time Paul and Ringo had played together on-stage since

The Free As A Bird video

For the promo video of The Beatles' 1995 single "Free As A Bird", imaginative advert director Joe Pytka came up with the idea of a hallucinatory bird's-eye flight over Liverpool and London with myriad Beatles references throughout. The result was perhaps one of the most brilliant and most viewed pop promos ever made. It was a clever move which captured the imagination of Beatles fans who can't help but try and join the dots of hidden meaning in The Beatles' work (despite Lennon's admonishment of them in "Glass Onion"), simply because it was fun. There are between eighty and a hundred allusions to The Beatles' story, music and lyrics in the video. Here are a few:

- The sound of a bird's wings flapping can be heard (**Across The Universe**)
- In front of the picture of George on the mantlepiece there is an **Old Brown Shoe**
- The sun comes through the window (**Here Comes The Sun**)
- People run and hide their heads (**Rain**)
- The bouncer at The Cavern has a noticeable "flat-top" (**Come Together**)
- There is a Silver Hammer store next to the bakery (**Maxwell's Silver Hammer**)
- See how they (the kids) run (**Lady Madonna**)
- An eggman unloads eggs (**I Am The Walrus**)
- The video has a barrow in the marketplace (**Ob-La-Di, Ob-La-Da**)
- A nurse sells poppies in a tray; both a fire engine and a barber appear (**Penny Lane**)
- There's a 64th birthday cake (**When I'm Sixty-Four**)
- A crowd of people stand and stare (**A Day In The Life**)

The Beatles, though they subsequently reunited seven years later, at a New York concert promoting transcendental meditation in schools, playing "With A Little Help From My Friends".

Despite all the Beatles product disinterred in the post-split years, there remained unfinished business. In November 2003, the long-threatened de-Spectorized *Get Back* album finally arrived in the guise of the newly selected, mixed, processed, edited and programmed *Let It Be ... Naked* which was generally reviewed favourably, if guardedly. The movies *A Hard Day's Night* and *Help!* received Apple-approved DVD releases in 2002 and 2007 respectively, though official *Magical Mystery Tour* and *Let It Be* DVDs remain conspicuously absent. The CD box-sets *The Capitol Albums Volume 1* (2004) and *Volume 2* (2006) satisfied those American fans who wanted to relive the early records as they grew up with them.

The resignation of Apple Corps Ltd chief and faithful friend **Neil Aspinall** in 2007 and his replacement with ex-Sony vice-president **Jeff Jones** marked the beginning of a new era of Beatles business. Beatles songs (albeit re-recorded) became available to TV advertisers for the first time ever in 2008 and the much-trumpeted remastered catalogue was released in 2009, featuring spanking new packaging and mini-documentaries along with the crisp audio (though not the *Yellow Submarine Songtrack* style remixes some had hoped for).

However, the two most significant Beatle-related products of the last decade were the Cirque Du Soleil Las Vegas show *Love*, which opened in 2006 – and inspired much waving and smiling from Paul, Ringo, Yoko and Olivia – and the computer video game *Beatles Rockband*, launched in 2009. These brilliant collisions of Beatlemusic, imagination and technology ensure that the Fabs' music lives on, while their legend grows ever larger.

Decades after they split, the reputation of The Beatles has never been higher. Every new generation is made aware of them in school as part of their musical/cultural studies, and each generation of pop musician recognizes the benchmark that has been set. There are already signs of their music being accepted into the beyond-criticism pantheon occupied by Mozart and Beethoven, and anyone who expresses indifference to their legacy is suspected of shallow contrariness. As long as people remain interested in music, people will be interested in the four lads from Liverpool who shook the world. The Beatles, it seems, are forever.

Live At The BBC

BEATLE GREETINGS/FROM US TO YOU/RIDING ON A BUS/I GOT A WOMAN/TOO MUCH MONKEY BUSINESS/KEEP YOUR HANDS OFF MY BABY/I'LL BE ON MY WAY/YOUNG BLOOD/A SHOT OF RHYTHM AND BLUES/SURE TO FALL (IN LOVE WITH YOU)/SOME OTHER GUY/THANK YOU GIRL/SHA LA LA LA LA!/ BABY IT'S YOU/THAT'S ALL RIGHT MAMA/CAROL/SOLDIER OF LOVE/A LITTLE RHYME/CLARABELLA/I'M GONNA SIT RIGHT DOWN AND CRY (OVER YOU)/CRYING, WAITING, HOPING/DEAR WACK!/YOU REALLY GOT A HOLD ON ME/ TO KNOW HER IS TO LOVE HER/A TASTE OF HONEY/ LONG TALL SALLY/I SAW HER STANDING THERE/THE HONEYMOON

SONG/JOHNNY B GOODE/MEMPHIS TENNESSEE/LUCILLE/CAN'T BUY ME LOVE/FROM FLUFF TO YOU/TILL THERE WAS YOU/CRINSK DEE NIGHT/A HARD DAY'S NIGHT/HAVE A BANANA/I WANNA BE YOUR MAN/JUST A RUMOUR/ROLL OVER BEETHOVEN/ALL MY LOVING/THINGS WE SAID TODAY/SHE'S A WOMAN/SWEET LITTLE SIXTEEN/1822!/LONESOME TEARS IN MY EYES/NOTHIN' SHAKIN'/THE HIPPY HIPPY SHAKE/GLAD ALL OVER/I JUST DON'T UNDERSTAND/SO HOW COME (NO ONE LOVES ME)/I FEEL FINE/I'M A LOSER/EVERYBODY'S TRYING TO BE MY BABY/ROCK AND ROLL MUSIC/TICKET TO RIDE/DIZZY MISS LIZZY/KANSAS CITY-HEY! HEY! HEY! HEY!/SET FIRE TO THAT LOT/MATCHBOX/I FORGOT TO REMEMBER TO FORGET/LOVE THOSE GOON SHOWS!/I GOT TO FIND MY BABY/OOH! MY SOUL/OOH! MY ARMS/DON'T EVER CHANGE/SLOW DOWN/HONEY DON'T/LOVE ME DO

Apple; recorded March 1962–June 1965; released March 1994; currently available on CD

Between March 1962 and June 1965, The Beatles appeared in 52 BBC radio programmes with titles like *The Talent Spot*, *Swingin' Sound '63*, *Easy Beat*, *Saturday Club*, *Top Gear* and their own specials *Pop Go The Beatles*, *From Us To You* and *The Beatles Invite You To Take A Ticket To Ride*. They taped hundreds of performances, and this excellent album gathers 56 radio session performances (including thirty unreleased songs) from a variety of sources, including some privately taped home recordings. Interspersed with snippets of the BBC jocks jousting with The Beatles' cheeky chat – diverting enough for the listener to wish for a little more – the result is an enthralling glimpse into a lost broadcasting world and is probably the single most exciting of the post-split Beatles releases.

The performances catch the tidied-up Beatles in transition, somewhere between being hell-raising rockers and boundary-pushing pop pioneers. Along with an armful of familiar Beatles tunes, the repertoire consists of several beat-scene staples of Chuck Berry, Coasters, Little Richard and Carl Perkins material; though Ringo was reported to be "knocked out" by the album upon its release in 1994, he remembered "all the groups in Liverpool were doing the same numbers".

However, also featured are some proudly Beatle-excavated obscurities (Everly Brothers and Elvis album tracks, an Ann-Margret waltz) and a few customized exotic novelties like Paul tackling Theodorakis's deeply corny **Honeymoon Song**, and John delivering the rumba-rock of Dorsey Burnette's **Lonesome Tears In My Eyes**. The highlights, though, are probably **Some Other Guy** and **Thank You Girl**, two cuts recorded before a live audience in June 1963. With the energy level several notches up from the group's polite studio manner, there's a glimpse of the Cavern-era Beatles, the band who – in Lennon's view – no one in the country could touch when they played "straight rock".

Anthology 1

Disc 1

FREE AS A BIRD (NEW RECORDING)/'WE WERE FOUR GUYS... THAT'S ALL' (JOHN INTERVIEW, 1970)/THAT'LL BE THE DAY (THE QUARRY MEN, 1958)/IN SPITE OF ALL THE DANGER (THE QUARRY MEN, 1958)/'SOMETIMES I'D BORROW...THOSE STILL EXIST' (PAUL INTERVIEW, 1994)/HALLELUJAH, I LOVE HER SO (REHEARSAL, 1960)/YOU'LL BE MINE (REHEARSAL 1960)/CAYENNE (REHEARSAL, 1960)/'FIRST OF ALL...IT DIDN'T DO A THING HERE' (PAUL INTERVIEW, 1962)/MY BONNIE (TONY SHERIDAN SINGLE)/AIN'T SHE SWEET (STUDIO, 1961)/CRY FOR A SHADOW (STUDIO, 1961)/'BRIAN WAS A BEAUTIFUL GUY...HE PRESENTED US WELL' (JOHN INTERVIEW, 1971)/'I SECURED THEM...A BEATLE DRINK EVEN THEN' (BRIAN EPSTEIN NARRATION, 1964)/SEARCHIN' (DECCA AUDITION, 1962)/THREE COOL CATS (DECCA AUDITION, 1962)/THE SHEIK OF ARABY (DECCA AUDITION, 1962)/LIKE DREAMERS DO (DECCA AUDITION, 1962)/HELLO LITTLE GIRL (DECCA AUDI-

TION, 1962)/ 'WELL, THE RECORDING TEST...BY MY ARTISTS' (BRIAN EPSTEIN NARRATION, 1964)/BESAME MUCHO (EMI AUDITION, 1962)/LOVE ME DO (EMI AUDITION, 1962)/HOW DO YOU DO IT (UNRELEASED)/PLEASE PLEASE ME (EARLY VERSION)/ONE AFTER 909 (SEQUENCE)/ONE AFTER 909 (COMPLETE) (EARLY VERSION)/LEND ME YOUR COMB (BBC SESSION, 1963)/I'LL GET YOU (LIVE, LONDON PALLADIUM, 1963)/ 'WE WERE PERFORMERS...IN BRITAIN' (JOHN INTERVIEW, 1970)/I SAW HER STANDING THERE (LIVE IN STOCKHOLM, 1963)/FROM ME TO YOU (LIVE IN STOCKHOLM, 1963)/MONEY (THAT'S WHAT I WANT) (LIVE IN STOCKHOLM, 1963)/YOU REALLY GOT A HOLD ON ME (LIVE IN STOCKHOLM, 1963)/ ROLL OVER BEETHOVEN (LIVE IN STOCKHOLM, 1963)

Disc 2

SHE LOVES YOU (LIVE, ROYAL VARIETY SHOW, 1963)/TILL THERE WAS YOU (LIVE, ROYAL VARIETY SHOW, 1963)/TWIST AND SHOUT (LIVE, ROYAL VARIETY SHOW, 1963)/THIS BOY (LIVE, MORECAMBE AND WISE TV SHOW, 1963)/I WANT TO HOLD YOUR HAND (LIVE, MORECAMBE AND WISE TV SHOW, 1963)/ 'BOYS, WHAT I WAS THINKING...' (SKETCH, MORECAMBE AND WISE TV SHOW, 1963)/MOONLIGHT BAY (MORECAMBE AND WISE TV SHOW, 1963)/CAN'T BUY ME LOVE (EARLY VERSION)/ALL MY LOVING (LIVE, ED SULLIVAN TV SHOW, 1964)/YOU CAN'T DO THAT (EARLY VERSION)/AND I LOVE HER (EARLY VERSION)/A HARD DAY'S NIGHT (EARLY VERSION)/I WANNA BE YOUR MAN (STUDIO SESSION FOR AROUND THE BEATLES TV SHOW, 1964)/LONG TALL SALLY (STUDIO SESSION FOR AROUND THE BEATLES TV SHOW, 1964)/BOYS (STUDIO SESSION FOR AROUND THE BEATLES TV SHOW, 1964)/SHOUT (STUDIO SESSION FOR AROUND THE BEATLES TV SHOW, 1964)I'LL BE BACK (EARLY VERSION)/YOU KNOW WHAT TO DO (UNRELEASED)/NO REPLY (DEMO)/MR MOONLIGHT (EARLY VERSION)/LEAVE MY KITTEN ALONE (UNRELEASED)/NO REPLY (EARLY VERSION)/EIGHT DAYS A WEEK (OUT TAKES)/EIGHT DAYS A WEEK (EARLY VERSION)/ KANSAS CITY/HEY-HEY-HEY-HEY! (LATER VERSION)

Apple; recorded 1958–94; released November 1995; currently available on CD

From one perspective, the ***Anthology*** albums were a curious exercise. Low-fidelity, bootleg-quality alternate takes, demos and broadcasts deemed unfit for release at the time were mass marketed on the back of the two new "Beatles" tracks and a TV documentary series. It was hard to know what to expect for, as late as March 1993, the reliably punctilious George Martin was heard assuring the media that he'd "listened to all the tapes" and that the remaining Beatles material was "all junk, [you] couldn't possibly release it". By November 1993, however, he'd changed his tune and, announcing the imminent release of the ***Anthology*** CDs, he promised early versions of songs that are "well worth people hearing now". By the release of the first album, Capitol was describing it as "an unprecedented milestone in the history of rock'n'roll". What it failed to mention was the cocked-up intro on **Mr Moonlight**, Paul singing **All My Loving** out of tune on **The Ed Sullivan Show**, and an embryonic **And I Love Her** sounding useless without a bridge.

Of course, it made perfect sense for The Beatles freaks who had everything else: the ***Anthology*** albums were full of curiosity-sating ephemera they thought they would never hear. The fact that EMI/Capitol managed to sell so many millions of copies is partly a tribute to the marketing brilliance of the entire ***Anthology*** campaign, and partly to the widespread, continuing allure of the group itself. However, one has to wonder how often the ***Anthology*** discs get played.

Apart from the ELO-like **Free As A Bird** (see p.213), highlights of ***Anthology I*** (covering the years 1958 to1964) include all five cuts from a tremendous 1963 Swedish concert, a surprisingly raucous **Twist And Shout** from the Royal Command Performance and Little Willie John's **Leave My Kitten Alone** recorded during the ***Beatles For Sale*** sessions. ***Anthology I*** starts as if the CDs are going to be an audio documentary, complete with interview snippets, but that idea disappears as the tale reaches mid-1963 toward the end of the first CD, never to return. Instead, the compilers (overseen by George Martin) let musical segues (for instance, between two early takes of **I'll Be Back**) depict the song's evolution in the studio, telling their own fascinating story. It's a different kind of audio documentary. They also dabble with a composite technique ("flying" the original guitar solo from take 1 of "Can't Buy Me Love" onto the rhythm track of take 2, creating a single virtual alternate take) that would be used more and more over the coming discs.

Anthology 2

Disc 1

REAL LOVE (NEW RECORDING)/YES IT IS (EARLY VERSION)/ I'M DOWN (EARLY VERSION)/YOU'VE GOT TO HIDE YOUR LOVE AWAY (EARLY VERSION)/IF YOU'VE GOT TROUBLE (UNRELEASED, 1965)/THAT MEANS A LOT (UNRELEASED, 1965)/YESTERDAY (EARLY VERSION)/IT'S ONLY LOVE (EARLY VERSION)/I FEEL FINE (LIVE IN BLACKPOOL, 1965)/TICKET TO RIDE (LIVE IN BLACKPOOL, 1965)/YESTERDAY (LIVE IN BLACKPOOL, 1965)/HELP! (LIVE IN BLACKPOOL, 1965)/ EVERYBODY'S TRYING TO BE MY BABY (LIVE AT SHEA STADIUM, 1965)/NORWEGIAN WOOD (THIS BIRD HAS FLOWN) (EARLY VERSION)/I'M LOOKING THROUGH YOU (EARLY VERSION)/12-BAR ORIGINAL (UNRELEASED, 1965)/ TOMORROW NEVER KNOWS (EARLY VERSION)/GOT TO GET YOU INTO MY LIFE (EARLY VERSION)/AND YOUR BIRD CAN SING (EARLY VERSION)/TAXMAN (EARLY VERSION)/ELEANOR RIGBY (STRINGS ONLY)/I'M ONLY SLEEPING (REHEARSAL)/I'M ONLY SLEEPING (EARLY VERSION)/ROCK AND ROLL MUSIC (LIVE IN TOKYO, 1966)/SHE'S A WOMAN (LIVE IN TOKYO, 1966)

Disc 2

STRAWBERRY FIELDS FOREVER (DEMO SEQUENCE)/ STRAWBERRY FIELDS FOREVER (EARLY VERSION)/ STRAWBERRY FIELDS FOREVER (2ND EARLY VERSION)/PENNY LANE (ALTERNATE COMPOSITE)/A DAY IN THE LIFE (ALTERNATE COMPOSITE)/GOOD MORNING GOOD MORNING (EARLY VERSION)/ONLY A NORTHERN SONG (ALTERNATE COMPOSITE)/BEING FOR THE BENEFIT OF MR KITE (ALTERNATE COMPOSITE)/LUCY IN THE SKY WITH DIAMONDS (ALTERNATE COMPOSITE)/WITHIN YOU WITHOUT YOU (INSTRUMENTAL)/SGT PEPPER'S LONELY HEARTS CLUB BAND (REPRISE) (BASIC TRACK)/YOU KNOW MY NAME (LOOK UP THE NUMBER) (EXTENDED STEREO MIX)/I AM THE WALRUS (BASIC TRACK)/FOOL ON THE HILL (DEMO)/ YOUR MOTHER SHOULD KNOW (EARLY VERSION)/FOOL ON THE HILL (EARLY VERSION)/HELLO GOODBYE (EARLY VERSION)/LADY MADONNA (ALTERNATE MIX)/ACROSS THE UNIVERSE (BASIC TRACK)

Apple; recorded 1964–95; released March 1996; currently available on CD

Even the defenders of **Free As A Bird** found it hard to get enthusiastic about ***Real Love***, the second of the "Electric Beatles Orchestra" efforts to tart up a Lennon demo and the lead track of *Anthology 2*. The problem is not so much the record – which is competent and features some delicious Harrison guitar work – as the song. George's "presumptuous" (in Paul's view) argument for knocking this aspect of the project on the head – that Lennon "was going off a little bit toward the end of his writing" – is no better presented than here.

The ragged live cuts – from Shea Stadium in 1965 and Tokyo in 1966 – while full of atmosphere, do not bear comparison to *Live At The BBC*, the live tracks on *Anthology 1* or even *Live At The Hollywood Bowl* and confirm the band's view that in this period, they were simply "playing really bad".

Elsewhere however, *Anthology 2* (covering 1965 to early 1968) is probably the most interesting of the three double CDs, cataloguing as it does the fascinating early stages of some of the most highly evolved pop

music in history. Highlights include a compellingly dour early take of **Norwegian Wood**, an excellent Latin-folk version of **I'm Looking Through You**, a terrific discarded version of **Got To Get You Into My Life** and gorgeous instrumental mixes of **Eleanor Rigby** and **Within You Without You**.

George Martin and his team really go to town on the *Sgt Pepper* era material, especially **Strawberry Fields Forever** (granted a demo, early and alternate version lasting over eight minutes in total) and **A Day In The Life** (a composite alternative version). All these different versions and remixes can induce a sense of altered reality. Hearing the myriad directions in which such familiar songs could have gone, all of them emphasizing slightly different elements, it can sometimes feel as if you've stepped into some bewildering parallel universe.

At the same time, there's the pleasure of eavesdropping on The Beatles at work in their most creative period. It's captured in a tremendous, teasingly short, barely audible moment in **Being For The Benefit Of Mr Kite!**, where Paul can be heard encouraging a better vocal from John. No matter how much they give you, if you're in the mood you still end up wanting more.

Anthology 3

Disc 1

A BEGINNING (UNRELEASED INTRO TO 'DON'T PASS ME BY')/HAPPINESS IS A WARM GUN (DEMO)/HELTER SKELTER (EARLY VERSION)/MEAN MR MUSTARD (DEMO)/POLYTHENE PAM (DEMO)/GLASS ONION (DEMO)/JUNK (DEMO)/PIGGIES (DEMO)/HONEY PIE (DEMO)/DON'T PASS ME BY (ALTERNATE)/OB-LA-DI, OB-LA-DA (EARLY VERSION)/GOOD NIGHT (REHEARSAL/MASTER COMPOSITE)/CRY BABY CRY (EARLY VERSION)/BLACKBIRD (EARLY VERSION)/SEXY SADIE (EARLY VERSION)/WHILE MY GUITAR GENTLY WEEPS (DEMO)/HEY JUDE (EARLY RUN-THROUGH)/NOT GUILTY (UNRELEASED)/MOTHER NATURE'S SON (EARLY VERSION)/GLASS ONION (EARLY VERSION)/ROCKY RACCOON (EARLY VERSION)/WHAT'S THE NEW MARY JANE (UNRELEASED)/STEP INSIDE LOVE - LOS PARANOIAS (UNRELEASED AD LIB)/I'M SO TIRED (ALTERNATE COMPOSITE)/I WILL (EARLY RUN-THROUGH)/WHY DON'T WE DO IT IN THE ROAD (EARLY VERSION)/JULIA (EARLY VERSION)

Disc 2

I'VE GOT A FEELING (EARLY VERSION)/SHE CAME IN THROUGH THE BATHROOM WINDOW (REHEARSAL)/DIG A PONY (REHEARSAL)/TWO OF US (REHEARSAL)/FOR YOU BLUE (EARLY VERSION)/TEDDY BOY (REHEARSAL COMPOSITE, UNRELEASED)/RIP IT UP-SHAKE RATTLE AND ROLL-BLUE SUEDE SHOES (UNRELEASED)/THE LONG AND WINDING ROAD (BASIC TRACK)/OH! DARLING (REHEARSAL)/ALL THINGS MUST PASS (DEMO)/MAILMAN, BRING ME NO MORE BLUES (UNRELEASED)/GET BACK (LATER VERSION)/OLD BROWN SHOE (DEMO)/OCTOPUS'S GARDEN (EARLY VERSION)/MAXWELL'S SILVER HAMMER (EARLY VERSION)/SOMETHING (DEMO)/COME TOGETHER (EARLY VERSION)/COME AND GET IT (UNRELEASED DEMO)/AIN'T SHE SWEET (UNRELEASED)/BECAUSE (VOCALS ONLY)/LET IT BE (EARLY VERSION)/I ME MINE (UNEDITED VERSION)/THE END (REMIX)

Apple; recorded 1968–70; released October 1996; currently available on CD

Due to the fraught situation of the group at the time, there are fewer alternate takes on *Anthology 3*. There are some exceptions: a good but discarded **Ob-La-Di Ob-La-Da** and excellent early takes of **Sexy Sadie** and **Glass Onion**, and several fascinating solo sketches. There are seven of the famous acoustic recordings, taped at George Harrison's house in Esher in May 1968 to demo the mountain of songs written in India; George's lovely solo demos of **While My Guitar Gently Weeps** and **All Things Must Pass** (how did The Beatles let that one get away?); and McCartney's complete demo of **Come And Get It**, rattled off in an hour, which was offered to The Beatles but donated to **Badfinger**.

Two of the holy grails among Beatles' collectors – Lennon's oddball *White Album* reject **What's The New Mary Jane** and the original, Beatles recording of George's bitter **Not Guilty** – could hardly be said to be worth the wait, but they were certainly another piece in the jigsaw. Things go discernibly downhill with the **Let It Be** out-takes. Dreary, tired and uninspired, the rock'n'roll sags and everything else drags. Yes, John and Paul

sound like they're having a bit of fun here and there, but the general indiscipline makes one appreciate all the more Phil Spector's glossy 1970 salvage job on the original *Let It Be* album and the remarkable tidiness of the *Let It Be ...Naked* remake of 2003.

From the Abbey Road sessions, the multi-tracked three-part harmonies of **Because** are lovely to hear a capella, the alternate solos on **The End** further reveal the three distinctive guitar styles of Harrison, McCartney and Lennon, and Geoff Emerick's segue of a backward **A Day In The Life** piano chord with a straight one is an evocative conceit. For the most part, however, it's all the listener can do not to feel deflated.

Yellow Submarine Songtrack

YELLOW SUBMARINE/HEY BULLDOG/ELEANOR RIGBY/ LOVE YOU TO/ALL TOGETHER NOW/LUCY IN THE SKY WITH DIAMONDS/THINK FOR YOURSELF/SGT PEPPER'S LONELY HEARTS CLUB BAND/WITH A LITTLE HELP FROM MY FRIENDS/BABY YOU'RE A RICH MAN/ONLY A NORTHERN SONG/ALL YOU NEED IS LOVE/WHEN I'M SIXTY FOUR/ NOWHERE MAN/IT'S ALL TOO MUCH

Apple; recorded 1965–1968; released September 1999; currently available on CD

What else was there left to do? Well, this: putting all The Beatles' songs from the animated movie – including those from *Rubber Soul*, *Revolver* and *Pepper* – onto one album and having a "sacrilegious" bash at improving the mixes. As all the tunes were recorded on four-track machines, this involved the virtual undoing of George Martin's and Geoff Emerick's original reduction process.

In the 1960s, The Beatles' overdubs were achieved by filling all four tracks of one tape and mixing those onto one track of another machine, thereby freeing up three new tracks for further recording. This could occur several times in the process of an elaborate recording. Luckily, the original "filled" four-track tapes were retained at Abbey Road as a matter of course, which meant that Allen Rouse (the project's coordinator) and his team could put all the original music onto a modern multi-track and mix the sound with much more flexibility than was available to George Martin and his engineers.

The results speak for themselves. Clearer, sweeter and punchier with the original of necessity eccentric stereo – broadly, vocals on one side and instruments on the other – redesigned for a richer panoramic spread, it's gorgeous. The sumptuous stereo swell of the vocals on **Nowhere Man** and **Eleanor Rigby** is breathtaking, while the meticulous stereo placing of the elements, especially the four *Sgt Pepper* tracks, is thrillingly vivid. **It's All Too Much**, having been only available in "fake stereo" before, received the most radical audio overhaul, a process that, apparently, benefited from its composer George Harrison's enthusiastic input. In 1987 he had said he was "frankly a bit disappointed" with the *Sgt Pepper* CD transfer. Of the 1999 remixes he was happy to announce that the new *Yellow Submarine* mixes "really are good".

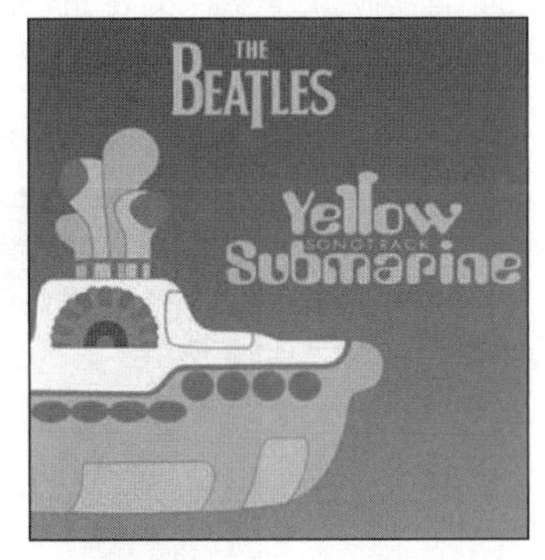

The outraged "tampering with history" arguments of Beatle purists might have more credence if the results were anything like, say, the attempts to add colour to the black-and-white movie classics of Laurel and Hardy. However, the months of painstaking work done by the

engineers (Peter Cobbin, Paul Hicks and Mirek Stiles) have resulted in something that sounds as it used to, only somehow more so. As Brian Wilson commented when hearing the results of a similarly revelatory exercise, the 1990s stereo mix of *Pet Sounds*, "More of what was there is there". *Yellow Submarine Songtrack* is a very good argument for an audio overhaul of the entire Beatles catalogue.

1

LOVE ME DO/FROM ME TO YOU/SHE LOVES YOU/I WANT TO HOLD YOUR HAND/CAN'T BUY ME LOVE/A HARD DAY'S NIGHT/I FEEL FINE/EIGHT DAYS A WEEK/TICKET TO RIDE/ HELP!/YESTERDAY/DAY TRIPPER/WE CAN WORK IT OUT/ PAPERBACK WRITER/YELLOW SUBMARINE/ELEANOR RIGBY/ PENNY LANE/ALL YOU NEED IS LOVE/HELLO GOODBYE/ LADY MADONNA/HEY JUDE/GET BACK/BALLAD OF JOHN AND YOKO/SOMETHING/COME TOGETHER/LET IT BE/THE LONG AND WINDING ROAD

Apple; recorded 1962–70; released November 2000; currently available on CD

Compiled according to the rather contrived idea that all Beatles singles hit the #1 spot somewhere on some chart or other (hence the title), it concentrates on the commercially successful side of the group's output. Yet despite the album's criterion precluding such essentials as "Please Please Me" and "Strawberry Fields Forever", this 27-track overview is the best single-disc Beatles compilation yet. The world certainly seems to think so – **1** has sold over 28 million copies to date.

Let It Be ... Naked

GET BACK/DIG A PONY/FOR YOU BLUE/THE LONG AND WINDING ROAD/TWO OF US/I'VE GOT A FEELING/ONE AFTER 909/DON'T LET ME DOWN/I ME MINE/ACROSS THE UNIVERSE/LET IT BE

Apple; recorded February 1968–January 1970; released November 2003; currently available on CD

After the McCartney–Lennon credit row (in which Paul conspicuously reversed the traditional Lennon/McCartney credit on the Beatles songs to appear on his 2003 *Back In The US* CD), this revisiting of a 34-year-old project was sensed by some to be further desperate Beatles revisionism to be foisted by an insecure McCartney on a Lennon-free world. However, far from a repositioning of the historical spotlight that Macca bashers will be so keen to detect, the *Let It Be* remix is not only a noble, entirely worthwhile exercise which enhances the reputation of all concerned, it also goes quite a way to putting right an episode which was, in Beatles terms, an historical wrong. The original *Let It Be* album was always a Lennon-instigated posthumous fudge, a cobbled-together compromise, finished by Phil Spector without McCartney's input or consent. For this version, McCartney (with Harrison's and Starr's approval) commissioned the Abbey Road team who remixed the Beatles for *Yellow Submarine* and the *Anthology* DVD to look once more at the session tapes and make the *Let It Be* album again, as they saw fit, but bearing in mind the original intention of an "honest" Beatles record unadorned with overdubs.

From sessions which featured hours of sloppy outtakes and dreary jamming (widely heard on bootlegs and excerpted on *Anthology 3*), only tidy performances of the core material were selected to comprise this 35-minute, eleven-track album. It's not exactly transformed into a classic – apart from a couple of McCartney's big hitters, it's the slightest selection of Beatles compositions after 1965's *Help!* – but the new *Let It Be* is nonetheless punchy, full of presence and powerfully involving.

Of the main differences, "Don't Let Me Down" is at last on the album it should always have been on – here represented by the passionate rooftop version. "The Long And Winding Road" is a later take with slightly different lyrics ("anyway, you've always known...") and "Let It Be" has no rolling toms in its final verse. The highlight of the record, however, may be the new (corrected speed) mix of 1968's "Across The Universe". It is just Lennon and his guitar with an increasingly, hauntingly processed tambura and a gorgeous new fade-out.

Of the myriad tiny differences that only Beatleheads who know the original album like the face of their mother will spot, more of Lennon's improvisational vocal yelps – and even more of McCartney's – are retained throughout; Billy Preston's keyboard licks are more prominent on "I've Got A Feeling" and Lennon's rhythm guitar and vocals are more defined generally. In fact there's an immediacy and muscle to the sound, particularly the rockers ("One After 909", always a good performance, now sounds huge) that gives the impression of everything being louder than everything else. Now that's a good mix.

Spector's edits on "Dig A Pony" and "I Me Mine" remain, though some may miss the raucous, always incomplete "Maggie Mae", the saggy improvised jam "Dig It" and Lennon's "Charles Hawtrey and the Deaf-aids" intros. As compensation, there's a twenty-minute bonus disc with around 25 items of other informal but fascinating studio flotsam, including Lennon singing McCartney's first ever song, "I Lost My Little Girl" and a snippet of a long-lost Ringo song, "A Trip To Carolina".

Ironically, in attempting to better create the spirit of pure unadulterated Beatles, the engineers used whatever modern editing and processing they needed to achieve the best album they could. In that respect, the results are probably no more "honest" than Spector's effort but what was previously an uneasy mix of medium-grade Beatles treated to glossy overstatement and irreverent editing is now simply a great little record.

The Capitol Albums Volume 1

Meet The Beatles

I WANT TO HOLD YOUR HAND/I SAW HER STANDING THERE/ THIS BOY/IT WON'T BE LONG/ALL I'VE GOT TO DO/ALL MY LOVING/DON'T BOTHER ME/LITTLE CHILD/TILL THERE WAS YOU/HOLD ME TIGHT/I WANNA BE YOUR MAN/NOT A SECOND TIME

The Beatles' Second Album

ROLL OVER BEETHOVEN/THANK YOU GIRL/YOU REALLY GOT A HOLD ON ME/DEVIL IN HER HEART/MONEY/YOU CAN'T DO THAT/LONG TALL SALLY/I CALL YOUR NAME/ PLEASE MR POSTMAN/I'LL GET YOU/SHE LOVES YOU

Something New

I'LL CRY INSTEAD/THINGS WE SAID TODAY/ANY TIME AT ALL/WHEN I GET HOME/SLOW DOWN/MATCHBOX/TELL ME WHY/AND I LOVE HER/I'M HAPPY JUST TO DANCE WITH YOU/IF I FELL/KOMM, GIB MIR DEINE HAND

Beatles '65

NO REPLY/I'M A LOSER/BABY'S IN BLACK/ROCK AND ROLL MUSIC/I'LL FOLLOW THE SUN/MR MOONLIGHT/ HONEY DON'T/I'LL BE BACK/SHE'S A WOMAN/I FEEL FINE/ EVERYBODY'S TRYING TO BE MY BABY

Apple; recorded February 1963–October 1964; original albums released 1964, box set released November 2004; currently available on CD

The Capitol Albums Volume 2

The Early Beatles

LOVE ME DO/TWIST AND SHOUT/ANNA/CHAINS/BOYS/ASK ME WHY/PLEASE PLEASE ME/P.S. I LOVE YOU/BABY IT'S YOU/ A TASTE OF HONEY/DO YOU WANT TO KNOW A SECRET

Beatles VI

KANSAS CITY/HEY HEY HEY HEY/EIGHT DAYS A WEEK/YOU LIKE ME TOO MUCH/BAD BOY/I DON'T WANT TO SPOIL THE PARTY/WORDS OF LOVE/WHAT YOU'RE DOING/YES IT IS/DIZZIE MISS LIZZIE/TELL ME WHAT YOU SEE/EVERY LITTLE THING

Help! Original Motion Picture Soundtrack

HELP!/THE NIGHT BEFORE/FROM ME TO YOU FANTASY (INSTRUMENTAL)/YOU'VE GOT TO HID YOUR LOVE AWAY/I NEED YOU/IN THE TYROL (INSTRUMENTAL)/ANOTHER GIRL/ANOTHER HARD DAY'S NIGHT (INSTRUMENTAL)/ TICKET TO RIDE/THE BITTER END-YOU CAN'T DO THAT (INSTRUMENTAL)/YOU'RE GONNA LOSE THAT GIRL/THE CHASE (INSTRUMENTAL)

Rubber Soul

I'VE JUST SEEN A FACE/NORWEGIAN WOOD (THIS BIRD HAS FLOWN)/YOU WON'T SEE ME/THINK FOR YOURSELF/ THE WORD/MICHELLE/IT'S ONLY LOVE/GIRL/I'M LOOKING THROUGH YOU/IN MY LIFE/WAIT/ RUN FOR YOUR LIFE

Apple; recorded September 1962–November 1965; original albums released 1965; box set released April 2006; currently available on CD

Aside from 1964's *Introducing the Beatles* on Vee-Jay and *A Hard Day's Night Original Soundtrack Album* on United Artists, up until *Sgt Pepper's Lonely Hearts Club Band* all The Beatles' albums in the US were compiled by EMI's American arm, Capitol. Recorded masters of all Beatles tracks were delivered, as they were completed, to Capitol's A&R department, who issued them in whichever way they saw fit. Mono, stereo and duophonic (fake stereo) tracks were spread across US-only singles and short albums which bore little resemblance to the British, Beatle-approved editions.

The American experience of the group was therefore subtly different. For example, contemporary British fans knew "Yesterday" as a classy, much-covered highlight near the end of the *Help!* album. Stateside fans knew it as a #1 single and an album track sandwiched between "Dr Robert" (appearing two months earlier than in the UK) and "Act Naturally" (appearing ten months later than in the UK) on a haphazard collection called *"Yesterday" ... and Today*. The US soundtrack albums for *A Hard Day's Night* and *Help!* featured George Martin's and Ken Thorne's incidental music and only half the songs of the UK album. *Something New* closed with "I Want To Hold Your Hand" sung in German, while the *Rubber Soul* album that inspired Brian Wilson to the greatest work of his career opened not with "Drive My Car", but "I've Just Seen A Face".

These box sets reissue the first eight Capitol albums in their original form on CD, for the first time ever. While the UK-released records have been subsequently embraced by US fans as the core catalogue experience, for American fans who lived through it all, hearing the playing orders that formed the soundtrack to their formative years will undoubtedly be a nostalgic experience. For everyone else, these records are most disorientating. In the world of random-play iPods, it shouldn't really be a big deal. But as various singles, B-sides and tracks from *With The Beatles*, *A Hard Day's Night* and *Beatles For Sale* are jumbled into unfamiliar and apparent haphazard order, the experience of hearing "Money" then "You Can't Do That" then "Long Tall Sally" in succession is surprisingly joyful.

Before the arrival of the 2009 remasters, the larger part of the appeal of this collection was the pristine original 1960s stereo mixes, most appearing on CD for the first time. When the first four UK Beatles albums were prepared for international CD release in 1987, George Martin remixed all of them into "sensible" stereo, except for the first four, which he considered better in mono. One can only assume that he didn't hear the tracks as we hear them now, because on *The Capitol Albums* they sound terrific. The original stereo panning was always a little eccentric – broadly speaking, instruments far left, voices far right – and the quirk was still present even on parts of *Sgt Pepper*. But the clarity and depth of sound is captivating and leaves the original mono mixes (also here) sounding thin and uninvolving. Lennon's voice fares especially well, the up-front sonics revealing afresh as exciting and extraordinarily impassioned a rock singer as ever there was.

Love

BECAUSE/GET BACK/GLASS ONION/ELEANOR RIGBY-JULIA (TRANSITION)/I AM THE WALRUS/I WANT TO HOLD YOUR HAND/DRIVE MY CAR-THE WORD-WHAT YOU'RE DOING/ GNIK NUS/SOMETHING-BLUE JAY WAY (TRANSITION)/BEING FOR THE BENEFIT OF MR. KITE!-I WANT YOU (SHE'S SO HEAVY)-HELTER SKELTER/HELP!/BLACKBIRD-YESTERDAY/ STRAWBERRY FIELDS FOREVER/WITHIN YOU WITHOUT YOU-TOMORROW NEVER KNOWS/LUCY IN THE SKY WITH DIAMONDS/OCTOPUS'S GARDEN/LADY MADONNA/HERE COMES THE SUN-THE INNER LIGHT (TRANSITION)/COME TOGETHER-DEAR PRUDENCE-CRY BABY CRY (TRANSITION)/ REVOLUTION/BACK IN THE U.S.S.R./WHILE MY GUITAR GENTLY WEEPS/A DAY IN THE LIFE/HEY JUDE/SGT. PEPPER'S LONELY HEARTS CLUB BAND (REPRISE)/ALL YOU NEED IS LOVE

Apple; recorded October 1963–August 1969, 2004-2006; released November 2006

It was thanks to George Harrison's friendship with Cirque du Soleil's Guy Laliberté that the concept of a theatrical presentation based on Beatlemusic developed. When Neil Aspinall vetoed the idea of using live musicians, George Martin and his engineer/producer son Giles were briefed to create ninety minutes of music using anything recorded with The Beatles between 1962 and 1969. There was some trepidation in the Abbey Road inner circle about fiddling with the holy scriptures and even George himself was wary of walking the "tightrope of taste" but once Paul, Ringo, Yoko and Olivia had heartily approved their early efforts, the chocks were whipped away and Giles got his wings.

All temptations to add beats or modernize the music were resisted. Other than a few sound effects and George Martin's new string arrangement on "While My Guitar Gently Weeps", there are no elements not already audible on existing Beatles recordings. Thus, with highly musical editing and reimagining, the *Love* music evolved into a fascinating, protean collage featuring bootleg-style mash-ups – one song's vocal over another's track – complete songs completely remixed and other songs represented only by iconic moments or disguised guest appearances in alien settings. "Drive My Car" is fused to "What You're Doing" and "The Word", "Blackbird" blended with "Yesterday" and, best of all, "Being For The Benefit Of Mr Kite" turned into a psychotic episode by introducing the mighty, churning coda of "I Want You/She's So Heavy".

Once you get over playing Spot the Source (130 individual recordings were used), you'll marvel at the sound and the new insight it brings to music you know too well. Returning to source takes where possible (as practiced successfully on *Yellow Submarine Songtrack* and *Let It Be ... Naked*) restores unbelievable freshness and clarity. Ringo's drums on "Come Together" sound like they were cut this morning, and guitars chime and clang anew alongside vocal performances that have never sounded more present.

The selected tracks favour the multi-hued nuances of mid-to-late-period Fabs and though there's a pervading undercurrent of darkness, drama and melancholy, there is inevitably great beauty too. Even the daft "Octopus's Garden" is given new majesty by the strings from "Good Night", one of many unexpectedly attractive conjunctions. Stimulating, moving and entertaining, it will be listened to much more than *Anthology*.

Part 3: The Solo Years

The Solo Years

It's generally agreed that as Lennon, McCartney, Harrison and Starr went about their post-Beatles lives and careers, as individual artists they mostly fell somewhat short of matching the best of their group achievements in the 1960s.

Lennon's output from 1970 to 1975 was wildly inconsistent, while his 1980 return from semi-retirement didn't bode especially well for any future music he might have made had his life not been cut tragically short.

While McCartney was prolific and popular, it was sometimes clear that he missed someone of Lennon's artistic clout he could respect enough to check his periodic, self-confessed "that'll do" tendency. Harrison began his solo career spectacularly but then displayed only erratic interest in music making over the years. Nothing much was expected of Ringo so anything he did achieve was received almost as a novelty bonus. And anyway, hadn't they already, as Lennon suggested, "given everything on God's earth"?

Yet John, Paul, George and Ringo remained charismatic, engaging figures as ex-Beatles and retained a certain commercial and artistic allure in their solo years. There was good, sometimes even great, work done in the post-Beatles period and, for those who cared, it was interesting to see these men engage with their battle to achieve individual reputations beyond the renowned four-headed monster. Though George Harrison in the early days after the split assured the world that they would strive to achieve "unity through diversity", as the years passed what characterized most of their work was an emphatic, but fascinating, apartness.

John Lennon

"The lesson for me is clear. I've already 'lost' one family to produce what? Sgt Pepper*? I am blessed with a second chance ... If I never 'produce' anything more for public consumption than 'silence', so be it. Amen."*

John Lennon, 1978

John Lennon's marriage to Yoko Ono unleashed an explosion of creative and expressive energy in him, often as wilful and wayward as it was sincere and impassioned. With Lennon playing, in varying degrees, the parts of primal rock'n'roller, avant-garde artist, surrealist revolutionary and hippie peacenik, John and Yoko's first two years together spurred them on to a remarkable range of artistic and political ventures.

Running parallel to The Beatles' latter years, Lennon's new-found zeal for using his celebrity for the promotion of world peace meant that in publicity terms, the adventures of John and Yoko easily eclipsed any Beatles events of the time. The laudable intentions and clear-headed media manipulation of their peace events – the two acorns sculpture (June 1968) and the bed-ins (March and May 1969) – ran hand-in-hand with oblique avant-garde art, obscure Warhol-style films and puzzling, obsessively self-referential sound-collage albums.

The first two solo Beatle singles were Lennon's. **Give Peace A Chance** (see p.93) was recorded at the Queen Elizabeth hotel in Montreal during John and Yoko's second Bed-In for Peace in March 1969. It was released in July that year and though unmistakeably Lennonesque in its earnest ambitions to become a mantra for humanity was nonetheless credited in traditional Beatles fashion to "Lennon/McCartney". John later said that he hadn't felt quite ready to break their old songwriting pact just yet.

The record was credited to the **Plastic Ono Band** – a group of no fixed line-up that would serve as a convenient umbrella for both Lennon's and Ono's records – as was his single of October 1969, **Cold Turkey** (see p.94), which had been premiered live in September at the Toronto Rock'n'Roll Revival Festival. Invited to appear at the last minute, Lennon hastily assembled a group (Eric Clapton on guitar, Klaus Voormann on bass and Alan White on drums), rehearsed unplugged on the flight over, and gave a performance split between amiable rock standards and Yoko's trademark caterwauling and feedback avant-garde music. Consistent with the couple's compulsive self-documentation of the time, the results were released on the album ***Live Peace In Toronto 1969***.

John and Yoko moved into Tittenhurst, a mansion in Surrey, in summer 1969 but remained constantly in the public eye. Various campaigns in late 1969 and early 1970 were endorsed by John and Yoko. There was the judicial protest, "Britain Murdered Hanratty" (Michael Hanratty was hanged for a 1962 murder many believed he didn't commit, and Hanratty's family persuaded John and Yoko to get involved). And the conceptually idealistic – the "War Is Over If You Want It" peace-promoting poster campaign that John and Yoko instigated. And the political – they donated locks of their hair to an auction raising money for black-power leader Malcolm X, and marched on CND rallies.

The punchy single of February 1970, **Instant Karma** (produced by Phil Spector), was written and recorded in one day. One of the best solo Beatles records, it prompted Lennon's only post-Beatles performance on *Top of the Pops*. John and Yoko, inseparable as ever, appeared on the TV show sporting cropped haircuts, Yoko wearing a blindfold and silently mouthing the word "breathe".

In the immediate aftermath of McCartney's making public The Beatles' split in April 1970 and the collapse of the mooted Montreal Peace Festival (which was to have been the climax of John and Yoko's peace campaign), Lennon retreated to Los Angeles with Yoko for four months of **primal scream therapy** with the renowned psychotherapist Dr Arthur Janov. The feelings of childhood hurt unlocked by the therapy (cut short by the expiration of his US visa) fuelled his harrowing debut solo album *John Lennon/Plastic Ono Band*, released in December 1970 to limited commercial success.

However, much attention was drawn to the record by one of the most notorious rock interviews ever, a sprawling, brawling rant which Lennon delivered to ***Rolling Stone*** editor Jann Wenner. It was run over two magazine issues in early 1971, and in it Lennon swiped mercilessly at Brian Epstein, Paul McCartney and the Eastman family, and railed against his schooling and upbringing. He vacillated between rage at the compromises and indignities he perceived himself to have suffered as a Beatle ("a fuckin' humiliation") and an intense pride in his old group.

Much of the Lennons' early 1971 was spent in legal wrangling over the custody of **Kyoko,** Yoko's daughter by musician and art promoter Anthony Cox. (Although they eventually won legal custody, Cox absconded with Kyoko and wasn't seen for years. Kyoko wasn't to reunite with her mother until the 1990s.)

The case took them to New York, where both John and Yoko had felt at home, and they found the time (and nerve) to jam with the sardonic, intellectual rock guitarist and "freak" **Frank Zappa** at the Filmore East. "We're treated like artists [in America]," he observed upon his return to the UK. "Here I'm like the lad who knew Paul, got a lucky break, won the pools and married the actress."

After finishing his second album, the well-received *Imagine*, at Tittenhurst in July 1971, John and Yoko left Britain for New York for good the following month. Settling first in the St Regis Hotel, later in an apartment in Greenwich Village, the Lennons fell in with **Yippie** radicals Jerry Rubin and Abbie Hoffman (of the fun and revolution Youth International Party), along with the militant street performer and marijuana evangelist David Peel. John and Yoko began their plans for a Hoffman-and-Rubin-inspired "movement for change in America", penning and performing politically charged songs that were subversive enough to attract the attention of the FBI and the CIA. Work permits were denied and deportation orders were filed against Lennon, actions ostensibly taken because of his marijuana conviction in the UK in 1968 although this, as Lennon suspected at the time, was subsequently proved to be politically motivated. The culmination of John and Yoko's radical energies was the collaborative album ***Sometime In New York City***, which appeared in mid-1972. It sold disappointingly and was uniformly savaged by the press. Even the FBI noted in their files that the album was "lacking Lennon's usual standards". Meanwhile, the US government redoubled its attempts to deport Lennon,

The radical Lennons

which he protested in the appeal courts. He also found himself in court having to defend himself against music publisher Morris Levy's claims of plagiarism, dating back to Lennon's borrowing two lines of Chuck Berry's **You Can't Catch Me** for his own **Come Together**. He eventually settled the case by agreeing to record three of Levy's songs for a future album of rock'n'roll oldies.

John and Yoko moved into a New York apartment in the Dakota Building on West 72nd Street in February 1973. When Lennon returned to the studio alone in mid-1973 to record ***Mind Games***, he made a record full of vague but sincere contrition for his recent bad behaviour. It was clearly not quite enough. By the album's release in October 1973, John and Yoko had split up.

It appears that around this time Yoko approached a young assistant of the Lennons', May Pang, to be John's lover, a singular move widely interpreted as an effort to keep Lennon on a long leash. In May's company, John hit Los Angeles in a dangerous party mood. Declaring he just wanted "to be a singer in a band", Lennon handed the reins of the Levy-assuaging rock'n'roll project to Phil Spector, who presided over two months of catastrophically overblown recording sessions and a studio full of drunken musicians, before absconding with the master tapes.

John meanwhile was seen carousing around town in the good-time, self-destructive company of The Who's drummer **Keith Moon** and the singer-songwriter **Harry Nilsson**, getting thrown out of nightclubs for drunkenly heckling the performers and brawling with waitresses. He managed to eventually pull himself together to produce Nilsson's *Pussy Cats* album ("One day I realised, Jesus, I'm the producer, they are going to be asking me where the tapes are"), before returning to New York to mix it during spring 1974.

Settling into an apartment with May Pang, over the summer of 1974 Lennon quickly wrote and recorded the songs that would become the *Walls And Bridges* album, before turning his attention back to the recently reacquired Spector tapes of the *Rock 'N' Roll* sessions. Depressed, in his newly sober state, by the shambolic music he heard – and with Morris Levy continuing to snap at his heels – Lennon finished the album in four days in October 1974 with his *Walls And Bridges* band.

In November 1974, Lennon took to the stage at Madison Square Garden as a guest of **Elton John**. Elton had sung on **Whatever Gets You Thru The Night** on *Walls And Bridges* and had made Lennon agree to join him live on-stage should the record get to #1. As luck would have it, it did (John's only solo #1 in his lifetime) and Elton held him to his promise. John hit the stage to a tumultuous reception and sang the hit along with **Lucy In The Sky With Diamonds** (which Elton had covered on the B-side of a 1974 single), and a song introduced by Lennon as being "by an old estranged fiancé of mine called Paul", **I Saw Her Standing There**. It was a wholly unexpected gesture. Even McCartney had yet to feature Beatles songs in his live set, let alone songs written by his former partner.

John had kept in touch with Yoko over the phone throughout his eighteen-month "lost weekend", but it was only after a backstage meeting with Yoko at Elton's gig that Lennon began the drift back into his wife's life. By early 1975 Lennon had moved back into the **Dakota** with Yoko and the couple had announced Yoko's pregnancy (although Lennon and May Pang carried on seeing each other from time to time until 1980).

In February 1975, Morris Levy, impatient for his payday, released rough mixes of the *Rock 'N' Roll* tapes as a shoddily packaged mail-order album called *Roots: John Lennon Sings The Rock 'N' Roll Hits*. This prompted Capitol to rush-release *Rock 'N' Roll* (shorn of two of the more out-of-tune tracks, **Angel Baby** and **Be My Baby**). Levy sued, citing a verbal agreement with Lennon; Lennon counter-sued, citing lost royalties and damaged reputation, and won. In a separate but rather more important legal victory, Lennon also won an action taken against Attorney General John Mitchell for "selective deportation based upon secret political grounds", earning the ex-Beatle temporary US residential status.

Yoko gave birth to their son Sean in October 1975, on Lennon's 35th birthday. The couple had wanted a baby for years, Yoko having suffered three miscarriages in the late 1960s and early 1970s, and Sean's birth marked the end of the Lennons' public life for almost five years. John declared himself uninterested in renewing his lapsed Capitol/EMI recording contract in February 1976 following the release of the retrospective ***Shaved Fish*** compilation. Yoko took over business matters while John took care of the baby and pottered around the house – just watching the wheels go round, as he would later sing.

The glut of tell-all memoirs by former Dakota employees (and acquaintances of former employees) that emerged after John's death, not to mention Albert Goldman's notoriously sensationalist biography of 1988, paint a bizarre picture of the Lennons' domestic life. It seems that between 1976 and 1980, John and Yoko had a cold, separate relationship, with John even having to make an appointment to see his wife through his own personal assistant from time to time. Yoko also purportedly had an affair with art advisor **John Green**, was addicted to heroin and planned to divorce John. Meanwhile John's moods, if the accounts are to be believed, alternated between violent rage and doped-up, self-absorbed indolence. Also, the couple apparently relied on tarot and horoscope readings to make important business and personal decisions, while John was instructed by Yoko to take month-long vows of silence and was sent on long solo holidays. While it's difficult to sort the truth from the hearsay and gossip, it's clear that life at the Dakota was far more complicated than the Lennons' later "babies and home-baked bread" PR made out.

> ***"Lennon's four-year battle to remain in our country is testimony to his faith in this particular American dream."***
>
> The US Court of Appeals, 1975

Lennon finally returned to the public arena in 1980. "Part of me is a monk," Lennon told **Newsweek** magazine, "and part performing flea." Inspired, apparently, at least in part by his hearing Paul McCartney's single **Coming Up** on the radio (which he considered his former partner's best work in years), the performing flea in Lennon was re-emerging. Lennon's return was welcomed by the public, although the autumn-released **Just Like Starting Over** single and ***Double Fantasy*** album, which alternated John's new songs with Yoko's material, was greeted by a mixed critical reception (see p.100).

However, John was clearly re-energized by his return to music. In the enthusiastic interviews he gave at the time there was talk of touring and a further two albums. He'd even scheduled a collaboration with Ringo for early 1981. December 1980 saw him dedicatedly producing Yoko's solo single **Walking On Thin Ice**. It was after a session for that record that Lennon was gunned down and killed by a deranged fan outside the Dakota on the night of December 8.

A psychotic Beatles fan called Mark Chapman, who had worked himself into a quiet frenzy of evangelical delusion that Lennon was a "phoney" who deserved to die, was arrested at the scene, pleaded guilty in July 1981 and was sentenced to twenty years to life in prison, where he remains to this day (see p.67). In the three months following the tragedy, the single **Just Like Starting Over** reversed its decline to top many charts worldwide, swiftly followed by the nine-year-old **Imagine**, and **Woman** from *Double Fantasy*. Even Yoko had a UK Top 40 with **Walking On Thin Ice**. In 1981, the *John Lennon Collection* was a huge seller, while the next few years saw posthumous Lennon ephemera of varying degrees of interest appear, including the "follow-up" to *Double Fantasy*, **Milk And Honey** in 1984 outtakes from the *Rock 'N' Roll* and *Walls And Bridges* sessions, ***Menlove Avenue*** in 1986 and the documentary movie *John Lennon Imagine* in 1988.

The elevation of Lennon to cultural icon has been steady. There's now a John Lennon museum in Hong Kong, a John Lennon Airport in Liverpool and there will continue to be, if Yoko Ono has anything to do with it, a growing global awareness of what she calls "John's spirit". "Many things are not being revealed yet, only because people are not ready for it or they don't have the wisdom to understand it," she has said. "When we all get wiser then we'll start to see that what he was saying was right. I think there's a lot that people are going to discover, not even just hidden things, it's right in their faces and they can't recognize it."

Those who find the knee-jerk, John-as-flawed-saint view, along with the dewy-eyed reverence for John's utopian hymn "Imagine", a little hard to swallow prefer to remember Lennon as a pioneering, inspiring pop musician with vision, conscience and a healthy dose of pomposity-pricking irreverence. Should we ever find ourselves lulled into fantasizing over John Lennon as some kind of spiritual guide, perhaps we should imagine what the man himself would have said to that.

Early singles

Give Peace A Chance

Apple; recorded March 1969; released April 1969; currently available on *Shaved Fish*, *Lennon Legend* and *Working Class Hero: The Definitive Lennon*

Recorded at John and Yoko's honeymoon/press conference for peace in a Montreal hotel room on a portable eight-track machine with Yoko playing percussion (banging a wardrobe) and bedside choral contributions from beat poet Allen Ginsberg and pop singer Petula Clark among others. With echoed beats added to steady Lennon's self-described wild sense of time, "Give Peace A Chance" was a concerted effort to write something as universal and inspiring as **We Shall Overcome** but with the power of a mantra. The impatiently throwaway, rapped list verses make clear that everything else, whether provocative ("revolution", "masturbation") or trivial ("Tommy Cooper"), is a mere distracting detail on the quest for peace and the perfect peace anthem. When TV reported half a million people singing the song outside the White House in Washington in protest against Vietnam in November 1969, Lennon described it as "one of the biggest moments in my life".

Cold Turkey

Apple; recorded September 1969; released October 1969; currently available on *Shaved Fish*, *Lennon Legend* and *Working Class Hero: The Definitive Lennon*

This blistering musical depiction of heroin withdrawal is built on the contrast between the thumping heartbeat of Voormann and Starr's rhythm section – bass and drums as indomitable life force – and Eric Clapton's nightmarish, needling guitar riff describing the physical agony of brick-wall drug deprivation. Lennon's grim blues vocal mutates into howling histrionics, inspired by his own experience of the pain of going cold turkey, and by Yoko Ono's pyrotechnic vocal technique. Offered to The Beatles, they unsurprisingly turned it down.

Instant Karma!

Apple; recorded January 1970; released February 1970; currently available on *Working Class Hero: the Definitive Lennon*

Written and recorded in one day, "Instant Karma" is a dazzling encapsulation – with the concise economy of a TV commercial – of John's belief in the sooner-rather-than-later effect of every individual's every action. Produced by Phil Spector, it's the first appearance of the trademark slap-back delay that Lennon admired on Gene Vincent's **Be Bop A Lula** and that characterized so much of Lennon's solo work. The abrupt ricochet of the vocal and drum echo (as if to say that's how quickly the consequences of your actions will come back to you) and the controlled impatience of Alan White's double-time drum fills, kick the track along with an apt propulsion, while the communal "We all shine on" chorus glows with a convincing inspiration and vision.

Power To The People

Apple; released March 1971; currently available on *Shaved Fish*, *Lennon Legend* and *Working Class Hero: The Definitive Lennon*

Written as a direct response to an interview by the left-wing *Red Mole* magazine: Lennon got off the fence about his position on revolution and warned menacingly (hear those tramping feet) that the exploited workers were on their way. **Power To The People**, being essentially a call for social justice, was the first and probably the best of Lennon's agitprop efforts. Its verse championing women's rights was a radical step for the time, even among the leftist underground. Spector's massive production and Lennon's gift for memorable, no-nonsense sloganeering ensured the music did its job well, though its composer later dismissed it as a record made out of guilt. "We kept all the royalties of course," he admitted.

Happy Xmas (War Is Over)

Apple single; released in UK November 1972; currently available on *Shaved Fish*, *Lennon Legend*, *Sometime In New York City* and *Working Class Hero: The Definitive Lennon*

Written during John and Yoko's peace-and-love phase over a year earlier, its UK release was delayed by a publishing squabble. (Northern Songs owner Lew Grade was as suspicious about John as he was about Paul, with regard to the co-crediting of their respective spouses on songs while Apple's income was frozen.) Both a perennial Christmas song and another of John's paeans to the power of collective consciousness, the two ascending key changes and the counterpoint of the two melodic themes has a rousing grandeur. Phil Spector – who knew a thing or two about Christmas records – decorates the proceedings with a mandolin orchestra and the Harlem Community Choir. Undervalued at the time (especially in America), its refusal to be straightforwardly sentimental means that, even now, it's unlikely to ever eclipse **White Christmas** as a festive favourite, despite the efforts of a 2003 remix and re-promotion.

Albums

Unfinished Music No. 1: Two Virgins

John Lennon/Yoko Ono

TWO VIRGINS NO. 1/TOGETHER/TWO VIRGINS NO. 2/TWO VIRGINS NO. 3/TWO VIRGINS NO. 4/TWO VIRGINS NO. 5/TWO VIRGINS NO. 6/HUSHABYE, HUSHABYE/TWO VIRGINS NO. 7/ TWO VIRGINS NO. 8/TWO VIRGINS NO. 9/TWO VIRGINS NO. 10

Apple; recorded May 19, 1968; released November 29, 1968; currently available on CD (Ryko)

Not quite the harmonious meeting of minds one might imagine, given the circumstances of its recording. Yoko's earnest yelping and retching noises awkwardly collide with John's electronic tapes, whistling and free-associative vaudeville-isms. "That's right dear, spit it out," suggests Lennon after one particularly guttural Ono offering. Yoko counters with a barbed "corny", in response to a glib Lennon piano glissando. As an audio verité account of two expressive people having a flirtatious jam it's moderately interesting. As avant-garde art, it's less convincing.

Unfinished Music No. 2: Life With The Lions

John Lennon/Yoko Ono

CAMBRIDGE 1969/NO BED FOR BEATLE JOHN/ BABY'S HEARTBEAT/ TWO MINUTES SILENCE/RADIO PLAY

Zapple; recorded November 1968–March 1969; released May 2, 1969; currently available on CD (Ryko)

"Cambridge 1969" is the ear-splitting duet (backed up by the established noise-jazzers John Stevens and John Tchicai) between Ono's squalling and Lennon's feeding-back electric guitar recorded in March 1969 at Lady Mitchell Hall, Cambridge. For all its uncompromising, howling cacophony, there's a coherence in John and Yoko's approach to the event that's an advance, if that's the word, on **Two Virgins**. Side two – mostly recorded onto cassette in the hospital room where Yoko was under observation during a risky pregnancy – documents the pair **improvising melodies** to various November 1968 newspaper articles about themselves, five minutes of foetal heartbeat and two minutes of silence representing Yoko's eventual miscarriage. This is then followed by twelve minutes of fiddling with a radio dial, which seems to say life goes on, art goes on. Self-obsessed artistic expression which recognizes no guidelines of taste or craft; indulgent doesn't quite cover it.

Wedding Album

John Lennon/Yoko Ono

JOHN AND YOKO/AMSTERDAM

Apple; recorded March–April 1969; released November 14, 1969; currently available on CD (Ryko)

Still in pain following the loss of their baby in November 1968, the couple recorded the experimental, cathartic track **John and Yoko** at Abbey Road, in which each called out the other's name for 22 minutes in various degrees of intensity accompanied by the reprised sound of a foetal heartbeat. In its own peculiar way it's oddly compelling, if you've got the time. **Amsterdam** is an insubstantial audio collage of press interviews, improvised songs and room-service phone calls documenting the events surrounding their March 1969 honeymoon "Bed-In". Somehow evading Klein's fat-trimming operation at Apple, it was packaged in a box with a cardboard piece of wedding cake and a copy of their marriage certificate. It sold in the dozens.

Live Peace In Toronto 1969

Plastic Ono Band

BLUE SUEDE SHOES/MONEY/DIZZY MISS LIZZY/YER BLUES/ COLD TURKEY/GIVE PEACE A CHANCE/DON'T WORRY KYOKO (MUMMY'S ONLY LOOKING FOR HER HAND IN THE SNOW)/JOHN, JOHN (LET'S HOPE FOR PEACE)

Apple; recorded September 13, 1969; released December 12, 1969; currently available on CD

Quickly routined on the plane to Canada, this recording of the Plastic Ono Band at Toronto's Rock'N'Roll Revival festival is surprisingly powerful. Alan White's drums, Klaus Voormann's bass (when he manages to keep up with the chord changes) and Lennon's rhythm guitar stoke up some deep rock grooves on **Money** and **Yer Blues**, and Clapton is on excitingly dangerous form throughout. Even Yoko's squawking – dominating side two but cameoing as early as **Dizzy Miss Lizzy** and central to the live reading of the mint-fresh **Cold Turkey** on side one – brings a further stirring dimension of energy to the proceedings.

John Lennon/Plastic Ono Band

MOTHER/HOLD ON JOHN/I FOUND OUT/WORKING CLASS HERO/ISOLATION/REMEMBER/LOVE/ LOOK AT ME/WELL WELL WELL/GOD/MY MUMMY'S DEAD

Apple; recorded autumn 1970; released December 1970; currently available on CD with extra tracks "Power To The People" and "Do The Oz"

During four months of primal scream therapy, Lennon had confronted his emotional pain and insecurities, exploring their deep roots in his troubled childhood. On this album Lennon showed his scars to his audience who, for the most part, preferred to look away. "Primal therapy allowed us to feel feeling continuously," he said at the time, "and those feelings usually make you cry." The shattering opener **Mother** sets the tone. Preceded by a tolling church bell – slowed down by producer Phil Spector for extra portent – Lennon howls an emotionally harrowing plea for his dead mother not to leave him and his absent father to return. The stark production, featuring brutal, gospelly piano chords, is as effective as a close-up in a movie, forcing all the listener's attention on Lennon's wounded vocals, line by tortured line. This and the album closer, the brief, bleak lullaby **My Mummy's Dead**, are as raw and affecting a pair of songs as any in popular music.

But he's not just hurt, he's angry too. **I Found Out** is a vicious, unpredictable track with fractious guitar and snarling vocals spitting out a list of his current bugbears: religion, drugs, "freaks" pestering him for attention and, once more, his parents. On **Working Class Hero** – a minor-key, Dylan-style waltz à la **Masters Of War** – Lennon's scattergun cynicism is at its world-weary best, as he makes a series of complex, ambiguous observations about social control, society's intolerance of the individual, and the contradictions of class and ambition.

The twice-used word "fuckin'" limited its radio play and the song was too ironic and downbeat to become the worker's anthem he hoped it would.

God delivers a seething list of religious, political and cultural icons Lennon no longer believed in – including John F. Kennedy, Elvis, Buddah, Jesus and, saved dramatically for last, The Beatles – before announcing that he now only believes in himself and his wife, and reclaiming his status as The Beatles' maker and breaker.

Among all the angst and vitriol, however, are several wound-licking interludes of calm in which Lennon's voice becomes a fragile, vulnerable coo. **Hold On John** is a salve of encouragement to himself and Yoko, dressed in comforting tremolo guitar. **Love** is a beautifully serene meditation which treads a fine line between haiku-like profundity and greeting-card sentiment. **Look At Me** recalls the finger-picking guitar tracks on *The White Album* (from which it dated) and pleads for a self-defining lover's gaze amidst attractive suspended chords.

Not especially popular at the time, Plastic Ono Band has retained a reputation among those who like their Lennon in extremis. Balanced compellingly between vital artistic expression and post-therapy self-indulgence, it remains a uniquely uncomfortable record.

Imagine

IMAGINE/CRIPPLED INSIDE/JEALOUS GUY/IT'S SO HARD/I DON'T WANT TO BE A SOLDIER MAMA/GIMME SOME TRUTH/ OH MY LOVE/HOW DO YOU SLEEP/HOW?/OH YOKO!

Apple; recorded 1971; released October 1971; currently available on CD (Parlophone)

On the surface, *Imagine* is a much more approachable album than its predecessor. Lennon was quick to characterize it as "Plastic Ono Band with sugar", lest the comparatively astringent meanings of the songs be overlooked. For instance, **Crippled Inside** is a polemic accusing more or less the entire world (including himself) of emotional hypocrisy, while disguising itself as a country ditty. On **Jealous Guy** Lennon confesses to a long-established and painful green-eyed inadequacy within an intimate relationship (which would often leave him seething with rage) with an apologetic musical bouquet, pungent with helpless, vulnerable justification.

Elsewhere, Lennon's sentiments were not so smartly dressed. **I Don't Want To Be A Soldier Mama** is a feverish, semi-coherent rant. **Gimme Some Truth** spits and sneers with an articulate self-righteous disgust, its tumbling, multi-syllable insults aimed at "hypocritics", politicians, chauvinists and prima donnas with all the anger and rhythmic precision of a rap lyric.

It was **How Do You Sleep**, however, that received the most attention. It is a witty but spiteful attack upon Paul McCartney (his music, his family and his reputation), and the listener's uneasiness is hardly helped by the fact it's one of Lennon's best solo recordings. Every element – George Harrison's snide slide guitar, Torrie Zito's insinuating strings, the grinding, downward minor-key chord changes, the rattlesnake echo on the vocal – is a caustic realization of Lennon's disenchantment with his former partner and friend. Lennon later variously justified it as "like a joke", as really an attack on himself and as a response to jibes made against him on McCartney's *Ram* album (Lennon went as far as including a postcard with the *Imagine* album showing him grappling a pig, a sarcastic reference to Paul's photo of himself playing the down-home shepherd on *Ram*'s cover). Most listeners, not least McCartney himself, were shocked. And yet, in a classic Lennon contradiction, despite all the sneering at McCartney and his "muzak", the next track on the album, **How?**, blatantly pilfers the distinctive rhythms of the suspended piano chords from Paul's **Long And Winding Road**.

The impact of *Imagine*'s famous title track has been somewhat dulled by over-exposure since Lennon's assassination. But its utopian radicalism nonetheless packs an impressive emotional punch. Some critics have pointed to the apparent contradiction of being encouraged to imagine no possessions by a multi-millionaire rock star from the "white room" in his mansion. Others argue that the song's meaning is a wistful question to self and listener – wondering if we actually can – rather than an imperative from a lofty political idealist (which he purported to be at the time) taking an off-putting moral high ground. (For Lennon's passionate, mature thoughts on the message of the song, hear his interview from

1980, included as a bonus track on the 2002 reissue of **Milk And Honey**.) The song's mainstream popularity and anthemic status were repeatedly confirmed at the end of 2000, as it was consistently voted to the top (or thereabouts) of various "Song Of The Millennium" polls.

Sometime In New York City

John Lennon/Yoko Ono

WOMAN IS THE NIGGER OF THE WORLD/SISTERS O SISTERS/ ATTICA STATE/BORN IN A PRISON/NEW YORK CITY/SUNDAY BLOODY SUNDAY/THE LUCK OF THE IRISH/JOHN SINCLAIR/ ANGELA/WE'RE ALL WATER/COLD TURKEY/DON'T WORRY KYOKO/WELL (BABY PLEASE DON'T GO)/JAMRAG/SCUMBAG/AII

Apple; recorded 1972; released September 1972; currently available on remixed and remastered CD which omits "Jamrag", "Scumbag" and "Aii" and adds "Listen The Snow Is Falling" and "Happy Xmas (War Is Over)"

This album reveals a John Lennon at the height of his grassroots, issue-specific politicking but is among the lowest artistic points of any Beatle. The **Yippie**-influenced off-the-peg radicalism did his songwriting no favours. **Attica State** sets its risibly naïve anarchist sloganeering to an unconvincing droning rant, while the sentimental **The Luck Of The Irish** has John providing the political propaganda and Yoko the condescending poetry, complete with leprechauns. More successful is **Sunday Bloody Sunday**. Lennon's lyrics, addressing the period's hottest of political hot potatoes, are more focused and his vocals are superbly menacing. Lyrically, **New York City** sets out to be the "Ballad Of John And Yoko II: The Big Apple". It rocks well enough but the words fall over themselves too often, never quite attaining that Chuck Berry style, freewheeling rock'n'roll poetry they aspire to.

The best track by some distance is **Woman Is The Nigger Of The World**, in which a man who had often confessed to uncontrollable, usually drink-fuelled violence when a young man, parades his new-found feminist solidarity, delivering an indignant lecture with all the self-righteous rectitude of the born again. A marvellously overblown production, Lennon sings magnificently, riding Spector's waves of sound like a magnificent warrior for the sisterhood.

The bonus album features two tracks from the War Is Over concert at the Lyceum in December 1969 and a live jam in New York from 1971 with Frank Zappa, of which **Well** (Lennon to audience: "I used to sing this in The Cavern") is the highlight. Otherwise it hardly warrants a single listen and was largely excised from the 2005 CD reissue. That *Sometime In New York City* took so long to receive proper digital attention and was unavailable in any form for some time is indicative of the general antipathy towards it.

Mind Games

MIND GAMES/TIGHT A$/AISUMASEN (I'M SORRY)/ONE DAY (AT A TIME)/BRING ON THE LUCIE (FREEDA PEOPLE)/NUTOPIAN NATIONAL ANTHEM/INTUITION/OUT OF THE BLUE/ONLY PEOPLE/I KNOW (I KNOW)/YOU ARE HERE/MEAT CITY

Apple; recorded summer 1973; released November 1973; currently available on CD with extra tracks "Aisumasen (I'm Sorry)", "Bring On The Lucie (Freeda People)" and "Meat City" (home versions)

After the debacle of *Sometime In New York City*, Lennon's artistic reputation was at a low. Undeterred, he entered the Record Plant studio, New York, with a crack team of session musicians and produced his slickest solo music to date. Eschewing the no-nonsense primitivism that had largely characterized his post-Beatles output, on *Mind Games* Lennon is back in touch with the subtler aspects of his craft. Whether paying vivacious tribute to his adopted homeland of NYC on **Tight A$** and **Meat City** or pressing home his "free your mind" brand of humanism on **Mind Games** and **Only People**, Lennon – unencumbered by either Spector or Ono – produces his most sophisticated arrangements and luxurious chord sequences since *Abbey Road*.

The voguish radicalism is limited to the anti-Nixon **Bring On The Lucie**, replaced with vulnerable, apologetic paeans to his wife on the eve of their eighteen months apart. The album cover Lennon eventually chose shows him walking away, bags packed, from a mountainous Yoko. The music has almost onomatopoeic powers of downbeat expression: **Aisumasen (I'm Sorry)** is a hanging-head of a song lurching joylessly from chord to chord; the harmonically meandering **One Day At A Time** limps tentatively from key to key, conveying not so much a satisfying journey as a vivid idea of someone who literally does not know where he is or where he's going. But, and this is often forgotten, the tunes are good.

The album was undervalued at the time and was the first by a Beatle to be relegated to EMI's budget label MFP. Its remastering in 2002, markedly improving the sound quality, did attract some long-overdue reassessment but it remains an underrated record.

Walls And Bridges

GOING DOWN ON LOVE/WHATEVER GETS YOU THRU THE NIGHT/OLD DIRT ROAD/WHAT YOU GOT/BLESS YOU/SCARED/NUMBER 9 DREAM/SURPRISE SURPRISE (SWEET BIRD OF PARADOX)/STEEL AND GLASS/BEEF JERKY/NOBODY LOVES YOU (WHEN YOU'RE DOWN AND OUT)/YA YA

Apple; recorded summer 1974; released October 1974; currently available on CD with bonus tracks "Whatever Gets You Thru The Night (Live)", "Nobody Knows You When You're Down And Out" (alternative version) and "John Interview"

The most significant music from his "lost weekend" in Los Angeles, *Walls And Bridges* was later slated by Lennon (significantly, from the position of a revitalized marriage) as the work of a "semi-sick craftsman" with "no inspiration". Those who thought that the honesty of expression in his post-Beatles music had sometimes been at the expense of the finer facets of his art disagree on the evidence of this music. Even as he sings of "drowning in a sea of hatred" on **Going Down On Love**, the carefully arranged, multi-thematic song confirms that he is also a man at one with his compositional dexterity. Ingredients are expertly chosen and blended into a series of compelling textures. **Old Dirt Road** shimmers like heat haze in the desert while **Scared** prowls with all the portent of an Orson Welles tracking shot. **Bless You** is the floatiest, jazziest thing Lennon has ever done while **Number 9 Dream** is a beautiful billowing cloud of a track; it's impossible to hear its nonsensical chant and not be uplifted.

While the lyrical content is almost uniformly downbeat, bordering on the paranoid, much of the music (the tough funk of **What You Got**, the jangle-soul of **Whatever Gets You Thru The Night**, the thumping instrumental **Beef Jerky**) rocks with big boots. Particularly notable on a biographical level is **Surprise Surprise (Sweet Bird Of Paradox)**, an ode to his lover May Pang. Compared to his many songs dedicated to Yoko, there's a certain restraint in the language, not least in the "well-waddaya-know" raised eyebrow of the title. But from the shuffle of the intro to the **Drive My Car** near-quote at the close, far from the hell on earth he was supposed to be having, Lennon sounds inspired, happy and relaxed.

Nobody Loves You (When You're Down And Out), however, is a wonderfully maudlin meditation on the fickleness of fame (in the face of recent unpleasant publicity and indifference to his art) and it corroborates his personal malaise. He may well have been miserable, but he still made a terrific record.

Rock 'N' Roll

BE BOP A LULA/STAND BY ME/READY TEDDY-RIP IT UP/YOU CAN'T CATCH ME/AIN'T THAT A SHAME/DO YOU WANT TO DANCE/SWEET LITTLE SIXTEEN/SLIPPIN' AND SLIDIN'/PEGGY SUE/BRING IT ON HOME TO ME – SEND ME SOME LOVIN'/BONY MORONIE/YA YA/JUST BECAUSE

Apple; recorded October–December 1973 and autumn 1974; released February 1975; currently available on CD with bonus tracks "Angel Baby", "To Know Her Is To Love Her", "Since My Baby Left Me" and "Just Because (Reprise)"

A patchy collection that can't quite disguise its compromised origins (Lennon's humiliating contractual obligation to Maurice Levy) or the quick-fix repair job Lennon made on the catastrophic Spector-produced sessions of autumn 1973.

Of the four Spector tracks which survived the album, three (**You Can't Catch Me**, **Sweet Little Sixteen** and **Just Because**) lumber along without grace or charm with only the monolithic take on "Bony Moronie"'s classic riff approaching any kind of style. However, delivered in a state of advanced intoxication, even Lennon's vocals sound foolish. Happily, Lennon was in marginally better voice for the tidier 1974 sessions, but whether the problem is messy double-tracking (**Rip It Up**), a half-hearted half track (**Peggy Sue**) or a rigid, groove-free non-arrangement (**Do You Want To Dance**), the whole betrays a certain lack of commitment to quality music making.

Among the few out-and-out successes are a great straight-rock version of **Ain't That A Shame** and a nifty **Ya Ya**. The highlight is probably **Stand By Me**, in which Lennon's gnarly, compelling singing transforms the tender Leiber/Stoller/Ben E. King plea for support into a snappy demand for attention. He announced he was getting back together with Yoko ("Our separation was a failure," he mused) the same day as releasing the track as a single.

Double Fantasy

John Lennon/Yoko Ono

JUST LIKE STARTING OVER/KISS KISS KISS/CLEANUP TIME/GIVE ME SOMETHING/I'M LOSING YOU/I'M MOVING ON/ BEAUTIFUL BOY (DARLING BOY)/ WATCHING THE WHEELS/YES I'M YOUR WOMAN/ WOMAN/BEAUTIFUL BOYS/DEAR YOKO

Geffen; recorded summer 1980; released October 1980; currently available on CD with bonus tracks "Every Man Has A Woman Who Loves Him", "Hard Times Are Over", "Help Me To Help Myself", "Walking On Thin Ice" and "Central Park Stroll"

Before John's tragic death gave it such unwelcome poignancy, the general response to *Double Fantasy* was disappointment. Not only because he had chosen to alternate tracks on his first album in five years with Yoko's, but also because Lennon's music itself was rather limp. On the retro-rock of **Just Like Starting Over** or the melodious, soft-centred dedications to Yoko (**Woman**) or baby Sean (**Beautiful Boy**), there seemed to be little to fire the imagination other than the pleasure of hearing the man sing again.

The original idea of the album was to create a musical dialogue – a "Heart Play" as the album's subtitle called it – between an intimate couple who, on one level, are John and Yoko, but on another somehow represent their whole generation of couples who "made it through" as Lennon said in interview at the time. As a musical experience, it is by turns idiosyncratic (Yoko's contributions) and underachieving (John's). But it nevertheless remains a fascinating pseudo-biography, especially in the light of post-assassination "revelations" about life in the Dakota, which suggested a much more complicated and strained emotional setup than is commonly supposed from the lovey-dovey photos and footage. The title of John's **Cleanup Time** seems to suggest that it wasn't always macrobiotic rice on West 72nd Street, while Yoko's **Kiss Kiss Kiss**, **I'm Moving On** and **Give Me Something** are full of words like "terror", "cold", "hard", and "phoney". John's **Just Like Starting Over**, **I'm Losing You** and **Dear Yoko** are all songs that imply John wasn't getting the attention he wanted from his partner, taking, respectively, a loving, an angry then a pleading tone. It's clear that the real ballad of John and Yoko is a very complex one.

Help Me To Help Myself, the bonus track on the 2000 reissue was a sweet, hymn-like 1980 demo. Its opening lines, full of startling premonition and portent, have an unwished-for pathos that hardly needs underlining. It isn't spectacular – those days were long gone – but it sounds like it could have been good. Could have been just fine.

Milk And Honey

John Lennon/Yoko Ono

I'M STEPPING OUT/SLEEPLESS NIGHT/I DON'T WANNA FACE IT/DON'T BE SCARED/NOBODY TOLD ME/O'SANITY/ BORROWED TIME/YOUR HANDS/(FORGIVE ME) MY LITTLE FLOWER PRINCESS/LET ME COUNT THE WAYS/GROW OLD WITH ME/YOU'RE THE ONE

Polydor; recorded 1980–83; released January 1984; currently available on CD with bonus tracks "Every Man Has A Woman Who Loves Him", "Stepping Out (home version)", "I'm Moving On" and "Interview December 8, 1980"

This was to have been the follow-up to *Double Fantasy*. Lennon and Ono were working on it when John was killed, and its rough vocals and early, undeveloped arrangements generate a similarly complex, if marginally cuddlier, dialogue between John's and Yoko's songs. There's nothing earth-shattering here, but on **I'm Stepping Out** and **Nobody Told Me** Lennon sounds genuinely excited to be working again, while Yoko's **Don't Be Scared** is a surprisingly exquisite reggae number. The 2001 remaster features a fascinating 20-minute interview conducted a few hours before John's death. Full of positivity and hope for the future of mankind, it may be the best thing on the disc.

Live In New York City

John Lennon/Yoko Ono

NEW YORK CITY/IT'S SO HARD/WOMAN IS THE NIGGER OF THE WORLD/WELL WELL WELL/INSTANT KARMA (WE ALL SHINE ON)/MOTHER/COME TOGETHER/IMAGINE/COLD TURKEY/HOUND DOG/GIVE PEACE A CHANCE

EMI; recorded August 1972; released February 1986; currently available on CD

A charity concert in aid of a New York school for mentally handicapped children, John and Yoko's final live appearance was recorded at Madison Square Garden on August 30, 1972. Maybe you had to be there (the video, released in 1986, is certainly entertaining), but as a record it barely holds up any better than the *Sometime In New York City* live bonus disc and probably isn't even as good as *Live Peace In Toronto*. The double-drummered Plastic Ono Elephant's Memory Band is thick-wristed and Lennon himself is distressingly cavalier with his delivery. **Come Together** is potentially the most interesting track ("You'll probably remember this better than me," announces Lennon) but, pitching it a full tone higher than the *Abbey Road* version, Lennon struggles to deliver the vocal and the overall effect is rather disheartening.

Menlove Avenue

HERE WE GO AGAIN/ROCK AND ROLL PEOPLE/ANGEL BABY/SINCE MY BABY LEFT ME/TO KNOW HER IS TO LOVE HER/STEEL AND GLASS/SCARED/OLD DIRT ROAD/NOBODY KNOWS YOU (WHEN YOU'RE DOWN AND OUT)/BLESS YOU

EMI; recorded 1973–74; released November 1986; currently available on CD

These outtakes from the Spector-produced *Rock 'N' Roll* sessions are mainly notable for the previously unheard Spector/Lennon collaboration **Here We Go Again** (a big production of a lightweight song) and the Lennon boogie of **Rock And Roll People**. The tracks that never made the finished album (**Angel Baby** and **To Know Her Is To Love Her**) suffer from the same problems as the ones that did: over-long, lugubrious arrangements and erratic singing (though **Since My Baby Left Me** generates an exciting party atmosphere). The early takes from the *Walls And Bridges* sessions of 1974 are little more than rehearsals, with half-decent vocals and bum bass notes from Klaus Voormann. If John's life had not been cut short, it's unlikely they would have seen the light of day. As it is, they're rather good to hear.

Lennon Anthology

Capitol/EMI; recorded 1968–80; released November 1998; currently available on CD

The same goes for this, a four-CD box of demos, out-takes, home versions, fragments of dialogue, and miscellaneous Lennon flotsam and jetsam. Those familiar with the American radio series from the late 1980s, the **Lost Lennon Tapes**, or even the audio verité of John and Yoko's late 60s records, will be at home with this documentary-like collection. It's less a musical treat than a way of bringing the man himself a little closer to the listener. A single CD, **Wonsuponatime**, while opting for the better of Lennon's solo highlights, loses some of the cumulative appeal of the whole box. Not for casual listeners perhaps, but compelling enough for anyone interested in Lennon the man.

Acoustic

WORKING CLASS HERO/LOVE/WELL WELL WELL/LOOK AT ME/GOD/MY MUMMY'S DEAD/COLD TURKEY/THE LUCK OF THE IRISH/JOHN SINCLAIR/WOMAN IS THE NIGGER OF THE WORLD/WHAT YOU GOT/WATCHING THE WHEELS/DEAR YOKO/REAL LOVE/IMAGINE/IT'S REAL

Capitol; recorded 1969–1980; released November 2004

Mostly culled from *Lennon Anthology*, this 16-tracker featuring John and his guitar demoing a selection of his solo tunes was never going to be an especially enlightening listen. However, the package is presented almost as a primer for aspirant players, complete with printed chord boxes and Yoko's dedication of the album to "all future guitarists". While Lennon's infamously wayward sense of rhythm (as displayed here on barely coherent versions of "Cold Turkey" and "Well Well Well") is hardly the most obvious model for students, some of his chord sequences certainly are, as is the pervading passion of his playing. For lay listeners, among the more diverting tracks is the alternate "Working Class Hero", perhaps even more vivid than the released version, a funky "What You Got" and a previously unreleased, unexpectedly lovely guitar demo of "Real Love".

Instant Lennon

Working Class Hero – The Definitive Lennon

(JUST LIKE) STARTING OVER/IMAGINE/WATCHING THE WHEELS/JEALOUS GUY/INSTANT KARMA! (WE ALL SHINE ON)/STAND BY ME/WORKING CLASS HERO/POWER TO THE PEOPLE/OH MY LOVE/OH YOKO!/NOBODY LOVES YOU (WHEN YOU'RE DOWN AND OUT)/NOBODY TOLD ME/BLESS YOU/COME TOGETHER/I'M STEPPING OUT/YOU ARE HERE/BORROWED TIME/HAPPY XMAS (WAR IS OVER)/WOMAN/MIND GAMES/OUT THE BLUE/WHATEVER GETS YOU THRU THE NIGHT/LOVE/MOTHER/BEAUTIFUL BOY/WOMAN IS THE NIGGER OF THE WORLD/GOD/SCARED/NUMBER 9 DREAM/I'M LOSING YOU/ISOLATION/COLD TURKEY/INTUITION/GIMME SOME TRUTH/GIVE PEACE A CHANCE/REAL LOVE/GROW OLD WITH ME

Recorded 1969–1980; released October 2005

This 2005 38-track compilation is the best Lennon solo overview yet, comparable to McCartney's excellent *Wingspan*. It's a comprehensive replacement for the earlier *Shaved Fish* (his 1975 kiss goodbye to EMI), *The John Lennon Collection* (the best-selling 1981 post-assassination set) and *Lennon Legend* (the 1995 single CD), though it should be noted that the CD version of *Collection* is the only place to get his oblique "lost weekend" message to Yoko "Move Over Ms L" (originally the B-side to "Stand By Me").

Paul McCartney

"From a purely selfish point of view, if I could get John Lennon back, I'd ask him to undo this legacy that he's left me."

Paul McCartney, 1981

Paul McCartney took the demise of The Beatles the hardest of the four. In the months following Lennon's announcement of wanting a "divorce" in August 1969, McCartney went to Scotland, thoroughly depressed, "the redundant man," as he later called himself. Yet when he returned to Cavendish Avenue, and his experiments with home recording – playing and singing everything himself – he soon found himself with an album's worth of music. His home-made approach extended to designing the cover himself, using Linda's pictures. He even stuffed the record sleeves personally, with his infamous press-release-cum-interview that the world took as the official announcement of The Beatles' break-up.

The record, *McCartney*, sold well, but in the gloomy atmosphere of The Beatles split in April 1970, many fans blamed Paul for the Fabs breaking up and the album was generally considered a disappointment, as was the anaemic February 1971 single **Another Day**. By the time the follow-up *Ram*, recorded in New York, came out in May 1971, Paul had sued The Beatles to dissolve Apple, and won. In an ironic comment on the legal proceedings, the cover of *Ram* showed two beetles copulating. McCartney later commented that the episode "certainly did not make me the most popular man in Britain" and ultimately *Ram* was no better received than his solo debut.

With Paul's future income frozen by the Apple receiver, he took to claiming songwriting co-credits for his wife. "If I have to just go out in another room and write, it's too much like work," reasoned McCartney. "If I can have Linda working with me, then it's like a game." Six of the songs on *Ram* were credited to Paul and Linda McCartney, which at least meant that 50 percent of the song's royalties would make their way into the McCartney bank account. Lew Grade's **ATV** (who now owned Lennon and McCartney's publishing via their acquisition of Northern Songs) would receive less of a cut and, suspicious, sued McCartney on the grounds that Linda wasn't a bona fide equal writing partner. McCartney and Grade reached a compromise, with Paul even re-signing to ATV in 1972 and agreeing to appear in an ATV television special, **James Paul McCartney**, which eventually aired in April 1973.

Missing playing in a regular band, in August 1971 McCartney announced he had formed

Wings. Comprising Linda on backing vocals and rudimentary keyboards, ex-Moody Blues man Denny Laine on guitar and New York session drummer Denny Seiwell, Wings' debut *Wild Life* was released in December to the worst critical hammering McCartney had ever received. Unperturbed, in February 1972 Wings, which now also featured ex-**Grease Band** member Henry McCullough on guitar, drove north and went on an unannounced tour of British universities. The kind of back-to-basics approach McCartney had wanted The Beatles to attempt in latter years, it was the perfect way for a new band to find its feet. Scrupulously avoiding Beatles songs, Wings played rock'n'roll numbers and *Wild Life* selections, stayed in unglamorous guest houses and got paid in bags of 50-pence pieces, the students' door takings from the impromptu lunchtime performances.

Some of the tour's later gigs were picketed by angry crowds of protesters, however, thanks to **Give Ireland Back To The Irish**, a song written as a spontaneous response to the Bloody Sunday massacres, and which was released in February 1972 as Wings' debut single. The record managed to irritate everyone, not least for its naïve, simplistic attitude to a complex situation (on a par with Lennon's similarly unconvincing perspective later that year), but also for its musical mediocrity. The BBC banned the record, granting it a notoriety disproportionate to its importance.

Wings' next single, **Mary Had A Little Lamb**, a ditty for the kids, had the critics sharpening their knives once more, but it was a respectable hit rather at odds with the unrespectable image the band had in mid-1972. Wings had been busted for possession of dope in Sweden on their August tour and McCartney had returned to his Scottish farm to find it had been raided by a Campbeltown police officer. McCartney eventually pleaded guilty to growing and possessing marijuana and was fined £100. He shrugged it off: "A fan sent us some seeds, we planted them and some of them came up illegal." Yet Wings' next single, **Hi Hi Hi**, earned them further infamy, being banned by the BBC for supposed drugs and sex references, although its flip-side, **C Moon**, was played regularly and sold well.

McCartney at last began to claw back his credibility in March 1973 with **My Love**, his most impressive post-Beatles offering since *McCartney*'s **Maybe I'm Amazed**. If the Wings LP that followed it, *Red Rose Speedway*, proved McCartney still struggled to maintain consistency over the course of an album, Wings' theme to the latest James Bond movie, **Live And Let Die**, released as a single in June 1973, was a commercial and musical triumph.

Wings had developed a certain panache as a live act during their 1973 British tour and released a swaggering October single, **Helen Wheels**, approaching rehearsals for a new album with confidence. However, a combination of McCartney's single-minded, domineering control of the group and his insistence in bringing his non-musician wife along at all times proved too much for McCullough and Seiwell, who quit the band on the eve of the Nigeria-based recording sessions. The remaining trio of Paul, Linda and Denny Laine pressed on with McCartney handling drums, though the visit was blighted by renowned African musician Fela Ransome Kuti accusing Paul of wanting to "steal the black musicians' music" and an unconnected, frightening knife-point robbery of the McCartneys. However, the resulting album of January 1974, *Band On The Run*, was a real coup for McCartney and was rapturously received as nothing less than the second coming of a much-missed musical talent.

Two hit singles from the album (**Jet** and **Band On The Run**) reached healthy chart positions in 1974 in both the UK and US. In October a stand-alone single appeared, **Junior's Farm**, featuring ex-Thunderclap Newman guitar prodigy Jimmy McCulloch and the drummer Geoff Britton, who had beaten 48 auditionees (including Mitch Mitchell, former Jimi Hendrix sideman) to become Wings' new drummer. Unfortunately, the clean-living Britton didn't gel with the partying rockers Laine and McCulloch and only lasted until February 1975, leaving during the New Orleans recording sessions for what became the *Venus And Mars* album. Presumably, he didn't hit it off with the pot-loving McCartneys either. Both were busted for marijuana possession by a California traffic policeman in March 1975 although Linda, mindful of her husband's visa, took the blame. She was ordered by the judge to attend psychiatric drug counselling in the UK.

The American drummer Joe English completed the album sessions and stuck with Wings at the height of their mid-70s popularity, beginning with the May 1975 release of the successful album **Venus And Mars** and continuing into the British and Australian live shows of 1975. With Wings now a well-drilled pop-rock unit sporting a fancy light show, and featuring a modest handful of McCartney's Beatle tunes among the increasingly persuasive Wings music, their live sets were received ecstatically.

So delighted was McCartney with the new line-up of Wings, he allowed each member of the band, including Linda, a lead vocal on the May 1976 album *Wings At The Speed Of Sound*. An LP which spawned his two biggest post-Beatles hits to date, **Let 'Em In** and **Silly Love Songs**, it formed the backbone of the Wings set he took to Europe and America. Between May and June 1976 they played 26 spectacular arena dates. Three million delirious fans saw the group on the **Wings Over America** tour, the entire show of which was released on a best-selling triple live album, with highlights appearing on the concert movie **Rockshow**. It was clear from concert attendances and record sales that Paul's 1970s audience was not just old Beatles fans, it was also new Wings fans.

Recording for the new album began at Abbey Road in January 1977 and continued on a series of chartered yachts in the **Virgin Islands**, but by mid-1977, Wings had lost their two newest members. Joe English missed his family and returned to the US, while the volatile McCulloch left the group following a series of violent, drug-fuelled tantrums. Within two years the 26-year-old McCulloch had died from a suspected drugs overdose.

Winter 1977 saw the single release of the sing-a-long Scottish-style waltz **Mull Of Kintyre** which, despite the presence of **Girls' School**, a naughty little rocker on the flip, did little for McCartney's credibility. He could console himself with the fact that it stayed at #1 for nine weeks and, selling over 2.5 million copies, became Britain's biggest-selling single ever. Outrunning **She Loves You**, the biggest Beatles seller, by two to one, it was eclipsed only by Band Aid's **Do They Know It's Christmas** seven years on. Oddly, the album released soon afterwards, *London Town*, failed to capitalize on "Mull"'s huge success. With no band to promote it and only some soft-centred singles leading the campaign at the height of the new-wave explosion, the LP was released in March 1978 to an equivocal critical and commercial response.

Ever resolute, McCartney hired Lawrence Juber on guitar and Steve Holly on drums and set to work recording a new album, **Back To The Egg**. In October 1978, a 19-strong collection of rock luminaries (including John Bonham, Pete Townshend, Hank Marvin, Ronnie Lane and Dave Gilmour) joined Wings at Abbey Road to be conducted through a couple of tunes by Paul as the Rockestra. However, even this extravaganza and a huge promotional push in June 1979 couldn't elevate the album from being only a moderate achievement and a disappointing seller. In fact, Wings' March 1979 stand-alone disco single **Goodnight Tonight** turned out to have been a better bet all round.

Wings across the Mersey, Liverpool

Wings embarked on a UK theatre tour in November 1979, which was generally considered to be an anticlimax, despite the live debuts of Beatles numbers like **Got To Get You Into My Life, Fool On The Hill** and **Let It Be.** "Paul hated the whole tour," remembered

Steve Holly. "Musically, there were definitely problems with some of the band." "I was bored," remembered Paul, years later. The tour climaxed with a reprise of the Rockestra at the **Concert For Kampuchea** at Hammersmith Odeon on December 29, 1979.

By January 1980, McCartney was looking forward to basking with Wings in the adoration of his Japanese fans for the first time since The Beatles were there in 1966. But Japanese customs put paid to that when they found marijuana in Paul's luggage at Tokyo airport. It has since been implied by several of the Lennons' former associates that Yoko informed them. When asked about it these days, Yoko is evasive whilst Paul shrugs off the whole thing.

Paul was arrested and imprisoned for ten days, the tour was cancelled and the McCartney family were understandably anxious. All, it seems, except for Paul. Though he felt foolish and scared lest he be separated from his family for long (there were threats of seven-year sentences), his unquenchable optimism got him through. "It was hell," he said later "but I only remember the good bits, like a bad holiday." Linda even reported him "laughing his way through his ordeal". It was perhaps the best example yet of McCartney's positive character. "Paul's an amazing guy," as Harry Nilsson once observed. "He just smokes his joints and whistles his way through life." McCartney detailed his prison adventures in a 20,000-word book ("like writing an essay for school" Paul said) and had one printed up for himself. It remains unpublished.

McCartney got the home-recording bug again in mid-1979 and cobbled together a cute, synthesizer-based single for the Christmas charts, **Wonderful Christmastime**. By spring 1980, his home keyboard doodling had evolved into a solo album *McCartney II* and a funky hit single **"Coming Up"**.

Though McCartney's press relations were usually effective ("a good PR man," Lennon once said of him, "the best in the world, probably"), Paul had suffered his share of criticism for his perceived bourgeois, non-rock gifts and his apparently glib charm. A careless understatement when a reporter's microphone was thrust at him in the hours after Lennon's assassination in December 1980 – "It's a drag" was his unprepared, unwilling comment – had the anti-Paul hounds out for a while. Recalling that a similarly stunned 14-year-old Paul who had blurted "What are we going to do without her money?" when his mother had died, some commentators chose to interpret this as evidence of a cold heart behind the doe eyes. Philip Norman's biography of The Beatles, *Shout*, published three months after John's death didn't help, portraying McCartney as a manipulating control freak, giving him little credit for any of The Beatles' achievements. This posthumous elevation of Lennon to a flawed saint and genius was an imbalance of perception that would eat away at McCartney for years.

Later in 1981, speculation that Wings had had its day was confirmed by Paul's next project – an album with George Martin in his Air Studios in Montserrat – which quietly turned into a McCartney solo album. But in the aftermath of John Lennon's death, Wings' demise was barely noticed. Indeed, the star-studded *Tug Of War* album of 1982 was considered by some reviewers as a musical rebirth for the former Beatle, although the #1 single **Ebony And Ivory**, a duet with Stevie Wonder and a plea for racial tolerance, was, like **Mull Of Kintyre**, another of McCartney's massive hits that ultimately ended up rather less loved than some of his other work. (Neither song, for example, is featured in McCartney's current live set.)

1982 also saw the beginning of McCartney's musical relationship with Michael Jackson. Jackson had already covered Paul's **Girlfriend** on his 1979 album *Off The Wall*. On *Thriller*, the 1982 album that confirmed Jackson's status as the biggest pop star on the planet, Paul sang with him on their co-written song **The Girl Is Mine**. Michael returned the favour on McCartney's 1983 album *Pipes Of Peace* with the co-written top-three hit **Say Say Say**. However, their "big brother/little brother" friendship soured in 1985 when Jackson decided to act on Paul's suggestion that it would be a good idea for him to get into music publishing. He bought the rights to the Lennon/McCartney catalogue, by purchasing ATV and Northern Songs (for $48m) from under the noses of Paul and Yoko. Granted, by this time McCartney and his company **MPL** owned the publishing of dozens of standard songs and musicals – he is one of the most business-savvy pop stars ever – but he currently only owns two Beatles songs, the first they ever released: **Love Me Do** and **P.S. I Love You**.

The year 1984 saw the release and universal panning of *Give My Regards To Broad Street*, McCartney's self-scripted $9m movie. The song **No More Lonely Nights** did manage to survive the wreck and was a hit single in the autumn. It was closely followed by a stand-alone novelty kids' single, **We All Stand Together**, which was taken from the MPL animated short *Rupert And The Frog Song* that accompanied *Broad Street* in the cinemas.

Following the demise of Wings, McCartney's relationship with erstwhile writing partner Denny Laine had descended into Laine giv-

Paul and Linda onstage, 1979

ing hurt tabloid interviews and publishing mean-spirited warts-and-all memoirs. Paul's next close collaboration went awry too when ex-10cc man Eric Stewart – who had co-written over half of 1986's *Press To Play* album – was upset not to be offered the co-producer's job. In 1987 however, McCartney invited **Elvis Costello** to co-write with him, a partnership that clearly inspired both men and resulted in around a dozen songs. Differences of opinion between them on how to arrange the music meant they never got as far as recording anything together, but several of their songs appeared piecemeal on various Costello or McCartney releases in the coming years.

From the mid-1980s onwards, McCartney became much more publicly involved in charitable events. He had been unable to attend the recording session for Band Aid's single **Do They Know It's Christmas?**, in aid of famine relief for Ethiopia, but he did appear at the climax of the Live Aid concert at Wembley Stadium in July 1985, where he sang **Let It Be** alone at the piano. Unfortunately, his microphone had been accidentally unplugged, which meant the first half of the performance, in front of 1.5 billion television viewers, was inaudible. He sang "Let It Be" again in recording, alongside a star-studded line-up, in aid of casualties of the 1987 Zeebrugge ferry disaster. Encouraged by his wife Linda, he was active in supporting various vegetarian and animal rights issues, and he used his first world tour in ten years, at the end of 1989, to promote the environmental charity Friends of the Earth. McCartney became, in the words of its president, "one of the earth's best friends." He was seen protesting for NHS funding for his local hospital, and even went as far as to describe his December 1990 single, **All My Trials**, as "an attack on eleven years of cruel Tory rule".

Back playing the world's big stadiums during touring stints in 1989, 1990 and 1992 in support of the albums *Flowers In The Dirt* (1989) and *Off The Ground* (1992), McCartney played his most Beatles-oriented set yet to the delight of record-breaking crowds, giving live premieres to **Eleanor Rigby**, **Sgt Pepper** and the closing sequence of **Abbey Road**, among many others. His efficient touring band comprised ex-Average White Band member Hamish Stewart on guitar and bass, ex-Pretender Robbie McIntosh on guitar, Linda and Paul "Wix" Wickens on keys and Chris Whitten on drums (replaced by Blair Cunningham in 1992). The tour albums *Tripping The Live Fantastic* (1990) and *Paul Is Live* (1993) were little more than tour souvenirs, though the 50-minute acoustic set filmed by MTV and released on record as *Unplugged: The Official Bootleg* (1991) was an entertaining set.

A significant event in McCartney's artistic life occurred on June 28, 1991, when his 100-minute **Liverpool Oratorio**, co-written over three years with the composer and conductor Carl Davis, was premiered at Liverpool Cathedral by an orchestra and choir of over 200 musicians. Critical opinion ranged from the generous to the condescending (the latter prompting a letter of support about the critics' "snobbery" to Paul from opposition leader Neil Kinnock) but the work has nonetheless been performed over a hundred times in two dozen countries. Other classical-style works followed: **A Leaf** (1995), a solo piano miniature; **Standing Stone** (1997), an orchestral piece written for the hundredth anniversary of EMI; and various other pieces, collected together on the album *Working Classical* (2000). Despite the predictably equivocal judgements of some music critics, McCartney's music is clearly earnestly realized and sells well. In 1995 the Royal College of Music awarded Paul an honorary fellowship and in 2007 he won the Best Album award at the Classical Brits for *Ecce Cor Meum*, his ambitious choral work.

McCartney spent much of the early 90s planning and fundraising to develop the site of his old school, the Liverpool Institute, into a "fame academy", the Liverpool Institute for Performing Arts, or **LIPA**. It was opened by the Queen in June 1996, and McCartney couldn't hide how proud he was about the project. When he was knighted in March 1997, an event wholeheartedly supported by the media, he confessed to feeling similarly overwhelmed. "I was much more impressed than I thought I was going to be," he admitted.

Though Paul has made his way into record-books as the composer of the world's most frequently played song (**Yesterday**) and for having played to the biggest stadium audience in history (184,000 in Rio de Janeiro in 1990), he often claims his (and Linda's) greatest achievement is the level-headedness of the McCartney children. Determined to keep their kids down to earth, Paul and Linda led as conventional a domestic life as they could: no nannies, no cooks. The children – Heather (from Linda's first marriage, but adopted by Paul), Mary (born 1969), Stella (born 1973) and James (born 1977) – were all sent to the local comprehensive school. The McCartneys' domestic equilibrium was knocked off kilter, however, by the detection of Linda's breast cancer in 1996. All of McCartney's wealth couldn't prevent his wife from succumbing to the disease – as his mother had 42 years earlier – in 1998. Linda's death prompted a grief-stricken retreat from public life, aside from his promotion of a compilation of Linda's songs, *Wide Prairie*, and a stated intention to continue her animal rights campaigning.

When his desire to work returned in 1999, in the form of an album of defiantly upbeat rock'n'roll covers called *Run Devil Run*, his optimism and life-affirming vigour were palpable. A new romance, with model turned charity fundraiser Heather Mills, blossomed in 2000 and inspired him to publicly support a new charity – Adopt A Minefield. Though their engagement in 2001 was reported to have caused some tension among the McCartney offspring, the whole family attended Paul and Heather's lavish, private wedding at Castle Leslie in County Monaghan, Ireland, in 2002. McCartney became a dad again aged 61 when daughter Beatrice was born in October 2003.

A late-flowering interest in painting, begun in 1983, culminated in a low-key exhibition in Siegen, Germany (1999), a book called *Paintings* (2000) and then more confident exhibitions in New York and Liverpool. In 2001, Faber and Faber published the book *Blackbird*

Singing, a collection of McCartney's poetry and lyrics. Specialist critics in both art and literature were, unsurprisingly, undecided as to the merits of either, although most applauded him for his creative bravery.

Among all this Renaissance-man activity and personal upheaval, he still managed to find the time to rattle off two albums – *Flaming Pie* (1997) and *Driving Rain* (2001). They appeared and, at least in part, sounded almost like afterthoughts, but there was no mistaking the gusto with which he returned to the American stage in the **Driving USA** tours of 2002 and the **Back In The World** European tour of 2003, or the love with which he was greeted. McCartney said that after 9/11 he felt it was part of his job to get out there and make people feel a little better. Historic gigs in Red Square, Moscow, and the Colosseum in Rome were just two highlights of his musical travels in 2003. In 2004, McCartney found himself back on the cover of the *NME* for the first time in decades as the music paper celebrated his acclaimed appearance at the Glastonbury festival. In 2005, Bob Geldof had Sir Paul open and close the "consciousness raising" Live 8 concert in recognition of his position as a musical giant and personal inspiration; Geldof misquoted McCartney's *Abbey Road* aphorism "and in the end the love you take is equal to the love you make", crediting The Beatles as "...where it all began".

For the next couple of years, Paul found himself in the papers on an almost daily basis as his marriage to Heather Mills unravelled. The UK tabloids delighted in the saga of Macca versus "Mucca" (as they dubbed Mills following revelations about her call-girl past) and their treatment of the estranged Lady McCartney was merciless. Heather and Paul were divorced in March 2008 in a settlement which cost McCartney £24.3m. He has since been seen in public with New York heiress Nancy Shevell.

It often seemed as if this most decorated, most rewarded, most popular of musicians was a little insecure about his place in history. Since John's death in 1980, Paul has watched Lennon's reputation as a genius overshadow his own and, in increasingly assertive moves, has sought to redress the balance. His official biography, *Many Years From Now* by Barry Miles, was published in 1997. Though it was full of fascinating detail, it was burdened by unbecoming "I was the cool one really" justifications and desperate percentage weightings over who wrote what. By the 2002 release of Paul's *Back In The US* live album and DVD, The Beatles' songs are credited pointedly to "Paul McCartney and John Lennon" rather than the traditional "Lennon/McCartney". Yoko objected but Paul seemed determined to see the matter through. It sometimes seems as though, if he could, he would have **Yesterday** and **Hey Jude** credited as being by "McCartney" alone – accurately, but perhaps against the spirit of John and Paul's original agreement. Some onlookers see his point but most are baffled. Bob Geldof, a huge admirer, but one infuriated by McCartney's defensiveness about who was the "groovy" Beatle, once told him: "There is no greater achievement in the twentieth century to beat what you and your mate did ... There are the great artists, you're one of them. Relax!"

If latterly Macca has relaxed his defensiveness about the past, he has not relaxed his work rate. *Chaos And Creation In The Back Yard* (2005) was his best album in ages, while *Memory Almost Full* (2007), released on the Starbucks label Hear Music, was his best-selling in years. The previously anonymous duo The Fireman – Paul with producer Youth – went public on *Electric Arguments* (2008), and garnered very credible reviews. Every concert – whether the BBC Electric Proms at the Roundhouse (2007), Liverpool 8 at Anfield (2008) or the Coachella Festival (2009) – makes international news, and there's no sign of him slowing down any time soon. "I'm in awe of McCartney," Bob Dylan told *Rolling Stone* in 2007. "He can do it all. And he's never let up ... He's just so damn effortless."

McCartney

THE LOVELY LINDA/THAT WOULD BE SOMETHING/ VALENTINE DAY/EVERY NIGHT/HOT AS SUN/GLASSES/JUNK/ MAN WE WAS LONELY/OO YOU/MOMMA MISS AMERICA/ TEDDY BOY/SINGALONG JUNK/MAYBE I'M AMAZED/KREEN-AKRORE

Apple; recorded November 1969–February 1970; released April 17, 1970; currently available on CD

This rough-hewn, home-grown trail run was inevitably disappointing for fans of McCartney's slick work on **Abbey Road** only months before. However, as a hastily recorded statement of independence at a difficult time, it has its moments. A pair of gorgeous melodies (**Junk**, **Every Night**) and one bona fide McCartney classic (**Maybe I'm Amazed**) stand alongside his best songs. And there's an appealing "don't sweat it" groove that Macca lovers would come to recognize as a solo signature and learn to enjoy. Certainly, the drumming on the bizarre blues-drone **Kreen-Akrore** is impressive, and the dirty guitar work on half-songs like **Oo You** has its admirers (Paul Weller, for one). If, in the end, too much of it sounds like jams to test the recording equipment to be a satisfying album, its lo-fi experimentalism has worn well.

Ram

Paul & Linda McCartney

TOO MANY PEOPLE/3 LEGS/RAM ON/DEAR BOY/UNCLE ALBERT–ADMIRAL HALSEY/SMILE AWAY/HEART OF THE COUNTRY/MONKBERRY MOON DELIGHT/EAT AT HOME/ LONG HAIRED LADY/RAM ON/THE BACK SEAT OF MY CAR

Apple; recorded early 1971; released May 1971; currently available on Parlophone CD with bonus tracks "Another Day" and "Oh Woman Oh Why"

Recorded in New York just as Lennon's infamous *Rolling Stone* interview was hitting the streets and just before The Beatles' court case, *Ram* shows Paul undoubtedly in a funny mood.

The first words on the punchy opener **Too Many People** appear to be "Piss off, yeah" (but may in fact be "piece of cake", heard elsewhere in the song) and from there Paul fashions a record jammed full of musical ideas with the funky looseness of *McCartney* but better played (partly by session guitarist and future Yoko Ono beau, David Spinoza), and with an attention to detail that the predecessor lacked. He has an obscure poke at his ex-bandmates on the ingenious blues **3 Legs** and puts in two of his most grotesque vocals ever on the vulgar rocker **Smile Away** and the deliriously surreal **Monkberry Moon Delight**. The lovely harmonies on **Dear Boy** are an arty nod to The Beach Boys and even the whimsical **Ram On** and **Uncle Albert–Admiral Halsey** sparkle with inspiration. The latter was an American #1 single, although the UK single choice, the earthily romantic paean to teenage sex **The Back Seat Of My Car**, stalled at a humiliating #39.

Ram was an album mostly dismissed at the time as more underachieving drivel served up by the guy who was breaking up The Beatles. In fact it's a quirky triumph and, for some, among McCartney's finest solo moments.

Wild Life

Wings

MUMBO/BIP BOP/LOVE IS STRANGE/WILD LIFE/SOME PEOPLE NEVER KNOW/I AM YOUR SINGER/TOMORROW/DEAR FRIEND

Apple; recorded mid-1971; released November 1971; currently available on CD with bonus tracks "Give Ireland Back To The Irish", "Mary Had A Little Lamb", "Little Woman Love" and "Mama's Little Girl"

A deeply misguided record, *Wild Life* still staggers in its apparently wilful determination to demolish McCartney's reputation as a musical craftsman of refinement and judgement. **Mumbo** (a two-chord grungy rocker with nonsense syllables in place of a lyric) and **Bip Bop** (a witless country blues) sound like McCartney was enjoying jamming with a band again and wanting to share the results. Unfortunately they're rollickingly, almost insultingly slapdash. Even the subtle reggae workout on Mickey and Sylvia's **Love Is Strange** or the virtuoso vocal hysteria of the triple-time plodder **Wild Life** can't save side one from being the longest twenty minutes in solo Beatledom.

Side two picks up a little with **Some People Never Know** and **I Am Your Singer** generating a certain amateurish charm, but it's thin stuff. **Tomorrow** is a sweet variation on the chord changes of **Yesterday** (get it?) and features the distinctive debut of the Denny Laine/Linda McCartney Wings backing vocal sound. The one genuine highlight (though curiously it didn't make it onto his 2001 *Wingspan* collection) is the haunting, sad-eyed piano-led elegy **Dear Friend**, which appears to quietly admonish John Lennon while simultaneously celebrating the profundity of Paul's new love for Linda.

Though the album has its apologists from those who enjoy their McCartney rough and ready, this one really is only for the curious who have got everything else.

Red Rose Speedway

Paul McCartney and Wings

BIG BARN BED/MY LOVE/GET ON THE RIGHT THING/ONE MORE KISS/LITTLE LAMB DRAGONFLY/SINGLE PIGEON/ WHEN THE NIGHT/LOUP (1ST INDIAN ON THE MOON)/ MEDLEY: HOLD ME TIGHT–LAZY DYNAMITE–HANDS OF LOVE–POWER CUT

Apple; recorded 1972–73; released May 1973; currently available on Parlophone CD with bonus tracks "C Moon", "Hi Hi Hi", "The Mess" and "I Lie Around"

Red Rose Speedway restored production values and discernibly more ambitious arrangements to McCartney's craft, with layered guitars, strings and backing vocals galore. However, some of the songs are either undercooked (**Big Barn Bed**), vacuously adept pastiche (the country ballad **One More Kiss** and the doo-wop **When The Night**) or experimental filler (**Loup**). Though the long medley at the end of side two shows off Mac's segue and melodic counterpoint skills, the dreary upshot is eleven and a half minutes of music that sounds rather less than the sum of its undeveloped parts. **Lazy Dynamite** indeed.

However, when it all comes together, like on the glorious romantic ballad **My Love** (featuring a memorably soaring Henry McCullough guitar solo) and the undervalued **Little Lamb Dragonfly**, it's terrific. Interestingly, the double A single of the period (the hip reggae-pop of **C Moon** and the boogiesome **Hi Hi Hi**) and the 1973 B-sides **The Mess** and **I Lie Around** (all are on the current CD issue of *Speedway*) are, all in all, a better bet.

Band On The Run

Paul McCartney and Wings

BAND ON THE RUN/JET/BLUEBIRD/MRS VANDERBILT/LET ME ROLL IT/MAMUNIA/NO WORDS/PICASSO'S LAST WORDS/ NINETEEN HUNDRED AND EIGHTY FIVE

Apple; recorded autumn 1973; released January 1974; currently available on CD with bonus tracks "Helen Wheels" and "Country Dreamer" and in a limited edition double set with extra interview CD

The justified critical gush that greeted this record was a veritable sigh of relief. Even John Lennon, who had blown raspberries at McCartney's earlier efforts, called it "a great album". With the help of only his wife and Denny Laine, McCartney produced a jewel. From the lustrous guitar twang and luxurious ride-cymbal groove of the opening song through the head-bobbing optimism of **Mrs Vanderbilt** to the apocalyptic climax of **Nineteen Hundred And Eighty Five** (delightfully undercut by an irreverent sing-a-long reprise of the title track's refrain), **Band On The Run** has a tangible vibe about it: McCartney's customary breezy confidence is, at last, once again matched by his muse.

The title track – a three-theme tour de force – is an irresistible statement of buoyant insubordination; **Jet** is his best rocker since **Back In The USSR** and boasts one of McCartney's all-time greatest vocals. **Bluebird** is almost a parody of McCartney's trademark acoustic beauty, and the ultra-repetition of the filthy guitar riff on **Let Me Roll It** becomes near-incantational. Even the question mark over his might-mean-something-probably-don't lyrics is answered by the delightfully sustained paean to rainfall, **Mamunia**, a dewdrop of attractively naïve, "even when things are bad, things are good" wisdom.

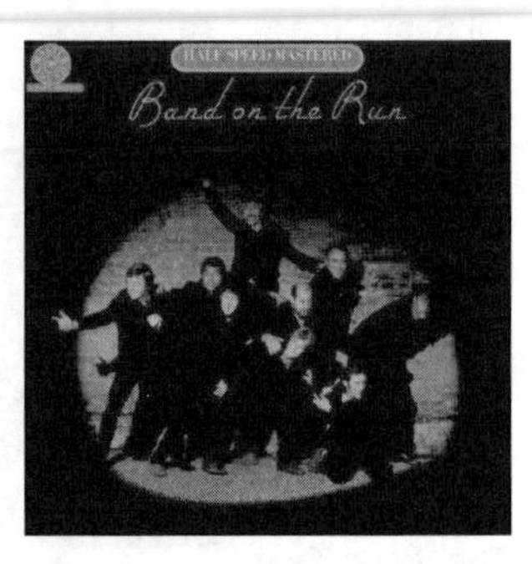

Picasso's Last Words (Drink To Me) is a fine example of Paul's talent of not letting the absence of a finished-off song get in the way of a great track. (It was written at a party after actor Dustin Hoffman told Paul that the last words reportedly spoken by Pablo Picasso were, "Drink to me, drink to my health, you know I can't drink anymore" and challenged Paul to write a song using these words, which McCartney did on the spot.) Denny Laine co-wrote the glorious slab of Wings harmony that is **No Words** and his husky tones are a valuable part of the fabulous vocal arrangements throughout. However, Laine's suggestion on the interview album accompanying the limited-edition 25th anniversary CD issue that "the contribution of the three people was, you know, very equal" sounds a touch fanciful. McCartney himself regards the record as "nearly a solo album". If so, it's probably his best.

Venus And Mars

Wings

VENUS AND MARS/ROCK SHOW/LOVE IN SONG/YOU GAVE ME THE ANSWER/MAGNETO AND TITANIUM MAN/LETTING GO/VENUS AND MARS (REPRISE)/SPIRITS OF ANCIENT EGYPT/ MEDICINE JAR/CALL ME BACK AGAIN/LISTEN TO WHAT THE MAN SAID/TREAT HER GENTLY (LONELY OLD PEOPLE)/ CROSSROADS THEME

Capitol; recorded 1974–75; released May 1975; currently available on CD with bonus tracks "Zoo Gang", "Lunch Box/Odd Sox" and "My Carnival"

The new Wings line-up put together a competent, self-assured record. Its high production values, motivic packaging (planet imagery abounds) and reprised musical themes made for an apparently coherent album. Closer inspection reveals, however, that beyond the impressive opening ten minutes (the atmospheric title track, the barnstorming "Rock Show" and the luxurious acoustic ballad "Love In Song") and the superior pop of **Listen To What The Man Said**, there's not an awful lot going on.

Call Me Back Again and **Letting Go** are inert sludge-rockers, the former an excuse to reprise Macca's **Oh! Darling** rock'n'roll howling, the latter an anonymous drone and a disastrous choice for a single.

Elsewhere it just feels a bit pointless: Jimmy McCulloch's **Medicine Jar** is uneventful, **Magneto And Titanium Man** silly and charmless and the Fred Astaire pastiche **You Gave Me The Answer** only works if you respond to the vaudeville aspect of McCartney's talent. And, God save us, there at the end is Tony Hatch's theme from the 70s UK TV soap **Crossroads**.

Recorded at the height of Paul's purported dalliance with cocaine (**Rock Show** itself refers to scoring an ounce), it clearly didn't do much for his judgement.

Wings At The Speed Of Sound

Wings

LET 'EM IN/THE NOTE YOU NEVER WROTE/SHE'S MY BABY/ BEWARE MY LOVE/WINO JUNKO/SILLY LOVE SONGS/COOK OF THE HOUSE/TIME TO HIDE/MUST DO SOMETHING ABOUT IT/SAN FERRY ANNE/WARM AND BEAUTIFUL

Capitol; recorded 1975–76; released April 1976; currently available on CD with bonus tracks "Walking In The Park With Eloise", "Bridge On The River Suite" and "Sally G"

This highly likeable album came out at the height of Wings' commercial success. It was also Paul at his most generous in sharing performance time with his bandmates. The two singles **Let 'Em In** and **Silly Love Songs** are expertly winning but the highlight is probably **The Note You Never Wrote**, a cryptically evocative McCartney jewel and one of Denny Laine's two lead vocal features (Paul had always liked his singing on the Moody Blues' **Go Now**).

Elsewhere **Joe English** does a charming job on **Must Do Something About It**, as does Macca on his sweetest, daftest love song **She's My Baby** and the perky acoustic lope **San Ferry Anne**. The big sensitive ballad **Warm And Beautiful** has a typically attractive melody but is uncharacteristically overstated here, in contrast to the rest of the record, which is admirably restrained, crafted rock-pop.

London Town

Wings

LONDON TOWN/CAFÉ ON THE LEFT BANK/I'M CARRYING/ BACKWARDS TRAVELLER/CUFF LINK/CHILDREN CHILDREN/ GIRLFRIEND/I'VE HAD ENOUGH/WITH A LITTLE LUCK/ FAMOUS GROUPIES/DELIVER YOUR CHILDREN/NAME AND ADDRESS/DON'T LET IT BRING YOU DOWN/MORSE MOOSE AND THE GREY GOOSE

Capitol; recorded 1977–78; released February 1978; currently available on CD with bonus tracks "Girls' School" and "Mull Of Kintyre"

At the time, during the height of punk and in the wake of the chart-dominating granny's fave **Mull Of Kintyre**, the adult pop of **London Town** (beautifully put together by a stoned millionaire and his chums on a cruise ship in the middle of the Virgin Islands) seemed a little irrelevant. Most of it has worn well though. Two cuts – **London Town** and **With A Little Luck** – are particularly memorable, full of the most sensitive pop synthesizer touches.

There's an attractive and rigorous folksy quality to the Laine/McCartney collaborations **Children Children**, **Deliver Your Children** and **Don't Let It Bring You Down**, songs powerful enough to suggest that that songwriting partnership has been unfairly undervalued. And the inclusion on the current CD issue of the best rocker Wings ever recorded, **Girls' School** ("Mull Of Kintyre"'s B-side), puts *London Town* among the more satisfying solo McCartney records. There's a story that an old friend of McCartney's was "excommunicated" for years for telling Paul at the time that "London Town" "wasn't very good", and that Macca admitted years later that he was right. They were both wrong.

Back To The Egg

Wings

RECEPTION/GETTING CLOSER/WE'RE OPEN TONIGHT/ SPIN IT ON/AGAIN AND AGAIN AND AGAIN/OLD SIAM, SIR/ ARROW THROUGH ME/ROCKESTRA THEME/TO YOU/AFTER THE BALL–MILLION MILES/WINTER ROSE–LOVE AWAKE/THE BROADCAST/SO GLAD TO SEE YOU HERE/BABY'S REQUEST

Capitol; recorded 1978–79; released June 1979; currently available on CD with bonus tracks "Daytime Nightime Suffering", "Wonderful Christmastime" and "Rudolph The Red Nosed Reggae"

The leader of the new line-up of Wings tries very hard to impress on *Back To The Egg*. But in the end, the record that started out as a "going-to-a-gig" concept album but ended as "just a bunch of songs", is a frustrating experience. The radio-tuning gimmick on the opening song is just lame, **Getting Closer** is warmed-over **Jet**, whilst Laine's **Again And Again And Again** is dull filler (perhaps included as compensation from Paul to him for being demoted from co-writing duties). The tougher post-punk stuff (**Spin It On**, **Old Siam, Sir**) is lacklustre and contrived, while the Rockestra tracks (**Rockestra Theme** and **So Glad To See You Here**) sound like they were more fun to play than to listen to.

Even when he's on to something, McCartney spoils it with poor judgement. Four perfectly reasonable songs in the middle of side two (**After The Ball–Million Miles**, **Winter Rose-Love Awake**) suffer from two apologetic segues, as if they weren't good enough to stand on their own. They were, especially the exquisite **Winter Rose**. And there's a beautiful theme trying to make itself heard on **The Broadcast**, but it's masked by plummy, spoken excerpts from the playwrights and novelists Ian Hay and John Galsworthy. As with most of the record, the question is "Why?" The new men's instrumental chops do make a superficial difference (Steve Holly's snappy snare-work on **Spin It On**, for instance, or Lawrence Juber's jazzy fills on the cute Mills Brothers tribute **Baby's Request**) but this group thing was starting to sound like a dead end.

McCartney II

COMING UP/TEMPORARY SECRETARY/ON THE WAY/ WATERFALLS/NOBODY KNOWS/FRONT PARLOUR/SUMMER'S DAY SONG/FROZEN JAP/BOGEY MUSIC/DARKROOM/ONE OF THESE DAYS

Capitol; recorded 1979–80; released May 1980; currently available on CD with bonus tracks "Check My Machine", "Secret Friend" and "Goodnight Tonight"

Recorded in Paul's Sussex and Scotland homes as a move away from group life, to be in "total control" and have some "private fun", as he had it. On those terms, it's reasonably interesting – like a documentary would be – to hear his attempts to turn synthesizer and drumbeat sketches into something resembling a song. As an album however, it's a dog, much less gratifying than his solo debut ten years earlier. There is a surfeit of scrappy instrumentals and rocking pastiches that should have stayed in the drawer. Fans of McCartney's distinctive songcraft will find only two real songs – the delicate **Waterfalls** and rather solemn **One Of These Days** – and a couple of doodles that got lucky, **Temporary Secretary** and **Coming Up**. That the fun-but-frothy latter track reportedly helped spur John Lennon back into action in mid-1980 doesn't say much for the standards of either man at that time.

Tug Of War

TUG OF WAR/TAKE IT AWAY/SOMEBODY WHO CARES/WHAT'S THAT YOU'RE DOING?/HERE TODAY/BALLROOM DANCING/ THE POUND IS SINKING/WANDERLUST/GET IT/BE WHAT YOU SEE (LINK)/DRESS ME UP AS A ROBBER/EBONY AND IVORY

Capitol; recorded 1981–82; released April 1982; currently available on CD

Tired of being perceived as not as good as he was – and starting to believe it himself – Paul turned to two of the men who had helped him get there in the first place: producer **George Martin** and engineer **Geoff Emerick**. Together they took the time to produce (or "goad" Paul into achieving, as Martin had it) McCartney's most considered and astute work for years. The high-quality sidemen (Steve Gadd, Dave Mattacks and Ringo Starr on drums, Stanley Clarke on bass, and Stevie Wonder on a couple of guest vocals) certainly helped, but the real revelation is Macca's writing. Whether catchy pop (**Take It Away**), poetic elegy (**Tug Of War**), off-beat rock (**Ballroom Dancing**) or heartfelt love song (**Here Today**, dedicated to John Lennon), it's all solo Macca on near top form. Even his written-the-day-before duet with Carl Perkins, **Get It**, hits the spot and although his Stevie Wonder assisted plea for racial tolerance **Ebony And Ivory** irritated as many as it delighted, its common-sense simplicity is nonetheless engaging in an **All You Need Is Love** kind of way.

Pipes Of Peace

PIPES OF PEACE/SAY SAY SAY/THE OTHER ME/KEEP UNDER COVER/SO BAD/THE MAN/SWEETEST LITTLE SHOW/AVERAGE PERSON/HEY HEY/TUG OF PEACE/THROUGH OUR LOVE

Capitol; recorded 1981–83; released October 1983; currently available on CD with bonus tracks "Twice In A Lifetime", "We All Stand Together" and "Simple As That"

Essentially *Tug Of War* part two – cuts from the same sessions with the same musicians and production team – there's an inevitable drop in quality, but it's by no means a disaster. The title track is majestic and **So Bad** approximates the R&B falsetto cool of **Girlfriend**, but elsewhere it's a tad humdrum. **The Other Me** is rhythmically clumsy, while Paul's attempt to empathize with the frustrated ambitions of everyman on **Average Person** is vaguely condescending.

The funky chant **Tug Of Peace** and **Hey Hey**, the dull instrumental co-written with **Stanley Clarke**, should really have been B-side bonus tracks on a 12" inch single; programmed together on side two, they virtually bring the record to a halt. Of the two duets co-written with **Michael Jackson**, **Say Say Say** was the disco-style hit, but **The Man**, complete with **Isley Brothers** style fuzz guitar and attractively breezy chord changes, is probably the more interesting song.

Give My Regards To Broad Street

NO MORE LONELY NIGHTS (BALLAD)/GOOD DAY SUNSHINE/CORRIDOR MUSIC/YESTERDAY/HERE THERE AND EVERYWHERE/WANDERLUST/BALLROOM DANCING/SILLY LOVE SONGS/SILLY LOVE SONGS (REPRISE)/NOT SUCH A BAD BOY/SO BAD/NO VALUES/NO MORE LONELY NIGHTS (BALLAD REPRISE)/FOR NO ONE/ELEANOR RIGBY/ELEANOR'S DREAM/LONG AND WINDING ROAD/NO MORE LONELY NIGHTS (PLAYOUT VERSION)/GOODNIGHT PRINCESS

Capitol; recorded 1984; released October 1984; currently available on CD with bonus tracks "No More Lonely Nights" extended and dance mixes

The record certainly turned out better than the film. The re-recording of several Beatles songs was not the profane travesty it could have been and indeed is more successful than the new arrangements of solo and Wings-era tunes. (And it's worth noting that Lennon had also expressed the desire to re-record "every last one" of his Beatle songs, given the chance.) Truncated versions of **Yesterday** and **Here There And Everywhere** are beautifully recorded, dressed with a discreet brass ensemble. Interestingly enough, the Martin/McCartney recasting of **The Long And Winding Road** is not so different from the Phil Spector treatment (complete with heavenly choir and the works) that Paul got so irate about in 1970. The hit single **No More Lonely Nights** is vintage mature solo McCartney, and the live thrashes **Not Such A Bad Boy** and **No Values** generate genuine pop-rock joy.

Press To Play

STRANGLEHOLD/GOOD TIMES COMING-FEEL THE SUN/ TALK MORE TALK/FOOTPRINTS/ONLY LOVE REMAINS/ PRESS/PRETTY LITTLE HEAD/MOVE OVER BUSKER/ANGRY/ HOWEVER ABSURD/WRITE AWAY/IT'S NOT TRUE/TOUGH ON A TIGHTROPE

Capitol; recorded 1985–86; released September 1986; currently available on CD with bonus tracks "Spies Like Us" and "Once Upon A Long Ago" (note: "Write Away", "It's Not True" and "Tough On A Tightrope" were not on the original vinyl issue)

By no means the most obvious of McCartney's albums (and conspicuously lacking a big hit single, though the elegant **Only Love Remains** was close), ***Press To Play*** repays attention mainly due to the intricately layered, superbly played arrangements and taut 1980s-style production by Hugh Padgham. The songs are a mixed bag, though a few of the eight co-writes with 10cc's Eric Stewart are good. **Stranglehold**, an unusual, dense acoustic rocker, and the haunting **Footprints** are especially intriguing, full of elusive musical detail and carefully constructed lyrics. Too often, however, the writing simply isn't interesting or scrupulous enough. The impression is that Paul is enjoying hanging with people he gets on with, rather than pushing himself. Nothing wrong with that, but one could hardly expect a great record to be the result.

Flowers In The Dirt

MY BRAVE FACE/ROUGH RIDE/YOU WANT HER TOO/ DISTRACTIONS/WE GOT MARRIED/PUT IT THERE/FIGURE OF EIGHT/THIS ONE/DON'T BE CARELESS LOVE/THAT DAY IS DONE/HOW MANY PEOPLE/MOTOR OF LOVE/OU EST LE SOLEIL

Capitol; recorded 1988–89; released May 1989; currently available on CD with bonus tracks "Back On My Feet", "Flying To My Home" and "Loveliest Thing" (note: "Ou Est Le Soleil" was not on original vinyl issue)

Hailed by some as a return to top form, it's certainly the best McCartney record since *Tug Of War* seven years previously. No huge hits on it, just a consistency of achievement with a variety of producers (Trevor Horn, Mitchell Froom, Neil Dorfsman) that makes for a surprisingly even album. The highly anticipated writing collaboration with **Elvis Costello** produced some rather peculiar songs. There were a couple of heavy waltzes – **You Want Her Too** on which Costello possibly overdoes the Lennon-style acerbic commentary to McCartney's "dumb twit" lines, and **That Day Is Done**, an affecting gospelish dirge. There was also the self-consciously, pleasingly Beatlesque **My Brave Face** (though the best McCartney/Costello song is probably **So Like Candy**, which appeared on Elvis's 1991 album *Mighty Like A Rose*).

The album's highlights, however, are McCartney's alone. The sumptuous **Distractions**, arranged by Clare Fischer, is one of Macca's best latter-day love songs, while **Put It There** and **Motor Of Love** are two contrasting tributes to his late dad. The former is a delightfully straightforward, traditional-sounding song of paternal encouragement to a young boy, the latter a synth-swept cry of thanks to his "heavenly father". A tad over-hyped thanks to huge, tour-driven promotion, *Flowers In The Dirt* is nevertheless solid, grown-up McCartney.

Off The Ground

OFF THE GROUND/LOOKING FOR CHANGES/HOPE OF DELIVERANCE/MISTRESS AND MAID/I OWE IT ALL TO YOU/ BIKER LIKE AN ICON/PEACE IN THE NEIGHBOURHOOD/ GOLDEN EARTH GIRL/THE LOVERS THAT NEVER WERE/GET OUT OF MY WAY/WINEDARK OPEN SEA/C'MON PEOPLE

Parlophone; recorded 1992; released February 1993; currently available on CD

Following his triumphant tour of 1990–91, it was inevitable that Paul would take his new favourite people, the group, into the studio with him for his next album, with the equally inevitable result that standards slipped a little. The flexi-personnel and multi-textured effect of *Flowers In The Dirt* is sacrificed somewhat for a tougher band sound which works well enough on daft rockers like **Get Out Of My Way** and **Biker Like An Icon** (a groovy, unassuming song with a couple of clumsy rhymes that some took as evidence of Macca having lost the plot entirely) but does little for plain material like **Winedark Open Sea** and the distressingly ordinary title track.

There's an appealing, optimistic feel to the lyrics of songs like **Hope Of Deliverance** and **Peace In The Neighbourhood** that's matched by the music's light, melodic assurance, but a couple more leaden, triple-time Costello co-writes drag things down a little. McCartney gives them a go but the tenacious depictions of dark relationships in **Mistress And Maid** and **The Lovers That Never Were** sit on him like a suit made for someone else.

The angry animal-rights rant **Looking For Changes** and call for global optimism **C'Mon People**, while clearly heartfelt, end up being a shade embarrassing. But he had just played to millions of people who love him, and he was about to play to millions more. It can turn a fifty-year-old's head.

Flaming Pie

THE SONG WE WERE SINGING/THE WORLD TONIGHT/IF YOU WANNA/SOMEDAYS/YOUNG BOY/CALICO SKIES/FLAMING PIE/ HEAVEN ON A SUNDAY/USED TO BE BAD/SOUVENIR/LITTLE WILLOW/REALLY LOVE YOU/BEAUTIFUL NIGHT/GREAT DAY

Parlophone; recorded 1995–97; released May 1997; currently available on CD

A good home-brewed album in the McCartney tradition of do-it-yourself fun featuring deep-groove drums, bluesy guitar and the full gamut of his vocal range in particularly marvellous form. Of the "see what happens" jams, "Flaming Pie" is the best, while **Really Love You** (made up in the studio with Ringo) is a bit mad and indulgent, but kind of happening. Only the duet with Steve Miller – a slinky Texas twelve-bar blues, **Used To Be Bad** – palls.

The Song We Were Singing has an enchanting stoned elegance, **Heaven On A Sunday** is prime, dreamy Macca, whilst **Souvenirs** is a soulful, lazy, oddball beauty. There are three finger-pickin' numbers: **Calico Skies**, a solemn little love song which develops into an anti-war

prayer; **Somedays**, a portentous song of doubt, always threatening to mean something, beautifully decorated by George Martin's string arrangement; and **Great Day**, a sweet, throwaway piece of unfeasible optimism. They ain't **Blackbird**, but they're fine.

With Jeff Lynne co-producing over half the tracks, McCartney sounds more like himself on ***Flaming Pie*** than he has for years. Sporting his eccentric primitive miniaturist colours, this album's a fine reminder of how much they suit him.

Driving Rain

LONELY ROAD/FROM A LOVER TO A FRIEND/SHE'S GIVEN UP TALKING/DRIVING RAIN/I DO/TINY BUBBLE/IT MUST HAVE BEEN MAGIC/YOUR WAY/SPINNING ON AN AXIS/ABOUT YOU/ HEATHER/BACK IN THE SUNSHINE AGAIN/YOUR LOVING FLAME/RIDING INTO JAIPUR/RINSE THE RAINDROPS/ FREEDOM

Parlophone; recorded 2001; released November 2001; currently available on CD

It seems that with his painting, his poetry and his classical pieces soaking up his creativity, there was less left over for Macca's pop music. And, hoping for some inspired spontaneity, he didn't show his new band of young US session musicians his songs until the day of recording: "My favourite way of working with The Beatles", Paul explained. Macca's determination to get in and out of the studio in five weeks, leaving the music with a "raw freshness", means that anyone hoping for a musical feast will have to be content with this plate of small sandwiches. Any album that contains the couplet "1-2-3-4-5/Let's go for a drive" (**Driving Rain**) requires a certain modification of expectations.

But as ever, there is always at least something on offer you'll wish there was a bit more of. **Tiny Bubble** is Wings-catchy, **Your Loving Flame** is almost a good love song, and **Heather** is a pleasing semi-instrumental. What's perhaps most interesting is the inexplicit but potent mix of material that reflects the emotional complexity of Paul's old love, new love situation, and the medium-gloss production seems to underline the transitory, work-in-progress nature of this stage of his life. With that in mind, repeated plays reveal a resonance and detail that are hidden during the first few listens. As Paul wrote to journalist Penny Valentine in 1970, after she expressed such disappointment with his debut album, "Even at this moment it is growing on you." And this one still is. How does he do that?

Chaos And Creation In The Back Yard

FINE LINE/HOW KIND OF YOU/JENNY WREN/AT THE MERCY/ FRIENDS TO GO/ENGLISH TEA/TOO MUCH RAIN/A CERTAIN SOFTNESS/RIDING TO VANITY FAIR/FOLLOW ME/PROMISE TO YOU GIRL/THIS NEVER HAPPENED BEFORE/ANYWAY
Parlophone; recorded 2003–2005; released September 2005; currently available on CD

No downwardly adjusted expectations needed for this one. In choosing (at George Martin's suggestion) and bravely sticking with a tough-love partner in producer **Nigel Godrich**, McCartney allowed himself to be challenged, criticized and inspired into producing some of his most substantial, eccentric work for decades.

McCartney, as is his wont, initially wanted to record with the touring band that had been sending shock-waves of pleasure around various enormodomes of the globe since 2002. Godrich soon realised that this boys-club arrangement (from which the producer felt excluded anyway) was not conducive to Paul's quality control. The band was sacked, with Nigel insisting on an intimacy and honesty between artist and producer not based on being mates ("I don't want to be your friend," 32-year-old Godrich told the ex-Beatle) but on creating good art. That relationship involved Godrich rejecting some of Macca's songs as "not very good". At first McCartney was naturally hurt, rattled and not a little angry. But ultimately, to his enormous credit, he took it on the chin, dug deep and delivered.

There are breezy Macca specialities such as the beautiful, "Blackbird"-like **Jenny Wren**, the tongue-in-cheek refinement of **English Tea** ("very twee, very me," he winks in the lyrics) and the best song yet inspired by Heather, the exotic acoustic rumba of **A Certain Softness**. But overall *Chaos And Creation* is a stark, haunting record full of musical subtlety and dark corners hinting at shadowy troubles. The album is bookended by songs conveying a sense of estrangement: "We all cried when you were driven away," he sings in **Fine Line**; "You can make that call," he pleads in **Anyway**. Elsewhere he bitterly castigates someone for eschewing friendship in **Riding To Vanity Fair**, he admits he'd "rather run and hide than face the fear inside" on **At The Mercy**; and he has been "waiting on the other side for your friends to go" on **Friends To Go**. The cumulative effect of these songs, with their bone-dry vocals and spooky electronic soundscapes haloing McCartney's excellent guitar and piano work, is somewhere between a deliciously overstated man-child neurosis and a genuinely heart-tugging emotional frailty. How much of McCartney's work can you say that about?

This is a genuinely rich, thoughtful record, quite a distance from much of Paul's middleweight solo moments and crowd-delighting live antics. If McCartney continues to suffer a little more for his art, as he clearly had to here, his autumnal recording years will be fascinating.

Memory Almost Full

DANCE TONIGHT/EVER PRESENT PAST/SEE YOUR SUNSHINE/ ONLY MAMA KNOWS/YOU TELL ME/MR. BELLAMY/GRATITUDE/ VINTAGE CLOTHES/THAT WAS ME/FEET IN THE CLOUDS/ HOUSE OF WAX/THE END OF THE END/NOD YOUR HEAD
HearMusic; recorded 2006–2007; released June 2007, deluxe version released November 2007 includes "In Private", "Why So Blue", "222" and a DVD

The album Paul abandoned to make *Chaos And Creation In The Back Yard* was finished off and released less than two years later. While not as darkly rich or as rigorous as the McCartney/Godrich record, *Memory Almost Full* has an equally personal tone in the lyrics and, musically, is a winning blend of the artful and the frivolous.

The mandolin strummer "Dance Tonight" (added as an afterthought when Paul noted how excited his three-year-old daughter Beatrice got when he played it) is almost a parody of how lightweight McCartney can be. Yet a couple of hearings in and it makes total sense, especially after having heard it played on Jools Holland's 2007 New Year's Eve *Hootenanny*. Similarly, "Ever Present Past" is Macca in ultra-pop mode, and just as you're about to dismiss it, you realize you can't stop yourself humming it; he still appears to know what he's doing.

McCartney freaks detected that the title (actually an inspiringly resonant message from a mobile phone) was an anagram of "for my soulmate LLM", LLM standing for Linda Louise McCartney. However, the delightfully encouraging love song "See Your Sunshine" and the uninhibited *cri de coeur* "Gratitude" were apparently written for Heather. Though going through marital trauma at the time of recording, McCartney decided to leave the songs inspired by his estranged second wife untouched.

There is a series of nostalgia songs towards the end of the album, of which the stream-of-consciousness rocker "That Was Me" is the best. The record's highlight, however, is "The End Of The End", a poetic meditation on death that is breathtakingly poignant. Typically, he undercuts his own seriousness by ending the album with "Nod Your Head", a "Why Don't We Do It In The Road" style throwaway. The leave-'em-smiling trick works as well here as it did on *Abbey Road*.

Rock'n'Roll Macca

Choba B CCCP The Russian Album

KANSAS CITY/TWENTY FLIGHT ROCK/LAWDY MISS CLAWDY/BRING IT ON HOME TO ME/LUCILLE/DON'T GET AROUND MUCH ANYMORE/I'M GONNA BE A WHEEL SOMEDAY/THAT'S ALL RIGHT MAMA/SUMMERTIME/AIN'T THAT A SHAME/CRACKIN' UP/JUST BECAUSE/MIDNIGHT SPECIAL

Melodiya; recorded July 1987; released in Russia only 1988; released worldwide September 1991; currently available on CD with extra track "I'm In Love Again"

Run Devil Run

BLUE JEAN BOP/SHE SAID YEH/ALL SHOOK UP/RUN DEVIL RUN/NO OTHER BABY/LONESOME TOWN/TRY NOT TO CRY/MOVIE MAGG/BROWN EYED HANDSOME MAN/WHAT IT IS/COQUETTE/I GOT STUNG/HONEY HUSH/SHAKE A HAND/PARTY

Parlophone; recorded March 1999; released October 1999; currently available on CD

Recorded in two sessions over two days and available exclusively in Russia for three years ("I extend the hand of peace and friendship to the people of the USSR"), ***Choba B CCCP*** was Paul's anticipated return to his rockin' roots. However, it was as faintly disappointing in its workmanlike, pub-rock way as Lennon's bloated *Rock'N'Roll* album. Only sporadically sparking into life (an ingenious rocking arrangement of Duke Ellington's **Don't Get Around Much Anymore**, and a kicking version of Fats Domino's **I'm Gonna Be A Wheel Someday**), Macca's and the band's strolling energy sags in places.

Twelve years on and **Run Devil Run** is another prospect entirely. Retaining the searing guitar of The Pirates' Mick Green but adding Pink Floyd's Dave Gilmour for a terrifying double-axe attack, he gives the band a week to nail things and it makes all the difference. Startlingly loud, the music is unfussy, tight and direct with more than a hint of menace. It's rock'n'roll looking for a fight. Also, as Paul's first musical statement following

Linda's death (aside from ***Rushes*** by his ambient-music alter ego **The Fireman**), it's impossible not to hear this remarkable record as a defiant, cathartic cry of life-affirming positivity. And as no one in the world sings "yeah" like Paul McCartney, it thrills you to your boots.

McCartney Live

Wings Over America

VENUS AND MARS/ROCK SHOW/JET/LET ME ROLL IT/ SPIRITS OF ANCIENT EGYPT/MEDICINE JAR/MAYBE I'M AMAZED/CALL ME BACK AGAIN/LADY MADONNA/THE LONG AND WINDING ROAD/LIVE AND LET DIE/PICASSO'S LAST WORDS/RICHARD CORY/BLUEBIRD/I'VE JUST SEEN A FACE/BLACKBIRD/YESTERDAY/YOU GAVE ME THE ANSWER/ MAGNETO AND TITANIUM MAN/GO NOW/MY LOVE/LISTEN TO WHAT THE MAN SAID/LET 'EM IN/TIME TO HIDE/SILLY LOVE SONGS/BEWARE MY LOVE/LETTING GO/BAND ON THE RUN/HI HI HI/SOILY

Capitol; recorded 1976; released in December 1976; currently available on Parlophone CD

Tripping The Live Fantastic

SHOWTIME/FIGURE OF EIGHT/JET/ROUGH RIDE/GOT TO GET YOU INTO MY LIFE/BAND ON THE RUN/BIRTHDAY/EBONY AND IVORY/WE GOT MARRIED/INNER CITY MADNESS/ MAYBE I'M AMAZED/THE LONG AND WINDING ROAD/ CRACKIN' UP/FOOL ON THE HILL/SGT. PEPPER'S LONELY HEARTS CLUB BAND/CAN'T BUY ME LOVE/MATCHBOX/PUT IT THERE/TOGETHER/THINGS WE SAID TODAY/ELEANOR RIGBY/THIS ONE/MY BRAVE FACE/BACK IN THE USSR/I SAW HER STANDING THERE/TWENTY FLIGHT ROCK/COMING UP/ SALLY/LET IT BE/AIN'T THAT A SHAME/LIVE AND LET DIE/IF I WERE NOT UPON THE STAGE/HEY JUDE/YESTERDAY/GET BACK/GOLDEN SLUMBERS/CARRY THAT WEIGHT/THE END/ DON'T LET THE SUN CATCH YOU CRYING

Parlophone; recorded 1990; released November 1990; currently available on CD as *Tripping The Live Fantastic (Highlights)*

Unplugged – The Official Bootleg

BE BOP A LULA/I LOST MY LITTLE GIRL/HERE THERE AND EVERYWHERE/BLUE MOON OF KENTUCKY/WE CAN WORK IT OUT/SAN FRANCISCO BAY BLUES/I'VE JUST SEEN A FACE/ EVERY NIGHT/SHE'S A WOMAN/HI-HEEL SNEAKERS/AND I LOVE HER/THAT WOULD BE SOMETHING/BLACKBIRD/AIN'T NO SUNSHINE/GOOD ROCKIN' TONIGHT/SINGING THE BLUES/JUNK

Parlophone; recorded 1991; released in May 1991; currently unavailable

Paul Is Live

DRIVE MY CAR/LET ME ROLL IT/LOOKING FOR CHANGES/ PEACE IN THE NEIGHBOURHOOD/ALL MY LOVING/ROBBIE'S BIT (THANKS CHET)/GOOD ROCKIN' TONIGHT/WE CAN WORK IT OUT/HOPE OF DELIVERANCE/MICHELLE/BIKER LIKE AN ICON/HERE THERE AND EVERYWHERE/MY LOVE/ MAGICAL MYSTERY TOUR/C'MON PEOPLE/LADY MADONNA/ PAPERBACK WRITER/PENNY LANE/LIVE AND LET DIE/KANSAS CITY/WELCOME TO SOUNDCHECK/HOTEL IN BENIDORM/I WANNA BE YOUR MAN/A FINE DAY

Parlophone; recorded 1993; released November 1993; currently available on CD

Back In The US Live 2002

GOODBYE/JET/ALL MY LOVING/GETTING BETTER/COMING UP/LET ME ROLL IT/LONELY ROAD/DRIVING RAIN/YOUR LOVING FLAME/BLACKBIRD/EVERY NIGHT/WE CAN WORK IT OUT/MOTHER NATURE'S SON/VANILLA SKY/CARRY THAT WEIGHT/THE FOOL ON THE HILL/HERE TODAY/SOMETHING/ ELEANOR RIGBY/HERE, THERE AND EVERYWHERE/BAND ON THE RUN/BACK IN THE USSR/MAYBE I'M AMAZED/C MOON/ MY LOVE/CAN'T BUY ME LOVE/FREEDOM/LIVE AND LET DIE/ LET IT BE/HEY JUDE/THE LONG AND WINDING ROAD/LADY MADONNA/I SAW HER STANDING THERE/YESTERDAY/SGT PEPPER/THE END

Parlophone; recorded 2002; released November 2002 (US); *Back In The World* released March 2003 (UK) with "Vanilla

Sky", "C Moon" and "Freedom" replaced by "Let 'Em In", "She's Leaving Home", "Michelle" and "Calico Skies"

Twenty-five years of live Macca with, as time passes, increasingly liberal Beatles selections. Take your choice from four versions of **Yesterday**, three of **Blackbird** and **We Can Work It Out** and two of **Hey Jude** and **Fool On The Hill**. Look closely enough and you'll find rare live cuts of **Magical Mystery Tour**, **Getting Better**, **Drive My Car** and **Mother Nature's Son**. The triple vinyl *Wings Over America* was a big event upon release, and perhaps one of the all-time great live albums, but the subsequent tour collections *Tripping* and *Paul Is Live* are progressively less interesting. *Unplugged*, however, is a subtle gem, but was always intended as a limited edition and was deleted soon after release. The latest, *Back In The US Live 2002/Back In The World*, is a delightfully boisterous document of an extraordinary sixty-year-old delivering a stupendous show featuring one of the most ridiculously illustrious set lists in concert-giving history.

Classical Mac

The Family Way

Decca; recorded 1966; released January 1967; currently unavailable

Liverpool Oratorio

WAR/SCHOOL/CRYPT/FATHER/WEDDING/WORK/CRISES/PEACE
EMI; recorded 1991; released October 1991

Standing Stone – A Symphonic Poem

EMI; recorded 1997; released August 1997

Working Classical

JUNK/A LEAF/HAYMAKERS/MIDWIFE/SPIRAL/WARM AND BEAUTIFUL/MY LOVE/MAYBE I'M AMAZED/CALICO SKIES/GOLDEN EARTH GIRL/SOMEDAYS/TUESDAY/SHE'S MY BABY/THE LOVELY LINDA
EMI; recorded 1999; released October 1999

A Garland For Linda

SILENCE OF MUSIC/PRAYER FOR THE HEALING OF THE SICK/WATER LILIES/MUSIC DEI DONUM/THE DOORWAY OF THE DAWN/NOVA/I DREAM'D/FAREWELL/THE FLIGHT OF THE SWAN/ A GOOD-NIGHT
EMI; recorded 1999; released February 2000

McCartney's soundtrack, arranged by George Martin for the Boulting Brothers' 1966 movie *The Family Way*, isn't really part of his classical output. But it does reveal his initial efforts to express himself in purely instrumental terms. One of the most elusive items of the Beatles years, it has seldom been on general release, although one of its themes did get a rare outing in 2001 when it was used as the wedding march for the marriage of Paul and Heather Mills.

The lavishly scored and sung *Liverpool Oratorio* (written with Carl Davis) contains some revealing meditations on aspects of family relationships and bereavement but as far as the tunes go (surely the reason people will want to listen to it) it's a bit of a disappointment. By no means bad – there are emotive moments in **Crypt** and **Father** – there's nothing here with quite the memorable sweep of McCartney's best dramatic melodies like **She's Leaving Home**. And in taking a determinedly serious tone for the majority of its ninety-odd minutes, too much of it is plain dreary.

A product of the digital age, his seventy-minute ***Standing Stone*** could have only been brought into being with the help of a computer and three classicos – the composers Richard Rodney Bennett and David Matthews, and the saxophonist John Harle – to help McCartney with structure, orchestration and score editing. However, the work is rigorously realized, complex and in places, rather difficult both to play and listen to. Many of his paintings of the period were adorned with Celtic crosses, and *Standing Stone* too was inspired by Paul's Celtic roots (his parents were Liverpool-Irish): there is much droning in fifths in the strings, reels on the fiddle and jigs on the flutes. There's also sometimes a sense that he's enjoying playing with the texture of the orchestra and chorus, perhaps at the expense of a memorable melody or a convincing form (with the exception of the rousing final theme), but there's no denying the power and excitement of the piece.

The three specially conceived works on *Working Classical* are probably the most engaging half-hour of Macca's classical output to date. Each lasts just over ten minutes and was scored for orchestra by John Fraser. **A Leaf**, originally a charming piano miniature, has become a capricious, utterly captivating piece, while **Spiral** and **Tuesday** feature moody, mature tonalities unlike anything else in McCartney's canon. Similar in texture to John Barry's introspective orchestral works like *The Beyondness Of Things*, it is if anything denser and more mysterious. Elsewhere on the album, McCartney's string-quartet arrangements of his own pop tunes like **Junk**, **Maybe I'm Amazed** and **My Love** are less successful. One's ears are too often drawn to the awkward phrasing of the strings (sticking too literally to the lyric-driven rhythms) than to the beauty of the melodic lines. However, it's a lovely sounding record.

A Garland For Linda actually only features a single McCartney composition (**Nova**, arranged by John Harle for the Joyful Company of Singers) among other elegiac commemorative pieces by modern composers, but it's very beautiful – better than the similarly toned pieces from *Liverpool Oratorio* – and easily holds its own among some heavyweight company.

Ecce Cor Meum

SPIRITUS/GRATIA/INTERLUDE (LAMENT)/MUSICA/ECCE COR MEUM

EMI; recorded March 2006; released September 2006; available on CD

While some critics sniffed at a mix-and-match approach to the choral tradition (a bit of Handel here, a bit of Mozart there), *Ecce Cor Meum* (Behold My Heart) is probably McCartney's most straightforwardly enjoyable classical effort to date. With a couple of big tunes emerging from the mature, evolved music, there is much atmosphere and a beautiful central soprano performance from Kate Royal. It was voted Classical Album of the Year by Classic FM listeners in 2007.

Macca experiments

Thrillington

EMI; recorded 1971; released 1977; currently available on CD

Strawberries, Oceans, Ships, Forest

EMI; released 1994; currently unavailable

Rushes

Hydra; released 1998

Liverpool Sound Collage

WAR/SCHOOL/CRYPT/FATHER/WEDDING/WORK/CRISES/PEACE

Hydra; released 2000

Electric Arguments

NOTHING TOO MUCH JUST OUT OF SIGHT/TWO MAGPIES/SING THE CHANGES/TRAVELLING LIGHT/HIGHWAY/LIGHT FROM YOUR LIGHTHOUSE/SUN IS SHINING/DANCE 'TILL WE'RE HIGH/LIFELONG PASSION/IS THIS LOVE/LOVERS IN A DREAM/UNIVERSAL HERE, EVERLASTING NOW/DON'T STOP RUNNING

One Little Indian; recorded 2006–2008; released November 2008

Many years before lounge music was considered hip kitsch, in 1971 McCartney commissioned Richard Hewson to orchestrate the entire *Ram* album in an easy listening, "classy" style and the result was *Thrillington*. Released six years later without fanfare and credited to Percy "Thrills" Thrillington, the only indication that this clever exercise in orchestral whimsy was a McCartney product was a faint painted reflection of his face on the back cover. It saw a CD release briefly in the 1990s, became a collectors' item for a decade or so, but was reissued in 2004. A remix session for the *Off The Ground* album gave birth to **Strawberries, Oceans, Ships, Forest**, a series of techno dance tracks designed by McCartney and producer Youth using old Macca samples as source material and released under the name **The Fireman**. The secret wasn't kept for long and the specialist reviews were grudgingly complimentary, but it remains the lowest-selling McCartney-related record ever. The second Fireman album **Rushes** four years later was a more considered affair all round and, in favouring an avant ambient direction, was favourably reviewed along the lines of "a record worth listening to (if you're taking a hefty amount of drugs)". *Liverpool Sound Collage* comprises cut'n'paste doodles and loops from McCartney and the Welsh psychedelic band **The Super Furry Animals**, with actual Beatles studio chatter thrown into the mix. The first creations using officially sanctioned Beatles samples, the results have a certain curiosity value, but most listeners will have better things to do. **Electric Arguments** was the third Fireman album after a gap of ten years, and the first to feature vocals. McCartney went public with the project, cranked up the promo and got rave reviews in the mainstream media. It was super spontaneous: Paul improvised and Youth edited and processed one track per day. There's bags of energy and loose, experimental invention, though listeners who like McCartney for his melodies may get restless.

Instant McCartney

Wingspan Hits And History

LISTEN TO WHAT THE MAN SAID/BAND ON THE RUN/ ANOTHER DAY/LIVE AND LET DIE/JET/MY LOVE/SILLY LOVE SONGS/PIPES OF PEACE/C MOON/HI HI HI/LET 'EM IN/ GOODNIGHT TONIGHT/JUNIOR'S FARM/ MULL OF KINTYRE/ UNCLE ALBERT–ADMIRAL HALSEY/WITH A LITTLE LUCK/ COMING UP/NO MORE LONELY NIGHTS/LET ME ROLL IT/ THE LOVELY LINDA/DAYTIME NIGHTIME SUFFERING/ MAYBE I'M AMAZED/HELEN WHEELS/BLUEBIRD/HEART OF THE COUNTRY/EVERY NIGHT/TAKE IT AWAY/JUNK/MAN WE WAS LONELY/VENUS AND MARS /ROCKSHOW/BACK SEAT OF MY CAR/ROCKESTRA THEME /GIRLFRIEND/ WATERFALLS/ TOMORROW/TOO MANY PEOPLE/CALL ME BACK AGAIN/TUG OF WAR/BIP BOP/HEY DIDDLE/NO MORE LONELY NIGHTS
Parlophone; released 2001; currently available on CD

It took a while to get right. Even at the height of Wings' post **Mull Of Kintyre** popularity in 1978, *Wings Greatest* looked like a strangely meagre collection. No **C Moon**, no **Helen Wheels**, no **Listen To What The Man Said**.

1990's *All The Best* benefited from the more generous playing time of the CD era, but still took the "best" to mean the charting singles, favouring semi-hits like **Once Upon A Long Ago** over inspired album cuts like **Maybe I'm Amazed**. 2001's *Wingspan*, however, was a canny double-CD: a forty-track selection featuring, along with the hits, **Heart Of The Country** from *Ram*, **Daytime Nightime Suffering** (B-side of **Goodnight Tonight**) and no fewer than five tracks from his maligned 1970 debut. In acknowledging less obvious solo and Wings-era McCartney achievements, *Wingspan* is by far the most reliable place to begin exploring post-Beatles Macca.

George Harrison

"I'm just another human who can play a little bit of guitar. I can write a little bit. I don't think I can do anything particularly well, but somewhere down the line I feel there is a need for me to be what I am."

George Harrison, 1971

Perhaps more than either Lennon or McCartney, George Harrison's solo career began from within The Beatles. Though Paul's quasi-solo efforts (**Yesterday**, **Eleanor Rigby**) were considered Beatles music (written, as most believed they were, by "Lennon/McCartney"), Harrison's singular work in The Beatles' mid-period, even contemporaneously, was widely received as "George" music. Indeed, from as early as 1966 he had relied on his own resources and creative energy to get songs like **Love You To** (which featured minimal group input) and **Within You Without You** (which featured none at all) off the ground and onto a Beatles record. That organizational vigour found a further outlet on the first Beatle solo album, *Wonderwall Music* (1968), for which George supervised sessions by Indian classical and British rock musicians in Bombay and at Abbey Road. *Electronic Sound* (1969), on the other hand, required little more preparation than switching on a Moog synthesizer and twiddling the knobs. It sounds like it too. "Avant garde a clue", as the composer himself put it.

Harrison was long resigned to but increasingly resentful of the fact that to have one of his compositions heard by the group "you'd have to do 59 of Paul's songs", so it's curious that both solo albums released within The Beatles' lifetime were instrumentals. Off-cuts from the burgeoning Harrison songbook found their way instead to Apple artists like Jackie Lomax (**Sour Milk Sea** was among the first Apple singles) and Doris Troy (**Ain't That Cute**). Cream even recorded **Badge**, a "quite silly" (adjudged Harrison) song written with Eric Clapton. Even **Something** was offered to Joe Cocker before being reclaimed for *Abbey Road*.

Of all The Beatles, Harrison moved in the hippest circles: co-writing with Clapton, hanging out and writing with Dylan, and touring with Delaney and Bonnie in late 1969. And after his notably mature contributions to *Abbey Road*, the arrival in November 1970 of the mighty triple album *All Things Must Pass* reinforced Harrison's reputation as the musical dark horse of The Beatles and was hailed as a magisterial accomplishment. Scoured by MOR balladeers for covers along the lines of **Something,** Matt Monro and Dana covered **Isn't It A Pity** and **Olivia Newton-John** sang **If Not For You,** though the biggie was the massive Harrison hit single of 1971, **My Sweet Lord,** which was quickly adopted as a genuine gospel classic.

Spending most of his time gardening and meditating at **Friar Park**, the Henley-on-Thames mansion he bought in early 1970, George was alerted in spring 1971 by **Ravi Shankar** to the suffering of the inhabitants of East Pakistan, later known as Bangladesh. The oppressive Islamist dictatorship of West Pakistan had caused thousands of refugees to flee to India, which had neither the food nor sanitation for such an influx, resulting in a humanitarian crisis. George agreed to front a high-profile fund-raising event, remembering later that "just that one decision to help Ravi ... took two solid years of my life". Harrison wrote an anthem which became a modest hit single **Bangla Desh**, and managed to cajole Bob Dylan out of hiding for two triumphant concerts at Madison Square Garden, New York, in August 1971. Ringo Starr also performed, making it the closest thing to a live Beatles reunion until Harrison's memorial concert in 2002. John Lennon bailed out at the last minute, apparently after rowing with Yoko (who was not invited to perform) and Paul McCartney also demurred, still in a post-split funk. The concerts were recorded and released on (another) triple album and a film.

George in 1971 with friend and musical mentor since 1966, Ravi Shankar

In a pioneering effort, George went to great trouble to try to persuade artists and record companies to waive royalties. Getting governments to waive purchase tax, to maximize funds for the relief effort, was harder. "The law and tax people do not help," he said. "They make it so that it is not worthwhile doing anything decent." Even though the concerts raised over £15 million, it was a disheartened Harrison who was forced to cover the tax due himself, to the tune of £1 million.

In 1973 George established his Material

World Charitable Foundation and donated a proportion of the considerable royalties generated by that year's album *Living In The Material World* to it. The following year, he set up his own record label, Dark Horse Records, and signed Splinter, a British acoustic pop duo, and Ravi Shankar. He also became the first Beatle to tour America, not quite in tandem with the release of his delayed album *Dark Horse*. With Ravi Shankar in support (and not going down well with George's audience), much exhortation to religious chanting, dour pronouncements from the stage (when an audience failed to chant "Hari Krishna" with him, George snapped "I don't know how it feels down there, but from up here you seem pretty dead") and Harrison's hoarse voice not up to concert-length performance, a critical backlash began. Even his friends had started calling George "His Lectureship". "It wasn't really that bad," countered George. "Every show was a standing ovation."

Harrison's final contractual obligation to EMI/Capitol was the under-cooked ***Extra Texture*** (1975), though the nadir of George's slipping solo reputation was reached in September 1976 when Harrison was found guilty of "subconscious plagiarism" in relation to the similarity of **My Sweet Lord** and The Chiffons' 1963 hit **He's So Fine**. He was eventually ordered to pay nearly $600,000 to Bright Tunes, The Chiffons' publishers. Contrastingly, Delaney Bramlett – who claimed to have got George started on **My Sweet Lord** in the first place – was resignedly philosophical at not being given a songwriting credit, let alone any remuneration.

George's troubles continued when, reportedly drinking heavily and following a bout of hepatitis, he was late with his 1976 album *Thirty-Three And A Third*. It was to be released on Dark Horse, but administered and bankrolled by **A&M**, who sued him for a fortune for "non-delivery of product". Warners swept up the mess, but the eventual emergence of the record did little to restore George's reputation in Britain. "I get the impression," he noted in interview, "that England is not particularly interested." America, on the other hand, was thrilled to witness a six-tune duet with Harrison and Paul Simon on TV's *Saturday Night Live* in November of that year.

His marriage to Patti had cooled long ago in the face of extramarital relationships on both sides (including George's dalliance with Maureen Starkey) and Harrison's paradoxical behaviour: devoutly religious while continuing to indulge in drugs and alcohol. "He has his black moods," Ravi Shankar once said of George, "and God help anyone who at that time incites his wrath." George eventually, and semi-amicably, gave way to allow his friend Eric Clapton and Patti to get together. Clapton had pined for Patti for years, written his famous **Layla** in her honour as far back as 1970 and sunk into a period of heroin addiction after she had initially rejected him.

George and Patti were divorced in June 1977 and in August 1978, George married Olivia Trinidad Arias, a former secretary at A&M, and the mother of his month-old son Dhani. In May 1979, Eric Clapton married Patti, an occasion that featured George, Ringo and Paul as part of an all-star wedding jam. The resultant music, including a version of **Get Back**, was "absolute rubbish," according to Denny Laine, who also played.

February 1979 saw the first Harrison music in two and a half years in the shape of the *George Harrison* album and its attendant minor hit single **Blow Away**. In August 1979, the exclusive publishers Genesis printed a collector's edition (2000 copies only) of George's Derek Taylor assisted autobiography *I, Me, Mine* retailing at £148. (It was later reprinted by mainstream publisher Simon and Schuster in 1982.) Perhaps the most notable thing about the book was John Lennon's reaction to it. With John barely mentioned, he claimed to have been "just hurt" at George's lack of acknowledgement of Lennon's influence on his life. "I was just left out as if I didn't exist," Lennon fumed in the autumn of 1980.

Although the rift of silence between the two Beatles hadn't been mended by December 8, 1980, all petty differences dissipated in the face of Lennon's death. "After all we went through together I had and still have great love and respect for John Lennon," ran Harrison's statement to the press on December 9. "To rob life is the ultimate robbery in life."

Three of The Beatles were finally reunited on record in those unhappy circumstances in January 1981 to overdub George's tribute to John Lennon, **All Those Years Ago**. A hastily rewritten song originally intended for Ringo, it became Harrison's biggest hit in a decade. The album for which it had been intended had already suffered the indignity of rejection by Warner Brothers but the hit single made *Somewhere In England* a successful, high-profile Harrison record in 1981.

The follow-up, however, *Gone Troppo* (1982), was under-promoted by both record company and artist, failed even to crack the Top 100 of the album charts and was virtually the last heard of George Harrison, musician, for over five years. Estranged from his religious associates and his friends – and amid reports of depression and a return to drugs, especially cocaine – George preferred to potter in his vast Friar Park garden and follow motor racing than compete in an industry he'd lost interest in, and for an audience that had apparently lost interest in him.

The highest profile activity of Harrison in the mid-1980s was as a film producer. As co-founder of **Handmade Films**, he had eased the birth of some of the most notable British-made films of the period including *Monty Python's Life Of Brian*, *The Long Good Friday*, *Time Bandits*, *Mona Lisa* and *Withnail And I*. He even fronted a PR charm offensive in 1985 for the ill-starred movie *Shanghai Surprise* to limit the damage done by the petulant behaviour of its husband-and-wife co-stars, Madonna and Sean Penn.

In the mid-1980s, a handful of rare live appearances evidenced Harrison's musical rejuvenation. In 1985, he guested on a TV tribute to Carl Perkins, enthusiastically banging out **Everybody's Trying To Be My Baby** ("George Harrison everybody!" bellowed a delighted Perkins. "Doesn't he look good?") and at a 1986 charity concert he shared the microphone with Robert Plant and Denny Laine on **Johnny B. Goode**. Summer 1987 saw George as the star guest of that year's Prince's Trust concert, singing **While My Guitar Gently Weeps** and **Here Comes The Sun** with Eric, Elton and Ringo there to help.

The comeback ("I've been here the whole time," shrugged George) culminated when the album *Cloud Nine*, produced by Jeff Lynne, hit the shops and charts in November 1987 in a blaze of confident Warners publicity and positive reviews. Harrison even scored a huge hit single on both sides of the Atlantic with James Ray's **I've Got My Mind Set On You**. An elated Harrison did his most intensive round of TV and press interviews for years. He was relaxed enough to attend and accept The Beatles' induction into the **Rock'n'Roll Hall of Fame** in January 1988. "I really don't have much to say," he remarked dryly in his speech, "because I'm the quiet Beatle."

Following the deliberately Beatlesque single **When We Was Fab**, the third single from *Cloud Nine* needed a B-side. What started as a Lynne and Harrison knock-out job at Bob Dylan's home studio with pal **Roy Orbison** guesting developed into a relaxed, five-superstar musician session with Dylan joining in along with Tom Petty, who had lent Harrison a guitar. The track produced – "Handle With Care" – was deemed too good to bury on a B-side and everyone agreed to repeat the experience. They recorded an album in two weeks during summer 1988, and **The Traveling Wilburys** were born.

The good-natured, retro-acoustic modesty of *The Traveling Wilburys: Volume 1* was popular, well received critically and won a Grammy, though plans for a tour were scotched by the death in December 1988 of **Roy Orbison**. The remaining four Wilburys put out a less successful follow-up album in October 1990 – waggishly entitled ***Volume 3*** – which was to be the final rock album with new Harrison material released in his lifetime.

In 1991 George was persuaded back to the stage by Eric Clapton. Clapton had suffered the loss of his 4-year-old son Conor in March, who had died after falling from the window of a New York apartment. Still coming to terms with his bereavement, Clapton felt in need of some low-profile distraction and offered to musically direct a backing band for a twelve-date tour of Japan in December. (Eric later explained the choice of country, commenting that "if [George] came to the US and he saw one bad review he'd go straight home.") Harrison, rumoured to be in need of some quick cash and fancying some light relief from business difficulties at **Handmade Films**, agreed. Basking in a warm audience reception and good reviews, he even enjoyed playing his old Beatles songs. "I've found that I like them," he said. "A few years ago, I might not have, but now I'm proud of them."

So energized was he by the experience, Harrison even conquered his fear of the "bitchy and nasty" British press to make his first-ever solo live appearance in Britain, an election fundraiser at the Royal Albert Hall in April 1992 for the **Maharishi Mahesh Yogi**'s Natural Law Party. Overwhelmed and gratified by the audience's response, he later spoke of his regret at not making it into a tour.

Of all The Beatles, Harrison was always the one who spoke of the past with the least affection. In the early 1990s, a series of catastrophic losses for Handmade Films forced Harrison to instigate a mismanagement lawsuit against Denis O'Brien, George's business manager since 1973 and partner in Handmade since 1979. That the financial wrangle coincided with George's apparent volte-face over involving himself in an updated Beatles legacy had the media speculating that Harrison's participation in the *Anthology* saga was less to do with a desire for historical truth, let alone nostalgic warmth, than sheer monetary necessity. Nevertheless, George's musical contributions to **Free As A Bird** and **Real Love** were widely acknowledged as the most characterful and distinctive aspects of the Threetles' two tracks.

The O'Brien suit was eventually settled in George's favour in February 1996 to the tune of eleven million dollars. "It's one thing winning," noted Harrison sceptically, "but actually getting the money is another thing." The massive profile of *Anthology* would have seemed the perfect time to weigh in with some viable product of his own. That George chose to spend his creative energy producing and playing on Ravi Shankar's ***Chants Of India*** in 1997 speaks volumes about his priorities and suggests *Anthology* had paid its way.

George underwent two cancer operations in 1997, one for a neck growth, another removing part of his lung (he had been a smoker for 35 years, quitting in 1992). By 1998, more cancer had been discovered in his throat. Responding well to treatment, George embarked on an intense period of writing and recording in his home studio. Yet the following year his life would again be threatened, in an unexpected and terrifying way.

Ever since the death of John Lennon, Harrison (and the other Beatles) had been subjected to various kinds of crank threats and security scares. But on the night of December 30, 1999, a man named Michael Abram broke into Friar Park. Abram suffered from schizophrenia and was convinced himself that The Beatles were "witches" and that George was "a witch on a broomstick, who talked in the Devil's tongue – an alien from Hell", as he later told his lawyer. He attacked George and Olivia with a knife, severely wounding and almost killing Harrison before police dragged him away. Though on the critical list for only 24 hours and back home by January 1, 2000, George was deeply shaken. He admitted later in a salty interview that he was ready to call his new album ***The World Is Doomed Volume 1***.

When the thirtieth-anniversary CD edition of ***All Things Must Pass*** was released in December 2000, genuine admiration for the record's artistry was tinged with a sentimental poignancy that time for George might be short. By mid-2001, rumours of recurring disease were confirmed as fact. He had developed a further growth on his lung and a brain tumour, and friends and family rallied round. In contrast to Lennon's shock demise, which left much unfinished personal business, McCartney and Harrison reportedly spent an emotional few hours together in November

2001 laughing, crying and holding hands.

George's death on November 29, 2001 prompted a media outpouring and a reassessment of the contributions of The Quiet Beatle, often focusing on his introduction of spirituality to the rock agenda, his pioneering work as rock'n'roll fundraiser and his pervasive dignity within an undignified business. A reissued **My Sweet Lord** returned to #1 for Christmas 2001, although by the time his final album ***Brainwashed*** was released a year later, mixed reviews and sales saw the final instalment of George's solo career back on a familiar road. It would neither have surprised nor worried him. "He was over the music industry ... He had no more desire to be famous," said his son Dhani. "He had absolutely no fears or worries left with him when he died." A year to the day after his death, *A Concert For George* was held at London's Royal Albert Hall. Musically directed by Eric Clapton and featuring contributions from Paul, Ringo, Jeff Lynne and Billy Preston among others, it was an extraordinarily moving evening. George's 1973 album *Living In The Material World* received the box-set treatment in 2006, and in 2008, Olivia created a Harrison-themed horticultural installation at the Chelsea Flower Show, "A Garden For George". At a 2009 ceremony attended by Olivia, his son Dhani, Paul McCartney, Jeff Lynne and Tom Petty, George received his own star on the Hollywood Walk of Fame, though the man himself would probably have been more impressed that the 50th-anniversary design of the Mini Cooper was dedicated to Harrison and his 1967 psychedelic motor-car.

Wonderwall Music

MICROBES/RED LADY TOO/TABLA AND PAKAVAJ/IN THE PARK/DRILLING A HOME/GURU VANDANA/GREASY LEGS/SKIING/GAT KIRWANA/DREAM SCENE/PARTY SEACOMBE/LOVE SCENE/CRYING/COWBOY MUSIC/FANTASY SEQUINS/ON THE BED/GLASS BOX/WONDERWALL TO BE HERE/SINGING OM

Apple; recorded November 1967–February 1968; released November 1, 1968; currently available on CD

An attractive sequence of Indian and pop vignettes that was the soundtrack for Joe Massot's swinging London movie starring Jane Birkin, *Wonderwall Music* has endured rather better than the movie itself. *Wonderwall Music*'s blend of Western and Eastern musical textures appeared to make its impact on the raga rock of **Kula Shaker** in the mid-1990s, while the title of the film was famously appropriated by Oasis's **Noel Gallagher** for one of his best songs.

Electronic Sound

UNDER THE MERSEY WALL/NO TIME OR SPACE

Zapple; recorded November 1968–February 1969; released May 2, 1969; currently available on CD

In the spirit of Lennon's avant-garde dabblings, these random musical scribbles made with the first Moog synthesizer comprised the second and final release on the experimental Apple imprint, Zapple. An interesting idea, but Harrison later regretted that the only records to appear on the label – this and Lennon/Ono's *Life With The Lions* – were "a load of rubbish".

All Things Must Pass

I'D HAVE YOU ANY TIME/MY SWEET LORD/WAH-WAH/ISN'T IT A PITY – VERSION 1/WHAT IS LIFE/IF NOT FOR YOU/ BEHIND THAT LOCKED DOOR/LET IT DOWN/RUN OF THE MILL/BEWARE OF DARKNESS/APPLE SCRUFFS/BALLAD OF SIR FRANKIE CRISP (LET IT ROLL)/AWAITING ON YOU ALL/ ALL THINGS MUST PASS/I DIG LOVE/ART OF DYING/ISN'T IT A PITY – VERSION 2/HEAR ME LORD/OUT OF THE BLUE/IT'S

JOHNNY'S BIRTHDAY/PLUG ME IN/I REMEMBER JEEP/THANKS FOR THE PEPPERONI

Apple; recorded May–October 1970; released November 1970; currently available on CD with bonus tracks "I Live For You" (outtake), "Beware Of Darkness" (demo), "Let It Down" (overdubbed demo), "What Is Life" (backing track), "My Sweet Lord" (2000 version)

Nominally overseen by Phil Spector in the wake of his **Let It Be** rescue sessions, George ultimately found the alcohol-dissipated personality of his producer more trouble than it was worth. However, it's clear that without Spector's wall-of-sound vision, mustering several drummers, bassists, guitarists, pianists and percussionists (sometimes all playing at the same time), this doorstep of a record wouldn't be the magnificently overblown item it is. A vinyl triple-album in a portentous monochrome box (gaily colourized for the CD reissue in 2000), it retailed at a conspicuously expensive £5 in the UK but nonetheless sold handsomely. It established George as the world's favourite ex-Beatle, a situation the magnificent **My Sweet Lord** and his Bangladesh efforts only enhanced.

However, even a casual listen reveals the triple album to contain only an album-and-a-half's worth of decent material. The third album comprises wearisome jams featuring messrs Clapton, Preston, Voorman et al, and even the main song set dips in the middle around the drearily whimsical **Ballad Of Sir Frankie Crisp** and the preachy **Awaiting On You All**. However, the best of it is surely some of the best music ever made by a single Beatle.

First of all, there's the sheer size of the sound. Almost threatening to trample both song and singer, the thunderous **Wah-Wah** (written after storming out of the **Get Back** sessions), **Let It Down** and **What Is Life** build up a head of steam that could only be generated by multiple live takes of dozens of musicians playing their hearts out. The roaring results mixed into Spector's customized echoey stew produced some memorable orchestral rock'n'roll.

Yet for all the impact of the sonic scale, it's perhaps the quieter moments that endure. The beautiful **I'd Have You Any Time** is Harrison at his most harmonically luxurious. Co-written with Bob Dylan, the song has George showing him his posh major-seventh chords and Bob respondong with the forthright middle eight. **Behind That Locked Door** – apparently concerning Dylan's elusive persona – is a delicate, touching country waltz, while **All Things Must Pass** – demoed way back in February 1969 – is a heart-rending piece of significant prescience which seems to take on more poignancy with every passing year.

Harrison confessed to feeling embarrassed at the overblown production when reissuing the album in 2000, and was sorely tempted to remix it. In the end he settled for reducing the pillowy Spectorness by mastering more attack into the sound. While there's a strong case to be made for issuing ***All Things Must Pass*** on a stupendous single CD (losing the pointless second version of **Isn't It A Pity** and the jam session), the thirtieth anniversary CD remaster managed to add material, including demos, instrumental mixes and the previously unissued **I Live For You**. Which is also good.

Concert For Bangladesh

INTRODUCTION/BANGLA DHUN – RAVI SHANKAR/WAH WAH/MY SWEET LORD/AWAITING ON YOU ALL/THAT'S THE WAY GOD PLANNED IT – BILLY PRESTON/IT DON'T COME EASY – RINGO STARR/BEWARE OF DARKNESS/BAND INTRODUCTION/WHILE MY GUITAR GENTLY WEEPS/JUMPIN' JACKFLASH/YOUNG BLOOD - LEON RUSSELL/HERE COMES THE SUN/HARD RAIN'S A GONNA FALL – BOB DYLAN/ IT TAKES A LOT TO LAUGH IT TAKES A TRAIN TO CRY – BOB DYLAN/BLOWIN' IN THE WIND – BOB DYLAN/MR TAMBOURINE MAN – BOB DYLAN/JUST LIKE A WOMAN – BOB DYLAN/SOMETHING/BANGLADESH

Sony; recorded August 1971; released December 1971;

currently available on CD with extra track "Love Minus Zero/No Limit" by Bob Dylan.

"Years before Live Aid," observed Tom Petty at George's posthumous induction into the Rock'n'Roll Hall Of Fame, "George invented the idea of rock'n'roll giving back to the people." Thirty-five years after the event, George's all-star fundraiser for Bangladesh is still giving – the royalties from the current CD issue continue to go to UNICEF – and the record is still worth hearing. Aside from the tough band versions of *All Things Must Pass* favourites "Wah-Wah" and "Beware Of Darkness" and a lovely solo performance of "Here Comes The Sun", the surprise appearance by the then-reclusive "friend of us all" Bob Dylan creates a genuine frisson.

Living In The Material World

GIVE ME LOVE (GIVE ME PEACE ON EARTH)/SUE ME, SUE YOU BLUES/THE LIGHT THAT HAS LIGHTED THE WORLD/ DON'T LET ME WAIT TOO LONG/WHO CAN SEE IT/LIVING IN THE MATERIAL WORLD/THE LORD LOVES THE ONE (THAT LOVES THE LORD)/BE HERE NOW/TRY SOME BUY SOME/THE DAY THE WORLD GETS ROUND/THAT IS ALL

Apple; recorded 1973; released June 1973; currently available on CD

A big-seller, this album has been characterized as the beginning of Harrison's unpalatable (not to say hypocritical, if tales of his less-than-holy behaviour of the period have any credence) preachy phase.

But, with the exception of "the law says" finger-wagging of **The Lord Loves The One (That Loves The Lord)** and the possibly over-mournful **The Light That Has Lighted The World**, Harrison conveys his struggle to reconcile a complex past to maintaining a spiritual present – with restraint and, in places, considerable grace and beauty. The "love" he's so desperate to express (**That Is All**, **Don't Let Me Wait Too Long**, **Who Can See It**) seems directed as much to an earthly relationship as to any God. And **Sue Me Sue You Blues** and **Try Some Buy Some** are wry, reasonable digs at symptoms of what Harrison sees as a diseased world.

His melodious gifts and distinctive ear for a harmony are in evidence throughout (he borrows from Pink Floyd's recently released Harrisonish song **Us And Them** for the graceful **Be Here Now**), though anyone who found **Long Long Long** or the big ballads on ***All Things Must Pass*** a bit tedious may lose patience with the determinedly shadowy, awed tone of the album.

Dark Horse

HARI'S ON TOUR/SIMPLY SHADY/SO SAD/BYE BYE, LOVE/ MAYA LOVE/DING DONG, DING DONG/DARK HORSE/FAR EAST MAN/IT IS 'HE' (JAI SRI KRISHNA)

Apple; recorded 1974; released December 1974; currently available on CD

A real dip in inspiration during a turbulent period of his life and a bout of laryngitis, *Dark Horse*'s best tracks are the cover of the Everly Brothers' **Bye Bye Love** (recomposed in a minor key and featuring pointedly customized lyrics to his wife "our lady" and friend "old Clapper" as well as featuring both Patti and Eric on backing vocals), **Far East Man** (a lovely co-write with another of Patti's recent suitors, Ron Wood) and the title track, in which George gamely struggles with a shot-to-pieces throat to deliver a pleasingly gruff vocal.

Featuring two of the worst songs he ever allowed out – **It Is 'He' (Jai Sri Krishna)** is George at his happy-clappy nadir, while **Ding Dong** is a risible New Year ditty that, incredibly, he saw fit to release as a single – the occasional contributions of crack sessioneers the LA Express only serve to wash Harrison's music of any distinctiveness. Though, really, he hadn't put much there in the first place.

Extra Texture

YOU/THE ANSWER'S AT THE END/THIS GUITAR (CAN'T KEEP FROM CRYING)/OOH BABY (YOU KNOW THAT I LOVE YOU)/WORLD OF STONE/A BIT MORE OF YOU/CAN'T STOP

THINKING ABOUT YOU/TIRED OF MIDNIGHT BLUE/GREY CLOUDY LIES/HIS NAME IS LEGS (LADIES AND GENTLEMEN)
Apple; recorded 1975; released October 1975; currently available on CD

After the disaster of the *Dark Horse* album and tour, Harrison perhaps piled into his next record a little earlier than his inspiration had kicked in. Wanting to be free of his EMI obligations sooner rather than later, he quickly recorded *Extra Texture* in LA, and the album appeared within ten months of its predecessor.

A marginal improvement, the record boasts some slick playing but the songs are either threadbare, such as **Ooh Baby** or **Can't Stop Thinking About You**, or medium-grade self-pastiche. **This Guitar Can't Keep From Crying**, for instance, feebly winks back at his other weeping guitar song, whilst **You** reheats his ***All Things Must Pass*** sound and adds a dash of Bruce Springsteen, without the requisite composition to carry it off. Things look up during **Tired Of Midnight Blue**, a sassy soft-shoe shuffle featuring Leon Russell on piano, and on the manically intricate tribute to the Bonzo Dog Doo Dah Band's drummer, Legs Larry Smith, on **His Name Is Legs (Ladies And Gentlemen)**.

While not quite the "grubby album" Harrison would later characterize it as, the good moments are enough to suggest he should have waited until he had a few more of them.

The Dark Horse Years

Box set released March 2004, including:

Thirty-Three And A Third

WOMAN DON'T YOU CRY OVER ME/DEAR ONE/BEAUTIFUL GIRL/THIS SONG/SEE YOURSELF/IT'S WHAT YOU VALUE/TRUE LOVE/PURE SMOKEY/CRACKERBOX PALACE/LEARNING HOW TO LOVE YOU
Dark Horse; recorded 1976; released November 1976

George Harrison

LOVE COMES TO EVERYONE/NOT GUILTY/HERE COMES THE MOON/SOFT-HEARTED HANA/BLOW AWAY/FASTER/DARK SWEET LADY/YOUR LOVE IS FOREVER/SOFT TOUCH/IF YOU BELIEVE
Dark Horse; recorded 1978–79; released February 1979

Somewhere In England

BLOOD FROM A CLONE/UNCONSCIOUSNESS RULES/LIFE ITSELF/ALL THOSE YEARS AGO/BALTIMORE ORIOLE/TEARDROPS/THAT WHICH I HAVE LOST/THE WRITING'S ON THE WALL/HONG KONG BLUES/SAVE THE WORLD
Dark Horse; recorded 1980–81; released May 1981

Gone Troppo

WAKE UP MY LOVE/THAT'S THE WAY IT GOES/I REALLY LOVE YOU/GREECE/GONE TROPPO/MYSTICAL ONE/UNKNOWN DELIGHT/BABY DON'T RUN AWAY/DREAM AWAY/CIRCLES
Dark Horse; recorded 1982; released October 1982

Cloud Nine

CLOUD NINE/THAT'S WHAT IT TAKES/FISH ON THE SAND/JUST FOR TODAY/THIS IS LOVE/WHEN WE WAS FAB/DEVIL'S RADIO/SOMEPLACE ELSE/WRECK OF THE HESPERUS/BREATH AWAY FROM HEAVEN/GOT MY MIND SET ON YOU
Dark Horse; recorded 1986–87; released November 1987

Live In Japan

I WANT TO TELL YOU/OLD BROWN SHOE/TAXMAN/GIVE ME LOVE (GIVE ME PEACE ON EARTH)/IF I NEEDED SOMEONE/SOMETHING/WHAT IS LIFE/DARK HORSE/PIGGIES/GOT MY MIND SET ON YOU/CLOUD 9/HERE COMES THE SUN/MY SWEET LORD/ALL THOSE YEARS AGO/CHEER DOWN/DEVIL'S RADIO/ISN'T IT A PITY/WHILE MY GUITAR GENTLY WEEPS/ROLL OVER BEETHOVEN
Dark Horse; recorded 1991; released July 1992

George established his own label in 1974 but didn't grace it with his recorded presence until 1976, when he was free of EMI. His independent Dark Horse years ought to have been a carefree bounty of unfettered Harrisongs. But as his health, outlook, business arrangements and ultimately his interest was seen to stutter and stall, much of the period is a disheartening continuation of the downward path Harrison's musical output had taken since *All Things Must Pass*. Amidst less-than-blue-chip musical settings, the consistency of his lyrical concerns – romantic/spiritual love, the reverential search for personal and global enlightenment and dry snipes at the modern world's shortcomings – palled even for avid

Beatlenuts. However, there are minor gems here and there – and even the occasional jewel.

Thirty Three And A Third (1976) appeared immediately in the wake of the "My Sweet Lord" "unconscious plagiarism" court case. The wry humour of his musical response – the minor US hit "This Song" – masked the blow to his confidence and inspiration; the rest of the oddly ordinary album, however, conveyed it all too clearly.

New loves – for Olivia and motor racing – delayed the follow-up a little, but when it came *George Harrison* (1979) was a freshly enthused, minor treat: an acoustic rock ten-tracker replete with sunshine melodies and gorgeous slide guitar. "Blow Away" perfectly conveys the breezy change of mood required to banish his sporadic blues, "Soft Hearted Hana" jazzily details his experiences with magic mushrooms, and the bitter *White Album* reject "Not Guilty" is varnished by producer Russ Titelman into a modest kind of splendour.

Somewhere In England (1981) was another semi-slump, however. It was rejected in its original form by Dark Horse distributors Warner Bros, prompting pointed commentary from George on "Blood From A Clone" ("I hear a clock ticking/I feel the nitpicking/I almost quit kicking at the wall"). While the rejigged record was by no means classic Hari, in the Beatles-hungry wake of John Lennon's demise and George's tribute single "All Those Years Ago", it did quite well. However, the best tracks were probably the amiably idiosyncratic versions of a pair of old Hoagy Carmichael songs "Baltimore Oriole" and "Hong Kong Blues", which sums it up.

Gone Troppo (1983) was a return to form of sorts. "That's The Way It Goes" was the sort of strumalong fatalistic shrug George had made his own. But this affable, light-hearted, tuneful music made by a bunch of mates with nothing to prove was perceived as the hobby record of a full-time gardener and film producer and was virtually ignored. George's brother Peter, in charge of the Friar Park grounds, was heard to say at the time, "I didn't know he had a new record out." It died unloved and unbought. Its failure was enough for George to bow out of record releases for five years.

But after this hiatus, George unexpectedly exploded back to the charts with a hit single, James Ray's "Got My Mind Set On You" and the fabulous album *Cloud Nine*, a very happy event. The break had done George immeasurable good, as had his recent friendship with producer Jeff Lynne. As with all Lynne's productions in the late 1980s and early 1990s (notably for **Tom Petty** and **Roy Orbison**), the album sometimes sounds as if George is leading a set of ELO tracks. But ultimately, the record is a credit to both men – to Jeff for his punchy, pop-rock production (despite the period preoccupation with the "big snare" sound) and to George for responding to it with his most focused songs and performances for years. There is the odd makeweight track, like the ordinary "Fish On The Sand", which just keeps the album from being premium Harrison work. Mostly though it's cocky rock (the sardonic swipes at the gossiping media on "Devil's Radio" and "Wreck Of The Hesperus"), spirit-lightening pop (the sublimely innocent "This Is Love" and the feel-good "Got My Mind Set On You") and archetypal yearning ballads ("Just For Today" and "Someplace Else"). There's also lots of juicy Harrison slide guitar and a quite brilliant "Walrus"-era Fabs pastiche, "When We Was Fab". It seems that Lynne was probably what George needed all along – a trusted musical pal who could record his voice properly, tidy things up at the back and encourage him to enjoy being an ex-Beatle. *Cloud Nine* is a heartwarming success.

Live In Japan is an unpredictably tough two-CD set of George's greatest Beatles and solo hits that suggests, if he'd wanted to, George could have had a ball on the US concert circuit in the 1990s.

Efforts to properly reassess the period following his death in 2001 foundered due to the extended unavailability of the albums. Now they're back – ironically, but as George apparently wished it – on EMI, beautifully packaged and remastered as individual albums and a handsome box set. While the bulk of George's Dark Horse output is hardly overdue for a revelatory critical repositioning, much of the music is very welcome and in places rather reassuring.

The Traveling Wilburys Volume 1

HANDLE WITH CARE/DIRTY WORLD/RATTLED/LAST NIGHT/ NOT ALONE ANYMORE/CONGRATULATIONS/ HEADING FOR THE LIGHT/MARGARITA/TWEETER AND THE MONKEY MAN/ END OF THE LINE

Warner; recorded 1988; released October 1988

The Traveling Wilburys Volume 3

SHE'S MY BABY/INSIDE OUT/IF YOU BELONGED TO ME/ DEVIL'S BEEN BUSY/DEADLY SINS/POOR HOUSE/WHERE WERE YOU LAST NIGHT?/COOL DRY PLACE/NEW BLUE MOON/YOU TOOK MY BREATH AWAY/WILBURY TWIST

Warner; recorded 1990; released October 1990

George's unexpected and most welcome late-1980s comeback continued with the fantastic success of the all-star hillbilly folk-pop of The Traveling Wilburys, featuring Harrison, Bob Dylan, Jeff Lynne, Tom Petty and Roy Orbison. *Volume I* is full of infectious, good-time stuff in which everything is treated as a bit of a laugh and everyone, including the listener, is in on the joke. The songs are half-daft, half-deft and damn catchy, especially Orbison's chest-beating feature "Not Alone Anymore" and the two hit singles "Handle With Care" (the elevated Harrison B-side from which the project sprang) and the stirring "End Of The Line". The slightly more self-conscious *Volume III* (they didn't bother with a Volume II) featured more Dylan, less George and no Roy Orbison (who had died in December 1988), and the results are a tad less enjoyable. Unavailable for a decade, in 2007 various formats of *The Traveling Wilburys Collection* box set appeared. Containing both albums and a making-of DVD, it went on to sell almost two million copies.

Brainwashed

ANY ROAD/P2 VATICAN BLUES (LAST SATURDAY NIGHT)/ PISCES FISH/LOOKING FOR MY LIFE/RISING SUN/MARWA BLUES/STUCK INSIDE A CLOUD/RUN SO FAR/NEVER GET OVER YOU/BETWEEN THE DEVIL AND THE DEEP BLUE SEA/ ROCKING CHAIR IN HAWAII/BRAINWASHED

Umlaut; released November 2002; currently available on CD

Begun in the late 1990s but unfinished at the time of George's death, it was left to producers Jeff Lynne and Dhani Harrison to complete the work, guided by the way George had spoken of the songs and by the extensive notebooks he kept to remind him what to do: "Sort out middle of 'Brainwashed'; cut down yew trees at back of lodge." The result is a mature and often profound record, comprising some of his most thought-provoking songs.

Events in the last years of his life evidently moved him to rigorous songwriting. There are powerful images quietly set inside these songs, often sweetened with humour: "I only hung around birds and bees/I never knew things exploded/I only found out when I was down upon my knees/Looking for my life." Also satisfyingly eloquent is the instrumental, **Marwa Blues**, a serene wash of guitar, autoharp and ukulele topped with George's trademark slide tracing a gorgeous melody. And on the chiming single **Stuck Inside a Cloud**, reminiscent of **My Sweet Lord**, he sings "Never slept so little, never smoked so much/Talking to myself, crying out loud/But only I can hear me while I'm stuck inside a cloud". These three tracks are followed by the expressive, philosophical **Rising Sun**, and all four run together building a cumulative power that is very moving for anyone who has ever loved George's music.

Better still is the final, title track, a Dylanesque rant about the way we live which suddenly dissolves into a lovely, meditative prayer. It seems the perfect expression of George's duality – continued anger at the lost modern world alongside a spiritual serenity – and somehow a comfortingly appropriate way of saying farewell.

Instant Harrison

Let It Roll: Songs of George Harrison

GOT MY MIND SET ON YOU/GIVE ME LOVE (GIVE ME PEACE ON EARTH)/THE BALLAD OF SIR FRANKIE CRISP (LET IT ROLL)/MY SWEET LORD/WHILE MY GUITAR GENTLY WEEPS (LIVE – BANGLADESH CONCERT)/ALL THINGS MUST PASS/ANY ROAD/THIS IS LOVE/ALL THOSE YEARS AGO/MARWA BLUES/ WHAT IS LIFE/RISING SUN/WHEN WE WAS FAB/SOMETHING (LIVE – BANGLADESH CONCERT)/BLOW AWAY/CHEER DOWN/ HERE COMES THE SUN (LIVE – BANGLADESH CONCERT)/I DON'T WANT TO DO IT/ISN'T IT A PITY

Capitol; released June 2009

George has been ill-served by compilations. He was rightly annoyed when EMI's 1977 *Best Of* – for many years the only one-stop Harrison shop - combined Beatle Harrisongs with solo cuts. They hadn't even done that with Ringo's *Blast From Your Past*. The excellent *Volume II – Best Of Dark Horse* went out of print quite quickly. At last, in 2009, a half-decent Harrison compendium, *Let It Roll*. This 19-tracker isn't a bad go at summarising solo George, but it doesn't quite feel definitive in the way Lennon's *Working Class Hero*, McCartney's *Wingspan* or even Starr's *Photograph* does; why not a double? With "Be Here Now", "You", "This Song", "Love Comes To Everyone" and several other Harrison highlights conspicuously absent, *Let It Roll* still feels like a bit of a fudge.

Ringo Starr

"A solo career? What do I do? I'm a musician and I made records, so now I'm gonna make them on my own ... with a lot of help from other people. A little help from my friends. And that's been the policy ever since."

Ringo Starr, 1998

Starr's solo persona – a genial, amateurish crooner with a certain instinctive wit – was first exposed to the public on Cilla Black's 1968 BBC TV show where he became the first Beatle to appear, on his own, as a showbiz guest. Over the coming years, his essential likeability and relaxed charm made him a TV chat show regular, especially in the US. He was offered a season in Vegas and there was even talk of a three-way TV special with Ringo, **Elvis Presley** and Raquel Welch, but talks folded and it was in acting that Starr began to make his mark.

Though Lennon was the first Beatle to try his hand at serious acting, playing Private Gripweed in Richard Lester's *How I Won The War*, filmed in 1966, it was Ringo who took it further than just a dabble. Having garnered a reputation as having some thespian talent thanks to his naturally doleful presence in ***A Hard Day's Night***, he found himself invited in 1968 to play the cameo role of randy Mexican gardener Emanuel, complete with Zapata moustache and broken English, in the Christian Marquand directed adaptation of Terry Southern's cult novel *Candy*. The Beatles' next move after the aborted *Get Back* project in February 1969 was delayed by Starr's filming commitments as second lead (to Peter Sellers) in another Terry Southern adaptation, the all-star *The Magic Christian*. Like the previous effort, the film suffers from the self-indulgent sex-and-satire tone of the period, though Ringo was (faintly) praised for the "innocence'"of his performance.

Spring 1970 saw various Beatles jostling for release dates with Ringo's debut, an album of old standards entitled ***Sentimental Journey***, very much the also-ran of the bunch. His quick follow-up in September, a Nashville-recorded set of contemporary country-and-western songs ***Beaucoup Of Blues***, fared better critically, but not much more so commercially.

He drummed on Lennon's *Plastic Ono Band* ("no real toe-tappers on it", he suggested) at the back end of 1970, but admitted later to feeling "absolutely lost" as it became clear The Beatles were not going to reconvene. Then, at the height of The Beatles' court case in spring

Ringo and Peter Sellers in *The Magic Christian*

1971, Ringo scored a surprise hit with the self-penned single **It Don't Come Easy**, which comfortably took its place high in the charts on the heels of Harrison's **My Sweet Lord** and McCartney's **Another Day**.

Rather than capitalize on this with an album, Ringo took another film role as yet another surly Mexican in the violent spaghetti western *Blindman*, which he rated as the "best film part I ever had". Most viewers, however, found it hard to swallow an overdubbed ex-Beatle being "real slimy" in a sombrero.

The thundering T Rex style rock of **Back Off Boogaloo** made it a #2 hit single in spring 1972. Again, rather than make the commercial most of it, Starr was compelled to finish *Born To Boogie*, a rockumentary/concert film Ringo was directing featuring Marc Bolan and T Rex, then the hottest of UK pop stars. The film emerged in late 1972 to fair reviews and good business.

He was also committed to co-starring with David Essex, playing a randy, corrupt Butlins teddy boy called Mike in the movie *That'll Be The Day*. Wearing his own "actual velvet -collared jacket", Ringo put in the acting performance of his life by essentially being his dry, laconic self. Coinciding with Essex's rise to pop fame, the film did very well in the UK in 1973 and Ringo got rave reviews. Starr passed on the follow-up *Stardust*, in which his character became manager of a teen idol, reportedly uncomfortable with the way the storyline developed into a dramatization of the potentially fatal madness of stardom.

Having been appointed head of Apple films, Ringo was further distracted from his solo recording career by producing *Son Of Dracula*. A "non-musical, non-horror, non-comedy comedy", Starr called it. Starring his drinking pal Harry Nilsson and directed by Hammer veteran Freddie Francis, it was a movie the public showed little interest in when it appeared in spring 1974.

By that time, his first proper solo album, *Ringo*, had been released to general acclaim and healthy sales. Starr was back in the charts at no lower than #1 in the US with the singles **Photograph** (co-written with George Harrison) and **You're Sixteen**. The album had tempted The Beatles to the closest they ever got to a reunion in Lennon's lifetime on the Lennon-penned track **I'm The Greatest**, which featured Starr, Lennon and Harrison. McCartney was apparently ready to contribute to the session, but was having visa problems following his recent drugs conviction. He later contributed a song and a kazoo solo elsewhere on the album.

Starr tried to repeat the *Ringo* formula with *Goodnight Vienna* toward the end of 1974 and had moderate hits with **Only You** and **No No Song**, but for the record-buying public the novelty was already wearing off. With recording sessions little more than an extension of his celebrity party lifestyle and his music lacking a solid artistic core, his final albums of the 1970s (*Ringo's Rotogravure* [1976], *Ringo The Fourth* [1977] and *Bad Boy* [1978]) yielded sharply diminishing musical, critical and commercial returns.

Starr was listless, drunk but mostly just plain bored. "You just try to fill the day," he once commented. Several of his business ventures – **Ring O' Records, Ringo Or Robin** furniture design – foundered almost before anything happened. In the mid-1970s he preferred to carouse with party pals Harry Nilsson, Keith Moon – and on his "Lost Weekend", John Lennon – than stay at Tittenhurst, the mansion he bought from John in 1973. Ringo's marriage to Maureen soon fell through and they were divorced in 1976. When Maureen sued her solicitors ten years later, for failing to secure better maintenance payments, she memorably characterized her ex-husband as "a sodding great Andy Capp".

Ringo jet-setted around with LA actress/model Nancy Andrews for a few years and dallied with singer Lynsey De Paul before meeting and falling for actress and former Bond-girl Barbara Bach in 1980 on the set of the prehistoric comedy ***Cavemen***. Their romantic bliss was interrupted firstly by a near-fatal car crash – after which Ringo proposed and Barbara accepted – then secondly by Lennon's death in December 1980. A shaken Ringo and Barbara were among the first visitors to the Dakota after the tragedy but when they were married, in April 1981, Yoko was not invited to the ceremony, or to witness the gathering of the three remaining Beatles. Yoko suggested perhaps "it was really not the right time to encounter people being happy ... but it would have been nice to have been told about it".

Caveman opened in April 1981 in the US to fair reviews for Ringo's wordless performance as a grunting Neanderthal, though the attendant publicity rounds didn't especially help the fortunes of his ***Stop And Smell The Roses*** album. Not even the presence of a Harrison song, two of McCartney's or the release of an MPL-sponsored eleven-minute movie short *The Cooler,* spotlighting three album cuts, could tickle the public's interest. A further lack-lustre, under-performing shot at the recording game, the Joe Walsh produced *Old Wave* (1983), wasn't even released in the UK or USA. Later projects produced by Chips Moman and Elton John were aborted by Ringo himself. *Old Wave* was to be the last new Starr album for a decade.

Instead, for the want of something to do, he and Barbara accepted parts in the 1983 TV movie of Judith Krantz's ***Princess Daisy*** and McCartney's disastrous *Give My Regards To Broad Street* in 1984. The Starkeys had become a glamorous couple, famous for being famous and seen at many a showbiz bash, movie premiere and restaurant opening. Yet Ringo found himself a celebrity in his own right once more, to a whole new generation of young fans, by becoming the narrative voice of the animated UK TV show *Thomas The Tank Engine and Friends*. When it was adapted for the US in 1988 as *Shining Time Station*, with Ringo as Mr Conductor, he was nominated for a "Best Performer In a Children's Series" Emmy. "John had the intellectuals; Paul had the teenies and George the mystics," commented Ringo at the time. "I always got the mothers and babies."

The Starkeys mostly lived an apparently aimless, boozy life in the late 1980s. Though Ringo had started showing himself on stage at various tributes (including the televised Carl Perkins special in 1985) and charity dos (the Prince's Trust of 1987) and Barbara – retired from acting and modelling – was involved with a range of charity activities, by 1988 both had to face up to their misery, induced mainly by alcohol but also cocaine addiction. Amid garish tabloid headlines ("Beatle and Wife in Booze Hell"), they committed to a severe clean-up programme and emerged evangelical about the transformation in their health.

So energized was Ringo by his sober state, he formed a group of celebrity musicians (Jim Keltner, Billy Preston, Dr John, Clarence Clemmons, Levon Helm, Joe Walsh, Nils Lofgren and Rick Danko) to tour North America as Ringo's All-Starr Band in summer 1989. In the nostalgia-friendly climate, the amiable, slightly chaotic show – featuring a balance of Ringo-related Beatle numbers, Starr hits and big hits from members of the band – was well received and netted a respectable $5 million.

Ringo took the show to Japan in November 1989, pursuing a similar endeavour in summer 1992 (this time with **Todd Rundgren**, Dave Edmunds and drumming son Zak Starkey in the line-up) in the US and Europe, including a triumphant return to the Liverpool Empire. He even produced an album in 1992, ***Time Takes Time***, which was received as Ringo's best recorded effort since 1973's *Ringo*. However, while thousands turned out for his good-natured live appearances, fewer were interested in his new record.

Ringo's new success as a variety-show rocker became a good-cheer spreading, biennial routine. Ringo's All-Starr Band was back on tour in 1995 (with John Entwistle and Randy Bachman), 1997 (with Jack Bruce and Gary Brooker), 1999 (Bruce, Brooker and the return of Todd Rundgren), 2001 (Sheila E, Ian Hunter, Howard Jones, Greg Lake, Roger Hodgson), 2003 (Paul Carrack, Colin Hey of Men At Work and Sheila E again), 2006 (Richard Marx, Billy Squire, Rod Argent) and 2008 (Colin Hay, Edgar Winter, Hamish Stuart). Over the years he has released an incredible ten live albums, which is five more than McCartney. Ringo's albums, including *Vertical Man* (1998) and *Ringorama* (2003), came and went the commercial way of most of his other studio efforts, though his 1999 seasonal offering ***I Wanna Be Santa Claus*** was applauded as an endeavour suited to his singular gifts. In 2003, he published a Beatles book, *Postcards from the Boys* (see p.227). However, perhaps the biggest news in the recent career of Richard Starkey, MBE, is that in 2005, Stan Lee – founder of Marvel Comics and the creator of Spiderman and The Hulk – announced plans to develop an animated superhero based on Ringo, with Starr himself providing the voice.

Though mostly seen performing live in the US and largely resident in Monaco and Los Angeles, Ringo nonetheless received a hero's welcome upon arriving on stage at the Royal Albert Hall for the George Harrison tribute concert in November 2002. He was also welcomed back to UK chat shows both on TV (Frank Skinner) and radio (Steve Wright) on the back of some good reviews for his 2005 album *Choose Love*. Ringo's genial image took a bit of a knock however while promoting his 2008 album, *Liverpool 8*, when he admitted to missing nothing about his home town, where he had just been helping to celebrate its City of Culture status. Merseyside was unimpressed. The same year he broadcast a video message on his website that because he was too busy, all future fanmail to him would be "binned". That he signed off this stern announcement in his blithe "peace and love" fashion was hilariously lampooned on Chris Moyles' BBC Radio 1 show.

Whenever asked, he will pronounce that "life is just grand" and that he's having "a lot of fun". As the *New York Times* observed at an All-Starr show, "He seemed content behind his drums as his mates took their turns, acting like just another guy lucky enough to make the charts sometimes."

Sentimental Journey

SENTIMENTAL JOURNEY/NIGHT AND DAY/WHISPERING GRASS/BYE BYE BLACKBIRD/I'M A FOOL TO CARE/STARDUST/ BLUE TURNING GREY OVER YOU/LOVE IS A MANY SPLENDOURED THING/DREAM/YOU ALWAYS HURT THE ONE YOU LOVE/HAVE I TOLD YOU LATELY I LOVE YOU/LET THE REST OF THE WORLD GO BY

Apple; recorded November 1969–February 1970; released March 27, 1970; currently available on EMI CD

Recording this in the absence of anything else to occupy him ("What shall I do with my life, now that it's all over?") and to please his mum, Ringo got George Martin to produce and some real heavyweights (Quincy Jones, John Dankworth, Elmer Bernstein) to arrange a series of 1930s and 1940s standards for him to croon on. Considered an embarrassment at the time, there's a certain car-crash fascination in hearing Richie flat-footedly navigate the staircase melody of **Stardust** or make some sense of Oliver Nelson's crazy version of **Blue Turning Grey**. But generally, the cavernous discrepancy between the lavishness of the backing tracks, the quality of the songs and the foolishness of the singer makes this Ringo's best comedy record.

Ringo's two smash hits

It Don't Come Easy/Early 1970

Apple single; released April 1971

Back Off Boogaloo/Blindman

Apple single; released March 1972

A pair of thumping hit singles meant that for a while Ringo eclipsed the other Beatles as a commercial entity. Strange days. "It Don't Come Easy" was given a big push by Apple and the surprise of hearing Ringo singing some half-decent pop took it high into the charts. Self-penned (though from the sound of the chords, George Harrison may have been in the room when it was written) and with the help of Badfinger on backing vocals, it blunders agreeably and memorably along.

"Back Off Boogaloo" has more than a hint of Ringo's then-pal Marc Bolan about it and is as subtle and repetitive as a football terrace chant. Produced, like the first, by George Harrison, it sees Starr apparently (if obscurely) joining in the musical sniping at Paul McCartney. Both remain favourites of the All-Starr Band live shows.

Beaucoups Of Blues

BEAUCOUPS OF BLUES/LOVE DON'T LAST LONG/FASTEST GROWING HEARTACHE IN THE WEST/WITHOUT HER/ WOMAN OF THE NIGHT/I'D BE TALKING ALL THE TIME/$15 DRAW/WINE, WOMEN AND LOUD HAPPY SONGS/I WOULDN'T HAVE YOU ANY OTHER WAY/LOSER'S LOUNGE/WAITING/ SILENT HOMECOMING/

Apple; recorded June 1970; released September 1970; currently available on CD with bonus tracks "Coochy Coochy" and "Nashville Jam"

With his well-known affinity for country music (**Act Naturally** and **What Goes On** were two of his Beatles features), Ringo's mournful tones were marginally better suited to this authentic Nashville-recorded country set featuring Pete Drake, Charlie Daniels and many other Nashville sessioneers. But really, he's no less outclassed on this than he was on his debut. His fast-track graduation from leading a novelty feature on the best records around to leading his own albums was simply not working.

Ringo

I'M THE GREATEST/HAVE YOU SEEN MY BABY/PHOTOGRAPH/ SUNSHINE LIFE FOR ME (SAIL AWAY RAYMOND)/YOU'RE SIXTEEN/OH MY MY/STEP LIGHTLY/SIX O'CLOCK/DEVIL WOMAN/YOU AND ME (BABE)

Apple; recorded 1973; released December 1973

Goodnight Vienna

(IT'S ALL DA-DA-DOWN TO) GOODNIGHT VIENNA/ OCCAPELLA/OO-WEE/HUSBANDS AND WIVES/SNOOKEROO/ ALL BY MYSELF/CALL ME/NO NO SONG/ONLY YOU/EASY FOR ME/GOODNIGHT VIENNA (REPRISE)

Apple; recorded 1974; released November 1974; both albums currently available in the US on Capitol

With a little help from his fab friends (Harrison co-writes several, Lennon and McCartney contribute a song each and everyone appears at some point, though not all together), on *Ringo*, the drummer fronts a genuinely entertaining, varied pop album with much to recommend it. Apart from The Beatlesque moments (of which Lennon's sly **I'm The Greatest** is the most vivid), the Harrison/Starr-written hit **Photograph** is memorable and **You're Sixteen** is one of the great party records. There's also the out-and-out disco of **Oh My My** and the twinkle-toed **Step Lightly** (with Ringo taking a tap-dance break). A definite musical achievement and commercial triumph, and everyone involved deserves credit, with a special thumbs-up for producer Richard Perry.

Goodnight Vienna used the same producer and the same idea (a couple of oldies plus lots of special guests – Elton, Lennon, Allen Toussaint – writing and playing) but the songs weren't as good, so neither was the record.

Ringo's Rotogravure

A DOSE OF ROCK'N'ROLL/HEY BABY/PURE GOLD/CRYIN'/YOU DON'T KNOW ME AT ALL/COOKIN'/I'LL STILL LOVE YOU/ THIS BE CALLED A SONG/LAS BRISAS/LADY GAYE

Polydor; recorded 1976; released September 1976; available in the US on CD

Ringo The 4th

DROWNING IN THE SEA OF LOVE/TANGO ALL NIGHT/ WINGS/GAVE IT ALL UP/OUT IN THE STREETS/CAN SHE DO IT LIKE SHE DANCES/SNEAKING SALLY THROUGH THE ALLEY/ IT'S NO SECRET/GYPSIES IN FLIGHT/SIMPLE LOVE SONG

Polydor; recorded 1977; released September 1977; available in the US on CD

Bad Boy

WHO NEEDS A HEART/BAD BOY/LIPSTICK TRACES (ON A CIGARETTE)/HEART ON MY SLEEVE/WHERE DID MY HEART GO/HARD TIMES/TONIGHT/MONKEY SEE-MONKEY DO/OLD TIME RELOVIN'/A MAN LIKE ME

Portrait; recorded 1977–78; released April 1978; currently unavailable

A new label with a new producer, Arif Mardin, *Rotogravure* attempted to repeat the success of Ringo's star-studded formula, but was only partially successful. Ringo's take on Bruce Chanel's **Hey Baby** was spirited enough (and the song's revival as a party tune in 2001 suggests that he had been on to something) but Lennon's contribution, **Cookin'** (his last recorded song before four years as a house husband), was a sorry indication of the feeble turn his writing would take when he returned. *Ringo The 4th* largely consisted of Starr/Vini Poncia co-writes and with Mardin at the helm quickly descended into anonymous disco. Its commercial failure saw him at Portrait for *Bad Boy*, inexplicably released only half a year later, but the only people buying this dreary product by now were Beatle nuts and even they must have questioned why.

Stop And Smell The Roses

PRIVATE PROPERTY/WRACK MY BRAIN/DRUMMING IS MY BUSINESS/ATTENTION/STOP AND TAKE THE TIME TO SMELL THE ROSES/DEAD GIVEAWAY/YOU BELONG TO ME/SURE TO FALL IN LOVE WITH YOU/YOU'VE GOT A NICE WAY/BACK OFF BOOGALOO

Boardwalk; released October 1981; currently unavailable

Old Wave

IN MY CAR/HOPELESS/ALIBI/BE MY BABY/SHE'S ABOUT A MOVER/I KEEP FORGETTIN'/PICTURE SHOW LIFE/AS FAR AS WE CAN GO/EVERYBODY'S IN A HURRY BUT ME/GOING DOWN

RCA Canada; released June 1983; currently unavailable

Time Takes Time

WEIGHT OF THE WORLD/DON'T KNOW A THING ABOUT LOVE/DON'T GO WHERE THE ROAD DON'T GO/GOLDEN BLUNDERS/ALL IN THE NAME OF LOVE/AFTER ALL THESE YEARS/I DON'T BELIEVE YOU/RUNAWAYS/IN A HEARTBEAT/WHAT GOES AROUND

Private Music; released May 1992; currently unavailable

Vertical Man

ONE/WHAT IN THE . . . WORLD/MINDFIELD/KING OF BROKEN HEARTS/LOVE ME DO/VERTICAL MAN/DRIFT AWAY/I WAS WALKIN'/DE DA/WITHOUT UNDERSTANDING/I'LL BE FINE ANYWHERE/ PUPPET/I'M YOURS

Mercury; released April 1998; currently available on CD

I Wanna Be Santa Claus

COME ON CHRISTMAS, CHRISTMAS COME ON/WINTER WONDERLAND/I WANNA BE SANTA CLAUS/THE LITTLE DRUMMER BOY/RUDOLPH THE RED-NOSED REINDEER/ CHRISTMAS EVE/THE CHRISTMAS DANCE/CHRISTMAS TIME IS HERE AGAIN/BLUE CHRISTMAS/DEAR SANTA/WHITE CHRISTMAS/PAX UM BISCUM (PEACE BE WITH YOU)

Polygram; released October 1999; currently available on CD

Ringorama

EYE TO EYE/MISSOURI LOVES COMPANY/INSTANT AMNESIA/ MEMPHIS IN YOUR MIND/NEVER WITHOUT YOU/IMAGINE ME THERE/I THINK THEREFORE I ROCK'N'ROLL/TRIPPIN' ON MY OWN TEARS/WRITE ONE FOR ME/WHAT LOVE WANTS TO BE/LOVE FIRST, ASK QUESTIONS LATER/ELIZABETH REIGNS/ ENGLISH GARDEN

Koch; released March 2003; currently available on CD

Choose Love

FADING IN FADING OUT/GIVE ME BACK THE BEAT/OH MY LORD/HARD TO BE TRUE/SOME PEOPLE/WRONG ALL THE TIME/DON'T HANG UP/CHOOSE LOVE/ME AND YOU/ SATISFIED/THE TURNAROUND/FREE DRINKS

Koch; released June 2005, currently available on CD

Liverpool 8

LIVERPOOL 8/THINK ABOUT YOU/FOR LOVE/NOW THAT SHE'S GONE AWAY/GONE ARE THE DAYS/GIVE IT A TRY/TUFF LOVE/HARRY'S SONG/PASADOBLES/IF IT'S LOVE THAT YOU WANT/LOVE IS/R U READY

EMI; released January 2008

Most listeners have got the measure of Ringo's talent by now. No matter how competently made his records are – and he manages to attract some considerable talent to come and help out – they are still Ringo records. And other than a blip of commercial credibility in the early to mid-1970s, the public has voted with their feet and stayed away in their millions. Which is a shame in a way because they're not bad, but it's also understandable because they're not that good either.

1981's *Stop And Smell The Roses* nearly recaptured the *Ringo* magic, with two new McCartney songs, but not quite. 1983's Joe Walsh produced, defiantly titled *Old Wave* is the rarest of Starr discs, unreleased in the US until 1994, now deleted, and never released in the UK, but well regarded by Ringo cognoscenti. 1992's Don Was produced *Time Takes Time* was made with a new generation of collaborators. The first to capitalize on the fun-loving audiences wooed on his All-Starr tours, the record favoured a Beatles-meets-"Back Off Boogaloo" contemporary retro sound which suited Ringo well. He pursued this approach on 1998's *Vertical Man*, and also, surprisingly but effectively, on his *I Wanna Be Santa Claus*, his 1999 Christmas album. How come he took so long to get round to that one?

Mark Hudson, Ringo's by now regular producer, gathers one of Starr's more illustrious cast-lists (Eric Clapton, Willie Nelson, Van Dyke Parks) and fashions a tough, Beatlesque bounce for 2003's ***Ringorama***. However, it may be ***Choose Love*** (2005) that displays Ringo's latterday solo formula of upbeat anthems set to Fabs musical gestures at its most refined and entertaining. A falling-out with Hudson during *Liverpool 8* (2008) saw ex-Eurythmic Dave Stewart installed as "re-producer", resulting in another OK album. But the music's strengths (Ringo's amiable personality) and weaknesses (Ringo's amiable personality) remain the same.

Instant Ringo

Photograph

PHOTOGRAPH/IT DON'T COME EASY/YOU'RE SIXTEEN/ BACK OFF BOOGALOO/I'M THE GREATEST/OH MY MY/ONLY YOU/BEAUCOUPS OF BLUES/EARLY 1970/SNOOKEROO/NO NO SONG/GOODNIGHT VIENNA/OO-WEE/HAVE YOU SEEN MY BABY/SIX O'CLOCK/WEIGHT OF THE WORLD/NEVER WITHOUT YOU/ACT NATURALLY/WRACK MY BRAIN/FADING IN AND FADING OUT

EMI; released August 2007

Three-quarters of this useful 20-tracker were recorded in Ringo's best solo period (1970–75), while a handful of decent latter-day cuts makes up the rest. It replaces 1975's *Blast From Your Past* as the best place to sample solo Starr.

Part 4: The Beatles on Screen

The Beatles on Screen

The Beatles on TV (1962–68)

Some clips are available in the video *The Beatles Live Ready Steady Go! Special Edition* and DVD of *The Beatles' Anthology*

Britain in the early 1960s was still learning to love television. There were just two channels, broadcasting in black and white from late afternoon (aside from morning schools broadcasts) until midnight at the latest. The BBC still respected the edict of its founder, Lord Reith, that public broadcasting should be improving and serious. Independent or commercial TV offered some second-channel choice from the mid-50s – "What's on the other side?" – with programming that was generally more populist than the BBC (though ITV was hampered by being divided into regional stations which didn't always broadcast programmes simultaneously).

Even to contemporary eyes, the entertainment both channels provided was old-fashioned stuff, variety shows peopled with stage comics and nightclub singers, and delights like the bellowing cockney bandleader Billy Cotton, and the Black and White Minstrels, who dragged light entertainment high-kicking back to the 1890s.

When The Beatles first appeared, there were a few signs of change afoot; *That Was The Week That Was* was considered shocking for poking fun at politics in 1962, but the 1960s spirit we understand today was still a few years off. That The Beatles could introduce some sort of youth culture into the nation's living rooms via the **Royal Command Performance** and delight an audience aged from 8 to 80 says something about both their impact and their uniqueness. Their value as a link with a new world shouldn't be underestimated. If they'd done nothing else but play **Twist And Shout** in front of the **Queen Mother** they'd have made a difference, so austere and entrenched was Britain at the time.

This was the message that, consciously or not, they beamed into homes across Britain when they hit TV: "We are the right thing at the right time. It's in all our interests that the future is exciting and here it comes: homegrown, funny, classless and sexy." **Cliff Richard and the Shadows** and **Tommy Steele** had been a once-removed reaction to the impact of Elvis

Presley – a revolutionary sound born to another culture – and were quickly absorbed into the status quo. The Beatles were fresh local produce who ushered in a new status quo and drew up new templates that they bequeathed to the groups who followed them. Their TV performances were polite, well-groomed, unthreatening affairs (Lennon's occasional notorious "spastic" imitations notwithstanding) but The Beatles were a Trojan horse concealing the future. And the beautiful part was, while Britain was as dumbly welcoming as the Trojans, The Beatles were probably as oblivious to what they were carrying as was the wooden horse.

All they knew was that they needed the exposure, and the programme makers quickly discovered that booking The Beatles resulted in a measurable surge in the ratings. This being the case, the group was able to call the shots from early on. They were given more airtime than other groups ever had, and were rarely forced to endure the sometimes patronizing treatment other pop acts accepted to appear on TV. You could sense established programmes trying hard to understand this new thing and how it should be presented to make everyone look good, or "with it" as they said then.

Its regional emphasis meant that it was independent television that was first to embrace the group. The Beatles made eleven appearances on northern magazine programmes like *People and Places* (their first broadcast was on October 17, 1962), and the programme that took over its slot, *Scene at 6.30*, before securing a booking on the BBC's *625 Show* in April 1963. Their other regular slot was *Thank Your Lucky Stars*, ATV's Birmingham-based show, which was the nation's favourite pop programme in the early 1960s. The Beatles' eight appearances on it in 1963 consolidated that status.

The BBC's Saturday teatime challenger to TYLS was ***Juke Box Jury***, where new records were played while the cameras scanned the audience and four panellists – usually comedians, actors, DJs or beauty queens – listened and tapped their toes before judging the songs either a "Hit" or a "Miss". This was riveting stuff in 1963. John was on the panel in June. All four made up the jury on December 7. Then a couple of hours later – under the title **It's the Beatles!** – the BBC broadcast a full live set from the Empire Liverpool. The Beatles were so popular that the BBC was happy to devote the majority of an entire Saturday night's viewing to them.

The station could do this with confidence because in October The Beatles had topped the bill on ITV's top-rated *Sunday Night at The London Palladium* and then, in November, had stolen the show at The Royal Command Performance. There had also been major documentaries on the rise of The Beatles and Mersey Beat on both channels. There was nothing hotter in the world of entertainment.

Sure enough, 23 million people tuned in to the all-Beatles edition of *Juke Box Jury*. This represented a kind of fame that artists today, with huge amounts of TV exposure – whole channels devoted to pop and several daily outlets – can only dream of. The entertain-

Backstage, McCartney shows Ed Sullivan the bassline to "All My Loving", February 1964

ment establishment, in the form of **The Variety Club of Great Britain**, had no choice but to award The Beatles the title of "Showbusiness Personalities of 1963".

In 1964, the visit to America would result in nothing less than a piece of TV history. Reports of Beatlemania had cropped up on US news bulletins in November 1963, and a clip of the group performing **She Loves You** for the BBC's *Mersey Sound* documentary (shot in August 1963) had been seen on the popular *Jack Paar Show* on January 3, 1964. It featured the tidily honed choreography which, along with the record, had seduced the UK:

• Lennon singing lead crouching alone at the left mic, dangerously open-legged; Paul harmonizing on the right

• George stepping forward to share Paul's microphone for his "I saw her yesterday" harmony; Paul politely making way; George stepping back again (repeated as necessary)

• Paul and George shaking their moptops on the "oohs" inducing knicker-wetting frenzy from the female audience

• Final "yeah" chord rings with a flourish of guitars, followed swiftly by a beautifully coordinated low bow.

Perhaps that's all it took to make their then current US single leap from #43 to #1 in the US charts a fortnight later and thus inspire 73 million Americans to tune in to The Beatles' debut on *The Ed Sullivan Show* on February 9. That incredible figure remains an unbeaten record for a variety show.

Back home, the pleasure in this triumph swelled to national pride – so much so that the BBC was happy, perhaps obliged, to interrupt the hallowed Saturday afternoon sports show *Grandstand* with a thirteen-minute report on the group's arrival back on British soil, and an interview with presenter **David Coleman**. Only someone who lived in Britain during the 1960s can fully appreciate how momentous that was. The next day they taped their second appearance on variety show *Big Night Out* and, soon after, their first on *Top of the Pops* – the BBC's superior new answer to *Thank Your Lucky Stars* and *Ready Steady Go!* Only The Beatles were ever asked to play both sides of a new single, in this case **Can't Buy Me Love** and **You Can't Do That**.

One of the costume requirements for *Around The Beatles*, April 1964

In April, they guested on *The Morecambe and Wise Show* (filmed in late 1963), fooling around with Eric and singing barbershop quartet with Ernie. On May 6 a sixty-minute special, *Around The Beatles*, became their first and last variety TV special as hosts, during which they played a short set and donned clownish costumes for a spoof of Shakespeare's *A Midsummer Night's Dream*.

By July of 1964 The Beatles were world famous and had released their big-screen debut, *A Hard Day's Night*. The need for constant promotional TV appearances was less pressing and they began to thin out. Occasionally, they would make one when a single was due – George and Ringo returned to *Juke Box Jury* and the group performed on a few more variety and award shows – but by 1965 the cosy world of family entertainment was looking less

The Beatles' cartoon series

In November 1964, **King Features Syndicate**, a well-known American distributor of TV cartoons and comic books, announced that work had begun on an animated Beatles TV series. The shows would follow the tone of *A Hard Day's Night*. Each half-hour show contained two songs and took a total of seventy artists a month to complete. In the UK 26 were made by Soho animation house **TVC**, and another 26 were divided between teams in Australia and Canada. Originally it was hoped that The Beatles themselves would improvise dialogue for the series, but this proved impractical, so two actors were hired to be The Beatles. American Paul Frees tackled John and George while British comic actor Lance Percival was Paul and Ringo. Neither sounded remotely like any of them.

An artist named **Peter Sander** drew up the templates for the animated Fabs designed to capitalise on the caricatures of the group as suggested by *A Hard Day's Night*. His stylesheets included the following guidelines:

- "John pulls funny faces especially after giving orders. Slightly queer showbiz gestures can be used in long shot. Gives the feeling that John doesn't take his job as leader seriously."
- "Paul is the most poised and stylish Beatle. He always looks straight at whoever he's talking to. He's the one who gets excited when John says anything."
- "George never looks at who he is talking to. Nearly always gives the impression of frowning. Always leans against something. Shoulders hunched, hands in pockets, legs crossed."
- "Ringo looks a bit disjointed whether walking or standing. Keep upper lip protruding. Keep hair at back long and shaggy. Keep mouth in a wavy line. When Ringo laughs, having made a funny remark, he squints."

Plot lines tended to be daft fantasies which prefigured ***Help!*** and were usually contrived to fit around the two songs selected for each episode. Shows produced in Australia had an unpleasant tendency to include evil, "Yellow Peril" stereotypes as the villains, and seem more than a little xenophobic. However, the show was a smash hit in the US when it premiered in September 1965, easily topping the ratings.

The Beatles themselves hated it – Lennon was heard to complain of being made to look like "the bloody Flintstones" – and it was never properly broadcast in Britain, bar a few episodes being shown on regional commercial stations in the mid-1970s and late 1980s. King's archive of scripts and animation cels were destroyed in the early 1990s; Apple since bought out the rights to the programmes but shows no signs of making them available again.

relevant to their ambitions.

During the American tour of that year, they paid a final visit to *The Ed Sullivan Show*. Sullivan's production company sent a film crew to **Shea Stadium** on August 15 for an engrossing colour record of the event in an hour-long slot. *The Beatles at Shea Stadium* was first shown in the UK on March 1, 1966, and in the US, oddly, on January 10, 1967. Back home, 1965 ended with a television special, *The Music of Lennon & McCartney*, featuring guests as varied as Cilla Black, **Peter Sellers** and flamenco dancer Antonio Vargas.

The following year they did hardly any TV at all. Their *Top of the Pops* performance playing **Paperback Writer** and **Rain** on June 16, 1966, marked both their first live appearance on the show and their last live TV pop show appearance anywhere. Once ubiquitous on our TV screens, The Beatles, now also retired from touring, were suddenly distant and unreachable.

In 1967 *Our World*, a huge pan-global live broadcast on June 25, marked the arrival of satellite facilities to link the world's TV networks. It seemed only fitting that Britain's contribution to this worldwide get-together should be the world's most famous pop group unveiling, less than a month after *Sgt Pepper*, their new single, **All You Need Is Love,** before an audience estimated to be around four-hundred million viewers.

With rococo "flower child" clothing and freshly psychedelicized guitars, The Beatles sat on high stools in the middle of Abbey Road studios in a mock-up of a recording session, surrounded by beaded-and-belled friends and celebrities (including **Mick Jagger**, **Eric Clapton** and **Marianne Faithfull**), who gazed adoringly upward and sang along. The Beatles were never so affiliated in the public's mind as part of the peace-and-love generation as here. If it hadn't already, the Summer of Love went global from this moment.

That Christmas, the dubious pleasures of *Magical Mystery Tour* premiered a new kind of TV show, which neither The Beatles nor anyone else felt inclined to pursue afterwards. On September 9, 1968, a pre-filmed insert of the group part-miming **Hey Jude** for David Frost's *Frost on Sunday* was their final musical TV appearance. Subdued, seated and, for much of the song, surrounded by audience members singing along with the chorus, they looked little like the young masters of the box who stole a nation's hearts in black and white, less than half a dozen years earlier.

Beatles movies

A Hard Day's Night

1964; currently available on digitally remastered two-disc DVD, with several extra hours of interviews with cast and crew (note: an earlier VHS release featured the cut "You Can't Do That" performance)

Known in Italy as *Tutti per uno* (*All For One*) and in France as *Quatre garçons dans le vent* (*Four Boys In The Wind*), The Beatles' first movie was immeasurably better than it need have been, thanks to several factors.

One of them was the personal charisma and energy of The Beatles themselves, which had prompted George Martin to sign them in the first place, and which transferred itself to screen, and therefore the world, charmingly.

There was also the fact that **Dick Lester** was precisely the sort of "kick bollock and scramble" director who could convey and enhance The Beatles' natural qualities. Furthermore, Alun Owen's script was both plausible, and funny, with an authentic vernacular wit. Then there was the crisp black-and-white photography, amking the movie look like a kooky but credible arthouse movie, rather than a business-driven cash-in. Add to that the songwriting flair the group had developed in eighteen months and *A Hard Day's Night* had little problem enchanting both the public and the critics. "I must say," sputtered the amazed *Village Voice* film critic Andrew Sarris, "I enjoyed even the music enormously."

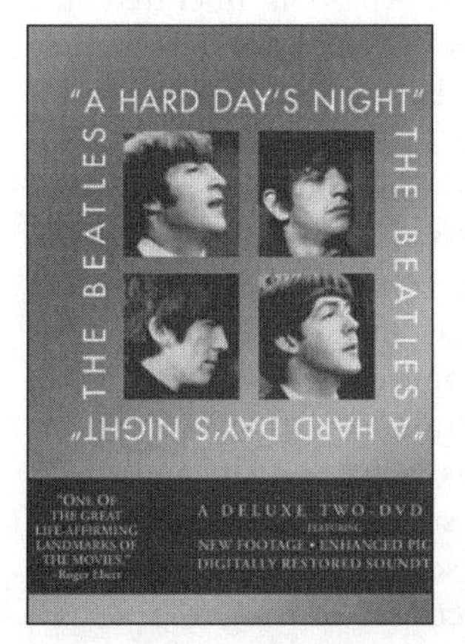

The film came about thanks to **George "Bud" Ornstein**, an American executive for **United Artists** based in London in 1963 and an enthusiastic socialite and anglophile. When UA employee Noel Rogers suggested there might be some mileage in a movie of the pop group that was dominating the culture in Britain that year, Ornstein appointed producer **Walter Shenson** and they approached Brian Epstein with a three-picture deal in the autumn of 1963. UA would make the films and, if the group took off in the US, would keep rights to the soundtrack albums too.

For its day this was a radical suggestion. Pop films were pot boilers at best. Flimsy plots would be threaded together by cameos from lame comics or DJs and awkward-looking performances by usually ephemeral singers. Many of these movies were modelled on 1950s rock'n'roll cash-ins like ***The Girl Can't Help It***, though were seldom as good. Nevertheless, UA calculated a low budget would make money on the film's British income alone and began negotiations. Epstein thought he was striking a hard bargain for The Beatles' share by starting the bidding at 7.5 percent. However, The Beatles' lawyer, David Jacobs, subsequently secured 25 percent.

In February 1964, The Beatles made their triumphant debut in America. So by the time the eight-week shoot began on March 2, the film's worldwide success was assured. Though the decision had been made to shoot in black and white to save money, United Artists took orders for 500,000 soundtrack albums while shooting was still in progress, making back the modest budget of £200,000 before the movie was even finished. By release day, 2.5 million copies of the album had been advance-ordered.

Walter Shenson hired Richard Lester (whom he'd worked with on a typically silly British jukebox movie called *It's Trad, Dad*) and playwright **Alun Owen** and arranged a meeting in Paris in January 1964 as the Fabs began their season at the Paris Olympia. Philadelphian Lester was a musician and TV presenter who had moved to Britain in 1955 and briefly starred in his own TV series, *The Dick Lester Show* (which also featured Owen). A friendship with Peter Sellers and **Spike Milligan** of *The Goon Show* led to his directing them in *A Show Called Fred* on TV and a quirky short feature called *The Running, Jumping, Standing Still Film*. As when they first met George Martin, the Goons connection appealed to The Beatles and a rapport was struck.

Owen, a Welshman based in Liverpool, had met the group before and had already begun drafting ideas based on their very particular group dynamic. His initial script had a fantasy feel to it but, after Paris, he decided that the group's everyday existence was stranger than fiction and decided to try and capture that instead. The film had a variety of working titles, among them, *Beatlemania*, *What Little Old Man?* (a line of dialogue from the opening scene), *On The Move* and *Let's Go!* The phrase "A Hard Day's Night" was a Ringoism which had also appeared in John's book, *In His Own Write*, published a few weeks after filming began on March 23.

The plot, such as it is, centres around a day in the life of the group as they travel to London to film a TV show. With them on the train are road managers Norm and Shake (played by Norman Rossington and John Junkin, based nominally on Neil Aspinall and Mal Evans). Paul's grandfather (played by Wilfred Brambell, known in the UK for playing **Albert Steptoe** in *Steptoe and Son*) proves to be a disruptive influence, sneaking off to wreak havoc in a gambling club, a press conference and the TV studio where he needles Ringo who then goes AWOL, jeopardizing the TV appearance. After a series of solo adventures, including a fight in a pub and eventual arrest, Ringo is liberated just in time for the live TV slot for which they sing several songs before a screaming audience. Then it's onto a helicopter and off to the next show. As individuals, The Beatles had variable success at losing their self-consciousness in front of the camera. John had an obvious presence tinged with slight menace but appeared physically awkward. Paul, the most theatrically aware (thanks to recent playgoing with his actress girlfriend), was sweet-looking but stiff and it was his unsuccessful "signature scene" – a meeting with a "Shakespearean actress" during the search for Ringo – which was cut, being considered one contrivance too far. George, according to Dick Lester the most "accurate" of the four, breezed through it. Ringo was singly praised for his Buster Keaton-like melancholy on the Thames towpath scene, though he confessed later his performance had much to do with having an enormous hangover.

Although the group would come to resent the inevitable stereotypes that Owen's "enhancements" of their characters presented in the film (Paul – charming; John – witty and cynical; George – deep; Ringo – funny and cute), the film was an enormous help for the world to perceive The Beatles as identifiable individuals beyond being identikit moptops with "something of the 'Midwich Cuckoos' about them", as Jonathan Miller observed.

Together, however, their tightly scripted ensemble scenes generated an attractive, intriguingly intimate exclusivity (very much the "four-headed monster" that **Mick Jagger** remembered meeting in Richmond in 1963), while their on-screen presence as a group had an immense, gawky appeal. Why the sight of four young men in tight suits running around in a field or up a London street, all flailing limbs and unfeasible hair, should cause such pleasure is unclear. It just does.

A late hiccup in an otherwise smooth production was a United Artists suggestion after an early screening that The Beatles' Liverpudlian voices be re-dubbed by American actors. Happily, Lester and Shenson flatly refused, though the final edit was ready only a few days before the "Royal World Premiere", held at the London Pavilion on July 6. Opening in five hundred American theatres in August, the movie was a hit worldwide, mustering over $14 million in its first run and winning rave reviews everywhere. Andrew Sarris famously anointed it "the *Citizen Kane* of jukebox movies".

Help!

1965; currently unavailable in the UK; available on VHS and DVD in the USA

By the time their second movie was due, The Beatles were so enormously famous that the prospect of capering about on screen didn't

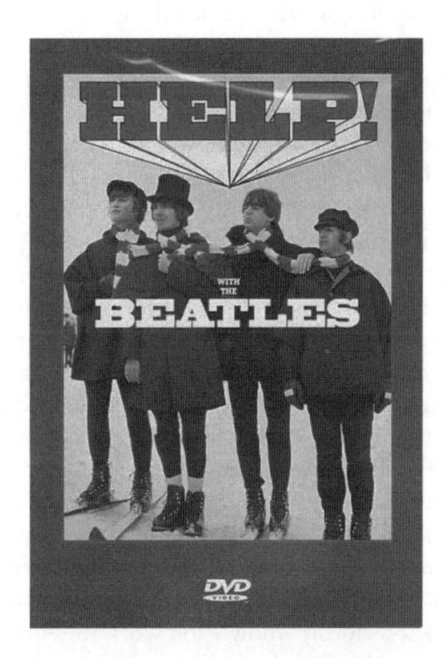

hold the appeal for them it once had. "None of us are very good in movies," Paul told a reporter shortly after *A Hard Day's Night* was released, before admitting that John and Ringo weren't bad. The reporter remarked that people thought Paul was good too. "Well they're wrong," he replied. "I thought I was terrible actually."

"I hope there are no songs in it," George said when the new film was announced in October 1964. "And I don't mind colour in a film if it doesn't mean dancing about in a red shirt, like in one of Cliff's. I don't like that." The plan for the follow-up, then, was to have more screen-time taken up with sub-plot, to focus on Ringo, who seemed the least reluctant screen presence, and to visit exotic locations so that there could be an element of holiday about the shoot.

Director Richard Lester was hired again but decided against "professional Liverpudlian" (as Lennon called him) Alun Owen for the screenplay this time. With friend Joe McGrath, Lester came up with an intriguing plot line: Ringo is told he is terminally ill and hires a hit man to kill him suddenly and painlessly. But the next day, he's informed the diagnosis was a mistake, thus changing his mind about being bumped off early, but being unable to contact his putative killer. With hilarious results.

Unfortunately, this turned out to be the plot of another film being shot at the same time (*Les tribulations d'un chinois en Chine*, starring **Jean-Paul Belmondo**). So screenwriter Marc Behn (previously known for work on Audrey Hepburn's *Charade*) came up with another Ringo-in-peril tale involving his inadvertent ownership of a sacred ring, which makes him the sacrificial target of a bungling religious sect led by **Leo McKern**. Lester felt the result lacked Englishness and approached Charles Wood – who had scripted Lester's other hit of 1964, *The Knack* – to graft a British quality onto the transcontinental capers.

The eleven-week shoot began in Barbados on February 22, 1965. The budget was three times the size of *A Hard Day's Night*, but still only in the medium range of about £600,000. The film's working title was ***Eight Arms To Hold You*** (a neat double-reference to the Fab Four and the multi-armed statue of the goddess Kali that rises out of the sea in the movie), but Lester had wanted to use the title *Help, Help*. He finally settled for the single word with exclamation mark in April. The title song was written by Lennon less than thirty hours later.

Completed in May and premiered in London on July 29, ***Help!*** was lusher, sillier but definitely inferior to its predecessor. One or two of the set pieces sparkle (the speedily edited comic tableaux of the "Ticket To Ride" skiing scene, the beautifully lit "studio recording" of "You're Going To Lose That Girl"), but the story-line is banal and borderline racist, and the sidelined wacky larks of the lads seem particularly forced. When they weren't singing, The Beatles simply weren't very good. For all of *Help!*'s occasional cartoon-style energy – and with much screen time given to the supporting players, presumably to compensate for the main attractions' thespian ineptitude – the film feels long and uninteresting.

Doing well to stay upright whilst filming *Help!* in the Bahamas

"*Help!* was a drag," said Lennon later. "We were on pot by then and all the best stuff, with us breaking up and falling about, was left on the cutting room floor." A long sequence with comedian **Frankie Howerd** was among the discarded footage. "Frankie just couldn't work with The Beatles," remembered Lester. "To him, The Beatles were just on another planet." Even the laid-back Lester lost patience trying to get sensible performances out of the giggling group. Lester was still dismayed, however – when he came to look for the unused tape for ***Help!***'s video release – to discover it had been destroyed in 1966 when the studio's storage space was being reorganized.

Critics were justifiably less enthusiastic than they had been for ***A Hard Day's Night***. Even Lester was offhand about it in the press. "You'll find nothing new about Help! There's not one bit of insight into our times. It's a comic strip adventure." But audiences flocked to see it anyway and its flashy, mildly surreal pop-art style was a massive influence on several seminal 1960s TV series, notably ***Batman*** and, of course, ***The Monkees***.

Magical Mystery Tour (1967)

1967; currently available in the US on DVD

After they made the decision to stop touring, The Beatles discussed other ways to reach their public when they weren't releasing records. The obvious answer appeared to be television. Specials by entertainers like **Frank Sinatra** were

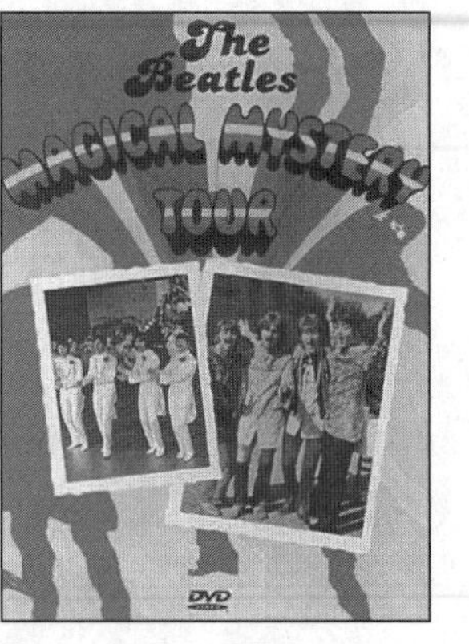

commonplace in the 1960s and The Beatles saw a chance to gate-crash the medium and do something unusual at the same time.

Paul had been visiting Jane Asher in the US. In a park in Denver, with Mal Evans, he came up with the idea of a chara-banc trip peopled by a motley bunch of character actors, comics, musicians and freaks, a **Magical Mystery Tour** where the participants would create the film: they'd plan a few activities en route, write a few songs, just let things happen organically and shoot the ensuing fun. There was possibly an element of **Ken Kesey** and his **Merry Pranksters** about the idea, too. Kesey, famously, had been wandering around America with a bus full of hippies compiling a movie (that never appeared) called *The Merry Pranksters Search For A Cool Place*. Paul, who'd just been hanging with **Jefferson Airplane** in San Francisco, would undoubtedly have heard of it.

On the plane back to the UK, Paul and Mal drew up a pie chart of what might take place in an hour-long film – a song here, a dream-sequence there – and each Beatle would be given a scene to write or a song slot to fill. Shot in colour, the project would eventually also yield an unusual six-song double EP with a lavish book of pictures, cartoons and lyrics, making a pricey but delightful Christmas bonanza from the Fabs to their fans. Planning began under Brian Epstein. Budgets were approved and the title song was recorded in April. After Brian's sudden death, The Beatles decided to continue, with much of the organizing, directing and editing left to Paul. But the hiring of crew and talent was a skill none of The Beatles possessed and it was rather haphazardly done. Little thought was given to whether the cast would mix or even understand the concept, let alone whether anybody would generate the kind of footage they needed.

Nevertheless, there were some good ideas in the mix and The Beatles attacked the project with gusto. Shooting took place in Devon, Cornwall, and on an abandoned airbase near Maidstone, Kent. The cast included Scottish poet **Ivor Cutler**, music-hall comic Nat Jackley, and absurdist rockers **The Bonzo Dog Doo Dah Band**. The budget was £40,000, but the anticipated two-week edit ended up taking eleven weeks and Paul approached the BBC with little time to make the Christmas slot he was after. They got Boxing Night (and a second, colour, showing on BBC2 on January 5) although, because of the unusual nature of the film, they were paid only £9000 by the BBC. (It was subsequently sold all round the world, however, and was shown in cinemas in the US, generating millions of dollars in rentals.)

When it premiered on BBC1 it was shown in black and white, which rendered sequences

The Fabs roll up for the Mystery tour, September 1967

Certain sequences remain entertaining, though. John's cameo as a waiter serving Ringo's corpulent Aunt Jessie a wheelbarrow full of spaghetti is one. Paul's **Fool On The Hill** interlude (shot in late October in Nice, France, while editing was well underway) has a sweet trippiness to it, and the closing big production job on **Your Mother Should Know**, where the Fab Four turn Fred Astaire and high-kick dressed in white tuxedos, is cute. Less engaging today are the **I Am The Walrus** segment, which looks like an amateurish video, and the boys' capering about as wizards in the clouds, controlling the tour.

like the psychedelic cloud ballet that accompanies **Flying** utterly pointless, but its main failing was its inappropriateness for its slot. More French New Wave than family Christmas viewing, it baffled a British public expecting easily digestible light entertainment from the loveable moptops. Reviews panned it for being a giant home-movie, self-indulgent and embarrassing. Seen now, in colour, and judged in the avant-garde, stoned spirit in which it was made, it fares slightly better, but is undoubtedly flabby and, generally, dull.

But Paul and John remained proud of the results. "I enjoyed the fish and chip quality," said John, "the fact that we went out with a load of freaks and tried to make a film is great, you know?"

"I really had to carry the can when it got bad reviews," says Paul. 'But by the same argument I can now take credit for the cool little film I still think it is."

The biopics

Various aspects of The Beatles' story have been enacted on the screen down the years. Though there is a certain embarrassment in viewing a series of young actors struggle with often inelegant caricatures of the Fabs in imaginary or amusingly simplified dramatic reductions of the tale (especially in the handful of made-for-TV movies about John Lennon), most are oddly watchable for the very same reasons.

The atmospheric Hamburg-to-Beatlemania ***The Birth Of The Beatles*** (1979) was the only one made in Lennon's lifetime. Shot on location, it employed Pete Best as technical advisor, but that didn't stop it being – like all these films to some degree – an error-laden fiction.

The Hours And Times (1991) was a sensitively handled chamber-piece about Lennon and Brian Epstein, concentrating on their trip to Barcelona in 1963. Ian Hart was especially acclaimed for his performance as John Lennon and reprised the role for ***Backbeat*** (1994). Covering a similar period as *The Birth Of The Beatles*, the focus on Stuart Sutcliffe's story brought a welcome unfamiliar slant to the story. Featuring intelligent direction, good performances and a decent soundtrack, it's one of the better biopics.

Two Of Us (2000) takes as its setting the evening in 1976 when Lennon and McCartney spent the evening together in Lennon's home in New York watching Lorne Michaels' offer to reunite The Beatles on *Saturday Night Live*. Speculating wildly as to the dialogue and emotional significance of the meeting, the film veers dangerously close to sentimental wish-fulfilment. However, at least it had the advantage of being directed by Michael Lindsay-Hogg who, as the director of ***Let It Be***, had observed both men closely in real life.

Yellow Submarine

1968; available on digitally remastered DVD

Canadian **George Dunning**, co-founder of a small Soho animation house, **TVC**, had doubts about the offer to make a full-length cartoon feature for The Beatles. It came from **Al Brodax**, producer at **King Features**, the American company that had employed TVC to work on their Beatles TV series. George was worried that there wasn't much steam left in the frolicsome boys who'd peopled their cartoons. While the project was being discussed in the spring of 1967, George Martin invited him and TVC partner **John Coates** to Abbey Road to hear the album The Beatles had just completed. One listen to ***Sgt Pepper's Lonely Hearts Club Band*** was all it took to convince Dunning of the project's viability.

Pepper tipped them off that this film could and should be more ambitious than anything they'd attempted before. The Beatles themselves expressed anxiety about the project, given their dislike of the animated TV series. They didn't want a cartoon bearing their name to be twee or to smack of Disney. TVC agreed. Not that a Disney-scale production was an option. By the time the contracts had been signed, there were only eleven months left to complete the film – the night of the premiere had been booked for

July 1968 – and a budget of just £385,000. Absorbed in *Sgt Pepper*, and beginning work on *Magical Mystery Tour*, The Beatles had had no time to be involved in the film's genesis. Brodax's search for a suitable screenplay writer unearthed young **Lee Mintoff.** The Beatles met and approved him, but rejected much of his fairytale script. Around forty writers contributed to the script, among them Liverpudlian poet **Roger McGough**, colleague of McCartney's brother Mike from Merseyside comedy group The Scaffold, who was hired to provide credible Liverpudlian dialogue; and **Erich Segal** – a young American English professor who was working with composer Richard Rodgers and went on to write *Love Story* – was employed as a script doctor. A final script wouldn't be assembled until the film was actually complete, a few days before the premiere.

Meanwhile, TVC began work anyway. A team of Britain's best animation directors were hired to tackle separate sequences, having come up with the idea that different animations for different songs would be linked by an overall story line. Work began on some of the musical numbers but the appearance of The Beatles themselves hadn't been finalized. Special-effects director Charlie Jenkins brought in a copy of an impressive German magazine called ***Twen***, and suggested they contact its gifted Czech art director Heinz Edelmann. Within a fortnight, Edelmann delivered drawings that stunned the animators. Recognisably the Fabs, the figures captured the spirit of the time with their vivid colours and soft, balloonish graphics. Edelmann would also suggest the villains of the piece, the **Blue Meanies**, and did much to outline the atmosphere of the whole film.

A few weeks into production, Brian Epstein died. The Beatles withdrew and were unavailable to provide the voice-track needed to begin shooting the group scenes, so TVC found actors who could mimic their voices. Almost every young animator in London was employed on the project: over two hundred animators, artists, tracers, colourists and background painters. A special nightshift was bussed in from London's art schools. Such a concentration of bright young things in one place in the Summer of Love had inevitable consequences: some thirteen babies were conceived during the making of ***Yellow Submarine***.

The film concerns the invasion of an underwater paradise, **Pepperland**, somewhere in the Sea of Green, by its neighbours, the Blue Meanies, who hate anything to do with music, colour or positive vibes. They silence Sgt Pepper's Lonely Hearts Club Band and literally petrify the locals, but one man, **Young Fred**, escapes in the vessel of the country's founding fathers – a yellow submarine. He turns up in Liverpool, where he follows Ringo and recruits The Beatles to help restore order in Pepperland. They return via various underwater distractions – The Sea of Time, The Sea of Monsters and The Sea of Holes, which provide opportunities to break into song and pick up Nowhere Man, Jeremy the Boob, to defeat the Meanies and rescue their doubles in Sgt Pepper's band by singing **All You Need Is Love.**

The interest of The Beatles themselves grew

as they saw the quality of the rushes. They would occasionally visit TVC and monitor progress and agreed to be filmed for the film's closing sequence. The last of their contracted four new songs was delivered late, however. The **Hey Bulldog** sequence was shot hurriedly in the final weeks of production. After the UK premiere it was decided that the ending dragged and this slapstick sequence – the closest in spirit to the TV series – was removed before the US premiere, consequently baffling American purchasers of the soundtrack album.

Perhaps its psychedelic mood already seemed dated by July 1968, perhaps United Artists' marketing of *Yellow Submarine* as a children's cartoon was misguided. Whatever, distributors Rank quickly scaled down the number of theatres the film was shown in and doomed it to modest receipts in Britain. But it was enthusiastically reviewed in America and did much better business there. A riot of visual delights, which still looks extraordinary even after the advent of computer animation, *Yellow Submarine* is a rare document of its time that has matured as the years have passed.

Promotional films (1965–69)

Most clips available on *The Beatles Anthology* video and DVD

We Can Work It Out/Day Tripper/Help/Ticket To Ride/I Feel Fine

As The Beatles tired of touring, so did they tire of TV appearances, and in late 1965 they turned to promotional films, the forerunner of the pop video, to visually plug their music without the group having to drag themselves from studio to studio. Inspired by *The Music Of Lennon & McCartney*, the Granada TV special in which they had taken part on November 1–2, 1965, The Beatles hired Twickenham Studios and a production team headed by director **Joe McGrath**. Over a single day, November 23, 1965, The Beatles filmed two black-and-white video versions each, of five different songs. The multiple promos policy enabled them to offer different films to different programmes. Ranging from straightforward mimed group performances in their Shea Stadium suits to semi-surreal clips involving some half-hearted horseplay with gym equipment and a white umbrella, most of the footage was rather bland and lackadaisical, though they did their job in that all the films were shown around the world except one: Brian Epstein blocked the version of **I Feel Fine** which showed the group eating fish and chips, making no attempt to mime whatsoever.

Paperback Writer/Rain

Michael Lindsay-Hogg had already filmed The Beatles for *Ready Steady Go!* several times and was hired to shoot promos for both sides of The Beatles' June 1966 single. Gathering at Abbey Road studios on May 19, 1966, two black-and-white (UK TV was to broadcast only in monochrome until late 1967) performance promos of both sides of their current single were shot. The following day, in the grounds and gardens of Chiswick House, West London, colour promos were filmed for showing in the US on *The Ed Sullivan Show*, complete with insert sequences in which the group sent spoken messages to their American fans apologizing for not being there in person: "Everybody's busy these days," said Ringo, "with the washing… "

Lindsay-Hogg went some way to conveying the deeper mood of The Beatles' new music by going for many facial close-ups showing the startlingly shaggy Fabs looking moodily inscrutable in their shades. However, the cutaways to the uncomfortable group miming with their guitars in a huge greenhouse (made even more absurd by Ringo – drumless – sitting around redundant) betray the fact that no one was yet taking these promos particularly seriously as a credible aspect of The Beatles' art.

Strawberry Fields Forever/Penny Lane

Recommended by Klaus Voormann, Swedish pop TV director **Peter Goldmann** was trusted with the job of introducing the new moustachioed Beatles to the world in early 1967. Selecting National Trust land in Knole Park, Sevenoaks, Kent, he filmed The Beatles there on January 30–31 cavorting around a huge dead oak tree that was attached to a piano with hundreds of strands of cobweb-like string for "Strawberry Fields Forever". Beautifully and spookily lit – especially in the sequences filmed at dusk – much attention is given to close-ups of The Beatles' faces and facial hair, as if the viewer is invited to contemplate the significance of the newly furry Fabs. There's an appropriately surreal air about the film (John wears a tie across his face, McCartney – in a reversed sequence – flies effortlessly backwards from the ground onto a tall tree branch) which, when experienced simultaneously with The Beatles' extraordinary new music, is deliciously disorientating. The final scene of The Beatles pouring pots of coloured paint onto the "piano" is oddly shocking, but brilliantly memorable as a statement of iconoclastic artistic intent.

On February 5 The Beatles were filmed in East London on horseback, and John was filmed walking up and down Angel Lane, Stratford, for the gentler "Penny Lane" promo. These scenes were interspersed with shots of the actual Penny Lane in Liverpool (the shelter and the barber's shop), although The Beatles themselves were not present. The shoot culminated back at Knole Park, where the red-hunting-jacket-adorned group were filmed taking tea at an outdoor dinner table. Bewigged Renaissance waiters present them with their guitars whereupon John, in another iconoclastic gesture, up-ends the table and its contents. Compared to the "Strawberry Fields" promo, "Penny Lane" seems little more than an extra-curricular afterthought, but as a further document of the revolutionary times, it's good to see.

A Day In The Life

On February 10, 1967, seven hand-held cameras were put in the overall charge of NEMS employee Tony Bramwell at Abbey Road studios to capture the "event" that was the orchestral overdub of "A Day In The Life". The rather disordered but atmospheric results – featuring the orchestra (instructed by The Beatles to wear evening dress, false noses, wigs and plastic nipples) and an invited host of swinging London celebs – were going to be part of a promo for the song but, after it was banned by the BBC, the footage was to be made part of a 1967 *Sgt Pepper* TV special which never materialized. The freaky footage wasn't seen generally until the ***Anthology*** series nearly thirty years on and is a fascinating artefact of an important recording session that was also a "happening" of sorts.

Hello Goodbye

Directed by Paul McCartney at the **Saville Theatre**, performance promos for The Beatles' winter 1967 single were filmed on November 10 with the group wearing their *Sgt Pepper* outfits. Mixed together with shots of the group in their 1963 collarless jackets, rather stiffly "waving goodbye" to old-style Beatles, the promos climaxed with Hawaiian-style dancing girls for the "Hey-la, hey-la aloha" finale and much comic frugging from the boys. Unfortunately, as far as the UK was concerned, it was wasted effort; the films were never shown at the time because of a June 1966 British Musicians' Union ban on promotion in which the performers were seen to be miming to pre-recorded music.

Lady Madonna

Shot by Tony Bramwell in a hybrid promo shoot/recording session at Abbey Road in February 1968. Film of The Beatles recording **Hey Bulldog** (with yet another new look – John with mutton-chop sideburns) was edited by Bramwell into a non-mimed, non-performance collage of clips to promote their February single **Lady Madonna**, thereby skirting around the stringent Musicians' Union rules. Because the images have nothing to do with the music heard, the best way to watch the film – arresting jump-cut shots of The Beatles at work and play in the studio – is probably with the sound off and in slow motion.

Hey Jude/Revolution

Filmed at Twickenham on September 4, 1968, this featured three hundred extras posing as an audience of beautiful people who crowd around The Beatles for **Hey Jude**'s chanted fade-out. It was directed once more by Michael Lindsay-Hogg; David Frost attended the filming to add his own introduction, thereby giving the impression that it was an exclusive Beatles appearance for his TV show. Despite the appearance, for the benefit of the Musicians' Union, of a live performance (complete with amps, a 36-piece orchestra and David Frost announcing it as their first "live appearance in goodness knows how long") for **Hey Jude**, only McCartney's vocal was actually live, the remainder of the music being a backing track. **Revolution**, in its rockier B-side version, was mimed in a stand-up performance fashion, but benefits from a superb, live Lennon vocal featuring the lyric of the as-yet-unreleased album version.

The Ballad Of John And Yoko/Something

For the June 1969 single **The Ballad Of John And Yoko**, home-movie and newsreel clips of John and Yoko on their wedding, honeymoon and peace events were combined with only a brief glimpse of The Beatles on the **Get Back** set at Twickenham. By the time the single **Something** was released in October 1969, The Beatles were not getting together for anything, let alone a promo. The film, coordinated by **Neil Aspinall**, significantly comprised entirely independent shots of the four individual Beatles in pastoral settings with their respective partners.

Ringo and Maureen cavort on mopeds, George and Patti look lovely in a garden, and John and Yoko walk towards the camera sporting black capes. McCartney, in virtual estrangement on his Scottish farm, filmed the rural segments of himself, Linda and Martha the sheepdog by tying the camera onto his tractor. A surprisingly touching film, it manages to underline both the song's expression of romantic commitment and – months before it was public knowledge – The Beatles' apartness.

Behind-the-scenes Beatles

Let It Be

1970; currently unavailable (though there is talk of a DVD release)

This downbeat document of The Beatles' penultimate sessions was conceived as a joyous return to their roots, an attempt to rekindle the simple joys of getting together and making music, which had dissipated as their fame and influence grew. *Get Back* was going to be a new, no-frills album, heralded by an hour-long TV special edited together from three shows at London's **Roundhouse Theatre** and a short TV documentary of the rehearsals, gigs and recording.

The plan was sound but it depended on an equality of enthusiasm from all the participants. Paul, who had suggested it, was the most keen. John was prepared to go along with it, as long as Yoko was at his side. Ringo would do anything to keep the peace (with the exception of going abroad, that is). George, however, was less than thrilled at the prospect of playing live and kicked against this aspect from the outset.

So, before the group started rehearsing in the cold and cavernous Twickenham Studios on January 2, 1969, under the watch of director **Michael Lindsay-Hogg** and his crew, discussions took place about where they might play the climactic show. Exotic locations, cruise ships and the Houses of Parliament were dismissed for practical and financial reasons, before John suggested just shooting a performance before an invited audience in the studio at the end of the rehearsals. The chilliness of the sound-stage at Twickenham is evident and matched by the frostiness that develops between the members of the band as the sessions become more tedious and obviously less productive than they'd hoped. Due to union regulations, they were unable to shoot in the evenings and had to start work first thing in the morning, which annoyed John in particular. Yoko's constant presence on set undermined the "four lads go back to basics" flavour Paul had intended and, because it was his idea and someone needed to keep hold of the reins, Paul tended to assume charge, which upset George, in particular. The infamous row between them, which partly sparked George's early departure, was caught on film and is particularly uncomfortable.

The music is a mix of rather uninspired new material, like John's **Dig A Pony**, and weary revisits to their roots – snippets of rock'n'roll covers and old faithfuls like "Besame Mucho". There's a glimmer of fun when John and Yoko waltz around the set while the band plays, but nothing much happens to stimulate the group or lighten the heart of the viewer. Notable producer **Glyn Johns**, who worked as an engineer on the sessions, has said that the atmosphere was actually really upbeat, that Lennon was hilarious and that the film concentrates unnecessarily on the gloomy moments. But he seems to be alone in this assessment. Lennon himself once commented that "Even the biggest Beatles fan couldn't have sat through those six weeks of misery. Nobody was into it at all. It was just a dreadful, dreadful feeling."

Things pick up a bit once the band decamps to the basement studios in Apple and George returns, bringing their old friend from Hamburg, Billy Preston, to play keyboards and deflect some of the intra-band grumpiness. The final rooftop sequence is a joy, tantalizing in its depiction of how a late-period live Beatles show might have felt, with the added spice of the cops turning up to poop the party.

At the end of the month they had over ninety hours of footage. Unfortunately, this meant that editing the final movie would take the best part of a year. When it transpired that ***Yellow Submarine*** didn't after all fulfil the group's three-film contract with United Artists, the decision was made to hand the documentary footage to them for theatrical release. By the time it and its ill-starred soundtrack album were ready for release, The Beatles had split. The change of title for the project said it all. Running only 82 minutes, *Let It Be*, though obviously a fascinating peep behind the scenes, feels a lot longer, and for some viewers, will be too painful and feel too intrusive to ever actually enjoy.

Beatles Anthology

1995; currently available on an eight-tape VHS box set and five-DVD set

Twenty-five years after they split, The Beatles' official video autobiography finally appeared. Geoff Wonfor, creator of the groundbreaking 1980s TV pop show **The Tube** and already a veteran of a couple of McCartney promos, was appointed director. Over several years in the early 1990s Paul, George and Ringo (and, to a lesser extent, George Martin and Neil Aspinall) took part in hours of interviews that were interspersed with archive recordings of John Lennon interviews and myriad clips of the group in the 1960s. (Sadly, some sequences proved impossible to locate, including the group's 1963 takeover of ***Juke Box Jury*** and, predictably, any substantial footage related to their 1966 Manila tour disaster.) The three remaining Beatles' appearances culminated in a low-key but fascinating gathering at George's house, filmed in mid-1994, but mostly unused until the DVD in 2003.

The TV series was sold to over 110 countries and hyped in the US as "an extraordinary event" on ABC. Producer Chips Chipperfield commented, "I can't think of a bigger series in terms of international broadcasting." Rather than a nippy visual retelling of The Beatles story, which is probably what the public would have preferred, *Anthology* the series was little more than a stroll through the best of the available Fab footage which, though fascinating in itself, didn't provide much in the way of narrative, while the participants' affectionate, lucid but slightly anodyne reminiscences of the "they were great days" variety didn't help. It made for curiously sluggish, uninvolving TV without the kind of bite you might expect in the story of history's most phenomenal pop stars. Reviews were average and initial viewing figures were respectable but tailed off as the series progressed. However, too much was not enough for some, and the eight hour-long episodes were expanded to 75 minutes each for the video edition of the series.

The trick, it turns out, is not to watch it the way it was made. The DVD reveals *Anthology* to be a superb resource, perfectly suited to not-necessarily-linear viewing, allowing you to drop in on The Cavern, the Budokan or the making of *Sgt Pepper* and enjoy all the relevant, extant footage any sane fan could wish for – the *Day In the Life* super-8, *Nowhere Man* live in Munich, the promo for **Rain**, home-movies shot in Greece and Rishikesh and the *Our World* broadcast in colour, for example – without worrying too much about narrative thrust or historical depth. There seems to be more interview material too (though still not enough of John). An early story about them in the van on the way home from a show having to lie on top of one another to keep from freezing to death when their windscreen

The Rutles (1978)

All You Need Is Cash currently available on DVD; *The Rutles* (1978) and *Archaeology* (1996) available on CD (Virgin and Rhino respectively)

The Rutles was the brainchild of Eric Idle, former member of the surreal Oxbridge comedy troupe Monty Python's Flying Circus and in the mid-1970s, writer/performer in the BBC comedy series *Rutland Weekend Television*. The Rutles' music was written by Neil Innes, former member of anarchic musical comedy group The Bonzo Dog Doo-Dah Band, who had themselves appeared in *Magical Mystery Tour*. Paul McCartney had even produced their 1968 UK hit **I'm The Urban Spaceman** under the pseudonym Apollo C. Vermouth.

The Rutles first appeared in embryonic form in a segment of *RWT* called *A Hard Day's Rut* performing the janglesome **I Must Be In Love**. Encouraged by *Saturday Night Live* producer Lorne Michaels to produce an hour-long movie tracing the mythical history of the imaginary group, Idle wrote the script and Innes the songs of *All You Need Is Cash*, which appeared in 1978. The film traced the progress of the pre-fab Four – Ron Nasty, Dirk McQuickly, Stig O'Hara and late addition Barry Wom (who had changed his name from Barrington Womble) – through their discovery by Leggy Mountbatten and development through Rutlemania, their introduction to tea by Bob Dylan, their second movie *Ouch!*, their album *Sgt Rutter* ("a millstone in popular music history") and their swansong, "Shabby Road". Other career highlights included their first major flop *Tragical History Tour* ("not the strongest idea for a Rutles film: four Oxford professors on a hitch-hiking tour of tea shops in the Rutland area") and the rooftop concert in their final movie Let It Rot.

Managing to be an off-beat, ingenious parody of The Beatles' story as well as a satire on the way it was often presented (particularly by portentous, mid-1970s rockumentaries like Tony Palmer's *All You Need Is Love*), its credibility was enhanced by straight-faced appearances by Mick Jagger (remembering how Dirk McQuickly was always hustling songs), Paul Simon shattered is particularly charming and vivid.

Those already in possession of the expensive video set will be dismayed to know that the cheaper DVD set adds a delightful eighty minute disc of extra material, topped by an extended sequence from the summit meeting in George's garden. Sitting on a picnic blanket, Paul and George sing early compositions like **Thinking Of Linking** with ukuleles while Ringo slaps his knees, and they shoot the breeze about old times. Next, you see them together at Abbey Road, reviewing old tapes while the *Anthology* albums are being compiled (George, hearing **Golden Slumbers:** "What album was this on?"). Watching them listen to the elements of **Tomorrow Never Knows** is particularly fascinating. This material has a warmth that's harder to locate in the original films, with the added thrill of witnessing their combined charisma one last time. "It's been really beautiful and moving," says Ringo, preparing to leave George's place. "I like hanging out with you guys." Most viewers will feel the same.

and even Idle's friend George Harrison, who appeared as an interviewer outside 3 Savile Row, itself masquerading as a pillaged Rutle Corps. So subtly pervasive have some of the jokes become over the years, it came as some surprise to this writer (viewing the film twenty years after first seeing it) that it was in fact Dirk McQuickly talking about the formation of Rutle Corps and not Paul McCartney talking about Apple who said, "We want to help people to help themselves."

Innes's brilliantly detailed musical pastiche (written apparently from memory) was sometimes an inventive amalgam of Beatles-esque gesture (**Hold My Hand** alludes to at least three moptop-era classics), sometimes song-specific: "Doubleback Alley" strongly evoked **Penny Lane,** while **Get Up And Go** was dangerously close to "Get Back". In the end, Lew Grade, then owner of The Beatles' songs, forced Innes to give up fifty percent of his royalties to Grade's ATV music. In 1996, Innes reformed The Rutles – minus a disapproving Idle – for the *Anthology*-era cash-in *Archaeology*, and wisely kept the songs a little vaguer.

As for The Beatles themselves, Lennon was "fascinated" according to Innes, though McCartney has barely spoken on the subject, save a "No comment" in 1978 when he was promoting *London Town*. Ringo was said to have enjoyed the happy stuff, but not the sad stuff. Indeed, the film lingers rather heartlessly on The Rutles' manager **Leggy Mountbatten**'s private life and tragic acceptance of an Australian teaching post in 1967. Harrison was always the film's chief advocate, even clearing the use of some authentic Beatles footage. He noted that "The Rutles liberated me from The Beatles in a way" and suggested that of all the made-for-TV Beatles documentaries "it was actually the best, the funniest and most scathing, but at the same time, it was done with the most love".

Harrison would still be heard on 1980s chat shows blackly echoing one of the film's catchphrases, usually in relation to discussing the death of John Lennon, where he would admit to feeling "shocked ... and stunned."

Their First US Visit

2003; currently available on DVD

The Beatlemania/US invasion period is usually depicted in a montage of jump-cuts of screaming girls, limousines and waving from airport runways to the soundtrack of "I Want To Hold Your Hand". This Apple-approved documentary combines fly-on-the-wall footage shot in February 1964 at two hours' notice for Granada TV by US filmmaker **Albert Maysles** (who had no idea who The Beatles were) extended by ten tunes from the Ed Sullivan TV performances in New York and Miami and three from the Washington Coliseum show. The viewer therefore experiences at leisure some familiar scenes afresh and gets an enlightening glimpse inside the bubble of Beatlemania. McCartney sings lead on the first two numbers (and joint lead on the next two), as well as handling all the spoken introductions, and comes over as the impossibly perky leader of the group (Lennon doesn't sing lead until the third TV show). The performances are joyful, however, with the shambles of the stage arrangements in Washington – the boys repositioning the drum roster and amplifiers themselves in order to play to all four sides of the arena – still hard to believe. Maysles's preferred technique of eschewing interviews with his subjects means the boys are captured spontaneously riffing and joking in scenes that look almost like outtakes of *A Hard Day's Night*. There's a fine extra film featuring previously unseen footage with the intelligent Maysles in interview. Referring to how the film achieved such unusual intimacy – but also speaking for the whole of America – he says, "We liked these guys a lot." His film lets us see precisely why.

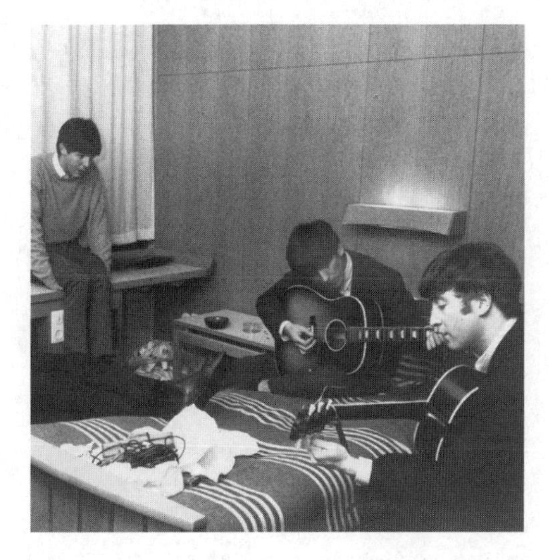

Part 5: The Canon

The Canon

50 greatest Beatles songs & the stories behind them

"... The Beatles are Divine Messiahs. The wisest, holiest, most effective avatars (Divine Incarnate, God Agents) that the human race has yet produced ... Prototypes of a new young race of laughing freemen. Evolutionary agents sent by God, endowed with mysterious power to create a new human species."

Timothy Leary, LSD guru, from his essay *Thank God For The Beatles* (1968)

1. Please Please Me

Lennon/McCartney; recorded November 26, 1962, EMI Studios, Abbey Road, London; available on *Please Please Me*, *1962–1966* and *1*

The young John Lennon had been intrigued by punning use of the word "please" in the old Robin/Rainger song **Please** as crooned by Bing Crosby in the 1933 movie *The Big Broadcast* and a song John's mother used to sing: "Oh please, lend a little ear to my pleas". In 1962, in the hands of Lennon, now a 21-year-old rock'n'roll songwriter, the dual meaning of the word took on more suggestive overtones, as he entreats his reticent girl to "please" him on an unspecified but clearly urgent ("Come on! Come on!") matter.

Musically, it began as a Roy Orbison style ballad along the lines of **Only The Lonely** and was offered to George Martin in mid-1962 as a possible follow-up to **Love Me Do**. Insufficiently impressed to change his mind that **How Do You Do It** should be the second single, Martin suggested further work was needed. In the coming weeks the song was speeded up and harmonica was added (as a reprise of **Love**

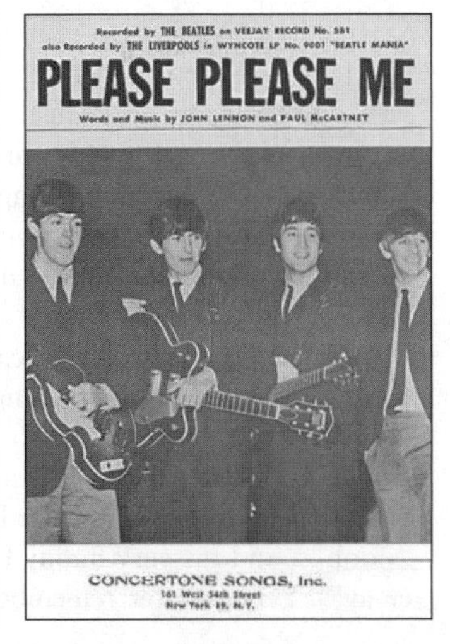

Me Do's instrumental signature). McCartney devised a static upper harmony in the manner of the Everly Brothers' **Cathy's Clown** (creating the distinctive "pealing" effect of the verse) and **Please Please Me** was transformed into a vibrant piece of work. Every element of the arrangement was an unforgettable hook – the guitar/harmonica lick, the surging guitar chords separating the verse lines, the impatient echo of the backing vocals, and the octave-leap explosion of the title line. Recognizing the rigorous, inspired job the group had done, George Martin famously told them, "Congratulations, gentlemen. You've just made your first Number One."

2. She Loves You

Lennon/McCartney; recorded July 1, 1963, EMI Studios, Abbey Road, London; available on *1962–1966*, *1*, and *Capitol Albums Volume 1*

Started in a Newcastle-upon-Tyne hotel room on June 26, 1963, before a show at the Majestic Ballroom and finished off soon after in Liverpool at Jim McCartney's Forthlin Road house, it was Paul's suggestion to avoid a simple "I love you" lyric with a scenario of romantic encouragement via messages from a third party.

It's a song full of wily musical detail ranging from the subtle (a heart-tugging C-minor-sixth chord on the second "She loves you" in the bridge) to the audacious (the answering "yeah yeah yeah"s of the chorus, the Isley Brother-ish "oooh"s, and the very Buddy Holly "yesterda-ee-ay"). Lennon later remembered, "We stuck everything in there – thinking when Elvis did **All Shook Up**, that was the first time I heard 'uh huh', 'oh yeah' and 'yeah yeah' all in the same song." They debuted the newly finished song to Paul's father, who liked it but disapproved of the Americanisms and suggested they might sing "yes, yes, yes" instead, much to John's and Paul's amusement.

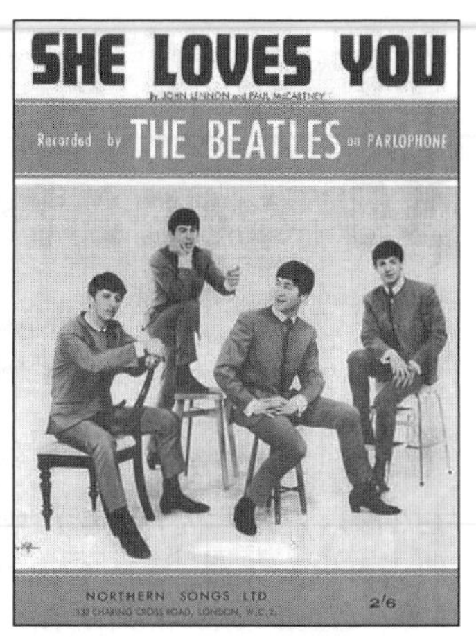

If the song was watertight, the record was something else again. Springboarding from a tom-tom roll straight into the chorus (at George Martin's suggestion), the sizzle of Ringo's hi-hats, the chiming fills of George Harrison's Rickenbacker guitar and the old-fashioned jazzy sixth chord at the end (which Martin needed convincing on) are all classic Beatles elements. Add the carefully choreographed presentation witnessed by fifteen million people on *Sunday Night At The London Palladium* and you have nothing less than the catalyst for Beatlemania. **She Loves You** remains The Beatles' biggest selling UK single.

3. All My Loving

Lennon/McCartney; recorded July 30 1963, EMI Studios, Abbey Road, London; available on *With The Beatles* (mono), *1962–1966* (stereo), and *Capitol Albums Vol 1*

Another epistolary song like **P.S. I Love You**, here's a rare instance of McCartney conceiving the words first, "like a piece of poetry". He got the idea while having a shave, developed it on the **Roy Orbison** tour bus on the way to a show and tackled the music on the backstage piano when he reached the theatre.

Taken at a medium-swing pace, the up-and-down-the-scale effervescence of the song (latterly rated by Lennon, in a rare outward display of respect for McCartney's efforts, as a "damn fine piece of work") is enhanced by a frantic 12/8 rhythm-guitar part by Lennon with which he was still pleased seventeen years on.

Its timeless melodiousness meant it was the first of The Beatles' tunes to receive serious cover attention from other artists, going on to attract over one hundred different versions. The song was rated highly enough to be the opening song of their inaugural *Ed Sullivan Show* appearance in February 1964, and McCartney remained sufficiently proud of it to still be pounding it out nearly forty years later in his 2002–03 live shows.

4. I Want To Hold Your Hand

Lennon/McCartney; recorded October 17, 1963, EMI Studios, Abbey Road, London; available on *1962–1966*, 1, and *Capitol Albums Vol 1*

Written "eyeball to eyeball ... playing into each other's noses" as Lennon recalled, their first American #1 was worked out on the piano in the basement of the Asher family home on Wimpole Street where Paul was staying in between tours in late 1963. John remembered getting excited when Paul fell onto "the chord that made the song" (probably the plangent B minor on "I think you understand") and cried, "That's it! Do that again."

Though the lyric is a more demure manifestation of **Please Please Me**'s carnal pressure, the music's immodest plethora of what Ian Macdonald calls The Beatles' "free-spirited unorthodoxies" makes **I Want To Hold Your Hand** one of the most exciting records the group ever made. From the disorientating intro (the bullish syncopations and non-home chords don't make sense until one has heard the repeated "I can't hide"s later

> ***"The outstanding English composers of 1963 must seem to have been John Lennon and Paul McCartney ... . One gets the impression they think simultaneously of harmony and melody, so firmly are the major tonic sevenths and ninths built into their tunes."***
>
> William Mann, *The Times* (1963)

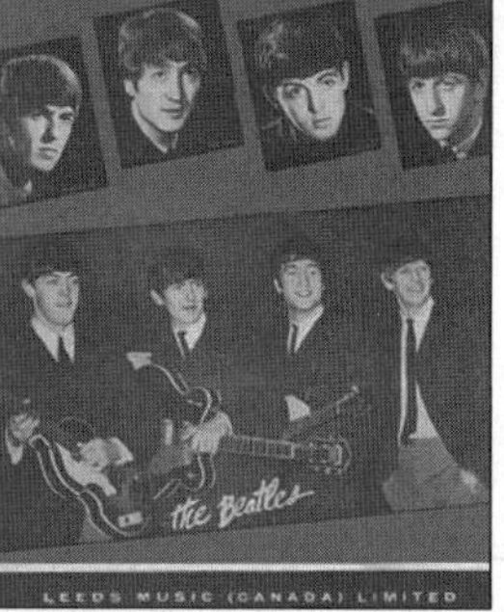

in the record) to the triple-time decelerations of the closing moments, the record is packed tight with arch Fabisms. There is a faint sense of a reprise of earlier songs in its mechanics (the octave jump between "your" and "hand" recalls **Please Please Me** and the middle revisits the chord changes McCartney was so proud to have stumbled upon for the middle of **From Me To You**) but even that contributes to an overwhelming sense of unique, spirit-lifting Beatleness. It went on to sell twelve million copies around the world.

Lennon barely reckoned the song at the time (he once asked *Melody Maker* journalist Ray Coleman to scribble out the forgotten lyrics before a show) and would look back in his sour, post-split reminiscences at this masterpiece (and others of the period) as mere "meat-market" music.

5. You Can't Do That

Lennon/McCartney; recorded February 25, 1964, EMI Studios, Abbey Road, London; available on *A Hard Day's Night* and *Capitol Albums Vol 1*

McCartney had nabbed the A-side of the single (**Can't Buy Me Love**) so this threatening blues of Lennon's was relegated to the B-side. Featuring some distinctive "rhythm-as-lead" guitar from Lennon (he would occasionally get bored with a traditional rhythm-guitar role) a chunky, four-beat groove (complete with cowbell and congas) and bold blue dissonances (in both the major/minor guitar lick and the arresting "told you before" sharpened ninth chords), this is Lennon at his belligerent best. Sounding like an authentic expression of John "Jealous Guy" Lennon's attitude to its subject (flirtatious girl gets left "flat" – see

Lennon strums away in his hotel room at The George V, Paris, January 1964

also *Rubber Soul*'s notoriously aggressive **Run For Your Life**). Its bullish swagger sets the tone for the Lennon-dominated *A Hard Day's Night* album and musically it's very much a companion piece to that record's **When I Get Home**.

Though Lennon later credited Wilson Pickett as inspiration, the great soul man's breakthrough hit **In The Midnight Hour** came several months after this was recorded, so it's likely Lennon was more generally inspired by the assertive sounds to be heard on Motown and Atlantic, recognizing the Pickett quality in retrospect.

Filmed as part of the final concert sequence in the movie *A Hard Day's Night*, it was left out of the original film and so consigned to the non-soundtrack side of the UK album release.

6. And I Love Her

Lennon/McCartney; recorded February 25–27, 1964, EMI Studios, Abbey Road, London; available on *A Hard Day's Night* (mono), *1962–1966* (stereo) and *Capitol Albums Vol 1*

As far as its composer was concerned, **And I Love Her** was "the first ballad I ever impressed myself with" and now, hundreds of McCartney songs later, it remains among the finest of all his melodies. Generally assumed to be written for Jane Asher, in later years the happily married Paul usually shrugged it off: "just a love song, it wasn't for anyone". Superficially hampered by clichéd romantic lyrics, the innocuous text actually works perfectly as a peg on which to drape the expressive tune. Repeating a yearningly upward movement for the first three lines, it tumbles downward by the fourth before a gorgeously unpredictable pay-off, the casual afterthought of the title. Pleased with this relaxed twist on a standard sentiment, McCartney was amused to note that Don McLean evidently liked it too, tweaking it for his own **And I Love You So**.

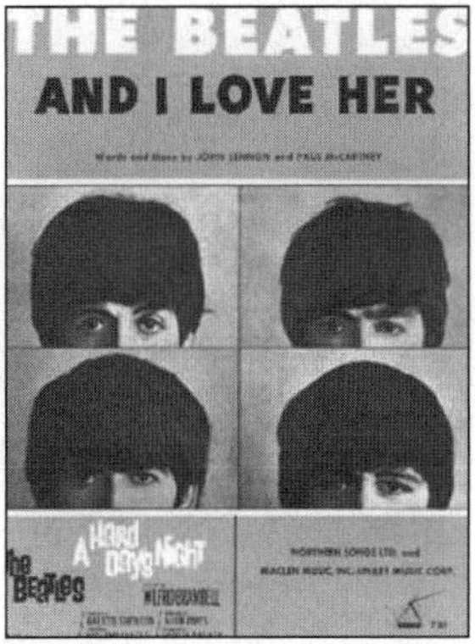

There were two days of false starts in its recording, and a bumpy, full-group run-through without a middle eight can be heard on *Anthology 1*. But it eventually inspired the subtlest Beatles performance to date, with delicate percussion, a resonant Harrison classical-guitar solo (upon the simple surprise of the mid-point key-change) and a beautiful harmonic left-turn into the closing chord.

If **All My Loving** was the first Beatle standard, then **And I Love Her** was the second, attracting dozens of adult pop covers by everyone from Julie London to Smokey Robinson. In a 1972 interview, Lennon claimed the middle eight as his own but by 1980 he had backed off, saying of McCartney's work, "I consider it his first **Yesterday**."

7. A Hard Day's Night

Lennon/McCartney; recorded April 16, 1964, EMI Studios, Abbey Road, London; available on *A Hard Day's Night* (mono), *1962–1966* and *1* (stereo) and *Capitol Albums Vol 1*

The phrase had already appeared in Lennon's *In His Own Write* but Dick Lester first heard

it in an off-the-cuff remark from Ringo on the set of the movie. (Alan Clayson suggests an obscure 1963 Eartha Kitt B-side, **I Had A Hard Day Last Night,** as its original coinage.) When it was adopted as the film's title, Lennon rushed home telling McCartney "I'll write it," and the newborn song was recorded the following day.

Journalist Maureen Cleave, present at the recording, remembers pointing out a weakness in the original lyric "I find my tiredness is through/And I feel all right", whereupon Lennon altered it, adding a little spiciness via the coyly undisclosed things that the song's muse does to make him feel all right. McCartney remembers helping with the middle in the studio but Lennon asserts Paul's contribution was simply to sing the climactic high notes Lennon himself couldn't hit.

Thematically, **A Hard Day's Night** belongs with **When I Get Home**, written in the same period. Both are full of bragging promises as to the delights awaiting "her" when her impatient hard-working man returns from a long day at the song mine. But there is also the sense of "home" being a comfort, and the lyrics convey just as much convincing autobiographical tone as Lennon's later cries for help.

Set to a driving groove (Lennon was particularly keen on the four-to-a-bar cowbell effect at the time), the tune, while an impressive Lennon vocal, is little more than a bluesy knot. It's no coincidence that the more effective covers of it are by rootsy performers, such as the 1965 soul-jazz reading by **Ramsey Lewis.** Sonically, however, it was the most powerful thing The Beatles had yet recorded. George Harrison's new Rickenbacker 12-string is to the fore, a sound which would have a huge impact on US West-Coast Beatles-freak Roger McGuinn and his group The Byrds. It makes its presence felt throughout, but it's especially potent on the striking opening chord and the nonchalantly mysterious jangling fade.

"I fell in love with The Beatles' music (and simultaneously, of course, with their four faces-cum-personae) … in whom I discovered the frabjous falsetto shriek-cum-croon, the ineluctable beat, the flawless intonation, the utterly fresh lyrics, the Schubert-like flow of musical invention, and the fuck-you coolness of these Four Horsemen of Our Apocalypse."

Leonard Bernstein, composer, introduction to *The Beatles* by Geoffrey Stokes, 1979

8. Baby's In Black

Lennon/McCartney; recorded August 11, 1964, EMI Studios, Abbey Road, London; available on *Beatles For Sale* and *Capitol Albums Vol 1*

Every now and again Lennon and McCartney would vocally harmonize on a song with such compositional purpose, it wasn't quite clear which of the notes sung was the actual melody and which was the harmony. The earlier **If I Fell** and **This Boy** would cause a solo singer some pause for thought before deciding on a single melodic line, while the final four bars of the middle of **You Won't See Me** present several equally appealing options, as the lead and backing vocals split like a fork in the road. **Baby's In Black** was another one of those songs. Written together, from the ground up, at Kenwood (their first "eyeball to eyeball" collaboration since **I Want To Hold Your Hand** almost a year previously) it is sung entirely in two-part harmony. McCartney proudly recalls getting enquiries from music-score transcribers as to which line should be prominent. "You could actually take either," was his answer.

It was only the second Beatles piece to be written in triple time (the doo-wop 12/8 of **This Boy** preceded it, though several imminent songs would be in a folksy 6 or 12 – notably **You've Got To Hide Your Love Away** and **Norwegian Wood**); McCartney remembers attempting "something a little bit darker, bluesy" in the song. While you can hear the "bluesy" element on the downbeat D7th chord on the title line, the "darkness" is really only evident in the title, though the scenario – singer is ignored by a girl who is distracted by an old love – is given marginal edge by the hint that the old love may be deceased. If he is indeed dead, that they sing her preoccupation with him is "only a whim" seems a little callous, especially, as some have suggested, if it was inspired by **Astrid Kirchherr**'s situation.

This interesting song never quite received the definitive reading on *Beatles For Sale* – Harrison audibly struggles with the guitar part – but its downbeat Dylanesque quality was central enough to what The Beatles were about in 1964–65 to be a constant of their live shows of the period.

9. She's A Woman

Lennon/McCartney; recorded October 8, 1964; EMI Studios, Abbey Road, London; available on *Past Masters 1* and *Capitol Albums Vol 1*

Another attempt by McCartney (witness **Can't Buy Me Love** earlier and **I'm Down** later) at injecting a bit more blues into The Beatles' sound, **She's A Woman** was devised while he was out walking around St John's Wood, and finished in the studio. While the chords and structure are simply long-form blues (24 bars as opposed to 12 bars, in the manner of Cliff Richard's **Move It**) with a four-bar bridge, there were other elements in the recording that make it an interesting item.

McCartney gives the song a terrifically chesty Little Richard vocal (criticized by some listeners, who missed the point that it was pitched deliberately out of his range in order to get that effect). A distinctive off-beat guitar part played by Lennon creates space for

a peculiarly disembodied piano part (beautifully played by Paul) and also to allow the bass to resonate as never before. George's highly prescribed solo (probably composed for him by McCartney) and Ringo's hi-hats zoom in and out in a flash; the whole is wound as tight as a noose. While certainly effective, it's tempting to hear the extraordinary "control" of the arrangement as musical expression of its composer's occasional dictatorial tendencies, increasingly exhibited whenever the rest of the group let their guard down.

Lennon, on the other hand, was just pleased to have the phrase "turns me on" in the lyrics, underground drug vernacular – a month or so after having first smoked marijuana – suddenly groovier and more subversive than the mild sexual slang it was probably taken for.

10. Ticket To Ride

Lennon/McCartney; recorded February 15, 1965, EMI Studios, Abbey Road, London; available on *Help!*, *1962–1966* and *1*

From **Misery** to **It Won't Be Long** to **I'll Cry Instead**, Lennon had been singing of how sad he felt, but it wasn't until the heaving slab of sound known as **Ticket To Ride** appeared could we hear it so clearly. A remarkable sonic achievement for its time, the music brilliantly conveys a depressed, heavy-lidded indolence.

A slow, chiming 12-string riff settles over a bed of droning fifths and a hanging-head, off-beat drum pattern. Expressing no particular desire to modulate chords, the track literally wallows in melancholic inertia before dragging itself to the closest cadence it can reach without actually getting up. The song's sullen reluctance to move is in the capable hands of Starr (directed by McCartney, but playing superbly), who gradually relaxes his grip on the reins of tension to install a secure backbeat as the song evolves (overtly in the bridge and more subtly on later verses) until the liberating double-time of the finale fade-out. His baby don't care, and frankly, neither does he.

"They are, in my mind, responsible for most of the degeneration that has happened, not only musically but also in the sense of youth orientation and politically, too. They are the people who made it first publicly acceptable to spit in the eye of authority."

Frank Sinatra, 1977

There are several levels of meaning in the title. The girl leaving the boy who is "bringing her down" has a travel ticket to Ryde, a town on the Isle of Wight where John and Paul had once visited Paul's cousin Betty. Also, she has been inspired to leave by the enlightenment felt "riding so high"; pot was her ticket to a new life. Furthermore, she's taking a new lover; a "ticket to ride" was how Lennon described the medical card carried by Hamburg prostitutes to prove the absence of venereal disease.

All this heaviness (Lennon would later claim it as one of the first "heavy metal" records) was enough for George Harrison to confess at the time that he was "worried" about **Ticket To Ride** being #1 material. It was, of course. However, indicating that those around The Beatles didn't quite know what they had, the song was featured in a fabulously inappropriate skiing montage in the movie *Help!*.

11. Help!

Lennon/McCartney; recorded April 13, 1965, EMI Studios, Abbey Road, London; available on *Help!*, *1962–1966* and *1*

"Help!" was started by Lennon as the title song of the new movie (after *Eight Arms To Hold You* had been dumped, to everyone's relief), and McCartney was on hand at Kenwood to help him finish it, providing the anticipation and echo of the counter melody in the backing vocals. Later, Lennon would claim it as one of his unconscious cries of pain emanating from his self-christened "fat Elvis" period. "You see the movie," he recalled, "he – I – is very fat, very insecure, and he's completely lost himself."

Prone to sporadic depression, the combination of Beatles pressure, marital malaise and "king of the world" over-indulgence (food, drink, pot, women) had tipped Lennon into a mid-20s crisis which would ultimately lead him both further inside himself in drug-inspired contemplation and further out in terms of his artistic expression.

For now, however, he had to sacrifice his medium-paced, personal Dylanesque strummer to The Beatles' beat machine. Sped up and given masterful Harrison arpeggiated jangles, the tidy recording also features a curious rhythm design with Starr playing his hi-hat cymbals and tom-tom/snare fills into the chorus in straight rock time, while Lennon's acoustic rhythm-guitar remains clearly in a country-swing feel. (This is the opposite of the "two-feels" contrast heard in Chuck Berry's recordings of tunes like **Sweet Little Sixteen**, where the rhythm section plays swing rhythm behind the straight-eight rock of Berry's rhythm guitar, which is the sound of rock'n'roll struggling to be born from the womb of rhythm and blues.) The result is a rhythmic tension unique in Beatles records and, in view of the song's tortured background inspiration, profoundly expressive.

12. Yesterday

Lennon/McCartney; recorded June 14–17, 1965, EMI Studios, Abbey Road, London; available on *Help!*, *1962–1966* and *1*

Rather taken aback by waking one morning at Wimpole Street to find an entire tune "complete" in his head, McCartney suspected it was some old standard and in the coming weeks played it to several people, asking if it was a song they already knew. Having been assured it wasn't (and after he'd driven Dick Lester to distraction by constantly doodling it on a piano on the set of *Help!*), he eventually got round to replacing his dummy lyric – "**Scrambled eggs**" – with words of vague but intense nostalgia.

He recorded a cool, vulnerable voice-and-guitar version later on the same day he'd screamed **I'm Down** onto tape and The Beatles had knocked off his **I've Just Seen A Face**. The others were impressed but at a loss as to how to approach it as a group. George Martin suggested strings and persuaded a reluctant McCartney (who feared Mantovani schmaltz) to give a string quartet a go. McCartney and Martin blocked out the arrangement together. Martin provided the authentic voicings, and McCartney the subversive "blue" seventh, which is played by the cello midway through the second bridge. At the recording session, in which the quartet overdubbed onto Paul's original performance, McCartney vetoed the excessive vibrato of the string players and the result was a recording that exuded class and originality.

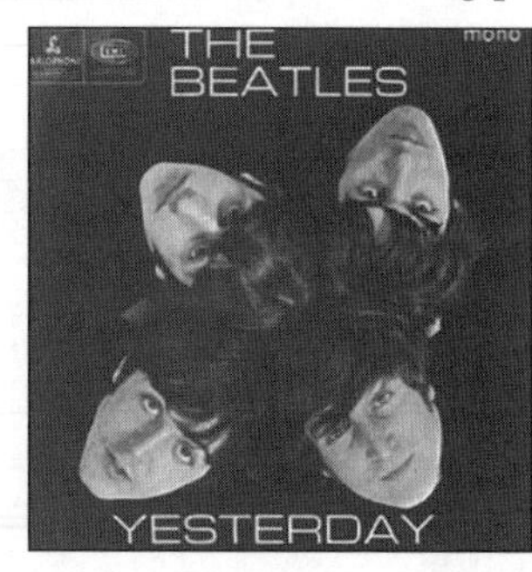

The world simply took it to their hearts. Everyone from Elvis to Sinatra sang it, old school musicians accepted it as inspired work, and musicologists fell over themselves discussing its perfection. **Yesterday** holds the record as the most recorded song in history, with over 2500 versions, and has been broadcast on American radio over seven million times.

True to form, McCartney has claimed the song to be about nothing in particular, though accepts there may be something in reading it as an unconscious paean to his late mother. Lennon had a mild grumble about the unresolved lyric but finally judged it "beautiful". When first playing it live again in the mid-1970s, McCartney was interested to note he was forgetting to play the reprise of the bridge and final stanza. "I quite like that," he said, "Not too precious with it."

13. Norwegian Wood

Lennon/McCartney; recorded October 12–21, 1965, EMI Studios, Abbey Road, London; available on *Rubber Soul*, *1962–1966* and *1*

The famously married Beatle had indulged in much extramarital activity to which Cynthia was entirely oblivious until 1968, when Lennon confessed his infidelities to his incredulous wife. "I must have had a mental block," she would write later. **Norwegian Wood** was started on a Swiss skiing holiday in February 1965 and began life as **This Bird Has Flown**, a veiled tale of one of Lennon's affairs. "I can't remember any specific woman it had to do with," its author said later, although Pete Shotton recalled it concerning a "sophisticated lady journalist". Back at Kenwood, McCartney recalls hearing the arresting open-

"...The Beatles gave us a seven-year lesson in the art of composition, along with a mini course in the development of music history. How could we help but want to master all the elements of the art with idols like this?"

James Russell Smith, composer/teacher, from *In My Life: Encounters With The Beatles* (Fromm), 1998

ing line and from then on, the song writing itself with a teasingly elusive scenario (Lennon: "gobbledegook") of an evening of unfulfilled sexual promise and an arsonist's revenge.

The song is set in folky triple-time with Lennon reprising his Dylanesque vocal delivery used on **You've Got To Hide Your Love Away** and playing excellent, truculently droning rhythm guitar, and The Beatles had to work to find a suitable arrangement, paring away through a couple of remakes to the stark finished track. Ringo's discreet percussion contribution features finger cymbals, tambourine and what sounds like thigh-slapping. The single most striking texture was the sitar line played by George Harrison on the "crummy" instrument he had bought in London after being intrigued by the Indian music he had heard on *Help!* If The Beatles were idolised before, this exotic ingredient along with the song's air of cool, menacing obscurity would inspire a whole new level of respect from their contemporaries.

14. Drive My Car

Lennon/McCartney; recorded October 13 1965, EMI Studios, Abbey Road, London; available on *Rubber Soul* and *1962–1966*

Started by McCartney as a "work job", the presence of the fatal phrase "golden rings" ("Rings always rhymes with things," recalled McCartney later. "I knew it was a bad idea.") did not bode well for the song's development. After a period of head-scratching (which McCartney would later describe as the closest he and Lennon ever got to a "dry session") the lyrics eventually evolved into a tightly devised scenario, drolly detailing a suggestive conversation between a manipulating aspirant "star" and a love-struck, would-be chauffeur, complete with a smart, winking pay-off. It also contained an irresistibly stupid hook – "beep, beep, beep, beep, yeah!" – which would be used for years as a radio sting and jingle for traffic news.

McCartney, burgeoning auteur, had got into the habit of arranging his songs in his head in advance of the recording session and instructing the group which parts to play. ("He'd never give you the opportunity to come out with something," George Harrison would recall.) However, at the **Drive My Car** session, Harrison suggested an involved guitar line (related to Otis Redding's **Respect**, which **Drive My Car** resembled) which was then doubled on bass, providing the bedrock for the track. The very particular two- and three-part vocal harmonies were the most advanced The Beatles had yet devised (the implied A7 sharp 5 sharp 9 at the end of each verse is especially startling) and were layered onto the backing. All this took the recording session past midnight for the first time (an occurrence that would soon be the norm rather than the exception) but the intricate, brisk results speak for themselves. The Beatles were moving from being simply recording artists to becoming artists of the recording studio.

15. Day Tripper

Lennon/McCartney; recorded October 16, 1965, EMI Studios, Abbey Road, London; available on *1962–1966* and *1*

Day Tripper followed **I Feel Fine** and **Ticket To Ride** to complete Lennon's trilogy of mid-period singles based on heavy electric-guitar riffs. It has the most assertive lick of the three, possibly based in part on Bobby Parker's **Watch Your Step**, but it also appears to reprise and slow the **Respect** motif borrowed for **Drive My Car**.

The lyric, completed with McCartney, was a dual attack on part-time hippies and sexually alluring but ultimately unforthcoming females, one of the sour "girl who thinks she's it" songs Lennon would feel the need to write from time to time (see also **Girl, Norwegian Wood, She Said She Said**); "she's a big teaser"soon became "she's a prick-teaser" in their live shows. Featuring blues chord changes up to a point, in lieu of a composed middle section, the track wigs out on a sustained B power chord with delirious ascending harmonies evoking a teasing rush to the temporary orgasmic relief, before crashing down once more to the grinding, earth-bound riff.

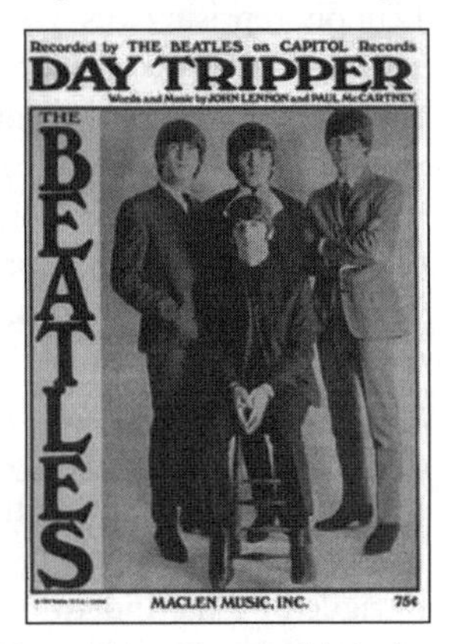

It was an odd, jeering choice for a single, but when the preferred **We Can Work It Out** came along Lennon was adamant that **Day Tripper** wouldn't be supplanted. A double A-side compromise was reached, the first of a few.

16. In My Life

Lennon/McCartney; recorded October 18–21, 1965, EMI Studios, Abbey Road, London; available on *Rubber Soul* and *1962–1966*

Although Lennon would later claim earlier songs like **I Don't Want To Spoil The Party**, **I'm A Loser** and especially **Help!** unconsciously indicated his depressed state, until **In My Life** he'd never consciously written an autobiographical song. Inspired by Dylan and stung by a remark made in late 1964 by British journalist Kenneth Allsop which unfavourably compared Lennon's lyrics to the literary efforts of his *In His Own Write*, Lennon sat down one 1965 day upstairs in Kenwood and made his first concerted effort to reflect his life in his art.

He struggled to force his Liverpool memories into a stanza before scrapping it. "It was the most boring 'What I Did On My Holidays Bus Trip' song," he remembered later, "It wasn't working at all." As he relaxed from his self-consciously literate endeavour, a poignant, balanced lyric came to him. Meditating on the emotional power of reminiscence and how change does not necessarily mean progress, the song ultimately recognises the limitations of nostalgia when compared to a now that can be shared with a loved one.

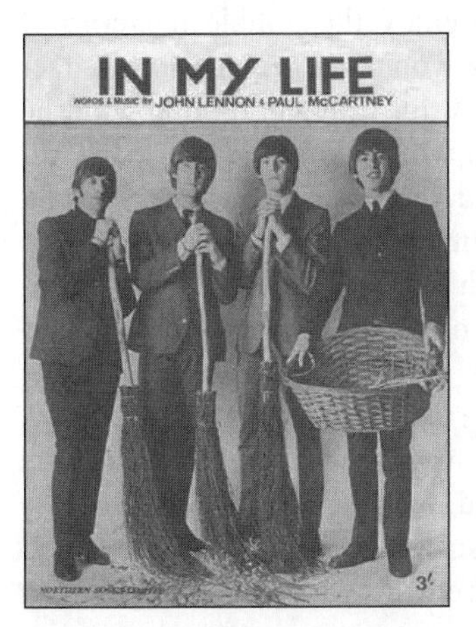

Though he credited Paul McCartney as assisting with the "middle eight musically" (possibly meaning the modulation to the relative minor that carries the three-line bridge to the title phrase, or perhaps using "middle eight" as a catch-all acknowledgement of McCartney's input), Lennon clearly regarded it as his own work. "The whole lyrics were already written before Paul had even heard it," he said, "signed, sealed and delivered." He rated the whole as "my first real major piece of work".

Paul McCartney claims it as a more collaborative effort than Lennon depicts it. McCartney remembers arriving at Kenwood to find Lennon had "the very nice opening stanzas for a song" but no tune, and that Paul himself composed the song on Lennon's Mellotron on the landing. **In My Life** is one of the few pieces about which Lennon's and McCartney's respective memories significantly differ.

The Beatles' recording is characterized by a plaintive Lennon vocal and a smartly arranged (and played) stop-start drum part which suggests the swing between reflection and revelatory forward momentum in the song itself. The band left the instrumental break empty until four days later, when producer George Martin came to the session early and filled it in. Following Lennon's suggestion for "something baroque-sounding", he tried an organ solo before slowing the tape to half-speed and playing a two-handed, Bach-style piano solo which, when replayed at the correct speed, approximated the sound of a harpsichord. Regarded variously as either a subtle underscoring of the song's tension between past and present, or as rather arch and inappropriate, Martin's effort remains for most listeners one of the most inspired of all Beatles instrumental passages.

The song was highly regarded; Gene Pitney, Judy Collins and Jose Feliciano were quick to cover **In My Life** and George Martin named his 1998 retirement album after it. There's something in the warm and measured wisdom of the song's sentiment and the seamless blend of heart and craft that mark it as one of the greatest Lennon/McCartney treasures.

17. We Can Work It Out

Lennon/McCartney; recorded October 20–29, 1965, EMI Studios, Abbey Road, London; available on *1962–1966* and *1*

In the common caricature of Lennon's and McCartney's distinctly evolving oeuvres, John's songs are often thought of as personal, almost private offerings from which his deeper feelings can be read, whereas Paul's songs are considered the facile but cooler work of a writer who "makes them up like a novelist" (according to John Lennon): McCartney is the dispassionate craftsman, Lennon the caustic soul-barer. While this view is clearly sustainable to a point, just as there are a number of later, tidily organized Lennon songs that mean next to nothing (**Sun King, Dig A Pony**), there are also several McCartney songs to indicate he was as capable as Lennon of accessing his not altogether noble inner thoughts as food for his art. Especially in late 1965.

For a while now, girlfriend Jane Asher had been showing more independence and desire to pursue her acting career than entirely suited Paul. Some observers say he was ready for her to settle to wifedom and motherhood, others that he couldn't understand why she wouldn't make him the centre of her universe. McCartney is calculatedly vague in his official biography *Many Years From Now*, while Jane Asher has never gone on record about their five-year relationship.

In autumn 1965 Jane left London to join the Bristol Old Vic theatre company (and, McCartney hints, a new boyfriend), whereupon the Beatle vented his frustration in song ("It saves you going to a psychiatrist", he would reason much later), two of which appeared on *Rubber Soul*. Both **I'm Looking Through You** and **You Won't See Me** deal with the trauma of rejection, though the latter still has the wherewithal to enjoy the double meaning of its title – "You won't see me" is both a fact and a warning. A third song grappling with the same emotional world, **We Can Work It Out**, was written and recorded in the same period and takes an outwardly conciliatory tone, but there's still a hint of steely threat in its "I'm-right-you're-wrong" stance which, interestingly, Lennon's pleadingly impatient middle manages to soften.

At eleven hours, it was the longest time The Beatles had yet spent recording a single song, yet the result was a beautifully restrained acoustic arrangement washed through with soothing harmonium chords. The most elaborate element of the record was a very particular tambourine part and an occasional lurch into four bars of German waltz time – Harrison's idea. It was ostensibly sharing the A-side of a single with **Day Tripper**, but airplay and public request soon ensured that **We Can Work It Out** came to be regarded as the lead track.

18. Nowhere Man

Lennon/McCartney; recorded October 21–22, 1965, EMI Studios, Abbey Road, London; available on *Rubber Soul* and *1962–1966*

Though considered at the time to be a critique of vacuous, directionless "straight" society, **Nowhere Man** is a further expression of Lennon's mid-career, mid-marriage, mid-suburbia malaise. Like **In My Life**, it came to him quickly after an unproductive session "trying to write a song that was meaningful and good". The self-flagellating tone is partially relieved by Lennon turning his beady-eyed insight on the listener, asking us to consider whether we are in fact that different from the Nowhere Man of the title, though the assuring second bridge can be heard as the song's most revealing moment of all. In Lennon's waiting to be lent a hand, he clearly anticipates external assistance in his crisis, whether through LSD, the Maharishi or ultimately the "dream girl" already alluded to in **Girl**, the "saviour" he eventually found in Yoko Ono.

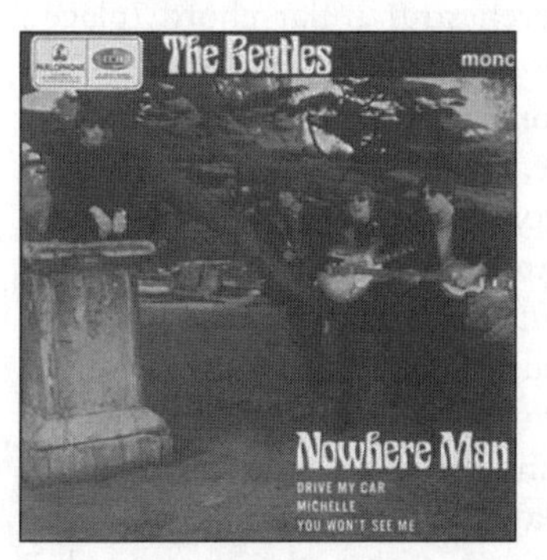

The powerful song was treated to luxuriously stacked harmonies and a glistening Fender Stratocaster guitar break from Harrison. Startlingly bright, the guitar sound was the result of the group encouraging the Abbey Road engineers to relax their established practice as to how "trebley" a recording should be.

19. Michelle

Lennon/McCartney; recorded November 3, 1965, EMI Studios, Abbey Road, London; available on *Rubber Soul* and *1962–1966*

Short of original tunes for *Rubber Soul*, Lennon reminded McCartney of a "joke" French-style song with nonsense French lyrics Paul used to do at art-school parties and encouraged him to develop it. Paul asked Jan Vaughan – wife of school friend Ivan Vaughan, the man who had introduced Paul to John eight years previously – to help with real French words (for which McCartney later apparently "sent her a cheque around") and John assisted with the

middle, inspired by the "I love you"'s of Nina Simone's **I Put A Spell On You**.

Probably the most harmonically adept of all Beatles songs, it features a reprise of their "ham-fisted jazz chord" (McCartney) learned from a guitarist in Liverpool (previously heard at the end of Harrison's **Till There Was You** solo and heard here on **Michelle** just before the line "my belle") among an impressively elegant welter of modulations and inversions. The fingerpicking style was the influence of Chet Atkins while the I–V–I rocking of the bass line against a chromatic descent in the guitar (heard on the intro and the end of the middle) McCartney credits to **Bizet**.

The sheer musicality of the piece made it a favourite among adult pop interpreters (The Overlanders' version hit #1 in January 1966) and the song went on to receive hundreds of covers and millions of radio plays. However, its light, tongue-in-cheek quality was regarded with suspicion by some as further evidence of a split in The Beatles' aesthetic between the parent-pleasing, cooing saccharine of McCartney and the anti-establishment wit and bile of Lennon.

20. Tomorrow Never Knows

Lennon/McCartney; recorded April 6, 7 and 22, 1966, EMI Studios, Abbey Road, London; available on *Revolver*

Written by Lennon in the wake of his LSD experiments in January 1966, the lyrics were adapted from the *Book Of The Dead*, a consoling, spiritually steering Tibetan Buddhist prayer to be murmured to the dying, as quoted in the acid-head's bible *The Psychedelic Experience* by **Timothy Leary**.

Composed as an arpeggiated, quasi-chant over a single droning C chord, the song was the first recorded for *Revolver* and quickly became an exercise in experimental sonic ingenuity. Dissuaded from his initial idea to have "thousands of monks chanting", Lennon settled for radical distortion of his singing voice first via Automatic Double Tracking, an Abbey Road innovation, then through the revolving Leslie speaker of a Hammond organ.

The backing track featured Starr's thundering, mesmeric drum pattern recorded using an extreme setting on the Fairchild limiter which, when cymbals were used, produced the effect that engineer Geoff Emerick described as "this whooshing, sucking noise" giving the impression of the drums being played backwards.

The extraordinary stereo storm of semi-random sound effects was achieved by five tape loops produced at home by the individual Beatles. These included the famous **screeching seagulls** (actually a sped-up recording of Paul laughing), an orchestral B-flat chord (placed with compositional judiciousness to create a haunting harmonic suspension) and an intense tamboura drone, created by removing the erase head on the recorder and saturating the tape.

The group and engineers all gathered in the control room, spooling the long pieces of tape with pencils while the producer worked the faders, mixing the loops with the backing track in real time direct to the stereo master. "There's no way I could re-create all those random loops going onto that two-track," remembered George Martin. "The actual mix itself was a performance."

By far the most radical music The Beatles had yet produced, its blend of rock with the avant-garde impressed most people, but not its composer. "It was a bit of a drag and I really didn't like it," he commented later. "I should have tried to get closer to my original idea, the monks singing. I realize now that was what I wanted."

21. Rain

Lennon/McCartney; recorded April 14 and 16, 1966, EMI Studios, Abbey Road, London; available on *Past Masters 2*

Written and recorded at the same time as *Revolver*, but appearing on the B-side of **Paperback Writer, Rain** enjoyed the same improved bass sound of the album (and its A-side). The audio improvement was due equally to McCartney's new Rickenbacker bass guitar and a new technique of recording that utilized a speaker as a microphone.

Indeed, McCartney's high and bold bass lines are dominant features of a track characterized by a droning, heavy, almost slow-motion feel. This mood was achieved by recording the backing track at a faster tape speed and slowing it on playback, creating a larger, more sonorous impact, especially from the drums. The process also accentuated any timing anomalies in the original performance and, with Starr's part virtually one long, elaborate drum fill, the track has a deliciously halting, woozy quality, almost threatening at times to stumble into the furniture.

Lennon, keen to sonically reflect his altered consciousness and weary of his natural sound, was impressed with anything that made his singing sound less like itself. The lead and the Eastern-sounding backing vocals were sped upward but Lennon was particularly delighted when he heard his voice played backwards. (Lennon claims to have discovered this himself at home, whilst George Martin remembers preparing and playing a tape for John at Abbey Road.) This remarkably appealing effect was used in the closing moments of the track and, though the technique was soon to become a psychedelic-era cliché, it was fresh enough in spring of 1966 to be used by the excited Beatles throughout *Revolver*.

The song itself amounts to a near-evangelical display of indifference to the physical world when the mind has been freed. "I can show you," Lennon is already knowingly announcing to the world, a whole year before he would tell it he'd "love to turn you on", though musically **Rain** is less the majestic manifestation of enlightenment than a blearily staggering stoner. Oasis would add a dash of Slade and base their entire style on it.

22. Taxman

Harrison; recorded April 20–22, 1966, EMI Studios, Abbey Road, London; available on *Revolver*

Appalled by the nineteen-and-a-half shillings in the pound (at the time, one pound was twenty shillings) top tax rate introduced by Harold Wilson's Labour government, George Harrison penned this sharp, caustic complaint (with some help from Lennon – notably the line advising the dead to declare the pennies placed upon their eyes) and set it to jarring, brittle-hard soul music.

Eleven hours of recording resulted in a track considered strong enough to open the *Revolver* album, a first for George. McCartney, whose whole-hearted contributions to Harrison's *Rubber Soul* songs had elevated their impact considerably, got right behind this song, playing some (by now, inevitably) excellent bass and a superb, scorchingly outraged guitar solo, sizzling with musical invention.

Far from feeling taken over, Harrison remembered being pleased by McCartney's interest and support. "It was like 'Great. I don't care who plays what. This is my big chance,'" he said. "If you notice, he did a little Indian bit on it for me."

Late additions to the arrangement were the "Ha ha Mr Wilson" backing vocals, immediately followed, lest The Beatles should be seen to be party political, by "Ha ha Mr Heath", a reference to the Prime Minster and the Leader of the Opposition, respectively.

23. Eleanor Rigby

Lennon/McCartney; recorded April 28–29 and June 6, 1966, EMI Studios, Abbey Road, London; available on *Revolver*, *1962–1966* and *1*

A lonely spinster, a lonely priest; she dies, he buries her. It's hardly **Love Me Do.** The combination of a lyric that was once memorably described by novelist A.S. Byatt as having "the minimalist perfection of a Beckett story", a chilly Bernard Herrmann-style arrangement for double string quartet by George Martin and a glassy-eyed vocal from McCartney makes **Eleanor Rigby** the bleakest and among the most brilliant of all Beatle works.

Even the story surrounding the name of the unfortunate heroine contains a spooky coincidence. Its main author McCartney claimed it was a blend of Eleanor Bron (the actress The Beatles worked with on *Help!*) and a Bristol wine shop called Rigby & Evans (spotted when visiting Jane Asher at the Old Vic), but there is in fact a gravestone in St Peter's Church, Woolton, Liverpool (where Lennon and McCartney first met), bearing the name Eleanor Rigby, who "died 10th October 1939, aged 44 years". McCartney claims to never have seen it.

The song was started by McCartney and finished at a stoned evening at Lennon's home in Weybridge with friends, and several people have staked claims on its development. Before settling on a name for the song and its central figure, Paul had considered, then rejected the name Miss Daisy Hawkins. The composer of the musical *Oliver!*, Lionel Bart, remembers at one point advising McCartney against calling it "Eleanor Hargreaves". Lennon claimed seventy percent of the lyric as his at one point, though neither McCartney nor Pete Shotton, who was at Kenwood that night, remember a single contribution from the host. Ringo apparently suggested Father McKenzie darning his socks, George the "all the lonely people" bit and Shotton, for his part, remembers coming up with the pay-off of Father McKenzie burying Miss Rigby in the final verse himself. Lennon's withering put-down at the time – "I don't think you understand what we're trying to get at, Pete" – was only partly assuaged by Pete discovering later that McCartney actually used the idea in the finished piece.

Generally celebrated as one of McCartney's masterworks, it has been covered over two hundred times, notably in progressive soul readings by Ray Charles and Aretha Franklin.

24. She Said She Said

Lennon/McCartney; recorded June 21, 1966, EMI Studios, Abbey Road, London; available on *Revolver*

When on tour in the USA in summer 1965, the entire Beatles team took LSD (except McCartney, who didn't partake until later – probably late 1966) at a celebrity party in LA with Roger McGuinn and David Crosby of **The Byrds** "and lots of girls" (Lennon). Having just watched, and been irritated by, the Jane Fonda movie *Cat Ballou*, a tripping Lennon was disturbed to overhear Jane's brother Peter Fonda soothing George Harrison (who, on his acid trip, thought he was dying) by telling him that he really knew what it was like to be dead, having nearly lost his life during a childhood operation.

Lennon, in a vulnerable state, was distressed by Fonda's morbid tone, but inspired enough by the incident to begin a song. Unsure at the time how to develop it ("it was meaning nothing'), it later received the additional 3/4 "when I was a boy" middle section in a moment of inspiration Lennon would later describe as "pure".

The bolted-together song was treated to a masterful group performance, with clusters of chiming guitars and a superb Ringo routine made more magical by a heavily compressed sound that made his cymbals emerge from the soundscape like slow-motion sea spray. The Beatles at their acid-rock peak.

25. Strawberry Fields Forever

Lennon/McCartney; recorded November 24, 28–29, December 8–9, 15 and 21–22, 1966, EMI Studios, Abbey Road, London; available on *Magical Mystery Tour* and *1967–1970*

Started in Almeria, Spain, while waiting between filming takes of *How I Won The War*, this affecting, ultra-Lennonesque jumble of nostalgia, egoism and insecurity was the beginning of the group's first post-touring recording project and it evolved, over an unheard-of 55 hours of studio time, into a magnum opus, perhaps the landmark Beatles record.

The garden of Strawberry Field – a Salvation Army orphanage near his childhood home – is where the young Lennon would be taken to summer fêtes by his Aunt Mimi and play with his mates Ivan Vaughan, Nigel Whalley and Pete Shotton. The chorus of the song has the effect of evoking a childlike place that is forever a haven while the verses explore more complex evocations.

Written in a deliberately halting, conversational style, the lyrics contrast a sharp lucidity with shrugging indifference and stumbling inarticulacy. He has a special insight, but then again, he says, so what? He could be a genius, he could be mad, he's learning to live with the isolation. Deciding it's all a dream anyway, now he doesn't know what to think. Remembering life was a lot easier in the childhood illusion of Strawberry Fields, he invites the listener to go there. These allusive fragments are set to appropriate this-way-that-way chords, and the whole is marvellously expressive of a trip through a hallucinatory hanging garden of the mind and memory.

Elaborately recorded to two entirely different states of near-completion, Lennon prevaricated as much as the character in the song ("I mean, er yes but it's all wrong") before asking George Martin to graft the first minute of version one to the back end of version two. Martin pointed out that the keys and tempi were different, to which Lennon replied, "You can fix it, George." Fix it he did, with careful varispeeding and astute editing, and the result was yet another watershed Beatle record.

In addition to conventional Beatle instrumental duties (including Harrison's gorgeous downward guitar slides and Indian arpeggios played on a swordmandel, a type of zither), there was an orgy of overdubs layering Mellotron (famously played by McCartney on the "flutes" setting), myriad percussion parts (including backward cymbals), cellos and traffic-parp trumpets. It could be argued that only some of this elaboration was in strict service of the song. Indeed, Lennon would once more complain of the record falling short of what he was after, accusing McCartney particularly of a cavalier experimentalism when recording Lennon's tracks while maintaining meticulous control of his own.

It was intended to be part of the *Sgt Pepper* album, but when Capitol pressed them for a new single the band stuck to their good-value general policy of not putting singles on albums, and **Strawberry Fields Forever** was extracted from the album, along with another milestone track, **Penny Lane**. George Martin would later describe this as the worst decision he took in the whole Beatles era. "We would have sold far more," the producer remembered, "if we had issued one of those with, say, **When I'm Sixty-Four** on the back."

Failing to reach #1 on either side of the Atlantic, **Strawberry Fields Forever** nevertheless set the standard and style for the entire psychedelic pop movement that would follow. It remains one of the single most impressive Beatles tracks in the entire canon and therefore, by definition, one of pop music's finest achievements.

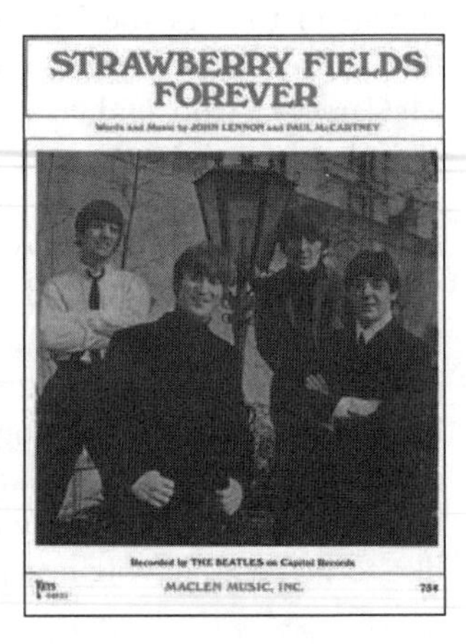

26. Penny Lane

Lennon/McCartney; recorded December 29–30 1966, January 4–6, 9–10 and 12–17, 1967, EMI Studios, Abbey Road, London; available on *Magical Mystery Tour*, *1967–1970* and *1*

McCartney had mentioned his intention of writing a song about Penny Lane (first alluded to in the Liverpool travelogue that was Lennon's first draft of "In My Life") as early as autumn 1965. In December 1966, work began on his semi-fictional whistle-stop tour of the Liverpool district. Jaunty psychedelic pop, its wry, "life's a gas" absurdism was the perfect flip-side to the shadowy uncertainty of Lennon's **Strawberry Fields** and when taken together (as on the double A-sided January 1967 single), they are the most vivid expression yet made of the differences in the respective composers' outlooks.

The recording of the song centred initially on overdubbing four unison parts for the on-the-beat marching piano chords (soon to become a McCartney trademark) but **Penny Lane**, like **Strawberry Fields Forever**, was soon subjected to another overdub extravaganza. Flutes, trumpets, oboes and cor anglais all played their part in an extraordinarily rococo track, but it wasn't until the brilliant crowning flourish of the piccolo trumpet solo played by David Mason (heard by McCartney playing Bach on television, and hired the following day) that the recording was considered complete.

The instrumentation (the fire-bell, for instance) and arrangement (a general air of Edwardian fussiness) serve the song rather more literally than they do in **Strawberry Fields Forever.** Even the two key-centres underline two distinct narrative states as the song cuts between the verses (in which a present-tense Penny Lane is "here") and choruses (in which the narrator sits "here", remembering Penny Lane "there") with the immediacy of a film flashback.

Though the locations (mostly real) and character eccentricities are story-book bright, many details, when not contradictory (the skies are blue, yet "pouring rain" occurs twice), are left teasingly unexplained. Why does the banker

"It is possible to see in The Beatles' music a synthesis in which one of the strongest elements has been a powerful and probably instinctive Englishry ... which goes back ... to pastoral pentatonic tunes and other revitalised archaisms."

The Times leader, 1967

never wear a mac? What does the fireman do with his hourglass? The hallucinatory images pile up (with the pretty nurse revealed as being "in a play", an equivalent to Lennon's declaring that "nothing is real" in **Strawberry Fields**) until three of the song's characters are brought together in the barber's shop thanks to personal grooming arrangements and a change in the weather. Elusively ear-catching, it's perhaps the most vivid and magical of McCartney's story-songs.

27. A Day In The Life

Lennon/McCartney; recorded January 19–20 and February 3, 10 and 22, 1967, EMI Studios, Abbey Road, London; available on *Sgt Pepper's Lonely Hearts Club Band* and *1967–1970*

Two news stories in the *Daily Mail* of January 17, 1967 – one concerning the coroner's report on the 21-year-old Guinness heir Tara Brown, a friend of Paul's who had died in a car crash in December, another about pot-holes in a road in Blackburn – inspired Lennon to some of his best sighing-sad verses. When McCartney's dapper everyman middle was added, the song evolved into a magnificently weary commentary about the dulling effect of commonplace consumption of the media and time-pressured routine, compared with the expansion of perception that drugs can bring. With its alluring "I'd love to turn you on" motif (suggested by McCartney), the song amounts to no less than an invitation to the straight world to join the high-flying Beatles on their cosmic journey of enlightenment.

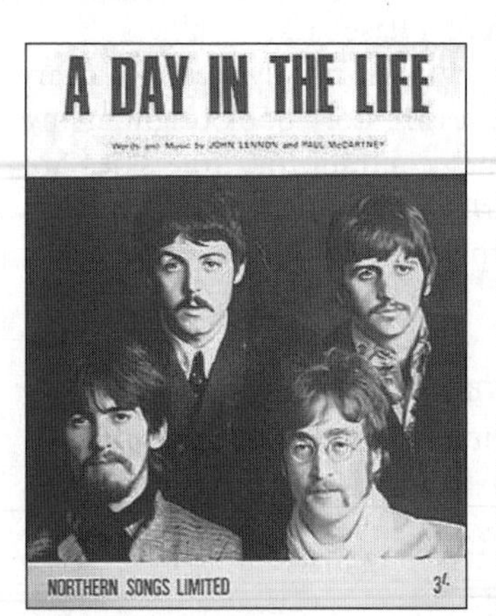

It might be easier to marginalize **A Day In The Life** as a Summer of Love relic (which it also is) if it were couched in the musical whimsy of the period like, say, Scott McKenzie's **San Francisco** of later that summer. However, dressed in the discreetly presented, neutral colours of acoustic guitar and piano, and featuring a superb drum part, comfortingly responding to Lennon's distressed "Oh boy"' (though Starr had to be cajoled into playing "lead drums"), it has an ambient timelessness that frees it from its place in history, while also being entirely reflective of it.

It's also memorable for a pair of remarkable overdubs. The transition between Lennon's verses and McCartney's bridge hadn't been devised so a gap was left in the recording with Mal Evans (still audible on the finished record) counting down 24 bars before allowing an alarm clock to ring, marking the end of the "moment" and appropriately heralding the "Woke up" bridge. Having come up with the "turn you on" line, McCartney wanted something suitably momentous to occur and requested a symphony orchestra to pursue one of his John Cage-like avant-garde ideas. He settled for half an orchestra and on February 10, 41 orchestral musicians, along with members of The Rolling Stones, The Monkees and various hangers-on attended EMI's cavernous Studio 1 for the event).

The players wore full evening dress and party novelties before attempting a mass, random instrumental ascension from their lowest possible note to climax on cue on their highest note belonging to the chord of E major. Overdubbed four times in all, the resulting swirling tornado of sound was used twice on **A Day In The Life**, once in the middle and once at the end. Still not quite considered finished, a final chord was needed and after abandoning a harmonized vocal hum, The Beatles went for four pairs of hands on three separate pianos all crashing down onto E major (overdubbed four times), which then resonates and fades for nearly a minute.

Highly regarded by Lennon even at the height of his anti-Beatles radicalism, **A Day In The Life** remains the enduring masterpiece of the greatest pop group of all, at the peak of their powers.

28. Sgt Pepper's Lonely Hearts Club Band

Lennon/McCartney; recorded February 1–2, March 3 and 6, 1967, EMI Studios, Abbey Road, London; available on *Sgt Pepper's Lonely Hearts Club Band* and *1967–1970*

Penned by McCartney as a way of introducing The Beatles' submerging of their identity behind a fictitious band, an orchestra tuning up and an expectantly murmuring audience heralds "Sgt Pepper's Lonely Hearts Club Band", the opening track of its eponymous album: an audacious blend of Hendrix-inspired rock (both McCartney and Lennon had attended a concert by the guitarist days before recording it) and huffing Edwardian horns. Hendrix later acknowledged The Beatles and McCartney in particular – he was invited to the Monterey Festival on Paul's recommendation – by opening his show with **Sgt Pepper** two days after the release of the album.

With McCartney welcoming us to the show in his best Little Richard holler to the sound of dubbed-in audience gasps, screams and laughter, the listener is instantly, happily confused as to whether Sgt Pepper's band is supposed to be The Beatles or the horn players or both. However, on the album, the alter-ego idea is never developed beyond Ringo being introduced as "Billy Shears" as the track segues into **With A Little Help From My Friends**.

While "Sgt Pepper's Lonely Hearts Club Band" may not be the subtlest or deepest of Beatles compositions, its recording has the colour and confidence of a Fourth of July parade and raises the curtain on the dizzying album to which it gives its name with genuine panache.

29. Lucy In The Sky With Diamonds

Lennon/McCartney; recorded February 28, March 1–2, 1967, EMI Studios, Abbey Road, London; available on *Sgt Pepper's Lonely Hearts Club Band* and *1967–1970*

When John Lennon asked his son Julian what one of his school drawings was about, the 4-year-old explained to his father it was his

nursery classmate Lucy, in the sky, with diamonds. Instantly reminded of one of his favourite authors, Lewis Carroll, Lennon used the title to start a surreal, *Through The Looking Glass* style song, finishing it off when McCartney arrived at Weybridge, bouncing imagery off each other, trading "newspaper taxis" with "kaleidoscope eyes".

In recording McCartney devised the gracefully unfolding arpeggios on a Lowry organ, an instrument whose notes had the glacial decay a Hammond wouldn't have given them. Harrison contributed the droning tamboura, which brings a weighty torpidity to the track. Starr was charged with the responsibility of shifting the song from drifting 3/4 into rocking 4/4 via the "clutchless gear change" (Martin) of three thumps on the drums. Otherwise, "Lucy" is generally considered the most Lennonesque of all the music on "Sgt Pepper".

In the face of later drug revelations in the press, the song's hallucinatory air, and the fact that the initial letters of the title's main words spelled out LSD, Lennon and McCartney found themselves having to deny many times over the years that "Lucy" was a veiled reference to acid. Given their forthright reminiscences about their drug experiences, the innocent explanation rings true. Later, Lennon preferred to consider it as an intuitive anticipation of the arrival of the woman who would "save" him. "Maybe it should be 'Yoko In The Sky With Diamonds'," he said.

30. She's Leaving Home

Lennon/McCartney; recorded March 17–20 1967, EMI Studios, Abbey Road, London; available on *Sgt Pepper's Lonely Hearts Club Band*

Inspired once more by a *Daily Mail* article, this time a story concerning the disappearance of a teenage girl ("I cannot imagine why she should run away," her father was quoted as saying, "she has everything here"), McCartney fashioned an exquisitely observed and executed vignette of the drift between generations. One of his most powerful lyrics, the condensed detail contains tip-of-the-iceberg resonance (there's a whole play in lines like those describing the girl's waiting to keep her appointment with the man from "the motor trade"), while Lennon's hand-wringing parental clichés, with their beautifully caught repetitions, suggest a serene empathy with a difficult situation.

McCartney, excited by his new composition, heard it as an arrangement rather than a Beatles performance and summoned George Martin to Cavendish Avenue to begin work. Martin demurred, being booked for a Cilla Black session. The Beatle, rather stung by Martin's decision to honour a previous commitment rather than jump to assist McCartney's latest masterpiece, phoned Mike Leander, whom he had met on Marianne Faithfull's **Yesterday** session (and who would go on to be Gary Glitter's co-writer and producer in the 1970s).

Leander did a fine job, full of dramatic details such as the agitated strings after "our baby's gone" suggesting SOS Morse code, ambulance sirens and ringing telephones. Though Martin confessed later to being deeply wounded at having been so casually supplanted, he recorded the arrangement with customary care, coaxing from the nine-piece ensemble one of the lushest Beatle orchestral sounds on one of the most mature of Beatle songs.

31. Within You Without You

(Harrison); recorded March 15 and 20, April 3–4, 1967, EMI Studios, Abbey Road, London; available on *Sgt Pepper's Lonely Hearts Club Band*

After scoring two strong songs on *Rubber Soul* and three on *Revolver*, George's preoccupation with Indian culture and LSD had left him even less musically productive than Lennon. His sole composed contribution to the *Pepper* sessions had been the quickly sidelined, clumsily dour joke **Only A Northern Song** (written to fulfil his contractual obligation to publishers Northern Songs, so he could establish Harrisongs). The arrival of **Within You Without You** was greeted with "a bit of relief all round" as George Martin remembered.

Begun after a long evening's stoned talk at the house of Klaus Voormann (the friend from Hamburg who designed the *Revolver* and, much later, the *Anthology* album covers), Harrison picked out the modal tune on his friend's harmonium, an instrument he had never played before. The resulting eastern melody Harrison credits to having the Indian exercises (sargams) he regularly practised constantly in his head in that period. That the lyrics (completed later at home) reflecting Hindu beyond-self-we're-all-one philosophy happened to connect with the acid generation's universality-through-ego-loss experience the author claimed as coincidence. "It's nothing to do with pills," he said at the time. "It's just in your own head, the realisation."

Even more of an exclusively George track than the Eastern-flavoured **Love You To** on *Revolver* before it, **Within You Without You** featured only Harrison from among The Beatles and uncredited Indian musicians from the Eastern Music Circle in Finchley, with Neil Aspinall caressing a tamboura. Georges Harrison and Martin both worked hard on the track, spending hours synchronizing Martin's superb string arrangement to the intricate dynamics and rhythms of the dilruba, the bowed Indian instrument carrying the melody in the 5/8 instrumental passage. The sonorous, serious result is some of the most exotic music released under The Beatles' name.

The other Beatles watched Harrison drill the Indian musicians with great tact and musicality. "There is his innate talent, he brought that sound together," said Lennon of Harrison's work on **Within You Without You**. "He's clear on that. His mind and sound are clear."

32. I Am The Walrus

Lennon/McCartney; recorded September 5–6 and 27–29, 1967, EMI Studios, Abbey Road, London; available on *Magical Mystery Tour* and *1967–1970*

The most extreme example of Lennon's penchant for obscurity, **I Am The Walrus** is regarded by some as the peak of Lennon's surreal genius, by others as a meaningless pit of nasty nonsense. Initially inspired variously by acid, a police siren (which gave him the seesawing tune) and a letter from a pupil from his old Quarry Bank School reporting that they were studying Beatles lyrics there in English lessons. Simultaneously amused and appalled, Lennon proceeded to juxtapose unrelated images to create bizarre wordscapes in order to deliberately confuse over-zealous interpreters. (This approach would reach a mean-spirited low on **Glass Onion**.) Delighting in the idea that the school that once said of the future Beatle "this boy is bound to fail" would soon be scratching their heads fathoming old boy Lennon's profundity, he composed the immortal line referring to semolina pilchard ascending the Eiffel Tower. "Let the fuckers work that one out," he told Pete Shotton.

However, with Lennon admitting later that the line describing a penguin "singing Hare Krishna" was a conscious criticism of the spiritual naivety of "putting all your eggs in one basket", the remainder of the text just about stands up to interpretation as a sorrowful, frothing, hallucinatory rant at the "straight" world's institutionalized authority, whether the police, religion, marriage, "experts" or teachers.

The "Walrus" derives from the character John wrongly assumed to be the "good guy" in Lewis Carroll's *Walrus And The Carpenter* poem from *Through The Looking Glass*. The "Eggman' was supposedly inspired by The Animals' **Eric Burdon**, who had a predilection for breaking raw eggs on the bodies of the girls with whom he consorted, an activity allegedly witnessed and excitedly encouraged by Lennon at an orgy. How either of the above connections fit with any interpretation of the song is hard to say.

Set to a peculiar sequence of shifting-sand major chords built from the white notes of a piano, the song thrilled George Martin, generally suspicious of The Beatles' current interest in "randomness as art", and he arranged a stormingly inspired score. Sliding, chugging cellos and berserk backing vocals for the **Mike Sammes Singers** more used to crooning Broadway melodies than shrieking, whooping and chanting "Oompah, oompah" made for a tour de force for all concerned.

33. The Fool On The Hill

Lennon/McCartney; recorded September 25–27 and October 20, 1967, EMI Studios, Abbey Road, London; available on *Magical Mystery Tour* and *1967–1970*

Sitting at his father's piano early in 1967, McCartney hit a D6 chord and from there composed a bewitching major-key melody that arced gently upward, settling "perfectly still" on serene high 6ths. He had used an unexpected switch to minor several times in songs from the period (**Penny Lane, Fixing A Hole**) but here the change of tonality hits precisely where the song reveals what the fool on the hill sees: the solemn, inner truth behind the foolish grin.

McCartney claimed the song was about "someone like the Maharishi," and he is known to have sung an early version to Lennon in March 1967 (The Beatles didn't meet the Maharishi until August), which gives credence to some commentators' detection of an autobiographical slant. However, part of the joy of the piece is the finely judged lyrical ambiguity that, along with the beautiful spaciousness of the arrangement (all flutes, recorders, bass harmonica and whispery brushes on the drums), allows a myriad of implied meanings to float beguilingly into the imagination of the listener.

> ***"Opposite poles generate electricity: between John and Paul the sparks flew. John's fiery iconoclasm was tempered by Paul's lyrical grace, while Paul's wide-eyed charm was toughened by John's resilience."***
>
> Wilfred Mellors, *Music And Musicians* magazine, 1972

34. Lady Madonna

Lennon/McCartney; recorded February 3–6, 1968, EMI Studios, Abbey Road, London; available on *Past Masters 2, 1967–1970* and *1*

McCartney's paean to the working-class female elevates womanhood, and especially motherhood, to the state of sainthood. Not an especially fashionable view among twenty-something northern men in the mid-1960s, but one that has perhaps endured more than other exhortations of the period.

A neat, Fats Domino-style piano boogie lick (along with a drum arrangement of double-time brushes plus backbeat) borrowed from George Martin's 1956 production of Humphrey Lyttleton's **Bad Penny Blues**, underpinning McCartney's disarmingly arch Domino/Presley hybrid vocal, made for a breezily rocking record, just the thing to shrug off the *Magical Mystery Tour* savaging only weeks before. It certainly didn't sound like a humbled Beatles; in fact it hardly sounded like The Beatles at all. Still doesn't.

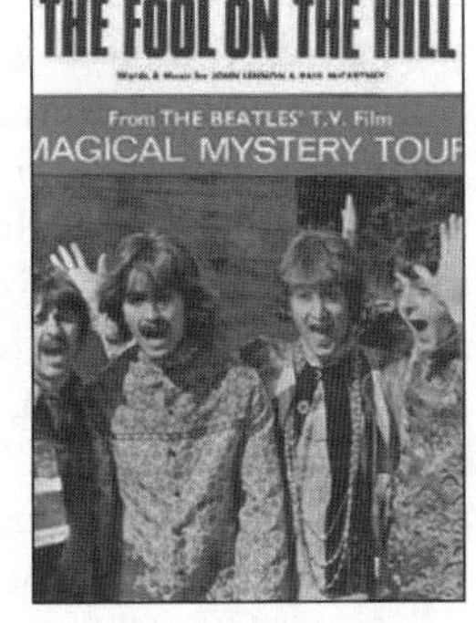

35. Revolution

Lennon/McCartney; recorded May 30–31, June 4 and 21, 1968, EMI Studios, Abbey Road, London; available on *The Beatles, Past Masters 2* and *1967–1970*.

Lennon's reaction to the revolutionary fervour sweeping Europe, particularly in France, supported by left-wing radicals throughout the counterculture, was remarkably cogent. Under pressure to nail his colours to the mast, Lennon instinctively resisted the ideas of extremism, self-appointed authorities (see **I Am The Walrus**) and change through violence. After all, he had been singing **All You Need Is Love** only ten months before he penned **Revolution:** he preferred to advocate a revolution in the mind. "Tell me one successful revolution," he wrote to a university magazine that had criticized his stance as "sloppy and irrelevant". "Who fucked up Communism, Christianity, capitalism, Buddhism, etc? Sick heads, and nothing else."

However, he was unsure enough at the time of the first recording of the song (which appeared on *The White Album*) to hedge his bets. The song is delivered amid a stoned, bluesy jam, with the vocals sung by Lennon lying flat on his back (later takes dissolved into full-on freak outs); the bleary singer obliquely (but perhaps appropriately given his state) suggests that as far as "destruction" is concerned, we can count him "out/in". The later version, recorded as a vibrant rocker in which the equivocal "In" is missing, has the effect of making his flower-proffering pacifism a positive, dynamic option rather than a soporifically waved white flag.

Another reason **Revolution** was entirely remade as a brighter and tighter track three weeks later was because Lennon hoped to make the song commercial enough to be the A-side of the new single. It rolled over in the face of **Hey Jude**, and the track's brutally overdriven guitars caused many a **Hey Jude** lover to attempt to return the record, imagining that there was something wrong with the B-side. Harassed record-department assistants were heard explaining, "It's called distortion, apparently. It's meant to sound like that."

36. While My Guitar Gently Weeps

Harrison; recorded July 25, August 16, and September 3, 5–6, 1968, EMI Studios, Abbey Road, London; available on *The White Album* and *1967–1970*

After coming across the phrase "gently weeps" on a randomly chosen page of a randomly chosen book, Harrison cast an eye around himself and, as usual (see also **Think For Yourself, Taxman, Within You Without You** or **Piggies**) found things wanting. Specifically, The Beatles. He later admitted that his **Not Guilty** (recorded in the same period but not released) expressed a very specific frustration at Lennon's and McCartney's dominance. It's difficult not to hear **While My Guitar Gently Weeps** in a similar light.

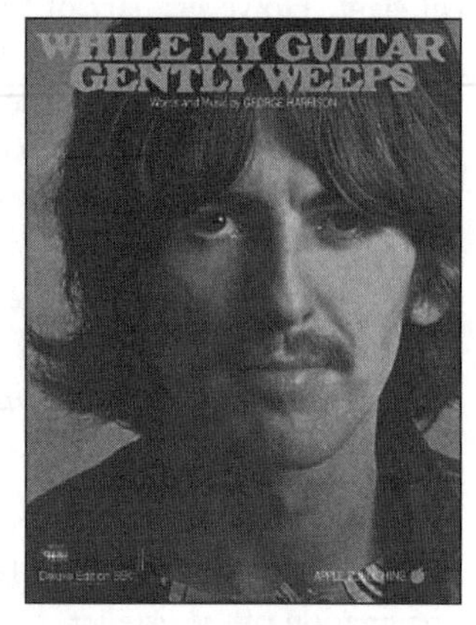

There's a peculiar sense throughout of an undervalued, under-involved, passive-aggressive junior partner observing sadly from the sidelines, especially in the excised lines about "doing nothing but ageing" while watching "a play' (to be heard in the demo version on *Anthology 3*).

Whether the group had gleaned the references to themselves, were just being true to condescending form or were genuinely uninspired by the dirge-like tempo, the doomy chords and the wailingly reproachful and self-pitying sentiments, The Beatles' initial efforts showed little enthusiasm. Frustrated in his painstaking attempts to capture a satisfying, crying, backwards guitar solo and determined to salvage the song from the band's apathy (Harrison: "I knew inside of me that it was a nice song"), George invited Eric Clapton to play lead guitar and was heartened to note that in Clapton's presence, "the other guys were as good as gold". Initially unsure of his role ("no one plays on Beatle records" Clapton remembered thinking), the guest guitarist delivered some excellent, aching blues lines but felt moved to suggest the application of ADT "wobble" on his guitar parts to make it sound more "Beatley".

The ominous result, sagging with reproachment, is one of the heaviest records The Beatles ever made; the resplendent major-key middle section is like a ton weight being lifted from the music. However, over thirty years on from the atmosphere that inspired it, while hardly one of the "finest love songs ever written", as inexplicably judged by Ringo, it is undoubtedly a Harrison classic of sorts.

37. Hey Jude

Lennon/McCartney; recorded July 29–31 and August 1 1968, EMI and Trident Studios London; available on *Past Masters 2, 1967–1970* and *1*

Conceived as McCartney drove out to Kenwood to show support for Cynthia, who was amidst the trauma of divorcing John, **Hey Jude** was initially a song of comfort for the Lennons' son Julian ("Hey Jules") but clearly evolved into a song of encouragement to an adult not to be afraid to act on feelings. Lennon believed, when he first heard it (and still believed just before his death), that it was McCartney's way of giving John and Yoko his blessing. McCartney, whose engagement to Jane Asher had recently ended and who was about to commit to Linda Eastman, assured Lennon it was about himself. (Lennon also saved a filler line that an embarrassed McCartney was going to change – "The movement you need is on your shoulder" – declaring it the most telling line [as in, "the solution to your situation is right there"] in a piece he would later call McCartney's best song ever.)

Featuring a masterful vocal performance that covered McCartney's entire range from the peaceful woody croon of the verse and chorus, to his inspired, hysterical howling improvisations in the coda, McCartney's baby got such enthusiastic group support that he found himself in the uncomfortable position of having to pare back Harrison's echoing riffs. "It was a bit of a number for me to have to dare to tell George Harrison, who's one of the greats, not to play. It was like an insult," remembered McCartney, admitting "It was bossy, but it was also ballsy. I could have bowed to the pressure."

McCartney always considered the chanted second section (the long fade of which made **Hey Jude** the longest single release to date at the time: over seven minutes) as an integral part of the song. After the soothing, brow-mopping

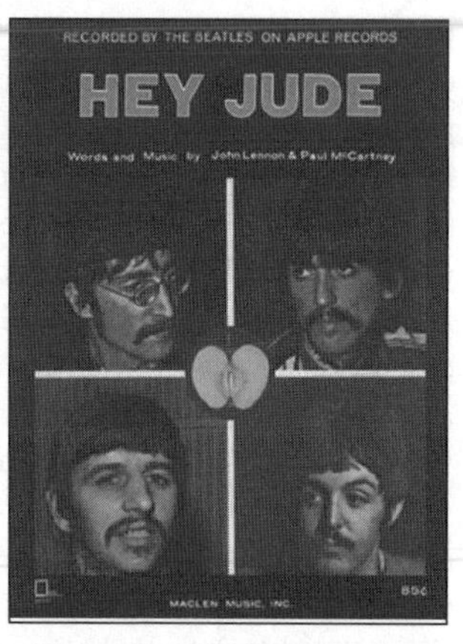

support of the song itself, it serves as an uninhibited terrace chant of encouragement, a veritable celebration of the excitement of letting go. Even the musicians hired for the orchestration of the chant were persuaded (with double their fee) to sing and clap along to the mantra-like repeated four bars that, to this day, achieve a full-hearted communality whenever the song is played.

38. Happiness Is A Warm Gun

Lennon/McCartney; recorded September 23–25, 1968, EMI Studios, Abbey Road, London; available on *The White Album*

Happiness Is A Warm Gun – both despite and because of its sinister mishmash of imagery and mood and its dementedly restless metric design – is perhaps the most arresting track on *The White Album*. The title was inspired by the headline of a gun magazine, itself an adaptation of the *Peanuts* comic-strip aphorism "Happiness is a warm puppy". It struck Lennon as "fantastic, insane ... a warm gun means you've just shot something," and he adapted it for his own sexually suggestive purposes.

Lennon once suggested to George Martin that he considered the art of songwriting to be making bits up and joining them together. That methodology was never more evident than on **Happiness Is A Warm Gun**, which comprises four distinct musical sections that never reprise and a series of unrelated, free-associated images that create a fantastical picture resonating beyond rationality. Derek Taylor, The Beatles' publicist, remembers suggesting many of the ideas himself at another stoned evening at Kenwood. "She's not a girl who misses much" was a saying of Taylor's mother to describe a particularly bright woman; another of the song's fanciful phrases took its inspiration from a shoplifter who kept a false pair of hands on the shop counter while pilfering under his coat; whilst the man who eats a "soap impression" of his wife before donating it to the National Trust was about defecating in public. What with that, the drugs ("I need a fix") and the sex ("my finger on your trigger"), it's quite a brew.

Perhaps stung by a comment Yoko felt compelled to make during the recording of **Hey Bulldog** in February 1968 about the monotony of The Beatles' beat, Lennon let his naturally wayward sense of time, and his attraction to rhythmic irregularity be formalized into the most complex series

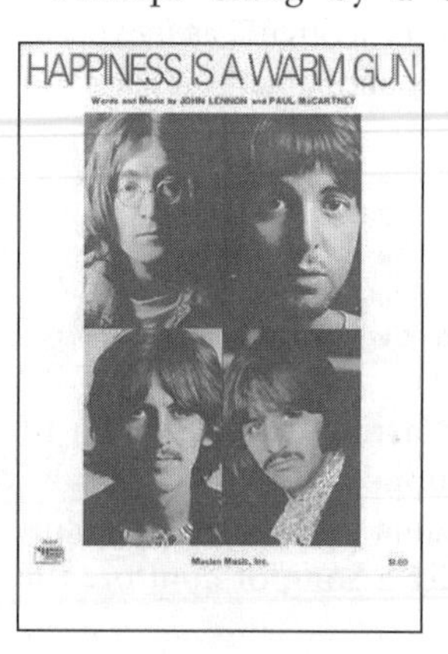

of time changes The Beatles ever attempted. A dogged band effort spread over fifteen hours and nearly one hundred takes (everyone liked the song – McCartney later pronounced it his favourite on *The White Album*), the resulting two minutes forty seconds of acid-folk, progressive rock and doo-wop was described by Lennon as "a history of rock'n'roll". It's not quite that, but certainly one of Lennon's final masterpieces for The Beatles.

39. Blackbird

Lennon/McCartney; recorded June 11, 1968, EMI Studios, Abbey Road, London; available on *The White Album*

Music inspired by Bach, words inspired by the civil rights movement, the modest delivery (acoustic guitar, metronome, birdsong) belies a wealth of compositional detail and full-hearted spirit. The parallel tenths of the guitar part spell out a gorgeously logical harmonic journey, rich with voice-leading tension and sweet resolve. The lyric is a beautifully restrained metaphor for struggle of any kind. (The black-rights connection was not publicly discussed until years later, though McCartney is heard mentioning it to Donovan on a bootleg recording from late 1968.)

With George and Ringo out of the country and John deep into the tape-loop extravaganza of **Revolution 9** with Yoko in Studio 2, Paul recorded his **Blackbird** alone in Studio 3. He would do something similar five months later, this time with only Ringo for company, on **Why Don't We Do It In The Road?** "I can't speak for George," remembered Lennon, "but I was always hurt when Paul would knock something off without involving us." McCartney, for his part, had felt excluded from **Revolution 9**. But as Lennon said, "That's just how it was then."

40. Helter Skelter

Lennon/McCartney; recorded July 18 and September 9–10, 1968, EMI Studios, Abbey Road, London; available on *The White Album*

McCartney was surprised when he heard a Who record – probably 1967's **I Can See For Miles**, which he'd read described as "wild" and "screaming" – to note that it was in fact "quite straight … very sort of sophisticated". (The inadequately approximate language of the UK music press of the time, struggling to keep up with pop's mid-1960s inventiveness, should have come as no surprise to McCartney. The *New Musical Express* once described the lugubrious **Ticket To Ride** thus: "It bounds along at a jaunty pace … at about much the same tempo as **I Feel Fine**.")

Feeling inspired to create the "loudest, nastiest, sweatiest" rock track imaginable himself, McCartney directed The Beatles appropriately on his vaguely threatening slip of a song, where the highs and lows of the named fairground ride serve, perhaps, as a relationship/drugs/sex metaphor. The Beatles were not really equipped with sufficient rock (as opposed to rock'n'roll) chops to be entirely convincing – much of the energy of the track comes from McCartney's hysterical vocal – though they gave it their best shot; one take of this out-of-tune thrash extended to 27 minutes, another – as part of what temporary producer Chris Thomas recalled as a "pretty undisciplined session" – ended with Starr shouting "I've got blisters on my fingers," a moment used on the final track. (Though not on mono copies of the album.)

An unhappy side-issue of the track is that lunatic cult-leader Charles Manson used it (and other songs on *The White Album*, particularly **Piggies**, Harrison's swipe at privilege and oppression) as "justification" for him and his followers to commit murder. The jury at Manson's 1971 trial were compelled to listen to the entire *White Album* to glean the "messages" heard by Manson as apocalyptic warning of an ensuing race war. The jury heard no such thing and Manson was sentenced to death, later reduced to life imprisonment.

41. Julia

Lennon/McCartney; recorded October 13, 1968, EMI Studios, Abbey Road, London; available on *The White Album*

In the flood of feeling that escaped him in the wake of his union with Yoko Ono, Lennon felt able to address his dead mother by name in a song, and to combine it with metaphors clearly alluding to his new love. Lennon credited Yoko with help on **Julia** (the "floating sky" and "silent cloud" imagery is very Ono) though equally influential was Donovan, the British folk singer and guitarist who had taught John the finger-picking style he uses here and elsewhere on *The White Album*.

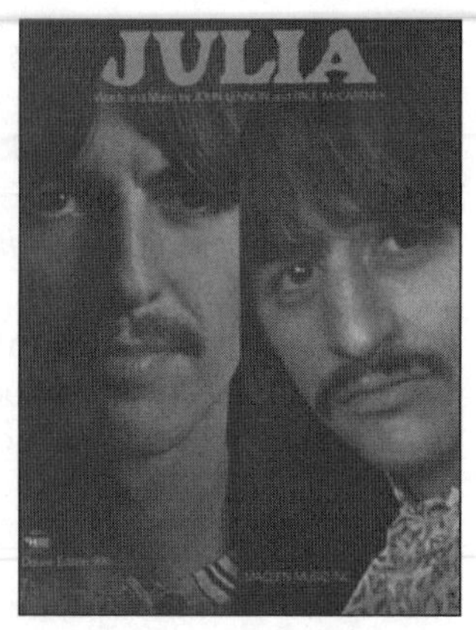

The less-than-assertive double tracking of the subtle guitar chords and vocal (it was the final song taped for the under-pressure album, and also a Lennon solo performance) makes for beautifully vulnerable music which touchingly conveys Lennon's hushed wonder at the depth of his emergent emotions. The Lydian surprise (a rare – in pop – sharpening of the fourth note of a major scale) of the middle ("shimmering") may be the most elegant musical moment of Lennon's entire catalogue.

42. Don't Let Me Down

Lennon/McCartney; January 22, 28 and 30, 1969, Apple Studios, Savile Row, London; available on *Past Masters 2* and *Let It Be ... Naked*

With an emotional directness that anticipated his Plastic Ono Band solo recordings eighteen months later, **Don't Let Me Down** was an unmistakable cry from Lennon's heart. Although excited by the possibilities his new life with his new partner afforded him, in his vulnerable moments Lennon felt, as McCartney recalled, very much "out on a limb". That vulnerability was exacerbated by his current involvement with heroin and the resultant *cri*

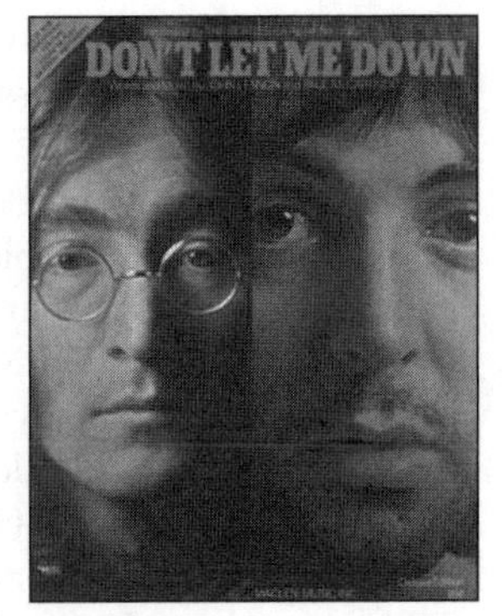

de coeur was like a feverish manifestation of the romantic insecurity previously drawn on five years earlier in **If I Fell**, only this time it's no polite enquiry, it's a howl of helplessness.

The simple-sounding "jamming" arrangement was hard won, the two-chord song having been subjected to dozens of McCartney's mostly rejected elaborative suggestions, the vestige of which can be heard in the convoluted bass and guitar unison lines in the middle. Lennon's passion and the group's re-evolving instinct for suitable ensemble backing win out in the end, though the effect of Billy Preston's musicianly electric piano on the polish of the final performance cannot be underestimated.

43. Get Back

Lennon/McCartney; recorded January 23, 27–28, 30 and February 5, 1969, Apple Studios, Savile Row, London; available on *Let It Be, 1967–1970, Past Masters 2, 1*, and *Let It Be...Naked*

The first and probably best track to emerge from the "as nature intended" *Get Back* project, the single release was a studio recording done the day after the slightly rawer take which appeared on the *Let It Be* album. Though both have their virtues, the slick ensemble work and lush studio sonics of the single are particularly pleasing to the ear. Starr's galloping, damped snare, Harrison's chopping on-the-beat rhythm guitar, Lennon's colourful rhythm/lead flourishes, Billy Preston's jazzy electric piano and McCartney's muted, nuanced vocals generate considerable momentum and style. **Get Back** is a great example of how to make mature rock music out of two or three chords.

Intended as a critique of British jingoism in the face of the late-1960s influx of Asian refugees, the original lyrics contained lines parodying racial prejudice but sung straight ("Don't dig no Pakistani taking all the people's jobs"). Deciding such an approach might easily be misconstrued and/or misappropriated (the National Front were by now an emergent neo-Nazi political force), they reworked the text to tell a cheerful, nonsensical tale of confused sexual identity and chasing good marijuana across America. That the two characters, Jojo and Loretta, neither get round to meeting each other (à la **Eleanor Rigby**, **Penny Lane** or **Rocky Raccoon**) nor to enjoying any third-verse exposition beyond their teasing introductions is symptomatic of the who-cares, in-rehearsal redraft the song became.

44. Let It Be

Lennon/McCartney; January 25–26 and 31, April 30, 1969, and January 4 1970, Apple and EMI Studios, London; available on *Let It Be*, *1967–1970* and *1*

Let It Be was written by McCartney in late 1968, a period when he remembers feeling "quite paranoid" and after a reassuring dream in which his late mother appeared to assuage his worries. Sharing the grandiose but calm gospel atmosphere of **Bridge Over Troubled Water**, Lennon later mistakenly assumed Paul Simon's tune was the song McCartney had been emulating; however, **Let It Be** was actually written a year or so earlier.

Over the course of the coming years, **Let It Be** was elevated to the status of a secular hymn. Bob Geldof requested McCartney sing it as the climax to his 1985 evangelically driven famine fund-raiser, Live Aid. But the churchy chords, the words of wisdom and especially the semi-coincidental evocation of the Virgin Mary (McCartney's mother was called Mary) also made it a favourite among believers.

There's an odour of sabotage about the way it was programmed on the *Let It Be* album, sandwiched as it was between Lennon's facetious spoken intro ("And now we'd like to do "Ark The Angels Come'") and his ramshackle version of a traditional song about a Liverpool prostitute, **Maggie Mae**. However, its release in March 1970 as the final Beatles UK single meant, during the trauma of The Beatles' split, it hung in the airwaves like a comfort blanket for the world.

45. The Ballad Of John And Yoko

Lennon/McCartney; April 14, 1969, EMI Studios, Abbey Road, London; available on *1967–1970* and *1*

On May 18, 1968, John Lennon called a meeting of The Beatles at Apple to announce, with apparent seriousness, that he was the current incarnation of Jesus Christ. The meeting was calmly adjourned to give everyone time to absorb the news. The following day, however, Lennon's life with Yoko Ono began and John being Jesus was never mentioned again.

This is but one of several occurrences in The Beatles saga where the names of John Lennon and Jesus Christ meet, the most famous and controversial of course being John's famous 1966 gaffe about The Beatles being more popular than Christianity. Not necessarily a judgement call, it was just a fact, though ill-judged PR.

However, in **The Ballad Of John And Yoko**, Christ is invoked twice. Once as a familiar, blasphemous expression of frustration to herald every chorus (which naturally resulted in an instant airplay ban) and, secondly, in Lennon feeling that the way things are going he is heading for martyred crucifixion too. Given that the song's lyrics were little more than self-aggrandising journalese in limerick form concerning their marriage, honeymoon and peace-promotion adventures in Europe, the Christ reference might seem at first a tad overstated. But there's little doubt that Lennon felt a connection between his peacenik activities and those of Jesus. "We're trying to make Christ's message contemporary," he said at one point during the marathon press conferences delivered during the Bed-In For Peace honeymoon in Amsterdam. "Christ made miracles to tell his message. Well today's miracle is communications, so let's use it."

Andrew Lloyd Webber and Tim Rice thought it appropriate to offer Lennon the part of Jesus in their new pop musical *Jesus Christ Superstar* in late 1969, while Yoko Ono would still be hinting at a higher purpose to Lennon's existence twenty years after his death. "There's a lot that people are going to discover about John, about John's spirit," she said.

Meanwhile, back on Earth in April 1969, Lennon brought the song to McCartney at Cavendish Avenue and persuaded him to come straight down to Abbey Road to record it. Despite their personal and business disagreements being at their height, McCartney agreed (one has to wonder whether Lennon would have offered McCartney the same support in a reverse situation) and, with George out of the country and Ringo filming *The Magic Christian*, it was up to just John and Paul to make the music, the first "Beatles" session in eight weeks.

On the unpretentious extended blues, John played guitars and sang, Paul sang harmony, played piano, bass and drums ("Good drums," said Starr later) and created some infectious modern rock'n'roll music. To some extent, friendly feelings were restored – just enough, perhaps, to allow them to contemplate pursuing another album. Harrison, the most openly opposed to the John and Yoko situation, especially in the studio, was unconcerned at not being involved. "It was none of my business," he said, later. "If it had been the 'Ballad Of John, George And Yoko' I would have been on it."

46. I Want You (She's So Heavy)

Lennon/McCartney; recorded February 22, April 18 and 20, August 8, 11 and 20, 1969, Trident and EMI Studios, London; available on *Abbey Road*

Lennon's expression of desire for Yoko Ono (coupled with obvious awe at what he has taken on), **I Want You** was the first track to be attempted following the *Get Back* debacle and it quickly abandoned that project's *au naturel* approach by editing three separate takes together to create a composite. It also was the last track, six months on, which all four Beatles worked on in the same room.

Clunking back and forth three times between a bluesy voice/guitar unison lick (sung and played by composer Lennon with some passion but varying degrees of accuracy) and an ominous, carefully designed, arpeggiated chord sequence, the song – perhaps surprisingly – inspired sophisticated instrumental work from the group. McCartney's bass is boldly rangy, Harrison was attracted enough to Lennon's chords to sit with him overdubbing them for hours and Starr plays a slinky latin groove in the verses.

The minimalist lyric drew criticism for its simplicity and repetition, for which Lennon had an answer. "When you're drowning, you don't say, 'I would be incredibly pleased if someone would have the foresight to notice me drowning and come and help me,' you just scream."

His near-demented desire is conveyed by the infatuated repetition of the guitar arpeggios for a full three minutes (bloating the track to over seven and a half minutes) with the infiltrating synthesizer effects taking the mesmeric reiteration to unnerving sonic extremes. Most shocking of all, just as it sounds as if it can't get any heavier, there is a brutal cliff-face of silence. Horribly compelling, Lennon's desire is made to sound more like an incurable disease.

47. Something

(Harrison); recorded April 16, May 2 and 5, July 11 and 16, and August 15, 1969, EMI Studios, Abbey Road, London; available on *Abbey Road*, *1967–1970* and *1*

Written on piano in an empty studio in Abbey Road during the *White Album* sessions, the song begins with Harrison's borrowed opening phrase from James Taylor's song **Something In The Way She Moves** (heard on the singer-songwriter's Apple Records debut of December 1968). Generally thought to be about his wife Patti (though George has refuted that), it evolved into a romantic but also complex and uncertain piece. With great emotional impact being generated from the simplest of chromatic melodic devices and a gorgeously understated delivery, it has a love-struck fulsomeness that even the equivocation of the "… I don't know" bridge can't diminish.

Written with someone like Ray Charles in mind, **Something** was first offered to Joe Cocker, who had done such a job with **With A Little Help From My Friends**, though by the time Cocker's version appeared, the song had already been released by The Beatles. Recorded with care by the group, it featured a lovely, limpid Harrison vocal and probably his most elaborately melodic guitar solo on a Beatles record. Opinions are divided on McCartney's extravagantly creative bass playing ("too fussy", judged the composer) but the jury returned its verdict on the song very quickly. It's Harrison's masterpiece.

The plaudits don't come much higher. Both Lennon and McCartney, in interviews given at the time, hinted at **Something** being the best track on *Abbey Road*, while Frank Sinatra sang it throughout the 1970s and 1980s, never failing to introduce it as "the greatest love song of the last fifty years" (also, for a while, blithely crediting Lennon/McCartney for it). It went on to be the most covered Beatles song after **Yesterday**. Even George Martin was faced with having to reassess Harrison's gifts and later

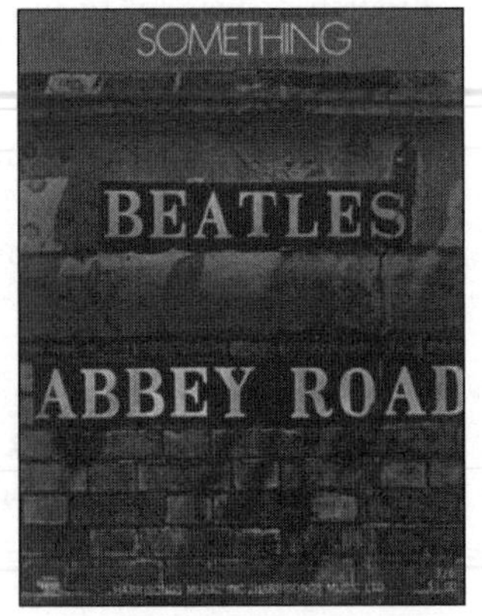

spoke of his guilt at undervaluing the guitarist in The Beatles' lifetime.

The selection of **Something** (by Allen Klein) as the *Abbey Road* single looked like nothing less than vindication for Harrison's patience, but by that time, it was too late. "Maybe now I just don't care whether you're going to like them or not," George was heard saying to the band at a meeting in Apple in Autumn 1969, "I just do 'em."

48. Come Together

Lennon/McCartney; recorded July 21–23, 25 and 29–30, 1969, EMI Studios, Abbey Road, London; available on *Abbey Road*, *1967–1970* and *1*

In its early incarnation, **Come Together** was a song written by Lennon for Timothy Leary's political campaign based around his slogan "Come Together – Join The Party". By the time it was offered to The Beatles, it had become an insistently funky, blues-spouting, semi-nonsensical description of a mysterious holy-rolling character with "juju eyeball" and "monkey finger". Heard variously as an oblique self-portrait, a picture of a counterculture guru and a disguised four-verse description of the four Beatles (as if Lennon would bother with that), even the term "spinal cracker" has been heard by critics to refer, by turns, to Lennon's and Ono's recent car accident, a Japanese technique to relieve back tension or simply to Lennon's "notorious abrasive humour" (Riley).

Most attempts at a coherent reading of the **Come Together** lyric beyond sex (the double entendre of "come"), drugs (Lennon appears to hiss "shoot me" on each spooky riff) and sporadically resonant gobbledygook (Lennon's term) are very hard work indeed. Adapting a line of Chuck Berry's **You Can't Catch Me** as a jumping-off point ["Here come a flat top"], Lennon later fell foul of Berry's publisher Morris Levy, who, in an out-of-court settlement in the 1970s, accepted Lennon's offer to record three of his published songs for his *Rock And Roll* project.)

Having not presented a song of his to The Beatles as a group since **I Want You** six months earlier ("There was no point in turning 'em out," he said. "I couldn't, didn't have the energy"), Lennon's final Beatles offering produced one of the great Beatles ensemble performances. Lennon's vocal is one of his most sinister and focused, better than most of his on *The White Album*, McCartney's inspired bass and electric piano is exactly what Lennon asked for ("swampy and smoky"), while Starr's expertly insouciant triplet-rolls around his hi-hat and heavily damped toms are a revelation.

In addition to being superbly played, **Come Together** is also beautifully recorded and mixed by George Martin and his team with a huge sonic presence, foggy-warm bass and sandpaper-dry snare. One of the best sounding Beatles tracks ever.

49. You Never Give Me Your Money/Sun King/Mean Mr Mustard/Polythene Pam/She Came In Through The Bathroom

Window/Golden Slumbers/Carry That Weight/The End

Lennon/McCartney; recorded May 6–18, August 1969, EMI Studios, Abbey Road, London; available on *Abbey Road*

George Martin had been saying to The Beatles for a while, "Think symphonically": longer forms, counterpoint, secondary themes, and recapitulation. *Sgt Pepper* had featured a reprise of the title track, but that had been an off-the-cuff idea by Neil Aspinall. "No one likes a smart-arse, Neil" was Lennon's response at the time. By mid-1969, rocker John was even less disposed to bigger musical ideas, so was initially unenthused by McCartney's suggestion to lash a bunch of half-finished half-songs together into a medley of jump-cuts, segues and cross-fades. George Martin was very keen, Harrison and Starr got on board and eventually Lennon committed himself to the point of submitting three of his bits of "garbage" (as he would invariably have them) to what became known as "The Long One".

While hugely entertaining musically, in thematic terms the middle section comprising Lennon's trio of characters – the Sun King who spouts tranquil Mediterranean gobbledygook, the miserly Mr Mustard who shouts rude things at the Queen and his curiously attired sister Pam – along with McCartney's tale of a fan's burglary of his St John's Wood home, is little more than diverting filler. The heavy heart of the medley lies in McCartney's work book-ending the medley.

You Never Give Me Your Money is a suite in itself, packing three distinct musical sections into four minutes, delivering a lyric that describes the agonizing turmoil of The Beatles' business troubles and the Klein-operated cash-flow as also representing a freedom of a kind, especially when he can drive around getting lost with new love Linda: "But Oh that magic feeling ..."

Eight minutes later and **Golden Slumbers** reveals he's worried again, he can't get home, and all he can do is comfort his companion that things will turn out all right while admitting in **Carry That Weight** how hard it all is to live through. But optimism wins out. There's just time in **The End** for a final celebration in which all four Beatles take their bow (via Starr's only recorded drum solo and McCartney, Harrison and Lennon swapping three lots of two-bar guitar solos) and a cosmic lyrical pay-off – a moment the composer hoped was the pop opera equivalent to a Shakespearean closing couplet.

When taken as a piece (**You Never Give Me Your Money/Golden Slumbers/Carry That Weight/The End**) it is nothing less than a subconscious, sorrowful farewell to The Beatles and probably McCartney's great interrupted masterwork.

50. Free As A Bird

(Lennon); recorded 1977 and February 1994, New York and Mill Studios, Sussex; available on *Anthology 1*

The *Anthology*-promoting single of 1995 featuring the three remaining Beatles – with ELO supremo Jeff Lynne producing – superimposed on a mid-1970s demo of Lennon's inspires wildly diverse reactions, often in the same listener. On the one hand, the record struggles to transcend its vinegar-and-brown-paper origins. Lennon's voice, extracted from a third-generation cassette, was time-stretched and processed into a distorted whimper, like ghostly reception on a distant radio station. Around him the Threetles plodded and poked in a Beatlesque but – creating music to a click track for the first time ever – palpably inhibited style. The sound of *Abbey Road* is evoked in places (the wobbly guitar arpeggios, the lush **Because**-style harmonies) as if to take up where they left off 25 years earlier, but Lynne's trademark clumpy drum sound and a frustratingly diffident McCartney bass part taint the remembered flavour.

And yet there is some magic at work that the ersatz process doesn't entirely suppress. The single held melody-note over the first three chords is a simple, evocative effect that is classic Lennon, Harrison's guitar work is plangent and unmistakable, the key change heralding the guitar solo is a delicious surprise and the accompanying vocal harmonies are almost heart-stopping.

This writer, dreading the moment when the "new" Beatles single was first aired, was simply relieved on first hearing that **Free As A Bird** wasn't embarrassing. On the second hearing, eyes were moist.

> ***"By reaching wide, The Beatles reached deep. It was the accuracy of their articulation of their age that allowed them to transcend that age, and to speak to us powerfully and privately today as they did two decades ago."***
>
> John Rockwell, *The New York Times*, review of The Beatles' albums box-set, 1982

Part 6: Beatles as authors & artists

Beatles as authors and artists

"If art were to redeem man, it could do so only by saving him from the seriousness of life, and restoring him to an unexpected boyishness."

John Lennon

"I think there's an urge in us to stop the terrible fleetingness of time. Music. Paintings ... Try and capture one bloody moment please."

Paul McCartney

As if being the ultimate trendsetters and standard-bearers in 1960s pop music weren't enough, the individual Beatles have seen fit to otherwise artistically express themselves down the years. Inevitably dominated, like the group, by Lennon and McCartney (neither Harrison nor Starr have shared very much of their non-musical output with the world, if indeed much was ever produced), the cumulative effect of the writings, drawings, happenings, films and paintings amounts to an impressive body of alternative work by two of the most diverting communicators of the twentieth century. Here is a selected chronological overview.

Lennon's early art and writings (1952–60)

The earliest examples of Lennon's art to have been generally seen are the 1952 paintings and crayon drawings he made available as part of the elaborate sleeve of the vinyl release of ***Walls And Bridges*** in 1974. Detailed depictions of cowboys, boats and footballers, the 11-year-old Lennon's graphic flair is unmistakable. Later in his school years, however, as he lapsed into disruptive behaviour and inattention, he ignored the efforts of his art teachers to marshal his undoubted abilities. In the heat of his post-primal therapy bitterness, he unfairly railed at his Aunt Mimi (to whom the *Walls And Bridges* paintings are clearly dedicated) for throwing out his juvenilia. "I never forgave her for not treating me like a fuckin' genius, or whatever

I was when I was a child," he frothed, "Why didn't they put me in art school, why didn't they train me?" In truth, young Lennon was virtually untrainable.

His most notable achievement in school was a series of exercise books filled with his poems and grotesque line drawings, which he called *The Daily Howl*. Most were ugly figures with deformities and warts, and even a self-portrait – "Simply A Simple Pimple: Short-sighted John Wimple Lennon" – depicted a figure with claws rather than human hands. The home-made periodical was a favourite among his fellow pupils and would get passed around the class under the desks. Even the teachers, themselves often caricatured within its pages, admired the cruel wit of the work. It was these drawings that head teacher William Pobjoy suggested Lennon use as his portfolio to present to Liverpool College of Art, which he attended between 1957 and 1960.

At art college, however, his behaviour was even more disorderly and contrary. One fellow student remembered Lennon deliberately distorting a sculpture after receiving praise for it. Another recalled his painting – apparently not good enough to admit him to the painting department – as "violent, noisy, semi-figurative work", which often featured a **Brigitte Bardot**-esque figure. Art teacher Arthur Ballard, who saved John from early expulsion, reckoned Lennon had "a lot of talent as an illustrator and cartoonist", adding, "if I had my way, he would never have been a Beatle. He would have been a professional artist." However, a report of the time says a lot about John's priorities. "Give up the guitar," it read, "otherwise you will never pass your exams."

Instead, by heading to Hamburg in 1960 with The Beatles, he virtually gave up his art for the time being, but not his writing. After having his semi-nonsensical prose piece about the "Dubious Origins Of The Beatles" published in its entirety by art college chum and *Mersey Beat* founder/editor Bill Harry in the paper's first edition, Lennon enthusiastically dumped a pile of poems, drawings and stories on Harry, which the editor used in a regular *Mersey Beat* column called "Beatcomber". When many were lost after the contents of a desk were accidentally thrown out, Lennon was said to have cried tears of frustration.

In His Own Write (1964)/ Spaniard In The Works (1965)

Lennon was encouraged in 1963 by Michael Braun (author of *Love Me Do*, one of the first books on The Beatles, and Lennon's favourite) to gather his writings and drawings into a book. Braun paved the way for Jonathan Cape to offer the Beatle a book-publishing deal, and *In His Own Write* was published in March 1964. Designed by Robert Freeman and featuring 57 pieces, the book comprised short stories, poems, playlets and line drawings. It was in a sense a formalized continuation of his *Daily Howl* and *Mersey Beat* style – even including several of his "Beatcomber" pieces – and the influence of Goon **Spike Milligan** and Stanley Unwin (a unique British comedian specializing in mangled-language monologues) was obvious. With wordplay and black humour to

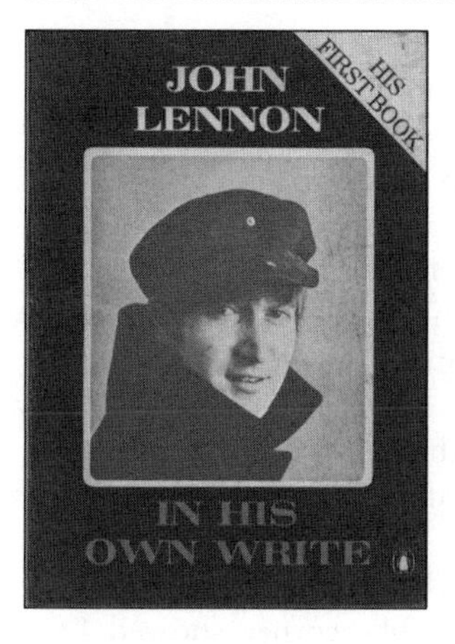

the fore, *In His Own Write* was a funny, edgy book full of grotesquery and absurdity that displayed much satirical character and sly imagination.

There was a darkness and bite to the material that was light years away from "I Want To Hold Your Hand". Peculiar, edgy humour about "cripples" abounds, reflecting the residue of Lennon's childhood phobia about physical and mental disability. Domestic violence features strongly, too. In **No Flies On Frank** a man beats his wife to death before attempting to deliver the fly-ridden corpse to his mother-in-law. One of several stories in that vein, others included "Henry And Harry", in which Mother is discovered burying Father; "Scene Three Act One", in which Mammy eats something that she says is Fatty's daughter; and "Randolf's Party", in which a lonely man is beaten to death in his house on Christmas Day.

Elsewhere there was an off-beat parody of TV surveys, "The Fringletoad Resort Of Teddyviscious"; an Enid Blyton pastiche, "The Famous Five Through Woenow Abbey"; and "A Surprise For Little Bobby", a charming tale of a one-handed man who receives a hook for his other arm for Christmas and so amputates his good hand.

The book was received with great enthusiasm, not so much by the mainstream Beatles fans (who bought it in droves, but probably found it a bit odd) but by the literary establishment. While noting the language was much bolder than that used for The Beatles' songs, critics also detected Lennon as belonging to a tradition that included **Finnegans Wake** era James Joyce, Edward Lear and Lewis Carroll, literate humorists with a nonsensical bent. Lennon would admit to a Lewis Carroll influence – *Alice In Wonderland* was his favourite childhood book – but hadn't read the other authors. When he did, he still couldn't see the connection, though later he would refer to reading Joyce for the first time as "like finding Daddy".

Lennon, a rocking rebel smack in the middle of pop superstardom, was dumbfounded to have his jottings received so well. "They took the book more seriously than I did myself," he said, "It just began as a laugh for me." But when publishers Jonathan Cape wanted another book quickly, he had no choice but to take it seriously; he was an author now. Without a backlog of work that he had effectively created for his own amusement, and probably with the *Times Literary Supplement*'s assessment that "Lennon shows himself well-equipped to take it further, he must write a great deal more" ringing in his head, the suddenly self-conscious Beatle found he had to hit the bottle to "loosen up".

The result, *Spaniard In The Works*, published in June 1965, was essentially more of the same without the novelty of being unexpected, and was received as such. Among the 56 pieces was a lampoon of the *Daily Mirror* column Cassandra ("Just my way of having a go back"), vaguely political satire in "The General Erection" and his longest piece yet in a **Sherlock Holmes** spoof entitled "The Singularge Experience Of Miss Anne Duffield", which ran to nine pages. "It seemed like a novel to me," Lennon said. "I couldn't do it, you know. I get fed-up. And I wrote so many characters in it I forgot who they were."

There were naysayers. Lennon's work was referred by Conservative MP Norman Miscampbell in Parliament as being "in a state of pathetic near-literacy" and evidence of how schools were failing the young. In a typically ungenerous assessment, biographer Albert Goldman dismissed the books as "nothing but send-ups of nursery tales and newspaper that John twists into sick jokes by encoding them in a stream of discombobulating puns".

Indeed, there was a hint, even in the raves – in *Book Week* **Tom Wolfe** called Lennon a "genius-savage" – that Lennon's literary gifts needed the bigger challenge to develop. It was a challenge Lennon never really rose to, but his two collections of grimly amusing miniatures from the mid-1960s remain strikingly individual and an essential aspect of Lennonilia. Both books are currently available in single Pimlico paperback.

The Tokyo Painting (a.k.a. Images of a Woman), 1966

Virtually imprisoned in their hotel rooms during their summer 1966 tour of Japan, The Beatles did their shopping from various traders who visited their presidential suite, all paid for by the promoter, Tats Nagashima. To pass the time, Tats suggested that the group do some painting and provided them with fine paper, paints and brushes. A large piece of paper was put on the table in the central sitting room of the suite with a table lamp placed in the centre. The Beatles each took a corner and over the course of the next few evenings, and with the inspiration of several joints, collaborated on their only non-musical artistic creation.

Photographer Bob Whitaker was present and commented that Paul's corner showed "the first stirrings of psychedelia", John's "paint was in relief, almost an inch thick in places", George's section was "stippled" and Ringo's contained "alien figures". When the paper was filled with paint, the lamp was removed, leaving a white circle within which all four Beatles signed. Whitaker was amazed by their focus and peacefulness. "Absolutely the best period I ever witnessed among The Beatles," he said. "I've never seen them calmer, happier and more content with themselves."

The painting, *Images of a Woman*, was donated to charity and was auctioned off several times down the years, most recently in May 2002.

McCartney's sound collages and home movies (1960s)

While Lennon, by virtue of his books and belligerence, became known as the dangerous intellectual of The Beatles in the mid-1960s, Paul McCartney was quietly getting involved with avant-garde London. Influenced by his friend Barry Miles, McCartney attended lectures by **Luciano Berio** and performances by **AMM** (the most radical free-form group of its day) and became intrigued by the random possibilities suggested by the methods of composers like Stockhausen and Cage.

The culmination of these left-field interests came when he was asked to provide some music for the underground rave called **Carnival of Light** at the Roundhouse, London. In January 1967, at a recording session earmarked for **Penny Lane** overdubs, he directed the other Beatles in 13 minutes 48 seconds of avant-gardening – complete with shrieking and gargling – before overdubbing distorted drums, organs and guitars. Played at the rave but unreleased at the time, it was blocked by George Harrison as a contender even for the *Anthology* releases and was the closest McCartney ever came to realizing his pipe-dream avant-garde album, *Paul McCartney Goes Too Far*. (Lennon, of course, strong-armed a comparably "challenging" collage done with Yoko – **Revolution 9** – onto The Beatles' *White Album* in 1968.)

Paul's home movies would be subject to similar experimentation. Around the time of *Revolver*, McCartney would be heard talking of the potential of distortion, "to take a note and wreck it and see in that note what else there is in it"; he applied the same principle to his private films with the techniques of overexposure, reversal and superimposition. A fan of Andy Warhol's "cheekiness", Paul would take long uninterrupted shots of a pavement, or use techniques such as double exposure. In one film, double-exposed shots of night-time traffic and a French peasant lady in a graveyard allow "a point of red light [to] appear in between her legs" which "just drifts very slowly like a little fart, or a little spirit or something, in the graves". He would further enhance the experience by allowing random sound synchronization with a record like Albert Ayler's version of "The Marseillaise". Pleased enough with his movies – called things like *The Defeat Of The Dog* and *The Next Spring Then* – to show them to *Blowup* director **Michelangelo Antonioni** one evening, McCartney lost all the films after fans broke into and burgled his house on Cavendish Avenue in 1968.

You Are Here (1968)

"Avant-garde is French for bullshit," Lennon once memorably declared. In July 1968, having fallen in love with arch avant-garde artist Yoko Ono, it was clear he had shifted his position. He mounted his first art exhibition at the Robert Fraser Gallery entitled ***You Are Here*** and in dedicating it to Yoko, also used it as a public declaration of their love.

Visitors had to navigate several charity collection boxes to get to a large, white, circular canvas with the words "you are here" written on it and were invited to contribute coins to a "for the artist, thank you" hat. Hornsey art students attempted a send-up of Lennon's efforts by delivering a **rusty bicycle** with a note saying "This was inadvertently left out"; Lennon immediately put it in the exhibition. White helium-filled balloons (365 of them) were released with a self-addressed tag. Most of the replies castigated John for his hair, for his wealth, for leaving his wife, and for the race of his new partner.

The critics were mostly indifferent, though Yoko was apparently impressed. "I thought, great," she said much later. "I don't think he had done too much avant-garde artwork but when he did, he was excellent; above the level of many so-called avant-garde friends."

"JohnandYoko" (1968–69)

Although they were virtually inseparable in private, John's and Yoko's public life became a series of conceptual art events which – with the brilliantly manipulated, barely comprehending collusion of a pruriently curious media – became perhaps the most publicized art in history. Perhaps deciding that art for its own sake on such a scale could hardly be justified, much of their notable output was well-intentioned **peace propaganda** that amounted to putting the word "peace" in the media as often as possible, simply because they could. Elsewhere they made records, films and staged "events" that were mostly a series of public-baffling self-promotions and self-celebrations seeking to blur the line between the art and life of "JohnandYoko". Here is a selection.

Acorn Event (June 1968)

This was apparently John's idea but was "so beautiful", said Yoko, "that I copied it." For the National Sculpture Exhibition, they offered the "living art" of two planted acorns; one facing east, the other facing west. Yoko described it as symbolizing "our meeting and love for each other and also the uniting and growth of our two cultures". Already marginalized from the rest of the exhibition by being obliged to publish their own catalogue, when attending the preview at Coventry Cathedral, they were told by Canon Verney that they couldn't plant in "consecrated ground" and that in any case the acorns were not real sculpture. Yoko was furious and demanded that leading artists be contacted to verify the authenticity of the idea. **Henry Moore**, unfortunately, was out. The acorns were eventually planted on a nearby lawn, stolen a week later in the night, with the second set guarded by security for the duration of the exhibition.

Smile/Two Virgins (1968)

"My ultimate goal in filmmaking," said Yoko in 1967, "is to make a film which includes a smiling face snap of every single human being in the world." Lowering her ambition a little for *Smile*, she shot a high-speed, three-minute shot of John's face alone, slowing it down on viewing to allow it to become a fifty-minute, soft-focus smile. John suggested that "The idea of the film won't really be dug for another fifty or a hundred years, probably." (Twenty-seven years on, filmmaker Kevin Godley borrowed the idea for the faces of The Beatles seen in the video of ***Real Love***.)

Two Virgins superimposes John's face on Yoko's. "In both films we were mainly concerned about the vibrations the films send out," said Yoko, "and the kind that was between us."

John and Yoko plug their "Bagism" concept on the TV show *Today* in 1969

Rape (1968)

Perhaps the most developed and unsettling of John and Yoko's films, it is a 72-minute movie in which a cameraman persistently shoots the actions of a Viennese girl, following her around the London streets, into a taxi and an apartment. At first she is flattered and amused, then increasingly disturbed and upset. The camera films on, ignoring her tearful pleas for mercy. "We are showing how all of us are exposed and under pressure in our contemporary world," said Lennon. "This isn't about The Beatles. What is happening to this girl on the screen is happening in **Biafra**, Vietnam, everywhere."

The *Evening Standard* was impressed. "This film does for the age of television," wrote Willie Frischauer, "what Franz Kafka's *The Trial* did for totalitarianism."

Bed-Ins For Peace (1969)

According to the book *Yes*, the weighty survey of Yoko's art, the bed-ins (see p.88) were remarkable international media events that drew upon "the philosophical and phenomenological aspects" of Ono's 1964 **Bag Piece** (people get into a bag, hidden disrobing occurs). *Yes* went on to assert that "they publicized the intimacy of the nuptial bed as a metaphor for cultural transformation, demonstrating the essential relation between private beliefs and public behaviour ... [wedding] erotic love and an intellectual desire for world peace with the ideological goal of ending the Vietnam war." Is this the same John Lennon who had said only four years earlier, "I'm not a do-gooder or anything"? Clearly not.

Self-Portrait (1969)

Fifteen minutes of Lennon's penis rising from flaccidity to tumescence and back again was filmed once more at high speed and slowed to the running time of 42 minutes. Reportedly performed with the aid of provocative poses from Yoko and a copy of **Playboy** (both out of shot), this epic went curiously unmentioned in *Yes*, an otherwise thorough career-survey of Yoko's artistic output, but the original programme notes assured us that "the result is translucent and hypnotic and mystifying".

Bag One (1970)

Encouraged by his new personal assistant and art advisor **Anthony Fawcett**, Lennon returned to line drawings in the form of this set of twelve lithographs, some of which portrayed John and Yoko's wedding and bed-in, while others concentrated on frank sexuality. Exhibited in London Arts Gallery, New Bond Street, in January 1970, most were confiscated under the obscenity laws, with 64-year-old chartered accountant George Holmes stating as a prosecution witness, "I honestly felt sick and angry that womankind should be depicted in such disgusting positions." Upon hearing of the confiscation Lennon commented, "It's a laugh".

The case was eventually thrown out when the magistrate judged that Lennon's work was "unlikely to deprave or corrupt". When exhibited in America, visitors (including **Salvador Dalí**, who was apparently keen to work with Lennon) were required to remove their shoes to enter the specially created environment at the Lee Nordness Gallery in New York.

It was produced as a limited edition of 300 signed sets in a white leather bag, with Lennon's signature imprinted in black, retailing at £550, one of which is on display at the Museum of Modern Art, New York. Among the large quantity of Ono-administered Lennon art that has emerged through Bag One Arts since his death, Bag One sets and individual prints are still for sale, but you have to "call for pricing".

I Me Mine (1979)

Years before **Bag One Arts** framed Lennon's lithographed lyrics and sold them at posh prices, George Harrison embarked on what he called a "little ego detour" by getting his compositional scribblings and transcribed autobiographical interviews bound by Genesis, publishers specializing in beautifully produced, expensive books. With 28 specially created colours, and gilded page edges, the books were hand-bound in leather, individually signed and retailed at £148. *The Daily Telegraph* called it, "an exquisitely packaged confection of thoughts, memories, snapshots, but above all, lyrics". The limited edition of two thousand copies sold quickly and though the book has been reprinted for the wider market several times, original prints have been known to fetch nearly $1500 at auction.

Skywriting By Word Of Mouth (1986)

Though carefully selected by the ever-vigilant Yoko, the posthumous publication of Lennon's late-1970s reminiscences of the "JohnandYoko" saga and his fight to stay in the US is sporadically revealing. He refers to **Power To The People** as "rather embarrassing" and characterizes their early 1970s revolutionary stance as "our biggest mistake." Elsewhere, there are 29 stories and sketches, broadly in his mid-1960s style, but denser, more personal and not as funny. Lennon mentioned these writings in one of his final interviews, but reckoned them to be "not right enough". In his absence, that they're available now is welcome, but they're certainly hard work.

Ringo Starr, artist

Ringo's first wife Maureen had an artistic bent and, when married, the couple collaborated on various forms of private artwork including photo collage, oil painting and simple sculpture. Continuing his private art pursuits through his life, the most public Ringo has gone with his work was in 1995 when he created a painting for the Private Issue credit card, the company that sponsored his summer tour. Describing himself as "not good at figurative painting", Ringo produced a face-cum-waterscape in a minimalist, "naïve" style for the Make A Wish Foundation benefiting terminally ill children, and it raised $33,000 when auctioned at the Guggenheim Museum.

The Beatles Anthology (book) (1999)

Apparently mistimed, coming over four years after the TV show and video, the book became a bestseller, proving the public were once more ready for another dose of the Fabs. The Beatles are the authors of the book in that, like the series, the only point of view given – in the form of hugely expanded interviews – is theirs (plus a little Neil Aspinall and George Martin). Some inevitably complained of a sanitized version of events (with Yoko having a quarter of the veto, the quotes pertaining to her are somewhat restrained), others unused to art-style books grumbled about how heavy and unfriendly the book was to use. It was artily designed in large format and on thick paper. It was also commented that the format, made up for the most part of quoted speech, assumes the reader knows the story already.

There's also the sense that some Beatles, George especially, used it to pummel home what it all means to him from where he is now (not much). Nevertheless, that it was done at all is a good thing and generally, it was done very well. There are many previously unknown details, especially about their individual early years, and the book is full of handsome unseen photographs and memorabilia. It's a 360-page Beatle feast that takes weeks to digest.

Paintings (2000)

Inhibited by Lennon's reputation and training as the artist of The Beatles, McCartney kept his artistic efforts to himself until letting some of his cartoonish line drawings out for 1981's book *Paul McCartney Composer/Artist*. After he took up oil and acrylic painting as a 40-year-old in 1983, two MPL-published collections quietly appeared in 1989 and 1994, but in September 2000, with his confidence boosted by the success of his first exhibition in Seigen, Germany, the previous year, the publicity for *Paintings* was stepped up.

Bold, colourful canvases of thickly applied paint, influenced by his friendship with abstract expressionist **Willem De Kooning**, the work sometimes reflects his early appreciation of Magritte's surrealism. Elsewhere it shows McCartney developing his own iconic code: crosses, penises, triangles and faces (John's, Linda's, Ringo's and the Queen's). Throughout there's a conspicuous, spontaneous physical enjoyment of the medium, which communicates itself instantly to the viewer. There's also a sense of McCartney's determination to have fun away from public judgement – he's getting closer to the essence of his own intuitively expressive self. "Humility and audacity are in the ring together," writes art critic Christoph Tannert in the book. "In his paintings, McCartney advances into realms that he never entered in his songs."

While it's traditional to have highfalutin

essays in art books, giving a stylistic context, explaining technique, and venturing interpretation, the book's writings from Paul's art-writer friends can't help but come across as a kind of in-house justification. In the end, he probably didn't need it. There is good, interesting, resonant work here.

Blackbird Singing (2001)

Aside from a few notable examples, McCartney's lyrics have not been the most praised aspect of his work. So it surprised some to see this book published, featuring poems and lyrics from 1965 to 1999. Selected by one of the "Mersey Poets", Adrian Mitchell, he reckons the best of Paul's lyrics can stand alongside Gabriel Rossetti, William Blake and Robert Burns. Indeed, in the formal, black-on-white poetry-book format, acknowledged lyrical achievements like **Blackbird** and **Eleanor Rigby** take on a new resonance. But what's really surprising is that so do **Junior's Farm, Yellow Submarine** and **Why Don't We Do It In The Road**.

Paul rediscovered writing poetry when he found it was the most natural way to express himself following the death of his old friend Ivan Vaughan in 1994. Although there are funny moments (**Hot As That, Dinner Tickets** and **Not On**) and lofty conceits (**Standing Stone**), it is his grieving pieces for Ivan and Linda (and John Lennon, in the lyric for **Here Today**) that ring out with the moving power of the intensely personal.

Richer than expected perhaps – the reviews used terms like "profoundly innocent", "passion" and "clarity and quirkiness" – *Blackbird Singing* will fascinate anyone interested in the evolving expression of Paul McCartney.

Postcards From The Boys (2004)

A Ringo book, this collection of 53 postcards and telegrams sent to the drummer by Paul, John and George over the years is slight stuff, but Starr's contemporary recollections of the artefacts and the circumstances surrounding them shed some touchingly personal light on familiar events and unearth some fresh anecdotes. From the card sent by Paul the day after the Apple rooftop concert in 1969 ("You are the greatest drummer in the world. Really.") to John's suggestion in 1979 that Ringo covers Blondie's "Heart Of Glass" to revive his flagging solo career, the boys' concern and affection for their erstwhile drummer is clear. Worth an hour of any Beatle fan's time.

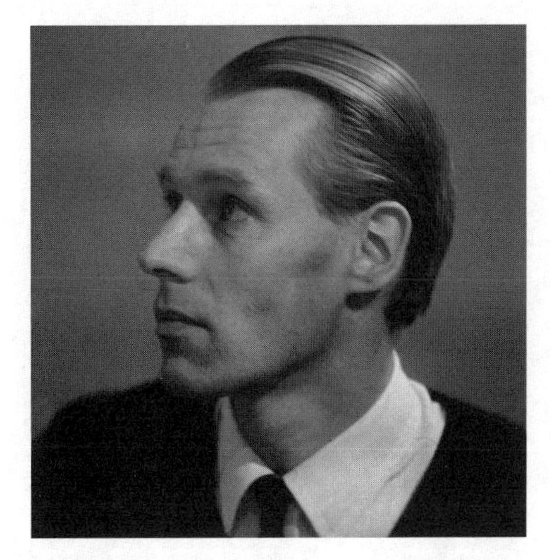

Part 7: The Fifth Beatle

The fifth Beatle

The phrase "The Fifth Beatle" was coined early in the band's history to describe satellite members of The Beatles' organization. These days the phrase has practically entered the language of the wider world as shorthand for anyone involved in a project outside of the limelight but in a notable way, whether they are the power behind the throne, the one who got left behind, the one who does the work but gets little of the recognition, or somewhere in between.

With their arrival in The Beatles' circle providing a chronological order of sorts, here are various Beatles people who, for one reason or another, and with varying degrees of credibility, have been dubbed "The fifth Beatle"...

Tommy Moore

Drummer

A fork-lift-truck driver at Garston Bottle Works and part-time drummer, Tommy Moore was recommended to The Silver Beatles in 1960 by Brian Casser – Cass of top Liverpool group Cass & The Cassanovas. Older than the rest of the group, Moore was late for his first appointment with The Silver Beatles – a May 1960 audition for Billy Fury with his manager Larry Parnes – and they were instead offered the second-string Scottish tour with Johnny Gentle.

Moore had to take time off work and had a miserable tour, aggravated by Lennon's provocative behaviour and coming off worst when their van crashed in Banff, a flying guitar knocking out one of his teeth. He was still concussed when dragged on stage by Lennon and the manager of Dalrymple Hall, Fraserburgh.

Back in Liverpool, £2 richer, he lasted a few more days in The Beatles before failing to show at the Jacaranda in June 1960. Driving to his house, the group were told by his girlfriend from a window to "piss off" as Tommy had a night shift at the bottle works and wouldn't be coming out to play anymore.

Stuart Sutcliffe

Bass player

John Lennon's best friend at Liverpool College of Art, Stuart Ferguson Victor Sutcliffe was a talented artist and a dedicated student of art history, but a reluctant Beatle. He was persuaded by Lennon and McCartney to invest his winnings from an art competition in a Hofner President bass guitar, even though he couldn't play one. Learning Eddie Cochran's "Summertime Blues" from a fellow student and Chuck Berry's "Thirty Days" from the

Stuart Sutcliffe

group, Sutcliffe was encouraged to turn his back and "do a moody" (McCartney) when playing in an attempt to disguise his difficulties, and the group would tease him mercilessly. "We were terrible," said Lennon. "We'd tell Stu he couldn't sit with us, or eat with us ... that was how he learned to be with us." Sutcliffe is also credited with suggesting the name Beetles. His vocal feature in the group was Elvis Presley's "Love Me Tender", but his real contribution was his Zbigniew Cybulski (the "Polish James Dean" and moody star of the film *Ashes And Diamonds*) good looks and style, which brought an air of bohemian cool to the stage.

It was this charisma that attracted the "Exis" in Hamburg, and Astrid Kirchherr in particular, who fell in love with him. "Here was I, feeling the most insipid working member of the group," wrote Stu, "being told how much superior I looked." Paul, already irritated by Stuart's lack of musical capability, was further niggled at being passed over by the gorgeous Astrid, and he and Stu, at the height of what McCartney would later call their "deadly rivalry", ended up in a fight on stage. "When I look back on it," admitted McCartney, "I think we were probably fighting for John's attention." When Stu decided to stay in Hamburg with Astrid in December 1960, effectively leaving the group, McCartney remembers a "sense of relief ... it seemed right that we all had to move on". Lennon kept up an intense correspondence with his friend, and even young George Harrison wrote to him. "Come home sooner," said Harrison in a letter to Stu a few weeks later. "It's no good with Paul, playing bass, we've decided."

Stu and Astrid hung out with The Beatles at the Top Ten club through spring 1961, with the boys much amused by his new Astrid-styled, combed-forward haircut. Within months, they had adopted the look themselves. In April 1962, after suffering excruciating headaches and blackouts for a year, Stuart died of a brain haemorrhage aged just 21 (see p.14).

Pete Best

Drummer

Summer of 1960 saw The Silver Beatles offered a residency in Hamburg, but only if they could find themselves a drummer. On August 6, 1960, 18-year-old Pete Best was playing drums for The Blackjacks in the Casbah, the club situated in the cellar of his home in West Derby and run by his mother Mona. The Silver Beatles had played a residency there in 1959 as The Quarry Men, and, having some time to kill after a cancelled gig, they visited the Casbah that evening for the first time in months.

Impressed with Pete's shiny kit, they briefly auditioned him on August 10 at Wyvern Social Club with **Shakin' All Over** and he was in. For the next two years, Pete was a Beatle and initially his mother was the band's chief hustler, badgering Ray McFall into booking the group into The Cavern. Pete was credited with developing in Hamburg a more solid, bass-drum sound than the "Shadows style"

British pop was using at the time, which was locally dubbed the "Atom Beat". He even had his own vocal feature, **Peppermint Twist**. And as The Beatles' local popularity rose, it became clear that Pete attracted a good deal of female attention, not to mention the purple prose of Cavern DJ Bob Wooler. In August 1961 in *Mersey Beat*, Wooler wrote of Best's "mean, moody magnificence" in a Beatles article in which the drummer was the only individual name-checked.

It was becoming clear within The Beatles, however, that Pete didn't quite fit in with the particular group synergy of John, Paul and George. News of disappointments or important developments – like the Decca rejection or the Parlophone audition – never seemed to reach Pete with any urgency and when, in June 1962, neither his drumming nor his personality impressed George Martin, his days were numbered. On August 16, 1962, Brian Epstein told him on behalf of the group that he was out. "They were jealous of him," asserted Mona. Brian issued an "amicable decision" statement and The Beatles never talked to Pete again.

Sporadically depressed, even suicidal, Pete stuttered on in showbiz until the late 1960s, when he became a civil servant. He published his story a couple of times but his boat finally came in during 1995 when the *Anthology 1* CD – featuring him on ten early cuts – sent substantial royalties in his direction and inspired him to appear all over the world with the new Pete Best Band, which he continues to do to this day.

Neil Aspinall

Assistant

Nominated for the honour "fifth Beatle" by George Martin himself, Neil Aspinall has been the group's closest aide and confidant for over forty years. "He's been a real solid guy for us," says McCartney, "but I don't think we've always been good for him."

He was born in Prestatyn, North Wales, on October 14, 1942, and was a classmate of Paul McCartney's at the Liverpool Institute in Mount Street, in the year above George Harrison. By the time of their GCE exams, John and Paul had been introduced and Lennon, attending the neighbouring art college, joined the informal "**Mad Lads**" gang, which included Paul, George and Neil.

When Neil left school to train as an accountant, he took lodgings in the Haymans Green home of Mona Best, the fiery, energetic mother of Pete and Rory. He helped the family convert the sprawling house's basement into a coffee bar, the Casbah Club, which opened in August 1959; its first band, formed on the night, comprised John, Paul, George and guitarist Ken Brown, the latest incarnation of Lennon's Quarry Men. The following year, when Pete joined as drummer, Neil, who by now was having an affair with Mona, was the natural choice for the band's driver whilst Mona looked after their bookings. Neil bought a cheap secondhand van and charged the boys five shillings each per gig to ferry them around and load their gear.

He was still taking them to gigs in 1962 when Brian Epstein summoned Pete Best to a meeting shortly after the Parlophone deal had been signed. Neil drove Pete to NEMS and was furious when he heard his friend had been sacked, threatening to quit too. Pete convinced him to stay with the group. Neil's relationship with Mo continued and she bore his child, Roag, Pete's half-brother (and who today manages the Pete Best Band).

Amazingly, throughout the heat and madness of Beatlemania, Neil and his colleague Mal Evans were the only full-time members of the road crew, acting also as lighting operators, security and personal assistants, among many roles. By 1968, Neil and Mona had split up and he married Suzy Ornstein, daughter of Bud Ornstein, the British head of United Artists, who gave ***A Hard Day's Night*** the go-ahead.

When The Beatles' company Apple became the hub of their business after Brian Epstein's death in 1967, Neil volunteered to run the Wigmore Street office. He began looking at capturing The Beatles' extraordinary story on screen, eventually compiling a two-hour documentary, *The Long And Winding Road,* from all the available Fabs footage. When the group split, Neil's film, though near completion, was shelved. Instead, he was listed as the producer of *Let It Be*.

Sidelined in the Apple organization during the Allen Klein years, Neil drifted into music supervision for movies, working on ***That'll Be The Day*** (starring Ringo, David Essex and Keith Moon). When Klein and Apple parted company, Neil returned as managing director, running a series of tiny Apple offices and surviving a bout of ill-health to oversee many ongoing legal disputes with third parties, notably EMI and Apple Computers. Throughout all the in-group legal bickering he remained a faithful, neutral retainer. He also quietly accumulated the rights to much of the extant audio and visual Beatles material so that, today, the copyright to the majority of photographs, likenesses, film and video footage of The Beatles belongs to Apple Ltd.

Aspinall – known to the inner circle as Nell – was a quiet, indeed reclusive curator of The Beatles' legacy, a trusted fellow-traveller who kept his unequalled knowledge of John, Paul, George and Ringo to himself. At George Harrison's posthumous induction into the 2004 Rock'n'Roll Hall of Fame, Olivia Harrison chose to thank on George's behalf only one person – "someone who looked after him, and all of them ... the mysterious Neil Aspinall".

Neil retired from Apple in April 2007, eleven months after losing Apple Corps' final lawsuit against Apple Computers. He died in March 2008 of lung cancer. McCartney and Starr were represented at his Twickenham funeral by daughter Stella and wife Barbara respectively.

Chas Newby

Bass player

A chemistry student and former rhythm guitarist with The Blackjacks, Newby played left-handed bass with The Beatles around Liverpool during his Christmas break in December 1960, as a temporary replacement for Stuart Sutcliffe. He performed at four gigs in all including the "Fabulous Beatles Direct From Hamburg!" date at the Casbah and the legendary Litherland Town Hall engagement on the December 27 at which the local excitement about the group was said to begin. Offered a permanent position in The Beatles, Newby declined and continued his studies, eventually becoming an industrial manager. Chas is currently a member of **The Racketts**, a Midlands-based charity-fundraising function band.

Brian Epstein

Manager

If there is one single factor that made the phenomenon of The Beatles possible, it is that Brian Epstein believed in them. His conviction in the importance of "his boys" seems almost supernatural. It's almost as if Brian – a lone believer – instinctively understood that he was the catalytic material from which the big bang would explode; that when he and The Beatles came together, there would be a starburst that would reverberate for as long as pop music would last.

Born in Liverpool on September 19, 1934, the first child of businessman Harry Epstein and his wife Malka (known to all as **Queenie**), Brian Epstein grew up a well-to-do but restive suburban Jewish boy. Unhappy at school and bored in the family's furniture store, he was conscripted as a clerk into the Royal Army Service Corps in 1952 and lasted only ten months before being discharged as "emotionally and mentally unfit to serve".

An urge to enter showbiz won him a place at RADA to study acting in 1954, but he soon dropped out. His homosexuality almost certainly exacerbated his sense of not fitting in anywhere, as did the expectations he felt as the eldest son in a Jewish household. Though Brian finally blossomed when put in charge of the music department of the family's electrical goods outlet, **North End Music Stores** (NEMS), he never shook off this unease. When he met The Beatles, it seems he discovered a previously unimagined purpose and a world filled with things he'd been unable to express: rebellion, theatricality, humour, creativity and youth.

Despite a rare knack for recognizing which records would sell, Brian was never especially a pop fan. He wrote a column for *Mersey Beat* from August 1961, but didn't seem particularly aware of the scene The Beatles emerged from. In fact, according to Alistair Taylor (Brian's assistant at NEMS who accompanied him to the show), when he first saw them at The Cavern on November 9, 1961, Brian was under the impression that they were German, as the flyers read "Direct from Hamburg"; but when they ambled on stage he realized these boys were regular customers at NEMS.

Immediately, Brian began declaring, somewhat improbably, that these scruffy local kids would soon be **"bigger than Elvis"**. Their arrival in his life changed, positively, the way he felt about himself: why shouldn't the rest of the world have the same response? Incredibly, it did. Two years after taking them on with the promise to raise their Cavern earnings from £5 a show to £10, Epstein was steering the most astonishing entertainment trend Britain had ever seen, with over £6 million worth of records sold. Soon he'd built an empire of Liverpool acts, which annihilated the rest of the pop business in 1963. With associates Taylor and Peter Brown, he moved NEMS to London. Chastised by John early on for making musical suggestions, Brian kept out of the group's artistic orbit and concentrated on the undoubtedly complex, day-to-day administration of the phenomenon.

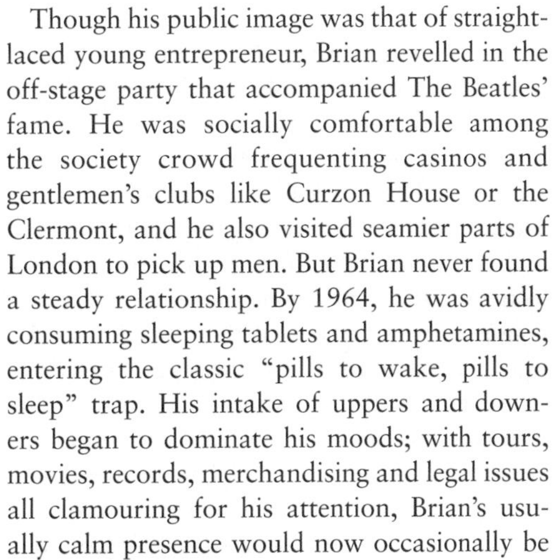

Though his public image was that of straight-laced young entrepreneur, Brian revelled in the off-stage party that accompanied The Beatles' fame. He was socially comfortable among the society crowd frequenting casinos and gentlemen's clubs like Curzon House or the Clermont, and he also visited seamier parts of London to pick up men. But Brian never found a steady relationship. By 1964, he was avidly consuming sleeping tablets and amphetamines, entering the classic "pills to wake, pills to sleep" trap. His intake of uppers and downers began to dominate his moods; with tours, movies, records, merchandising and legal issues all clamouring for his attention, Brian's usually calm presence would now occasionally be demolished by ferocious tantrums.

The Beatles' decision to stop touring was one Brian couldn't influence. He respected the boys' feelings, but some part of him felt he was being made redundant. On August 28, 1966, at LA's Dodger Stadium, the night before their last show, a contretemps involving Brian's errant lover, a Californian called **Diz Gillespie**, revealed the man to be little more than a hustler intent on preying on Brian's largesse. Betrayed, and feeling worthless and vulnerable on all fronts, Brian pitched into a deep depression.

Realizing he needed to concentrate on wider aspects of The Beatles' career, Brian spent the early part of 1967 renegotiating their contract with EMI, securing them a $2 million bonus from America and a nine percent royalty – a major coup in the age of three percent deals. But a break in Spain somehow ended in drug rehab at the Priory clinic in Putney, Brian emerging just in time for the release of *Sgt Pepper*. His contract with The Beatles coming up for renewal, Brian ought to have felt good about the way things were going, with a new recording deal in the bag and worldwide acclaim for *Sgt Pepper*, but when his father died suddenly, he was again rocked to his foundations.

On Friday, August 25, 1967, while George, John and Paul travelled to Wales to attend a seminar with the **Maharishi Mahesh Yogi** over the bank holiday weekend, Brian elected to spend it with friends at his country house, Kingley Hill in Sussex. However, when some of his guests cancelled, Brian returned to London that night in search of entertainment. On Sunday, he was found dead in the bedroom of his Chapel Street house.

The Beatles were told in Bangor. "I can't find words to pay tribute to him," John told the press as they left. "It's just that he was loveable, and it is those loveable things that we think about now." The inquest found that Brian had died accidentally of Carbrital poisoning, most likely having taken two barbiturate tablets to get to sleep, awoken in the night and taken two more. Mixed with the alcohol he'd ingested earlier, and perhaps because he'd been inactive for most of the day before, four pills were enough to prove fatal. Though Brian had a history of false alarms and botched attempts, suicide was ruled out (see p.291).

Some days after his death, his assistant Joanne, who had alerted the doctor who found Brian's body, came across two notes from Brian among his papers, one to his brother Clive and one to Queenie. They were dated some seven or eight weeks prior to his death, saying "Don't be sad. I'm okay. Take good care of yourself. I love you." It appeared that Brian Epstein may indeed have intended to take his own life – although probably not on the night he lost it. He was 32.

Since his passing, there has been much criticism of Brian's skills as a deal maker; on the one hand signing away merchandising rights for a pittance, on the other ensuring NEMS received a huge 25 percent gross of everything The Beatles generated. At the height (1970) of Beatles-split paranoia, even Lennon, who was closest to Brian, railed against his business dealings as self-serving: "He robbed us, he took all the fucking money and looked after himself and his family". For the most part, however, The Beatles have been loyal to his memory and notably affectionate in their reminiscences.

It's clear, as a personal manager and a catalyst for the group's extraordinary success, that he was undoubtedly the right man at the right time. And when they hit big, the group trusted and liked him sufficiently to be free to get on with the business of being Beatles. And it shouldn't be forgotten that there was no precedent for the kind of supergroup The Beatles became; it's unlikely there was anyone who could have guided them better in the circumstances.

So accustomed were The Beatles to the idea of Brian, a friend, being in charge, it took over a year after his death for them to address the question of finding a replacement. Their inability to agree on a suitable choice was a major factor in their eventual split.

George Martin

Producer

Finding a manager like Brian Epstein to battle for them was fortune enough, but in being lucky enough to end up with George Martin as record producer, The Beatles' story starts to look like destiny. It's impossible to imagine what The Beatles' records, indeed The Beatles' recording career, would have been like in the hands of someone less flexible, skilful and imaginative. And yet his greatest gift to the music of The Beatles may simply be to have selflessly recognized their genius and dedicated his professional expertise from

George and the boys parade the silver disc of "Please Please Me"

1963 until 1969 to serving it.

A graduate of the Guildhall School of Music but a failed classical pianist, George Martin first joined EMI in 1950 and was appointed assistant at Parlophone, the classical/jazz/comedy/light pop label. He was appointed the label's head in the mid-50s, and his work reflected his own off-beat tastes; he produced records for the likes of **The Goons**, Peter Ustinov, Flanders and Swann and the Beyond the Fringe team, as well as jazz artists **Stan Getz** and Johnny Dankworth and singers Judy Garland and Matt Monroe. He couldn't see much in **Tommy Steele**, however, and turned him down in 1957. Pre-empting the ironic reverse occurrence with The Beatles five years later, Decca signed Steele and made him a star.

Though it has been suggested that George Martin agreed to see The Beatles simply because Brian Epstein threatened to withdraw all EMI product from his shops, Martin has said many times over the years that he agreed to see them because he liked Brian and was won over by his enthusiasm, signing them simply because he liked them as people. "When you meet someone and you warm to them and you like being with them and they give you a kind of glow, when they leave you, you feel a little bit lost," Martin has said. "The Beatles had that effect on me."

Martin, despite his old-Etonian accent (learned in the Fleet Air Arm) and authoritative manner, won The Beatles over on their first session, when he was amused at George Harrison's cheeky crack about not liking his tie. He was like a schoolmaster they could have a laugh with. Yet, however charmed Martin was by them, when they fought him on **How Do You Do It**, it was his firm challenge to them to write as sure-fire a hit that spurred them to improve **Please Please Me**. In those early days, impressing someone they respected like Martin was undoubtedly an important yardstick in judging the quality of their own work. And when they did impress him, it is to his credit that Martin began to understand what he was dealing with: burgeoning, genuine talent.

Learning to trust Ringo's drumming and abandoning the idea that the group had to be seen to have a leader (he initially favoured Paul, as the prettiest), after The Beatles' initial hits Martin got landed with Epstein's entire NEMS stable of acts. The amazing result was that during 1963 Martin-produced artists occupied the UK #1 slot for 37 weeks of that year. With EMI failing to offer him a raise on his £3000 a year, or even give him a Christmas bonus from the reported £2 million profits, he eventually left the company in 1965 to form his own company **AIR**, Associated Independent Recordings.

Continuing to record at EMI's Abbey Road, The Beatles retained George as an independent producer. As the group developed, George noted that McCartney and Lennon required different things from him as producer and arranger. McCartney would sit with him and they would devise the arrangement together. "Lots of the arrangements to his songs were very much his idea," Martin said, "which I would have to implement." Lennon, on the other hand, would be more vague, often metaphorical. Leaving Martin with the suggestion that he wanted to "smell the sawdust" on **Being For The Benefit Of Mr Kite**, it was left to the producer to come up with splicing steam-organ tapes into the celebrated hallucinatory collage.

The Beatles, while happy to declare early on that George was "one of us", became more guarded about overstating his contributions, especially when *Sgt Pepper* was reviewed by one critic as "George Martin's best record". "Sometimes he works with us, and sometimes against us," Paul commented in 1967. "I don't think he does as much as people think. He sometimes does all the arrangements and we just change them."

George, though fascinated by their results on The Beatles' songwriting, didn't take drugs. The boys, knowing their producer would disapprove, would excuse themselves to the canteen or toilets of Abbey Road for a joint. On one occasion, George ingenuously escorted John, who suddenly felt "unwell", to the roof of the building for some fresh air, probably not the best place to take someone tripping on LSD.

By the time of *The White Album*, George was having less of an influence and was taking less interest, as his inmates took over the asylum. "I've changed from being the gaffer to **four Herberts from Liverpool**," he said in 1968, "to clinging on to the last vestiges of recorded power." Bored by the back-to-basics *Get Back* project, especially as the jaded group played so badly most of the time, his input was minimal until called upon to sort out a mobile studio in the wake of Magic Alex's organizational disaster at Apple. He had already warned them that without an "organizer", things could go wrong and it's clear that his return to the fold in summer 1969 – under the terms that discipline be restored and everyone worked like they used to, meaning as they had on *Sgt Pepper* – was the deciding factor in *Abbey Road* getting recorded at all.

By nature closer to Paul's organized approach to music, Martin nevertheless admired and pulled hard for Lennon's work, and was particularly hurt by John's post-split outbursts in interview. "I'd like to hear George Martin's music, please," Lennon snarled in 1970, "just play me some." Lennon apologized to him at dinner in 1973, saying he was out of his head. After Lennon's death, Yoko even went to the trouble of telling George that she wished he had produced *Double Fantasy*, which Martin was very touched by.

As the only Beatle to work with George Martin after the split, McCartney clearly felt the producer was part of the magic. "I've always had this lovely lucky feeling that when all The Beatles and George Martin signed off on a record," he remembered in 1996, "that meant it was fantastic." However, even as late as 1999, McCartney felt the need to assert that "George Martin was a great producer, no question of that, but most of the great ideas in The Beatles career came from The Beatles."

If George Martin had any regrets, they concerned his relative neglect of George Harrison. In the light of **Something** and **Here Comes The Sun**, the producer went out of his way to apologize to George for assisting Lennon and

McCartney to dominate over the years, giving them the majority of his attention and treating Harrison's work with a certain condescension. "I'm sorry George," the producer would say in interview many times, to the whole world as much as to the guitarist, "I should have encouraged you."

George Martin went on to produce dozens of records through the 1970s, 1980s and 1990s but, like everyone connected with the band, is not allowed to forget The Beatles. He wrote his autobiography, *All You Need Is Ears*, in 1978; *The Summer Of Love* (a *Sgt Pepper* reminiscence) in 1994; and he produced an entertaining all-star album of Beatlesongs as a farewell to his career, *In My Life*, in 1998. Reflecting on his career in the mid-1990s, he admitted that of all the great musicians and artists he'd worked with down the years, "None even begins to match the genius of those teenagers I met over thirty years ago." Now knighted and retired from producing, he has been seen on a lecture tour called "The Making of *Sgt Pepper*" and he acted as a wise old master of ceremonies at the Queen's Jubilee Concert in 2002. His latest Beatle-related activity was to score out the French-horn parts of "Sgt Pepper" from memory, just hours before McCartney, U2 and four horn players performed it as a curtain-opener for Live 8 in 2005 and, at the age of 80, collaborating with his son Giles to produce the *Love* album.

Dick James

Publisher

A former Parlophone recording artist, who hit #14 in 1956 with **Theme From Robin Hood** and had been produced by George Martin, James was recommended to Epstein as a hungry song publisher. He secured The Beatles' publishing by playing **Please Please Me** to a TV producer over the phone and getting the group their first national TV exposure. Epstein promised a long-term deal if the record hit #1, which it did, and Northern Songs (administered by Dick James Music for ten percent of the gross) was formed to copyright all future Lennon/McCartney compositions with a 50/50 royalty split between James on the one hand and Lennon/McCartney/Epstein on the other.

By June 1968, The Beatles had been forced to look into their finances seriously and decided that given their success, their publishing royalty was insufficient and invited Dick James to Apple to ask for a "raise". (This important meeting was made stickier by the presence of film cameras.) "We were trying to say, 'Look, you've done great,'" remembered McCartney. "From being the guy who sang **Robin Hood** to becoming the publisher of The Beatles." With James entirely non committal, McCartney asked him to "Come back with something that you know won't start this argument again."

The incident marked the start of James's disenchantment with Lennon and McCartney (hardly helped either by Lennon referring to him as "fascist pig" in his presence on the set of *Let It Be* in January 1969) and he eventually sold his share of Northern Songs, without informing John or Paul of his intentions, to Lew Grade's ATV Music in March 1969. James told a furious George Martin that he was "tired of being got at by The Beatles". When ATV acquired the extra shares to give them 51 percent, ie a controlling interest, Lennon and McCartney lost control of their songs forever.

Though James's perceived betrayal was just the first of many letdowns with regard to the Lennon/McCartney song catalogue, the composers were especially disappointed with the actions of their publisher, who had been struggling before making a fortune from their talent. "He's another one of those people," Lennon ranted in 1970, "who thinks he made us. And they didn't."

James probably didn't care, as he went on to publish Elton John, and release his records on his own DJM label. He died in 1986.

Mal Evans

Assistant

A Liverpool telephone engineer and gentle giant bouncer at The Cavern, Mal Evans – or "Big Mal" as The Beatles called him – was there for the group from mid-1963 until the end. His initial duties were as the gear humper and bodyguard, then in the studio years, as a general assistant who always seemed equipped with whatever the boys might need and seemed to revel in his place as quasi-servant. "He loved his job, he was brilliant," remembered George Harrison. "He was very humble but not without dignity; it was not belittling for him to do what we wanted, so he was perfect for us because that was what we needed."

Ever present and ever willing, Mal was on hand to contribute to several Beatles tracks including **You Won't See Me** (organ stabs), **Yellow Submarine** (chorus vocals), **Being For The Benefit Of Mr Kite** (bass harmonium), **A Day In The Life** (alarm clock and final piano chord), **What's The New Mary Jane** (sound effects) and, perhaps his finest hour, the filmed *Let It Be* rehearsals of **Maxwell's Silver Hammer** (anvil).

As Paul's housekeeper at Cavendish Avenue in 1966, he was around when Paul was writing **Sgt Pepper** and **Fixing A Hole** and quietly claimed a co-write. Explaining Paul didn't want Mal's name to disrupt the Lennon/McCartney credit, Evans said he was put on a royalty nonetheless. (This story is uncorroborated by McCartney's official biography *Many Years From Now*.)

The Beatles' demise saw him leave his family and lead a rootless existence in America. In Los Angeles in 1976, waving a gun in a drunken fit, he frightened his live-in girlfriend sufficiently for her to call the police who, unable to calm him, shot him dead. His gun was found to be unloaded. "He was not a nutter," McCartney said. "Any of his friends could have talked him out of it without any sweat."

Derek Taylor

Press officer

For many years he was their mouthpiece and spokesman and, as such, had much to do with the warm, optimistic and upbeat image of The Beatles. For these were qualities that pervaded Derek's journalism, poetry and books. There was something slightly dreamy and louche about his writing style but that was always tempered with strong wit, a good heart, a streak of mischief and charm to spare, and much the same was true of the man. He fitted right in with the 1960s hippie ethos and was the very soul of Apple's easy-come idealism. He seems to have been adored by everyone who knew him.

Taylor was born in Liverpool on May 7, 1932 and began his working career as a journalist on the *Hoylake and West Kirby Advertiser*, before graduating to the ***Liverpool Echo***. He married Joan Doughty in 1958. As The Beatles took off, he watched their rise from Manchester where he was showbusiness correspondent for the *Daily Express*. "As good as a rejuvenating drug for the jaded adult," he wrote of a Beatles show in that city in 1963, inadvertently setting the tone for much of his subsequent dealings with the group.

Interviewing Brian Epstein and documenting the history of the Hamburg years in the *Express*, he became known as the paper's Beatles correspondent, eventually ghost-writing a George Harrison column for them, and cementing a life-long friendship with George in particular. Epstein then summoned Derek to ghost his memoirs, ***A Cellarful Of Noise***. After this, Derek was offered the post of personal assistant to Epstein, a role that lasted five months until an argument over a limousine prompted Derek to resign.

Next, he moved to Los Angeles to work for a radio station, eventually becoming the press agent for a host of American acts who were enthralled by The Beatles, most notably The Byrds, Beach Boys (he coined the famous term "pocket symphony" to promote **Good Vibrations**) and Harry Nilsson, all of whom mingled with The Beatles after introductions from Derek. He also filed a weekly column for *Disc and Music Echo* in the UK. In 1968, he accepted another offer from The Beatles and returned to London with Joan and their children (there were six Taylor offspring) to run Apple's publicity department, leaving in 1970, shortly after the release of *Let It Be*.

For a while, he worked at Warner Bros and began producing records, by artists as diverse as George Melly, **Jimmy Webb**, Harry Nilsson and John Le Mesurier, and wrote an entertaining memoir, *As Time Goes By*, in 1973. But his association with The Beatles never entirely ceased; he worked on George's *I Me Mine* autobiography and returned to the fold full-time in the mid-1980s, working at Apple on the *Anthology* project. He was finishing work on the massive *Anthology* book when he died at his home in Suffolk, aged 65, after a battle with cancer. Tributes to him were warm and plentiful.

Taylor was always honest about life with

The Beatles and occasionally complained about being eternally linked with them. Ultimately however, he was convinced that the world was better for their existence (he wrote that The Beatles represented "the world's greatest romance") and that any pressure he endured being their conduit to the outside world was a small price to pay for being part of their story.

Murray The K

DJ

Murray Kaufman, a.k.a. Murray The K, was a scatter-mouthed New York disc jockey who tagged along with The Beatles during their first US tours, showing them the nightlife, bedding down in their rooms and babbling constantly about them on his shows. So ubiquitous was he, when it was asked at a Washington press conference what Murray The K was doing there, George Harrison replied, "Murray's the fifth Beatle". It was all Kaufman needed to constantly refer to himself in those terms with Epstein only desisting from legal action when he considered that, on balance, Kaufman's tireless publicity was probably worth it. Brian even considered Murray as compere of the April 1964 TV special ***Around The Beatles*** until Lennon, who distrusted the DJ, vetoed it.

His 1966 autobiography *Murray The K Tells It Like It Is*, Baby featured a forward by George Harrison; Murray was at the Montreal bedside when John and Yoko recorded **Give Peace A Chance**; and he was technical advisor for the 1970s Beatlemania stage show. He died in 1982.

Jimmy Nicol

Drummer

When Ringo went down with tonsillitis on the morning of June 3, 1964, during a photo shoot, Brian Epstein, in the face of a European and Australian tour, had to quickly find a temporary drummer "who looked like a Beatle and not an outcast". George Martin recommended Jimmy Nicol, whom he had recorded with **Georgie Fame** and NEMS act Tommy Quickly. Meeting The Beatles and sorting out the money (Nicol says £2500 per gig, other figures mention £500), they rehearsed the same afternoon and by the following evening, Jimmy was wearing Ringo's suit, sporting a new moptop haircut and playing with The Beatles in Denmark.

Thrust from obscurity into the centre of Beatlemania, Jimmy found it "strange and scary all at once," adding that "It's hard to describe the feeling but I can tell you it can go to your head. I see why so many famous people kill themselves. There is so little sanity to it all." So stunned by the bizarre change of surroundings was Nicol, McCartney remembers having to count him in for **She Loves You** several times before the drummer made his entrance.

Doing his best to party hard like a Beatle ("I was not even close to them when it came to mischief and carrying on"), Jimmy played ten shows in five cities before Ringo re-joined them in Australia. "I was hoping he would not want to come back," Nicol confessed, "I was having a ball, truly." Noticing the "wind had changed", Nicol was dropped out of the madness as quickly as he had been dropped into it. "When I was on the plane back to London, I felt like a bastard child being sent back home from a family that didn't want me."

Jimmy carried on in the music business for a few years, but lost heart. "When you've played with the best," he said, "the rest is just, well, the rest."

Yoko Ono

Muse, wife, business partner

Born into a wealthy Tokyo family in 1933, Yoko Ono was raised mainly by servants, as her international banker father, Yeisuke, was often abroad and her mother, Yasuda, was a chic but distant figure. A naturally imaginative and precocious child, Yoko was trained in formal music-making (German lieder, Italian opera and classical piano) with the encouragement of her music-loving father, who was later openly disappointed with her limited attainment.

In 1952 she began to rebel against what she termed the "Japanese pseudo-sophisticated bourgeoisie" by studying philosophy, being influenced and stimulated by the radical atmosphere in Japanese post-war thinking, especially that of the intellectual left-wing,

Jimmy and the gang in Amsterdam, June 1964

and the European existentialist influences of **Heidegger** and Sartre. She studied poetry and composition at Sarah Lawrence liberal arts college in New York before dropping out and eloping in 1955 with pianist Ichiyanagi Toshi, who became her first husband.

Through Toshi, who would go on to become one of Japan's highly regarded electronic composers, Yoko met John Cage and other avant-garde composers and artists, a disparate, loosely connected group of freethinking, Dada-influenced creators given the umbrella name of **Fluxus**. It was within this environment that Yoko began producing her broadly Zen-influenced and Cage-like "event scores", instructional poems, paintings and performances. They ranged from the simple ("Lighting Piece": "Light a match and watch til it goes out") to the implausible ("Sun Piece": "Watch the sun until it becomes square"), an Idea art, or Conceptual art: the point being that whatever mental response is inspired is the art.

In addition to the "instructionals" (collected in her famous 1964 book *Grapefruit*), there was her involvement in experimental improvisational music featuring what Lennon once called her "16-track voice" with **Ornette Coleman**. Further artistic activities of hers included the selling of bits of broken milk bottle tagged with a date in the future ("Morning Piece"); the removal of her clothing with scissors by the audience as she sat impassively on a stage ("Cut Piece"); and her film featuring 365 naked bottoms, with a commentary provided by the participants (*Bottoms*).

Provocative, sometimes whimsical, often humorous, usually philosophically complex as well as prodigiously productive, by the mid-1960s, Yoko had a certain name in the art world partly thanks to the support afforded her by second husband Tony Cox. However, there was resistance to her art even in the avant-garde because, as she considered, "The New York avant-garde was into cool art, not hot," and what she did was thought of as "too emotional ... in a way they thought it was too animalistic."

Intrigued by the positivism (the tiny word "Yes" painted on the ceiling, only visible from the top of a stepladder) and amused by the cheek (£200 for an apple on a stand) of her exhibition at London's **Indica Gallery** in 1966, John Lennon eventually recognized a kindred spirit and the pair became partners in life and art. Hooking up with Lennon did her reputation among the avant-garde no favours, but having the canvas of the world's media upon which to paint hastened her rejection of the exclusivity of the art world.

To John Lennon, Yoko Ono was far from the opportunistic dragon-lady hanging on to the coat-tails of a Beatle to further her career that some philistine and racist media coverage described; she was nothing less than "The Teacher" and the "Goddess of Love". From May 1968 until The Beatles ended sixteen months later, in a state of loving paranoia, he was obsessed with keeping her close to him at all times, whether at home, in the studio, or in the bathroom. Indeed, Yoko suggests that it is only because she agreed to accompany him to Abbey Road (Yoko: "If I'd said, 'I'm not gonna go, I'm gonna stay,' that would have been a scene") that the last three albums got made at all.

To the other Beatles, she was the first person outside the band's inner circle (the band, the studio men, Neil and Mal, essentially) who was allowed to stay around while they were working. Wives and girlfriends were discouraged from attending recording sessions and associates like Dick James and even **Brian Epstein** had been asked to leave Abbey Road at one time or another. Not only was Yoko not asked to leave, she was there all the time, usually within reaching distance of John. "We were always wondering how to say, 'Can you get off my amp,'" recalled McCartney, "without interfering with their relationship."

Irritation set in, not least because she would offer her views on the songs. "Suddenly she was in the band," remembered George Harrison. Indeed, though Lennon would later say, "That old gang of mine was over from the moment I met her", for a while he tried to combine old and new gangs. He collaborated with Yoko on the *musique concrète* of **Revolution 9** (which pointlessly retained a Lennon/McCartney credit) and insisted on the track appearing on *The White Album*. And when Yoko expressed the wish to do her own concerts ("There is no space where you are," she told John) he even offered The Beatles as her backing group. "You think they're just Liverpool and don't know anything, but they're pretty hip," Yoko remembers Lennon telling her. "They can really understand what you're doing and they can do it for you. It's a good band." Yoko demurred, probably saving face all round.

The nearest to an actual musical collaboration between Yoko and The Beatles occurred after George Harrison walked off the *Get Back* set at Twickenham on January 10, 1969, when John, Paul, Yoko and Ringo embarked on a long and furious, feedback-filled avant-garde jam. Ringo remembers "playing some weird drumming that I hadn't played before ... Our reaction was really, really interesting." When it was over, everyone left without speaking to each other.

Since John's death of course, Yoko, by proxy, has been the fourth Beatle as far as the business vote is concerned. The other three learned to live with it, with varying degrees of tolerance and harmony, though it was probably no more bumpy a ride than it would have been had John lived, or indeed than it has been with each other.

Billy Preston

Keyboards

Preston was born in Houston, Texas, in 1946, but brought up in Los Angeles; his mother was Robbie Preston Williams, a pianist and choir director, and Billy followed in her footsteps. Aged 10 he appeared as the young W.C. Handy in the biopic *St Louis Blues*, but mostly he was a child prodigy in the field of gospel music, notably with the influential Church of God in Christ Singers, fronted by Andre Crouch. In 1962, the 15-year-old wunderkind did a gospel tour of England and Germany with

Billy and George at the Oval Office with President Gerald Ford, December 1974

Little Richard. At the Hamburg dates he met The Beatles, just a few months before their big break with Parlophone.

After spells with Sam Cooke and some solo releases as an instrumentalist (notably **Billy's Bag**), Preston was touring with Ray Charles in 1969 when he met up with George again in London while Harrison was avoiding the *Get Back* sessions. George suggested that he join in when they moved to Apple studios, and Billy's presence both helped distract the group from its squabbles and added a soulful jazziness to The Beatles' sound.

His contributions can be heard on two-thirds of the *Let It Be* album and on **Something** on *Abbey Road*. Preston remains the only musician to play with The Beatles for longer than a single session and the only player to be credited alongside The Beatles when his name appeared on the single **Get Back**.

He subsequently signed with Apple, George producing the albums *That's The Way God Planned It* and *Encouraging Words*. When Apple folded, Billy signed to A&M, scoring #1 hits in the US with **Will It Go Round In Circles** and **Nothing From Nothing**. In the 1980s he toured with Ringo's All Starr Band, but in the 1990s he developed a cocaine habit, and thereafter a series of disasters ensued: a five-year suspended sentence for assault with a deadly weapon and cocaine possession in 1992, jail for violating probation in 1997, and a conviction for insurance fraud in 2001. He also suffered from kidney disease that year, but thankfully was well enough to attend the memorial concert for George Harrison late in 2002, where he gave a superb performance of **My Sweet Lord.** He died of kidney failure in June 2006.

Klaus Voormann

Bass player

A Hamburg-based illustration student and the boyfriend of Astrid Kirchherr until Stuart Sutcliffe supplanted him in late 1960, Klaus approached John Lennon about replacing Sutcliffe in The Beatles but was told, "Sorry mate, Paul has already bought a bass, we're going to stay as four people." Klaus moved to England and Brian Epstein signed his short-lived group Paddy, Klaus and Gibson, but Voormann spent much of the 1960s with **Manfred Mann**, and he also designed The Beatles' *Revolver* sleeve.

After the demise of The Beatles, Voormann appeared on several of Lennon's, Harrison's and Starr's solo records and there was even talk in the early 1970s of him joining up with them in a group called The Ladders. "There aren't any Beatles anymore," said Lennon in 1971, "but if you'd said that George, Ringo and John had an idea they might play a live show or two, then Klaus would be our man to play with us." However, the closest Klaus actually came to being McCartney's replacement was on the Lennon-penned Ringo track **I'm The Greatest** in 1973, which featured the other three Beatles, Voormann and Billy Preston. He is now a freelance artist. In the mid-1990s he designed the Beatles *Anthology* cover artwork and in 1999 published sketches and oil paintings of The Beatles in a book called *Hamburg Days*. He was persuaded, however, to get out his long-abandoned Fender bass once more for the Royal Albert Hall George Harrison tribute concert in November 2002.

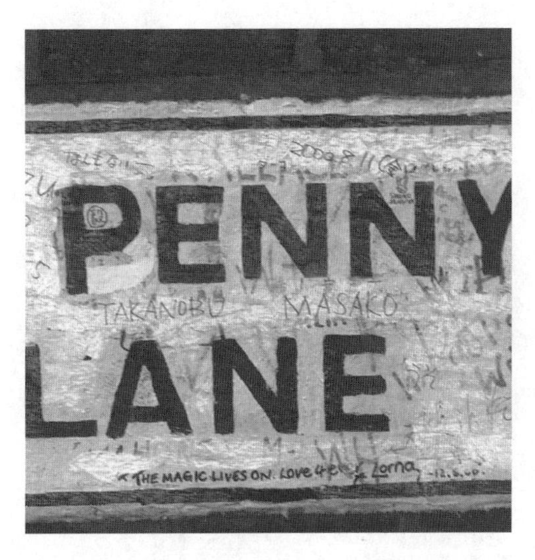

Part 8: Beatles Country

Liverpool

In the established tourism tradition of linking an area with popular cultural figures, just as Teeside is proudly "Catherine Cookson Country", the Yorkshire Dales "James Herriot Country", and Nottingham "Robin Hood Country" so Liverpool is, of course, "Beatles Country".

It wasn't always so. Through the 1970s, there was little recognition of the city's famous sons apart from Arthur Dooley's controversial 1974 **Four Lads Who Shook The World** sculpture in Mathew Street, which featured a Madonna figure and The Beatles as cherubs, one of whom – Paul – is flying away. In 1977, city councillors resisted calls for a monument of Liverpool's favourite sons on the streets of the city but, following the death of John Lennon in 1980, things changed.

Statues appeared both of John and of "Eleanor Rigby", the latter created by the original British showbiz rocker, Tommy Steele. Original clubs and even original homes related to Beatles history have now been revived, restored and re-created. Streets and places adopted appropriate names: in the eastern district of the city there is a John Lennon Drive off which runs the shorter Paul McCartney Way, George Harrison Close and Ringo Starr Drive. There's a bistro called Sgt Pepper's, a café called Lucy in the Sky with Diamonds, a bar called Lennon's and even Liverpool airport is now called John Lennon Airport with a tag line borrowed from **Imagine**: "Above us only sky".

Coach tours drive busloads of tourists to key addresses and there are gift shops, exhibitions and guidebooks ensuring that whatever you might expect from your Beatle-inspired visit, most of it has been anticipated and will be catered for, largely via www.visitbeatlesliverpool.com.

However, in addition to the pre-packaged must-dos, which require the cheerful surrender of all anti-herd sensibilities, there is still much of interest to be quietly savoured by those who prefer their tourist experiences to be a little less shepherded. A trek on foot around the backwaters of Liverpool will reveal pubs, streets and houses little changed since their connection with The Beatles story.

The Cavern and Mathew Street

In the 1980s, Mathew Street, where the Cavern Club was situated, was developed into a tourist-friendly Beatles Street, part of which, at a cost of £9 million, was turned into a shopping mall named **Cavern Walks**. A rose-and-dove fascia (representing John's favourite flower and his desire for peace) was designed by Cynthia Lennon. Just inside the doors of the mall is the Lucy in the Sky with Diamonds Café, which claims to be "exactly" where the stage of The Cavern was. Cavern Walks is also home to a rather lumpen bronze statue of the four Beatles in performance, by John Doubleday.

The Cavern Club itself was originally an arched brick cellar below a seven-storey fruit warehouse, which was used as an air-raid shelter in the war and became a jazz club in 1957. Beat music was disapproved of by the original owner, Alan Sytner, but under the ownership of Ray McFall, rock sessions were a common and popular occurrence by mid-1960. The Beatles appeared there nearly three hundred times between August 1961 and August 1963.

Spurred by a period of "where it all began" celebrity through the 60s, McFall expanded the club beyond his means and it closed in 1965 as McFall slid into bankruptcy. Reopened quickly under new ownership, it was forced to close for good in 1973 to make way for an underground railway ventilation duct. The warehouse was razed to the ground and a car park was built on the site.

The **New Cavern Club** opened for a while on the opposite side of the street, was re-named **Eric's** in 1976 and became a famous venue for a host of New Wave and New Romantic luminaries. In the early-80s aftermath of John Lennon's death, a full-scale re-creation of The Cavern was constructed at 10 Mathew Street, built on "75 percent of the original site" partly from bricks salvaged from the original club. A facsimile of the original painted back wall featuring all the names and signatures of the bands who played at The Cavern in the 60s was added to by Ringo Starr for a filmed documentary in the mid-80s, but the replica Cavern got the ultimate nod of approval in 1999 when Paul McCartney filmed a concert there as part of his Run Devil Run promotions.

Those who know complain that the building is the wrong way around and that the atmosphere falls inevitably short of the funky original. But most Beatles fans, if eyes close to the essentially ersatz quality of the venture, will undoubtedly get a frisson of pleasure from the experience. Continuing as a thriving live-music venue, admission is free for a visit during the day, while admission fees are payable when bands appear in the evening.

The club is owned by **Cavern City Tours**, the major players in Beatles tourism since the 1980s, whose website (www.cavernclub.org) also contains a wealth of info about their other concerns like the **Magical Mystery Tour** coach trip, an entertaining two-hour conducted bus tour of Beatles sites which, if it was twice the length, would still be too short. Their annual **Beatle Week** is an astonishing week-long Fabs orgy featuring dozens of international Beatles tribute bands and Beatles-associated personalities; previous guests have included Jackie Lomax, Tony Sheridan, ex-Wings members, the Fab Faux and The Rutles. A BBC documentary screened in January 2005 detailed Cavern City Tours' nightmare two-year struggle to secure the development of the Hard Day's Night Hotel, a 120-bedroomed Beatle-themed hotel on North John Street, around the corner from The Cavern. The £14 million pound project finally opened as a 4-star boutique hotel in February 2008, complete with a white piano in the "Lennon suite" (www.harddaysnighthotel.com).

In the early 60s, with The Cavern being a soft-drinks-only club, The Beatles and many other Liverpool musicians would gather between sets for a drink and to escape underage fans at the pub opposite. Still standing and open for business, **The Grapes** is also the pub a stunned Pete Best slumped into with Neil Aspinall after Brian Epstein told him he was no longer part of The Beatles. The one obvious concession to Beatle tourism is a discreet photo of the group in the pub circa 1961 in the corner where they sat when it was taken.

Elsewhere on Mathew Street, in addition to The Cavern and The Grapes, there is Liverpool's only dedicated Beatles-memorabilia establishment, **The Beatles Shop**, to purchase all things Fab, from postcards to rare copies of the Modern Jazz Quartet's *Under The Jasmine Tree* on Apple Records. Above the shop is the smart **Mathew Street Gallery**, which has some of John Lennon's art on permanent exhibition and which also features artwork by Klaus Voormann and photography by Astrid Kirchherr. **The Cavern Pub** has rock memorabilia, including a Hofner bass signed by Paul McCartney when he played The Cavern in 1999. Outside the pub is an impressively exhaustive Cavern Wall Of Fame featuring 1801 bricks embossed with the names of performers who appeared there. Right next to it is a statue of John Lennon, leaning in the same pose as the 1961 Hamburg photo that appears on the cover of his 1975 album *Rock And Roll*.

Albert Dock

Built in 1846 and revamped in the 1980s as a centre for arts, fashion, restaurant and retail, the dock houses **The Beatles Story** (www.beatlesstory.com), an enjoyable multi-media exhibition aimed at families and general tourists as much as Beatleheads. All visitors to The Beatles' Liverpool will want to see it. Featuring a mock-up of a Hamburg street, a re-creation of Bill Harry's 1961 *Mersey Beat* office and another facsimile of The Cavern, the exhibition has also snagged several credibility-enhancing items of memorabilia. These include George Harrison's first ever guitar, Colin Hanton's original Quarry Men drum kit and John Lennon's yellow-tinted spectacles, worn from 1971. An audio guide featuring the voices of John's sister Julia, Paul, Sid Bernstein, Allan Williams, George Martin and Brian Epstein certainly adds to the atmosphere. It's open every day 10am–6pm (except Christmas Day and Boxing Day). The **Magical Mystery Tour** coach trip leaves from here daily and tickets can be purchased in the shop along with a range of such essential Beatles Story merchandise as a "Love Me Do" teddy bear with pink T-shirt (£10) and a Rubber Soul wash-bag (£14.99).

Also at the Dock is the Tourist Office, which books the **National Trust tour** of Mendips and Forthlin Road (see p.326) and where passengers for the tour gather.

Just off Mathew Street is Stanley Street, where the local music shop **Hessy's** once stood at number 60. Run by Frank Hesselberg, it was where John's Aunt Mimi finally bought John a proper guitar – a Hofner Club 40 semi-acoustic – in 1959 for £17 (over £400 by today's standards). Stuart Sutcliffe bought his Hohner President bass guitar there and Brian Epstein, in one of his first moves as The Beatles' manager, settled The Beatles' outstanding instrument bills there in 1961 to the tune of £200. First opened in 1934, it finally ceased trading as a music store in 1995, though its 1970s shop sign can be seen at The Beatles Story museum. It's currently a clothes shop.

Stanley Street runs directly into Whitechapel, where **NEMS** (North End Music Store), the flagship shop of the Epstein family's chain of record shops around Merseyside, stood. Headlines in *Mersey Beat* (which was sold there), and several requests at the shop over a few days in 1961 for a record called **My Bonnie**, alerted Epstein to The Beatles. It was in a storeroom at the back of the shop on Sunday, December 3, 1961, that Brian convinced The Beatles to let him be their manager. For years a Rumbelows electrical retailer sporting a plaque proclaiming the building's historical importance, it is now an Ann Summers sex shop.

Lime Street, The Jac and The Blue Angel

North of the station, on Lime Street, lies the **Empire Theatre.** Here the boys unsuccessfully auditioned for Carroll Levi's *Search For The Stars* talent show: once in 1957 as The Quarry Men and again in 1959 as Johnny and the Moondogs. After several appearances as The Beatles, including the Chris Montez and Roy Orbison tours and a December 1963 preview of their Christmas Show, they gave their final ever Liverpool performance there in December 1964 where 40,000 people applied for 2300 tickets. (McCartney returned with Wings in 1973, 1975 and 1979 and, unannounced, in 2001 to sing an unaccompanied **Yesterday** at a tribute to George Harrison. Ringo brought his All-Starr Band here in 1992.)

The **Jacaranda**, at 23 Slater Street, is a few blocks south of Lime Street. Originally owned by Allan Williams, it was one of the many late-50s coffee bars in Liverpool following the example of London's famous "2 Is" where Tommy Steele had been discovered in 1956. Lennon, McCartney and Harrison hung out there as students and Stuart Sutcliffe (perhaps with Lennon's help) painted a mural there. The Silver Beetles played at The Jac a dozen times between May and August 1960 before their first trip to Hamburg, but having fallen out with Williams, didn't play there on their return to Liverpool. Known for years as the Maxie San Suzie, the Jacaranda name was restored in The Beatles-hungry 80s and remains a thriving watering-hole today, complete with the apparently authentic Sutcliffe/Lennon mural.

Another of Williams' clubs, the **Wyvern Social Club** (108 Seel Street) was the venue for the May 1960 audition of The Silver Beetles, among other Merseyside combos, to be the backing groups for Billy Fury and other Larry Parnes acts. Tommy Moore, the group's drummer at the time, was late for the audition and The Silver Beetles did half their set with Johnny Hutchinson of Cass And The Cassanovas. A combination of Moore's tardiness, age (he was several years older than the rest of the group) and Sutcliffe's tentative musicianship led to the lesser gig (Johnny Gentle) being offered to them. The Wyvern Social Club was also the venue of Pete Best's perfunctory audition in August 1960 for membership of The Beatles. When it became the **Blue Angel** in March 1961, The Beatles frequented the club as customers, though they never played there. It's still a popular Liverpool drinking and dancing club.

Art-school hangouts and Falkner Street

Ye Cracke (Rice Street) is a public house near Liverpool Art College where John Lennon, Stuart Sutcliffe, poet **Adrian Henri** and writer Bill Harry used to drink and talk art in the late 50s and early 60s. Art-college tutor Arthur Ballard was known to deliver lectures there. During a lunchtime college dance in 1960, John had asked fellow student Cynthia Powell to dance. She refused, saying she was engaged. John's reply was "I didn't ask you to fucking marry me did I?" Later, in Ye Cracke, their romance began, continuing later that day at Stuart Sutcliffe's **Gambier Terrace** flat. It is unspoiled today and entirely absent of Beatle memorabilia; the beer is good and the timeless, bohemian, student atmosphere remains. (The student halls of residence on Oxford Street, a few blocks away, at the end of Hope Street, were formerly **Oxford Street Maternity Hospital**, where one John Lennon was born on October 9, 1940. A plaque sporting a favourite "JohnandYoko" conceptual aphorism, "This Is Not Here", was mounted on the building to mark what would have been his sixtieth birthday.)

Near Rice Street is **Falkner Street**. Brian Epstein rented a ground-floor flat at number 36 in Liverpool's red-light district, during 1961 and 1962, for his private liaisons. He presented John and Cynthia (overwhelmed with gratitude) with the keys as a wedding gift on August 23, 1962, and Cynthia moved in that evening, while John went to play with The Beatles in Chester. With a possible reference to the nature of Brian's previous use of the flat, John wrote **Do You Want To Know A Secret** there. With John away so much, there was concern for a pregnant Cynthia stuck alone in Liverpool's seamier side of town, and she and John soon moved back to Mendips, Menlove Avenue, with John's Aunt Mimi, occupying the ground floor of John's childhood home.

Liverpool Institute (now **LIPA**), is on Mount Street. The "Innie", as it was known locally, was built in 1825 as a Mechanics Institute, becoming a fee-paying school in 1837 and a grammar school in 1944. After passing his 11+ exam, Paul McCartney was educated there from 1953, quitting in August 1960 in the middle of his A levels to play in Hamburg with The Beatles. George Harrison was there from 1954 and Len Garry, Neil Aspinall, Ivan Vaughan and Mike McCartney also attended. it was closed in 1985 after years of neglect, until in 1989 McCartney announced his plans to develop the building as the Liverpool Institute of Performing Arts. In 1995 LIPA was officially opened by the Queen and is currently attended by students from all over the world.

In June 1957, having been recommended by Quarry Bank headmaster William Pobjoy, John Lennon was interviewed for a place at **Liverpool College of Art**, on Hope Street, by college principal Mr Stevenson. He began his studies in September of the same year, meeting his future wife Cynthia, future Beatle Stuart Sutcliffe and future *Mersey Beat* editor Bill Harry. The art college was part of the same building as the **Liverpool Institute**, so John would often meet his young pals Paul and George from next door, to rehearse at lunch-times upstairs in the "life rooms". Absenting himself to tour Scotland with Johnny Gentle and The Silver Beetles in June 1960, he never returned to his art studies. It's currently part of the John Moore University facilities for their Art and Design provision.

Stuart Sutcliffe's first flat was at number 7 on the neighbouring **Percy Street**, at the back of the ground floor, which he occupied in 1957–59, paid for by his mother. He preferred to do all his painting here rather than at Liverpool Art College and even received tuition there from the art-college lecturer Arthur Ballard. He later moved to **3 Gambier Terrace**, an imposing Georgian terrace facing Liverpool Cathedral, and shared a first-floor flat there with art student Rod Murray and, from May 1960, John Lennon. The highly impressed Paul and George often hung out, ate, slept and rehearsed there. It was to this flat that the poet Royston Ellis returned – having been backed by The Silver Beatles at a poetry and rock event at the Jacaranda – and showed the boys how to get high from chewing the strip of benzedrine found on the inside of a Vicks inhaler. Liverpool Cathedral is itself of passing interest to Beatleheads. An 11-year-old Paul McCartney was turned down as a choirboy here in 1953, but was commissioned nearly forty years later to compose his "Liverpool Oratorio" for the cathedral choir. The work was premiered here in June 1991.

The Dingle

Richard Starkey, known as Richie to the family, later to be known by the world as Ringo Starr, was born in a Victorian terraced house on Madryn Street in the Dingle on July 7, 1940. (The house and surrounding district are due for demolition as part of a regeneration project. The council ignored protests from locals and Beatles historians, saying the site had no significance.) When his parents Elsie and Dickie Starkey split in the mid-1940s, Richie would hardly see his father again (despite the fact that Starkey senior continued to live on the same road and Elsie and Richie lived just around the corner). Ringo lived mostly with his mother (and latterly, her second husband Harry) at **10 Admiral**

Grove, another terraced house, from 1943 until he moved to London aged 23.

A severe bout of peritonitis led to him spending much of his seventh year at the Royal Children's Hospital, **Myrtle Street**. When he returned to school, he was placed in a class one year younger than him. Ronald Wycherley, later to be known as **Billy Fury**, was a classmate. The Starkeys' local pub, where Elsie was a barmaid, adjoins Admiral Grove. **The Empress** was immortalized in 1970 by being featured on the front cover of Ringo's first solo album *Sentimental Journey*. It's still standing and open for business. Ringo was the only Beatle not to attend grammar school, and went to **Dingle Vale Secondary Modern**, in Dingle Vale, sporadically in his teens, interspersed with bouts of serious ill-health. He left without qualifications. It later became Shorefields Comprehensive School.

Something to get hung about: Strawberry Field

Mendips, Woolton and Strawberry Field

Mendips, 251 Menlove Avenue, Woolton, was the home of Mary and George Smith (John's Aunt Mimi and Uncle George) and, from 1945 until 1963, apart from Hamburg, art school and his early marriage spells in Liverpool flats, the home of John Lennon. It was a comfortable home with a garden and leaded windows, and John was allowed to practise his guitar only in the porch, but he came to appreciate the acoustic reverberation there. After Uncle George died in 1954, John and Mimi lived there alone with occasional student lodgers, though Cynthia also had two periods there: once briefly in 1961 ("an impossible situation with Mimi") and again in 1962–63, when married to John and expecting Julian.

John bought his aunt a bungalow in Poole in 1965, but tried to persuade her not to sell his childhood home. Preferring a clean break, Mimi did sell it, but it was bought in 2001 by Yoko Ono and donated to the **National Trust**. Though for a long time it was an unvisitable quasi-shrine (a commemorative plaque wasn't mounted until 2000), Mendips is now restored to something approaching its 50s and 60s state and open to the public. A curiously cold exhibit compared to the **Forthlin Road** restoration, this is partly due to the new site being relatively undeveloped (old photos are in a book rather than on the wall and visitors are allowed twenty minutes flat), and possibly also to do with the visitor's recollection of the restrained emotional atmosphere of the household. Fresh flowers might help restore a sense of Mimi's gentility. Audio recollections of student lodgers help bring things to life, however. When visiting the legendary porch where John practised his guitar, beware interrupting awed Beatleheads having "a moment".

Near Mendips, on Beaconsfield Road, is **Strawberry Field** (Mimi: "He could see it from his window"). The garden of this Salvation Army orphanage was the site of many a childhood adventure for John Lennon and friends Pete Shotton and Ivan Vaughan. Visiting the annual fête every year, the boys would sell bottles of lemonade and pilfer from the stalls to the sound of the Salvation Army band. Later used as a metaphor for nostalgic escape in his song **Strawberry Fields Forever**, of all The Beatles shrines that emerged following Lennon's death, it is perhaps the most evocative and symbolic, linked as it is to one of his greatest musical creations. Mimi bought a tree to be planted there in John's memory and Yoko named

Forthlin Road and the National Trust Tour

Number 20, Forthlin Road, Allerton, is a three-bedroomed terraced council house that became the McCartney family home in 1955 when Paul was thirteen. McCartney remembers his mother being very proud to live there, though her premature death in 1956 from cancer meant Mary McCartney occupied it only for a matter of months and father Jim brought up Paul and Michael there alone.

Lennon and McCartney would play truant to write songs in the front parlour where the piano was while Jim was at work. **One After 909**, **Love Me Do**, **I Saw Her Standing There** and **When I'm Sixty-Four** were among the better-known songs conceived there.

It was still Paul's home in the early days of Beatlemania and he took to jumping into the neighbour's back garden and out the front door of number 18 to avoid the throng.

In 1964, Jim McCartney moved to Rembrandt, a house in Heswall bought for him by his Beatle son. 20 Forthlin Road was occupied by Mrs Sheila Jones and her family until 1998, when it was purchased (for £55,000) and restored to 1950s splendour (at a cost of £47,000) by the National Trust at the suggestion of then BBC chief John Birt. The audio headsets featuring Michael McCartney's reminiscences and the display of his evocative childhood photography make for a surprisingly vivid experience. A **National Trust Tour** currently takes in both **Forthlin Road** and **Mendips** (three to four daily tours, costing around £16 per person, operate Wednesday to Sunday, March to November. Details available at www.nationaltrust.org.uk/beatles, 0844 800 4791).

Lennon's memorial in New York's Central Park after it. A stop-off point for the **Magical Mystery Tour** bus passengers, the original orphanage building has gone and the stone pillars at the entrance are covered with the inevitable Beatles graffiti. Saved from closure once in 1984 thanks to a donation from Yoko, Strawberry Field finally ended its childcare provision in 2005.

At the north end of Beaconsfield Road is Church Road, where you'll find St Peter's Church. The church hall is the site of Paul McCartney's first meeting with John Lennon on July 6, 1957, after The Quarry Men had played their afternoon set at the garden fête in the field behind the church. A re-formed Quarry Men played there at the fortieth anniversary celebration of that meeting on July 5, 1997. The cemetery also has a tombstone marking the graves of the Rigby family, one of whom, Eleanor, appears to have died on October 10, 1939.

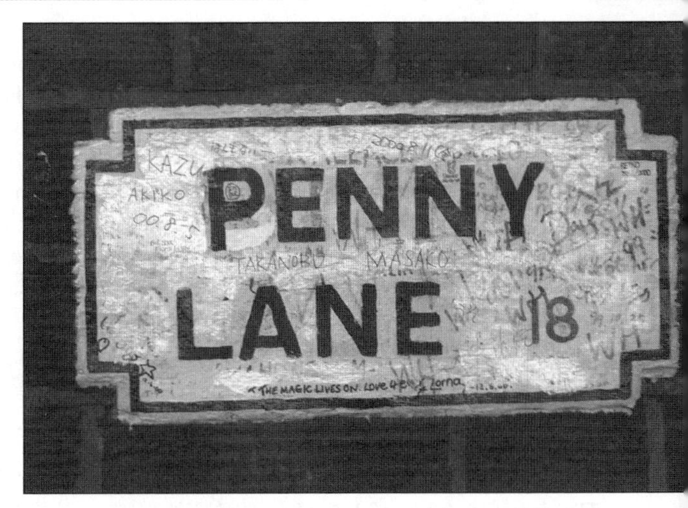

Penny Lane area

Across Calderstones Park from Strawberry Field was **Quarry Bank School**, founded in 1922. John Lennon entered the grammar school in 1952, soon got a reputation as a disruptive influence and received canings and detentions throughout his school life. He was streamed into the lower set and failed all his GCE O levels in 1956. A new headteacher, William Pobjoy, encouraged John's music and art by allowing The Quarry Men to perform at the school and arranging his interview with the Liverpool College of Art.

John Lennon had previously attended **Dovedale Primary School**, on Dovedale Road, from 1946 to 1951 after moving to Mendips. George Harrison was also there from 1948 to 1950 but, with three years between them, they are unlikely to have met at school. Fellow pupil and later TV comedian Jimmy Tarbuck remembered John as unusual and belligerent. Pete Shotton remembers an incident where Tarbuck strangled Lennon with his school scarf for "looking at him funny" and was pacified only when Shotton explained that John looked at everyone that way because of his short-sightedness.

Just around the corner is Penny Lane, a typical suburban street and district that happens to have been immortalized in song. There is indeed a bank on the corner, there was once Bioletti's the barber's (a contemporary hairdresser's on the street is called Tony Slavin), clean machines pass from time to time from the nearby fire station and the (tram) shelter in the middle of a roundabout houses a defunct Sgt Pepper's Café, a sorry indication of the area's inability to exploit its Beatle fame. John Lennon walked down Penny Lane to school, riding tram bumpers and occasionally thieving from the local shops.

Wavertree and Childwell

The first five years of John Lennon's life were spent at **9 Newcastle Road** over in Wavertree in a two-bedroom terraced house, with his mother Julia and various members of her family. With husband Fred emotionally estranged from his wife and absent at sea, Julia later set up home with John Dykins in a one-bedroom flat in Gateacre. Social services agreed with Julia's sister Mimi that both the accommodation and Julia's conduct were inappropriate for the raising of a 5-year-old boy and Mimi, with Julia's blessing, took John into her care. George Harrison was born not far away at **12 Arnold Grove**, a terraced house (two up, two down, outside toilet) on February 25, 1943, and lived there until he was six. When the Harrison family's name finally came up on the council housing list after eighteen years, they moved.

A five-bedroom house in the grander part of town, 127 Queens Drive, in nearby Childwell, is where the Epstein family lived for thirty years and where Brian was living with his mother Queenie and brother Clive when he met The Beatles. John Lennon became a regular visitor in the early days of Brian's involvement with the group and sat for long hours with Brian in the morning room, discussing the marketing of The Beatles. In June 1963, the house was host to a party to celebrate Paul McCartney's 21st birthday.

Other spots

The Casbah Coffee Club, West Derby

A huge fifteen-room Victorian house, it was the home of Mona and John Best and their sons Pete and Rory. The seven-room basement of 8 Haymans Green, West Derby, was converted by Mona into a coffee bar, the Casbah Club, in August 1959. It provided The Quarry Men with their first residency, which lasted until October 1959, when they quit after a row about money. It was here, in mid-1959, that Lennon and McCartney persuaded Stuart Sutcliffe to buy a bass guitar, rather than art materials, with his winnings from an art competition.

It was also here, in August 1960, that Lennon, McCartney, Sutcliffe and Harrison heard Pete Best playing with his band The Blackjacks. On their return from Hamburg, The Beatles decorated the walls and ceilings in the club and played at the Casbah throughout 1961–62. They met here with Mona – erstwhile manager, benefactor and all-round encourager – and Brian Epstein to discuss Brian's management contract in December 1961. They performed on the club's final night on June 24, 1962.

Following closure, the cellar became storage space again but the decor remained in its 1960s state until over thirty years later when the Casbah Club was restored to its former glory. With the house still in the Best family today, as the headquarters of the Pete Best Band, the Casbah is now open for tourism. Despite being slightly outside the "official" Beatles tourism circuit (for geographical and, it seems, political reasons), it is actually the most authentic Beatles site in Merseyside. With many original artefacts (microphones, guitars and amps) on display along with Paul McCartney's fully restored Rainbow ceiling, John Lennon's Aztec ceiling and Cynthia Lennon's silhouette of John, the atmosphere is uniquely vivid. Book a £15 visit at www.casbahcoffeeclub.com.

Litherland Town Hall, Hatton Hill Road, Litherland

The Beatles' third gig upon returning from their first trip to Hamburg was played here on December 27, 1960, and the excitement generated by the toughened, newly drilled rockers is regarded by many as a turning point in the group's fortunes. It was also the venue, on October 19, 1961, for a one-night-only joining of The Beatles and Gerry and The Pacemakers as **The Beatmakers**. It still hosts live gigs, particularly during Liverpool's annual Beatle Week in August.

London

The Beatles' home from 1963, London is almost as rich in Fabs locations as their birthplace. Their pads, their favourite clubs, their studio, and famous film and photo locations are all here and mostly still standing. Richard Porter's Beatles In London walks (www.beatlesinlondon.com) meet Sundays at 10.55am, Thursdays at 11am and Wednesdays at 2pm at Tottenham Court Road Underground (Dominion Theatre exit) with a separate walk meeting Tuesdays and Saturdays at Marylebone Underground at 11.20am (no booking required on either walk), and are recommended.

St James's and Piccadilly

The small area south of Piccadilly known as St James's is one of London's most select and least visited crannies. Its invariably quiet streets seem to house mostly solicitors' offices and art galleries. Tucked behind St James's Square is **Mason's Yard** (or Mason Yard as the older street sign hidden in an alley next to a pub reads), SW1, the kind of nook you wouldn't find unless you went looking for it. At number 6 was **The Indica**, a street-level bookshop and basement art gallery co-run by John Dunbar (then married to Marianne Faithfull), Barry Miles (notable underground journo and later McCartney biographer) and Peter Asher (brother of Jane and erstwhile pop singer). McCartney helped them set it up in 1966, decorating and designing Indica wrapping paper, while Lennon bought Timothy Leary's *The Psychedelic Experience* from the shop, finding within its pages inspiration for the song **Tomorrow Never Knows**. In November of 1966, John Lennon met Yoko Ono there for the first time on the eve of her "Unfinished Paintings and Objects" exhibition.

Diagonally opposite at number 13 stood **The Scotch of St James**, a favourite club of McCartney's in the 60s and the hippest of places for the pop scene. Number 6 is now occupied by a remodelled building looking like an old Dutch warehouse and housing another gallery, James Hyman Fine Art. The Scotch is now The Director's Lodge Club, a rather tatty-looking strip joint. The ugly abandoned electricity substation dominating the centre of the square, which was functioning in the 60s, has just been acquired by art impresario Jay Joplin to become a new five-storey gallery space, which suggests that the lost-world feel of this place is shortly to be, well, lost.

54 St James Street, W1, is where all Apple business moved to in 1972, with the exception of Apple Studios, which remained open at Savile Row during renovations and played host to some of George's sessions for *Living In The Material World* and Ringo's for *Ringo*. Starr's Ring O'Records was also housed here. (A downsized Apple moved up the road to 29–30 St James Street in 1975 and to **48 Charles Street** in 1983. In 1989 Apple moved around the corner to **6 Stratton Street** until 1993, when it moved to its present location at **27 Ovington Square, SW3,** where it shares space with George's publishing company Harrisongs and Olivia Harrison's Romanian Angel Appeal.)

Past Piccadilly Circus, **2 Lower Regent Street**, W1, was the address of the **BBC Paris Theatre**. This small theatre hidden in the depths of Rex House, a 1930s block at the quieter end of Regent Street, was used for many years by the BBC for recording radio comedy, quiz and music programmes. Beatle heroes The Goons recorded their famous shows here, so the boys were delighted that it was the location of sessions for their **Saturday Club** and other radio appearances between 1963 and 1965. Dezo Hoffman photographed the group outside the venue in April 1963, an image that became the cover for the 1994 release *Live At The BBC*. The BBC sold Rex House in the 90s and it was empty for several years. It has recently been refurbished as an office complex and there is a fitness centre in the basement formerly occupied by the Paris Theatre auditorium.

Off Regent Street, the grand, five-storey town house at **3 Savile Row** has been used variously as Lady Hamilton's residence (bought for her by her lover Lord Nelson), private gentlemen's club The Albany, bandleader Jack Hylton's headquarters and, from June 1968,

A Hard Day's Night and Help! locations

The first scene of **A Hard Day's Night** features The Beatles running down Boston Place next to **Marylebone Station**, NW1. From there they run through the entrance of the station, onto the concourse and along Platform 1.

The fire escape at the back of the 'TV Studio' (actually, the Scala Theatre on Charlotte Street, W1, destroyed by fire in 1970) belonged in reality to the **Hammersmith Odeon** (now the Apollo) on Queen Caroline Street, W6, the venue for many Beatles live appearances, including their 1964 Christmas shows. The boys gambol and frolic to the strains of **Can't Buy Me Love** on two locations: Thornbury Fields (Stanborough Road, Isleworth, Middlesex) and in a field at **Gatwick Airport**.

Ringo's solo adventure begins in Notting Hill Gate where he photographs a milk-bottle rack at **2 Lancaster Gate**, W11, is chased by girls around various streets in the area before darting into a corner shop at 20 All Saints Road, W11. His **This Boy** sequence was filmed at the Thames towpath at Ferry Lane, Kew, Surrey, while the pub in which he causes trouble is the **Turk's Head**, Winchester Road, Twickenham, Middlesex, still open for business. The boys are chased by policemen through **Newman's Passage**, W1. The exterior of the boys' four-door terraced super-pad in *Help!* was shot at Ailsa Avenue, Twickenham.

home of The Beatles' company Apple Corps and its extravagant doings. The basement was converted to a studio and is where The Beatles reconvened to complete the *Get Back/Let It Be* film in January 1969 following their abandonment of Twickenham Studios. The final live performance of The Beatles, shown at the close of *Let It Be*, took place on the roof of the building on January 30, 1969, as did the ceremony to change the name of John Winston Lennon to John Ono Lennon on April 22, 1969. John and Yoko housed their **Bag Productions** in a ground-floor office there in 1969–71.

The building was abandoned in 1972 when it was discovered that the absence of vital basement supports removed to create **Apple Studios** was causing the building to collapse. Refurbishments were to little avail and the building remained empty for years before finally being sold in 1984 to the Midlands Council Workers' Pension Fund, when an entirely new interior was constructed. It is currently the Building Societies Association building, and visits onto the rooftop are not possible.

Oxford Circus and Soho

From 1957, the elegant, early nineteenth-century house at 57 Wimpole Street, W1, was the five-storey home of Dr Richard Asher, Margaret Asher, and children Peter, Jane and Claire. When dating Jane in mid-1963, Paul missed the last train to Liverpool one evening and stayed at Wimpole Street. Jane's mother, Margaret, offered Paul use of the attic bedroom on the fourth floor whenever he was in town and the house became his London base until late 1965. With Paul being accepted into the household as a member of the family, the period spent at Wimpole Street was vital in the development of McCartney's cultural awareness.

Paul's room had a piano and it was here that the idea for **Yesterday** first came to him. Margaret, a music teacher whose former oboe students coincidentally included George Martin, had a music room in the basement. It was in this room that McCartney and Lennon collaborated on **I Want To Hold Your Hand** and Paul worked on many of his songs including **And I Love Her, Every Little Thing** and **I've Just Seen A Face**. Songs written in the heat of anger following an argument with Jane – **You Won't See Me** and **I'm Looking Through You** – were also written here.

In March 1964 Brian Epstein moved his company NEMS to the fifth floor of an office building situated at 5–6 **Argyll Street**, W1, next door to the **London Palladium**. Used for band meetings, press interviews as well as day-to-day business, this was Beatles Central until September 1967, one month after Brian's death. It has recently been reappointed as Sutherland House, suites of offices above a branch of Bar Logic. The fifth floor is now occupied by a company called G.L. Hearn.

The Bag o' Nails, at 8 Kingly Street, Soho, was a hookers' hang-out down the years, and in the 60s it was a drinking club with live music, a favourite watering-hole and place to "pull birds" for the swinging set, including The Beatles. Paul met Linda Eastman there for the first time in 1966 and did indeed pull her. It is now a hostess club called The Miranda.

In what looks like an alleyway off Wardour Street lies one of London's most important recording facilities: **Trident Studios** (Trident House, 17 St Anne's Court). To record **Hey Jude**, The Beatles decamped here in August 1968, primarily to try the studio's 8-track facilities, which EMI had yet to make available at Abbey Road. Over six days in October 1968, to break up the extended *White Album* sessions, The Beatles recorded **Honey Pie, Dear Prudence, Savoy Truffle** and **Martha My Dear** here. Later they returned to work on basic tracks for **I Want You/She's So Heavy**. In the early solo years, John's **Cold Turkey** and George's **My Sweet Lord** were also recorded

Paul's escape route

While living at Wimpole Street, in order to avoid the fans outside Paul would sometimes resort to an elaborate escape route devised by Dr Asher, and happily agreed to by the conspirators. It required McCartney to leave by the window of his attic room, across the narrow parapet to **56 Wimpole Street**, through an army colonel's flat to the lift, down to the basement, out through the back of the kitchen in a young couple's flat, emerging through a door near **10 Browning Mews**, before turning left through the archway onto **New Cavendish Street** and freedom.

here. (Other notable tracks at Trident include Elton John's **Your Song** and David Bowie's **Space Oddity**.)

After changing fortunes in the 1980s, Trident finally closed in the 1990s and the space was taken over by a post-production studio used mostly for TV and film voice-overs, called The Sound Studio. This has now been renamed Trident Sound Studios, and T-shirts celebrating its glory days and Beatle connections are on sale at reception.

In the neighbouring Soho Square, **MPL** has its headquarters. From the early seventies, the location of McCartney Productions Ltd, McCartney's song-publishing empire and still the most likely place to spot a Beatle, it features a replica of The Beatles' favourite number-two studio from Abbey Road in its basement.

Baker Street, Marylebone and Marble Arch

Like Liverpool, London has its own specialist Beatles shop, **The London Beatles Store,** to be found at 231 Baker Street (www.beatlesstorelondon.co.uk), where Beatleheads could easily spend their life savings on merchandise and memorabilia. It sells everything from rare fanzines to miniature ornamental Rickenbacker guitars, Beatles dolls, Lennon hats and even Beatles salt and pepper shakers, ensuring no lifestyle or household accessory is left unBeatled.

At number 94, a four-storey house built in the early nineteenth century on the corner of Baker Street and Paddington Street became the first proper home of The Beatles' new company Apple, which occupied the upper-floor offices in late 1967. From December 1967, the shop space below was the site of the Apple Boutique, "a beautiful place where you can buy beautiful things", as McCartney had it. A psychedelic mural designed by the Dutch artists collectively known as The Fool was painted over the entire building with the help of forty art students but against the wishes of Westminster Council, which forced Apple to whitewash it over within weeks. The boutique lost almost £200,000 in seven months and was closed on July 30, 1968, with the entire remaining stock given free to customers. Paul returned the following month to scrape the words "Hey Jude" on the inside of the whitewashed windows as publicity on the eve of The Beatles' August 1968 single release, but had to remove it after a local Jewish delicatessen-owner objected.

A few streets away is **Montagu Square**. The ground-floor flat at number 34 was Ringo's late-1964 address, and he retained the property following his and Maureen's move to Sunny Heights in 1965. Paul rented it off Ringo for a while in 1966 to set up an experimental recording studio for the underground Indica crowd and his own use. Guests, including **Jimi Hendrix** and **William Burroughs,** stayed there; Ringo had to redecorate the flat white after Hendrix trashed it while on acid. John and Yoko were living there in October 1968 when they were busted for marijuana possession. The landlords, appalled at the scandal, sued Ringo for "misuse of property", after which he sold the lease in February 1969.

Further south, past Marble Arch, is **Green Street**. Apartment L, at number 57, was The Beatles' first London apartment from summer 1963. Rented unfurnished by Brian Epstein originally for all four of them, it was quickly abandoned by Paul, who found it lacking in "homeliness", and John, who set up home with Cynthia and Julian when his marriage became public knowledge. Ringo and George stayed there until March 1964.

Belgravia to Kensington

Brian Epstein bought a five-storey Georgian house in December 1964 for £60,000 at **24 Chapel Street** in Belgravia, W1. He employed a chauffeur, butler and cook, and conducted his business from there in the latter years. It was the location for the ***Sgt Pepper*** press party in May 1967, which NEMS man Peter Brown described as a choice gathering of "ten of the most important representatives of the press to listen to the new album and enjoy a 'family' dinner with one or two of The Beatles around a dining table". On the afternoon of August 27, 1967, Brian's butler, unable to rouse him, raised the alarm and after breaking through two locked sets of doors, found Brian dead in his bedroom.

At **13 Emperor's Gate**, in West Kensington, SW7, the top-floor maisonette flat was the first London-based family home for the Lennons and baby Julian early in 1964 (*With The Beatles* photographer Robert Freeman lived in the same building). With only one way in, Cynthia would soon feel trapped by the fans – who quickly discovered the address and would congregate by the entrance – and by the students in the hostel opposite who would attempt to see into the flat and attract the Lennons' attention.

If you are in West London and feel like venturing a little further south, **Chiswick House** (Burlington Lane, Chiswick, W4; [020] 8742 1225) is well worth a visit. Its garden, designed in the eighteenth century, was the location for the **Paperback Writer** and **Rain** promo shoots and is open all year, from 8.30am until dusk. The garden's classical busts, sphinxes and columns justify a trip there in their own right but, like Abbey Road, it provides a good photo opportunity for a "Fabs tableau" – by the tree where The Beatles were filmed miming to **Rain**.

Abbey Road and Cavendish Avenue

Built as a nine-bedroom private residence in 1830, the Abbey Road building in leafy, well-to-do North London suburb **St John's Wood** has functioned as a recording complex since 1931 when it was opened by EMI. Apart from a handful of sessions, Studio Two – the medium-sized "pop" studio of the four – is the place where most of The Beatles' music was recorded from June 1962 until January 1970. With The Beatles' final album named after the street and the famous cover photograph being taken outside, the location has taken on an almost mythological quality among Beatles enthusiasts. During the group's time here it was known simply as EMI Studios, but a few years ago EMI finally changed its logo and external sign to the name by which it is known universally by fans and musicians. Still a thriving studio (now part of an EMI chain which includes **The Rolling Stones**' famous location Olympic Studios in Barnes), the building is not open to the public, so tourists have to content themselves with writing messages on the outside wall and photographing each other traversing the iconic zebra crossing. Both activities appear to be tolerated with benign indifference by studio staff and local traffic. The wall is repainted regularly and activities at the crossing are viewable via webcam on the website of the official **Abbey Road Café** (www.abbeyroadcafe.co.uk; [020] 7586 5404). The café is part of **St John's Wood** Underground station and sells Beatles and Abbey Road-related merchandise, as well as being a place to sip a cappuccino while listening to Beatles music.

When The Beatles were advised in early 1964 to invest in substantial property, McCartney was alone in staying in London. A detached, three-storey Georgian town-house up the street from Abbey Road studios, 7 Cavendish Avenue, NW8, was purchased in April 1965 for £40,000 and was Paul's London residence, after £20,000 worth of renovations, from March 1966.

Paul claims to have introduced **Mick Jagger** to marijuana in his music room there in 1966. The site of many a successful writing session (including **Getting Better** and **Hey Jude**) and a burgeoning collection of Magrittes, it was a favourite hangout, outside the large wooden gates, of Beatles super-fans the **Apple Scruffs**. One balmy summer evening in 1968, McCartney serenaded them from the window of his top-floor music room with a new song, **Blackbird**.

A burglary by rogue Scruffs in 1969 inspired McCartney's song **She Came In Through The Bathroom Window**. John Lennon reportedly drove there in 1971 to put a brick through the window when McCartney won the court case to begin the dissolution of Apple. Though McCartney stopped living there permanently in 1970, the listed building is still said to be owned by him and has been used by various Macca offspring down the years.

London suburbs and beyond

While McCartney plumped for a Georgian town-house in NW8 in the mid-60s, the other Beatles headed for Surrey and the Home Counties, splashing out on the kind of grand mansions that would become a cliché in the hands of future pop stars, soap opera actors and footballers. Kenwood, on St George's Hill in Weybridge, Surrey, was built in 1913 and John Lennon paid £40,000 for the stockbroker-belt, 27-room mock-Tudor mansion in July 1964, spending a further £30,000 on improvements. Stuffed with TVs and playrooms, cars and guitars, it was home to the Lennons and their staff for several years and the location for many a stoned writing session. John and Yoko recorded *Two Virgins* in the top-floor music room in 1968. It was sold after John and Cynthia's divorce in 1969.

George invested in **Kinfauns**, Esher, also in Surrey. A luxury bungalow set in a National Trust wood, it was George's home from June 1964 until 1969, when his taste in antique beds and recording equipment required more space. The exterior was treated to a lurid psychedelic design in 1967. Victim to several break-ins by fans, the house was also the location in May 1968 of a number of much-bootlegged Lennon, McCartney and Harrison post-India acoustic demos, some of which were released on *Anthology 3*. Ringo followed suit, purchasing Sunny Heights (Weybridge, Surrey), a large mock-Tudor home to the Starrs from 1965, overlooking St George's Hill golf course and around the corner from the Lennons. Both Ringo and John were interested in buying Brookfield House, Peter Sellers' fifteenth-century mansion in Elstead, Guildford (Surrey again). Ringo secured it for £70,000 in November 1968, staying there until December 1969.

George Harrison was the first Beatle to take the step of buying a country pile that wasn't in Surrey. **Friar Park** (Paradise Road, Henley-on-Thames, Oxfordshire) was Harrison's English home from February 1969 until his death in November 2001. It's a massive, rococo, 120-room Victorian mansion built in 1889 for London solicitor Sir Frank Crisp on the forty-acre site of a thirteenth-century friary. Surrounded by elaborate gardens and home to George's state-of-the-art recording studio, its sign on the gate – "Absolutely no admission" in ten languages – made little difference to the paranoid schizophrenic who broke in during December 1999 and stabbed George almost to death.

In mid-1969 Lennon bought Tittenhurst Park (Sunningdale, Berkshire) for £150,000. This 300-year-old Georgian mansion was home to John and Yoko until 1972, when they moved to America. Its seventy-acre grounds were the location for The Beatles' final photo shoot in August 1969. Lennon's *Imagine* was recorded there, at the studio he called Ascot Sound, and the house featured heavily in the making-of-the-album film *Gimme Some Truth*. It was sold to Ringo in 1973; the drummer converted the studio and renamed it Startling Studios, hiring it out to the public. Ringo sold Tittenhurst in 1990 for $9 million.

The McCartney family home since the mid-80s has been the 1500-acre Waterfalls Estate in Peasmarsh, Sussex. It's also the location of **The Mill,** where **Free As A Bird, Real Love** and Paul's 1997 album *Flaming Pie* were recorded.

Outside the UK

The extent of Beatles fandom is such that there are Beatles sites (of wildly varying degrees of relevance) all over the world. Among others, there are currently Beatles museums at Brescia in Italy, at Virginia Beach in the US and at Halle in Germany. There is also a fabulously pretentious, Yoko-approved John Lennon Museum in Tokyo. But, by and large, the main places of interest outside of England are Hamburg and New York City.

Hamburg

Hamburg's **Reeperbahn** is steeped in early-Beatles history. The **Top Ten Club** at 136, where they were living when George was deported, no longer exists but the **Kaiserkeller** (38 Grosse Freiheit), where The Beatles played such back-breaking sets for Bruno Koschmider in 1960, is still a live-music venue (although it has been enlarged and its interior redesigned). Koschmider's smaller venue, The **Indra Club,** was the first Hamburg club The Beatles played, at 64 Grosse Freiheit. There is currently a new Indra Club occupying the site. The **Star Club,** at number 39, where The Beatles played various bookings in 1962, closed in 1969 but the site does have a Star Club Café in what was once the club's interior and an engraved stone honouring The Beatles and other acts that played there. A couple of doors down you can find the **Gretel and Alfons** café, a favoured hangout of the Fabs in between sets.

A few blocks away from the Reeperbahn lies the site of the **Bambi Kino**. Another of Koschmider's properties, it was the scene of the "condom burning" incident that led to Paul McCartney and Pete Best getting deported in their first Hamburg trip in 1960. It is now an apartment building, though there is a tiny silver plaque commemorating the site. The nearby **Reeperbahn Police Station** is where Paul and Pete were taken shortly before deportation.

New York

The most explicitly Beatles landmark in New York is **Strawberry Fields,** a peaceful corner of **Central Park** just across from the Dakota building. A memorial to John Lennon, NYC's favourite adopted son, it was christened by Yoko Ono and its main feature is a circular mosaic of concentric stones (donated from all over the world) on the ground with the word "Imagine" at its centre. It has often served as a kind of unofficial message-board to register Beatles-related news for New Yorkers: following George Harrison's death it was decked out with flowers, condolences and tributes. Afer 9/11, and throughout the conflicts in Afghanistan and Iraq, it has attracted – predictably and fittingly – plenty of "Give Peace a Chance" messages.

The Dakota is at 72nd Street and Central Park West. When it was built in 1884, by Henry Hardenbergh, the West Side was seen as much less fashionable than the East, and it received its name as it was so far away from "the scene" that it may as well have been in the Dakotas. But it has been home to generations of the wealthy and the famous, including Lauren Bacall, Judy Garland and Boris Karloff, and it was where Roman Polanski's movie *Rosemary's Baby* was filmed. The Lennons moved there from a small West Village apartment (105 Bank Street) and it was their home for most of the 70s (Yoko still lives there). Lennon was murdered just outside the entrance. Rather ghoulishly, although perhaps inevitably, more people seem to take photos of the pavement outside than of the building itself.

On **Central Park South** at Fifth Avenue stands the **Plaza Hotel**. It was where The Beatles stayed in 1964 and it played host to many a scene of hysterical teenage Beatlemania. The **Ed Sullivan Theater** (1697 Broadway) is currently the headquarters of the chat-show host David Letterman, and is now known as the Late Show with David Letterman Theater. Sullivan's championing of The Beatles was instrumental in their breaking America – they made their first *Ed Sullivan Show* appearance two days after arriving in the US on February 9, 1964.

You can book a Beatles walk that takes in Strawberry Fields, the Dakota and the Plaza Hotel, along with other sites of Beatles significance on the **Fab 4 NYC** guided tour (see www.daytrippin.com for current timetable and reservations).

Part 9: Beatleology

Books

All listed publishers are UK publishers unless otherwise stated. o/p signifies out of print.

Billy Shepherd: **The True Story Of The Beatles**

(Beat Publications,1964; currently o/p)

"Brian Epstein couldn't believe his eyes when he first glimpsed 'that scruffy lot'. Now millions cannot feast their eyes enough on the fringed four." It was pearls such as this or nothing in early 1964, when *Record Mirror* journalist Peter Jones (writing under the pseudonym he used in *Beatles Monthly*) published the very first Beatles biography. Cheerful, reasonably informative and illustrated with peculiar drawings, it's a pot boiler with panache. Now extremely rare.

Michael Braun: **"Love Me Do" – The Beatles' Progress**

(Penguin, 1964; currently o/p)

This superb fly-on-the-wall documentary account was written by an American journalist granted access-all-areas at the height of British Beatlemania and during their triumphal entry into America. Braun (subsequently a film and stage-show producer) took them seriously when everyone else was dealing in fluff and delivered a unique record of the moment, with surprisingly candid chat from the boys, lots of humour and some fascinating curios – letters

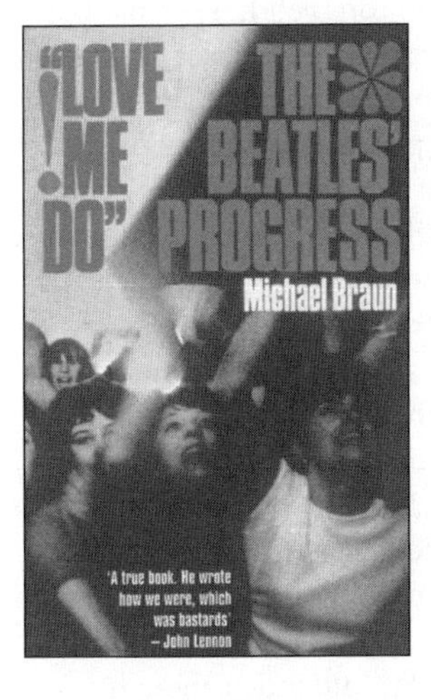

from fans, business telegrams, reviews and so on. "*Love Me Do* was a true book," John Lennon told *Rolling Stone* in 1970. "He wrote how we were, which was bastards – you can't be anything else in a position of such pressure." John overstated it a little, but certainly no writer ever got so close to the heart of the Beatles again.

Brian Epstein: **A Cellarful Of Noise**

(1964; reprinted Byron Press, 1998 in US)

Proficiently ghosted by Derek Taylor based on conversations with Epstein, this book convincingly conveys Brian's urbane modesty and deep wonder at the course of events. Necessarily selective, it is nevertheless a vivid account from a unique viewpoint.

Hunter Davies: **The Beatles – The Authorised Biography**

(1968; Cassell, 2002)

The accepted version of the story for years, the book's minor inaccuracies (including, famously, the wrong date for Lennon and McCartney's first meeting at Woolton Fête), sketchy business detail and political compromises (Lennon's Aunt Mimi insisted on an airbrushed portrait of young John whilst Epstein's homosexuality, and the drugs issues, are fudged) meant its reputation suffered for a while. However, Davies was the only journalist at the time (early 1967 to mid-1968) with almost unlimited access to the Beatles' world – he sat and watched them write **With A Little Help From My Friends** and record the *Sgt Pepper* album – and it is full of riveting, first-hand stuff. The 1985 revised version added a sketchily up-to-date postscript while the 2002 revision adds a fascinating essay on the writing of the book plus fetching black-and-silver illustrative photographs. Still no index though.

Jonathan Cott/David Dalton: **The Beatles – Get Back**

(1970; currently o/p)

Part of the original *Let It Be* box, this 150-page paperback is one of the handsomest Beatle books ever produced. The transcribed studio chatter from the *Get Back* rehearsals is baffling and inconsequential yet somehow fascinating, and Ethan Russell's candid full-colour glossy photos of the group are magnificent. Originally A4 size, some of it was used in the packaging of 2003's *Let It Be ... Naked*.

Jann Wenner: **Lennon Remembers**

(1971; reprinted Verso, 2001)

This is the complete *Rolling Stone* interview given to publicize **Plastic Ono Band**, but the mistake to make with this thrilling series of reminiscences is to take it at face value. This is Lennon at his most vulnerable, bitter and unforgiving. His blowtorch honesty is so persuasive it's easy to get swept up in it. However, anyone who hears the audio of his rant against his aunt for not recognising his genius is left with little doubt that this was a man on the edge. Interviewer Wenner published it as a book against Lennon's wishes, and Lennon ended up having to denounce most of it as "lies". A recent edition containing an insightful forward by Yoko: "not tactful, not calculated, and for once not even particularly clever", she correctly judges, before adding, "Get a whiff of his energy!"

Peter McCabe/Robert D. Schonfeld: **Apple To The Core**

(Sphere, 1972; currently o/p)

This book seeks to investigate how The Beatles business afairs unravelled by paying attention to the way they were run. It takes the view that The Beatles were mismanaged from the start; that Epstein, though enthusiastic and gifted, was erratic and effectively out of his depth from the beginning. The authors also take a dim view of the abilities of Allen Klein. Out of print, it's worth seeking out, if that's your prime interest in the group, though one suspects that the definitive book on Beatles business might never be written.

Richard DiLello: The Longest Cocktail Party

(1972; reprinted Canongate, 2000)

THE LONGEST
COCKTAIL PARTY
AN INSIDER'S DIARY OF THE BEATLES, THEIR MILLION DOLLAR 'APPLE' EMPIRE AND ITS WILD RISE AND FALL
Richard DiLello

American student Richard DiLello was employed at Apple in 1968 by Derek Taylor, who told immigration he was vital to the company as "the house hippie". By the time Apple closed, DiLello, who clearly adored Taylor, had effectively taken his role as Director of Public Relations. In the interim he kept a diary of the nuttiness unfolding around him and took plenty of pictures, compiling them into a fascinating, funny account of the whole folly, complete with the thoughts of *The Times* and the full text of McCartney's infamous self-interview which effectively announced the end of the group. Recently reissued, it's still a great, even essential read for anyone wishing to understand The Beatles' final months.

Derek Taylor: As Time Goes By

(Abacus, 1973; currently o/p)

"The riveting roving adventures of the publicist extraordinaire": the former reporter for the *Hoylake Observer* sets out his playful philosophy of life, telling tales of two tenures with the Fabs and an intervening stint in Los Angeles looking after The Byrds, Beach Boys, Nilsson et al. Taylor doesn't shy from noting his occasional displeasure at The Beatles and their people, though his love for them is luminous nonetheless. Candid, funny and quietly sage.

Roy Carr and Tony Tyler: The Beatles Illustrated Record

(New English Library, 1975; currently o/p)

An attractive set of reviews of The Beatles' records by 70s *New Musical Express* journos Carr and Tyler, displaying the kind of critical swagger and punch conspicuously absent from the *NME* in the 60s. A model of measured enthusiasm, the occasional cavalier moment (their dismissal of *All Things Must Pass* is a disgrace) only adds to the fun.

Allan Williams/Bill Marshall: The Man Who Gave The Beatles Away

(Elm Tree Books, 1975; currently o/p)

"Dear All … I understand that you only move around the stage when there is no audience – this is stupid and a suicidal attitude for any band to adopt." Thus The Beatles' first manager takes care of business by post while the boys play in Hamburg. Just one of a host of lively, occasionally lofty tales of the early years from the chap who advised Epstein not to touch the group "with a fucking bargepole". Ribald, tabloidy stuff in places, it is full of period flavour.

Anthony Fawcett: **John Lennon – One Day At A Time**

(1976; currently o/p)

Fawcett was Lennon's art advisor and personal assistant from 1968 until 1970, so his prose has an "I was there" energy when covering Lennon's activities of that period (Tittenhurst, the Acorn Event, Bag, etc), and he seems to have had access to fascinating tapes of 1969 Beatle meetings at Apple. Elsewhere, his cut'n'paste approach to the remainder of Lennon's 1970s – which he wasn't personally involved in – is capable and never less than astute.

Cynthia Lennon: **A Twist Of Lennon**

(1978; currently o/p)

Cynthia Lennon: **John**

(Hodder and Stoughton, 2005)

Patti Boyd: **Wonderful Today: George Harrison, Eric Clapton and Me**

Hodder Headline Review; 2007)

In the absence of any published reminiscence by Jane Asher or Maureen Starkey, Cynthia's and Patti's viewpoints are unique in Beatle literature. Cyn's first attempt at telling her story, *A Twist Of Lennon*, is a fascinatingly naïve account of life with Lennon from a woman who appeared to be out of her depth almost from the moment she met the bugger. Cynthia's tale – an intimidated fellow art-school student who became a neglected, secret wife in the middle of Beatlemania before being excluded from Lennon's drugged-out self-absorption – is a bit of a sorry one, of someone who was there but not there, somehow apart from all that was going on around her. However, throughout there's a modesty and warmth and, in the end, an uncalled-for generosity that is to her credit. Lennon attempted to stop its publication in 1978 (after a tabloid excerpt appeared) but the lack of sales and scandal indicated he hardly need have bothered. Out of print since before Lennon's death, it remains a touchingly personal domestic exclusive with some of its most cogent truths residing between the lines. Twenty-seven years on and Cynthia revisits the story in *John* as a wiser, less inhibited writer. Though riddled with factual inaccuracies about The Beatles' career, it's franker about her pervading affection for her ex-husband, her distaste for Aunt Mimi, the details of their marriage disintegration, the hurt inflicted on son Julian by his father's subsequent remoteness and Yoko's equally remote treatment of him after John's death. It's a more intense book all round. Patti Boyd's long-awaited autobiography is both candid and likeable, even as she charts the rather unpleasant, addled antics of her rock-star suitors. Life as a model in swinging London is vividly conveyed, as is George and Patti's peculiar, glamorous life at Kinfauns and Friar Park. It's easy to empathize with her puzzlement and hurt as she charts George's path from being a charming boyfriend to a coked-up control freak. Though famously succumbing to Eric Clapton's obsessive overtures while still married to the increasingly erratic Harrison, she interestingly notes in the end that she wishes she hadn't.

George Martin: **All You Need Is Ears**

(1979; reprinted St Martin's Press, 1995)

Urbane, warm and slightly stiff, just as you'd imagine, it is nevertheless crammed with technical insights and anecdotes that only the producer could tell. Covering his pre-Fab years as producer of Matt Monroe, The Goons et al, as well as many of the ground-breaking pop sessions with The Beatles, his older-brother affection and musical admiration for the group is obvious.

Philip Norman: **Shout! The True Story Of The Beatles**

(Corgi, 1981; reprinted Penguin, 1993; currently o/p)

John Lennon: The Life

(HarperCollins, 2008)

Despite McCartney's objections at being portrayed as "the great manipulator" and Norman's clear dislike for McCartney, which becomes a little wearing, *Shout* was rightly praised at the time of its publication for the rigour of its research and insightful reflection of the times. Readers wishing to know a bit more about the music, however, will need to look elsewhere. Twenty-seven years on and Norman tackles Lennon. Written with Yoko's cooperation (though not, in the end, her endorsement because he is "mean to John" – which he isn't), *John Lennon: The Life* is bold where Coleman was bland, insightful where Goldman was callous. Offering within its 800 pages several fresh angles (including Yoko's idea that Lennon may have desired an affair with McCartney), Norman comes close to having the final word on Lennon's life.

Andy Peebles: **The Lennon Tapes**

(BBC, 1981; currently o/p)

David Scheff: **The Playboy Interviews With John Lennon And Yoko Ono**

(New English Library, 1982; currently o/p)

Two of the extensive interviews Lennon gave just before his death, ostensibly to promote *Double Fantasy* but wide-ranging enough to serve as source material for researchers on a variety of Beatles matters. Now published as *All We Are Saying: The Last Major Interview*, the *Playboy* interviews are especially engaging as Lennon allowed himself to be grilled beyond the call of promotional duty in the autumn of 1980 as compensation to *Playboy* for slipping *Newsweek* the early exclusive. Full of energy and optimism, both transcripts are inevitably poignant now (the upbeat Peebles interview was conducted hours before Lennon's death) but, significantly, contain all the erudition and sharpness the music he was promoting conspicuously lacked.

Pete Shotton & Nicholas Schaffner: **John Lennon – In My Life**

(National Book Network, 1983; currently o/p)

Shotton was Lennon's school chum, an original Quarry Man, a frequent visitor to Kenwood at key moments (the writing of "Rigby" and "Walrus", the *Two Virgins* visit of Yoko) and the proprietor of the Apple Boutique. He also appears to have been Lennon's confidant on all manner of delicate matters (his infidelities and his relationship with Brian Epstein) and so may well have been the closest person to Lennon between Stuart Sutcliffe's death and Yoko Ono's arrival. His only occasional involvement in The Beatles saga means his voice is authentic, proud and sceptical Merseyside, full of endearing affection, delight and dismay.

Peter Brown & Stephen Gaines: **The Love You Make – An Insider's Story Of The Beatles**

(1983; reprinted New American Library, 2002 in US)

Ken Mansfield: **The Beatles, The Bible & Bodega Bay**

(Broadman and Holman, 2000)

Alistair Taylor: **A Secret History**

(Blake Publishing, 2001)

Denis O'Dell with Bob Neaverson: **At The Apple's Core: The Beatles From The Inside**

(Peter Owen, 2002)

Tony Bramwell: **Magical Mystery Tours: My Life With The Beatles**

(Robson, 2005)

Tony Barrow: **John, Paul, George Ringo And Me: The Real Story Of The Beatles**

(Andre Deutsch, 2005)

Six books written by people who were, in varying degrees of intimacy, part of The Beatles' inner circle. Peter Brown was an original NEMS and Apple employee and his sensationalist *The Love You Make*, coming three years after Lennon's death, was considered nothing short of a betrayal by the remaining Beatles; Harrison was furious, while Paul and Linda McCartney held a ritual burning of the book. Lennon (for whom Brown was best man) and Epstein (to whom Brown was very close) would undoubtedly have felt let down. Which means, of course, for anyone interested in the seamier side of The Beatles' story it's essential stuff – one of the most significant Beatles books of its sort ever written. The ones that (eventually) followed were bound to be relatively anti-climactic. Though Alistair Taylor's *A Secret History* was also written by a man who had made the journey from Liverpool to the centre of the universe with Epstein and The Beatles, his tale is nowhere near as vivid as Brown's. Taylor was present when Epstein first saw The Beatles (later turning down the offer of a percentage of their earnings in 1962, telling Brian, "All I need is a decent salary and I'll be happy") and went on to become the put-upon "Mr Fixit" at NEMS and Apple. His book is an informal, large-print ramble without the elegance of Brown's ghosted insights, but with a moderately effective, everyman immediacy. Tony Barrow was The Beatles' press officer from 1962 to 1968 and manages to write a book as insipid as his notorious sleevenotes. Denis O'Dell helped on *A Hard Day's Night* and was head of Apple Films, while Tony Bramwell was his assistant. Between them, they have a handful of fresh anecdotes among biographical padding and curiously uninvolving I-was-there bluster – but not many. Ken Mansfield spent part of his 30 years in the American music business as US manager of Apple Records and his book *The Beatles, The Bible And Bodega Bay* is an unusual, entertaining and unexpectedly moving account of his time with the group. He intersperses his accounts (sitting next to Yoko and Maureen Starkey watching the Apple rooftop concert, or playing a hilarious tennis match with Allen Klein to escape from his Apple contract) with meditations on the search for a Christian God. In all these books, the music is barely mentioned.

Ray Coleman: Lennon – The Definitive Biography

(1985; revised Pan, 1992)

The favourite of the adoring Lennon fans, of whom Coleman is clearly one, this selective, party-line book paints a wondrous picture. With access to Yoko, Cynthia and **Mimi**, as well as his own *Melody Maker* archives, both the strength and limitation of Coleman's book is its generosity when it comes to making sense of Lennon's art and personality. Coleman's dismissal of several other books with a less rose-tinted story to tell as being in "execrable taste" speaks volumes about his need to remember John with dignity. Leaving you with a warm glow, it would be lovely to believe it all.

Mark Lewisohn: Beatles Live

(1986; currently o/p)

Complete Beatles Recording Sessions

(1988; currently o/p)

Complete Beatles Chronicle

(Bounty Books, 1992)

Inspired by his work as a researcher on Philip Norman's *Shout*, Lewisohn's remarkable books are passionately detailed and are now considered to be standard works. *Live* unearthed many lost details and anecdotes about The Beatles' gigs. *Recording Sessions* was the result of Lewisohn listening to the entire Abbey Road archive of Beatles tapes. It chronicled, for the first time, every studio date, every take, every overdub, every reduction, every mix, every unreleased track and a load of things you didn't even know you wanted to know. Vociferous in its attention to the smallest facet of the recording process and sprinkled with quotes from engineers and producers, it is brilliant source material for specialists and researchers though Lewisohn's neutrally enthusiastic tone makes it an amazingly easy read. With the first two books (*Live* and *Recording*) truncated and amalgamated into the third (*Chronicle*), which adds film and TV sessions, Lewisohn's work represents the most authoritative research on this aspect of The Beatles' history available.

Albert Goldman: **The Lives Of John Lennon**

(1988; reprinted Chicago Review Press, 2001 in US)

A shocking book. Not because of what it purports to reveal about John Lennon so much as what it reveals about its author in the mean-spirited tone it adopts throughout. Its six years of research and alleged 1200 interviews cannot be ignored, though in sorting the factual wheat from the sometimes outrageously interpretive chaff means the reader should be on the alert the whole time.

Tim Riley: **Tell Me Why – A Beatles Commentary**

(Da Capo, 1988)

In a blow-by-blow account of what can be "heard" in The Beatles' music, Riley ventures some shrewd interpretations in among the exhausting detail, the doggedness of which recalls **Elvis Costello**'s description of music writing as being akin to dancing about architecture. However, a sporadically enlightening and inspiring read.

Alan Clayson

Ringo Starr

(Sanctuary, 1992)

George Harrison

(Sanctuary, 1996)

John Lennon

(Sanctuary, 2003)

Paul Mccartney

(Sanctuary, 2004)

Rather eccentric but usually entertaining, Clayson's books have been described as Beatles-flavoured teabags in a cup full of Clayson, containing as they do some of the author's harmless prejudices (Delaney and Bonnie always come in for a kicking for some reason), his simmering resentment at the indulgent mediocrity of some who made it "big" and determined references to his own musical associates Dave Berry and The Pretty Things. But as a second-generation veteran of the British beat scene, his point of view usually contains a certain authenticity and authority and his virtuoso labyrinthine prose makes for a lively read. Despite not having met him, Clayson's cut'n'paste job on George actually remains the best of a sorry bunch of Harrison biogs. His book on Ringo is a unique study and rather more interesting than you might imagine, though you sense that even the author is losing interest by the end. His Lennon and his McCartney – dashed off to complete the set, it seems – assume the reader is as jadedly familiar with their story as he is and he takes every opportunity he can to re-route things at some length into topics he's really interested in: Stuart Sutcliffe, the beat boom and Harry Nilsson.

Bill Harry: The Beatles Encyclopedia

(Virgin, 1992)

The John Lennon Encyclopedia

(Virgin, 2000)

The Paul McCartney Encyclopedia

(Virgin, 2002)

Don't be fooled by these books' dowdy, rather cut-price presentation. They're full of good stuff, unique accounts and first-hand information. Harry, the founder of *Mersey Beat* magazine, was there from the start and probably knew The Beatles as well as anyone in Liverpool. However, he's obviously had a few ups and downs with them since, and is not slow to occasionally take a view against the official line – he's particularly close to **Pete Best** for example – all of which makes his text much less objective than such a format usually requires. But it's generally more enjoyable for it. His Beatles-related database of facts, places and people is simply unmatched; there is material in this trio of thousand-page doorstops that can be found nowhere else.

Ian Macdonald: Revolution In The Head

(Pimlico, 1994)

The plaudits recognizing Macdonald's work as, finally, the book The Beatles' music deserved are entirely justified. An immensely erudite, approachable, thoughtful work in which the musical and biographical insight into The Beatles' oeuvre is as persuasive as its socio-political analysis of the 60s, it's a challenge to get out from under its authoritative shadow and have anything of note to add. Perhaps he overstates his idea that The Beatles matured at *Revolver* and *Pepper* then fell away. He also rather hammers the "lazily horizontal" Lennon and "vertical" McCartney theory of the pair's respective melodic style, but this is nit-picking. Knocking most heavyweight musical analysis books (eg *The Beatles As Musicians* by Walter Everett, *Every Sound There Is* edited by Russell Reising) into a cocked hat, it's a towering book.

Ray Coleman: McCartney – Yesterday And Today

(Boxtree, 1995; currently o/p)

Bland, in the author's customary style, but it has useful background on the business side of things, particularly in relation to the Lennon/McCartney publishing debacle.

Barry Miles: Paul McCartney – Many Years From Now

(Minerva, 1997; Owl Books, 1998 in US)

Full of hitherto unknown details about The Beatles' working practice and fascinating anecdotal wordage on the swinging 60s, due to the fact that Miles ran the Indica bookshop, edited *International Times* and worked for Apple – he was close to both Paul and John, and right at the heart of the post-moptop story. His own testimony is excellent, and he certainly extracts stories from Paul that have never been told before, some of them amazingly personal. And he's great at contextualizing or subverting a few myths where required.

However, as the culmination of years of frustration watching other authors (and Yoko) credit Lennon with inventing the wheel, *Many Years From Now* is often an uncomfortable read. McCartney virtually apologizes before he starts – "lest it be seen that I'm now trying to do my own kind of revisionism" – and then proceeds with 600 pages of what should have been called *My Own Kind Of Revisionism.* Swathes of interview quotes go to great trouble to claim his part of the songs (via faintly embarrassing percentage splits) and the story. No one questions his right to do it of course, but this book doesn't feel like quite the right way. Nevertheless, it remains an essential Beatles book.

Doug Sulphy & Ray Schweighardt: Get Back: The Beatles' Let It Be Disaster

(Helter Skelter, 1997)

To produce this pernickety document, Sulphy and Schweighardt have trawled their way through the hours upon hours of widely bootlegged audio tapes of The Beatles' January 1969 sessions, presumably so that no one else would have to. Every performance – from inconsequential noodles and fragments of oldies to complete run-throughs of songs – and every spoken word – from quiet asides to extended discussions – is logged and described like min-

utes of a meeting. Tedious, voyeuristic ephemera for some readers, undoubtedly, these snippets of minutiae will fascinate others. Although the *Anthology 3* excerpts of the notoriously sloppy music will be enough for most listeners, after reading these teasingly descriptive and speculative accounts of Beatles interactions, most fans will be firing up their BitTorrent and searching the Internet to try to hear precisely what John said before rehearsing "The Long And Winding Road", or listen to The Beatles having to discuss gig plans with Yoko in lieu of a strung-out Lennon, or the moment George quits. Another good example of the theory that states that, however much detail a Beatles fan gets, it's still not quite enough.

Steve Turner: A Hard Day's Write

(Carlton, 1999; reprinted Little Brown, 2003)

With little pretension to insight or analysis, this is nevertheless a terrific uncovering of the stories behind all The Beatles' songs, including some real scoops, like Turner's tracking down and interviewing the original runaway who inspired **She's Leaving Home**.

Keith Badman: The Beatles – After the Break Up

(Omnibus Press, 2000)

Off The Record – Outrageous Opinions and Unrehearsed Interviews

(Omnibus Press, 2001)

Off The Record 2 – The Dream Is Over

(Omnibus Press, 2002)

Badman is a leading Beatlehead (he was consulted on the *Anthology* series) and his three-decade pseudo-diary *After The Break Up* is an astonishing achievement of unreasonable dedication. Every individual Fab Four court case, press conference, tour, single and album is logged and chronologically entered. However, the lack of a cross-referencing index requires the reader to have some previous idea of the chronology to get the best from the book. The *Off The Record* books work well as companion volumes to the official *Beatles Anthology* book, telling the pre- and post-split story with well-chosen and mostly contemporaneous Beatle quotes and often casting a genuinely fresh light on familiar stories.

Hunter Davies: The Quarry Men

(Omnibus Press, 2001)

Davies returns to The Beatles with a delightful survey of the original Quarry Men in the light of their mid-90s re-formation. The reunited group's predictable welcome into crazed **Beatle Conference land** is somehow less interesting than the ordinary stories of the men whose lives were once part of The Beatles' story and then, for over 35 years, weren't.

Andy Babiuk: Beatles Gear

(Backbeat Books, 2001)

In a tremendous effort detailing the hardware of The Beatles' music-making, Babiuk brilliantly plugs a gap in Fabs minutiae. The book's fetishist devotion to the boys' Bigsby tremolo arms and Rodgers' Swivo-matic drum mounts, coupled with the porn-glamorous photography and rare anecdotes (John and George mysteriously swapping their Gibson J-160Es in mid-1963), is infectious beyond sense.

Roag Best with Pete & Rory Best: The Beatles: The True Beginnings

(Thomas Dunne, 2002)

This lush, arty presentation documenting Mona Best's contribution to the tale is written by her sons, pre-empting their 2004 re-launch of **the Casbah Coffee Club** as a Liverpool tourist attraction. Featuring fascinating reminiscences of the surviving players, there are lots of lovingly shot photographs of the restored club (including original McCartney-and-Lennon-decorated ceilings) and early 60s memorabilia – a valuable document of an underexposed aspect of The Beatles' story.

Dominic Pedler: The Songwriting Secrets Of The Beatles

Omnibus, 2003

An astonishingly rigorous and, for Beatlefreaks who happen to be familiar with music theory, highly readable treatise on the harmonic principles underpinning the Beatles' songs. If your thing is secondary dominants and parallel minor switches, there is enough astute chord-spotting here to keep you going for years. That Pedler devotes 42 pages of a 790-page book to investigating the mysteries of the opening chord to "A Hard Day's Night" is an indication of his thoroughness. That he quotes the author of *Rough Guide To The Beatles* thirteen times (from *Mojo* magazine's "Dr Rock" musicology column of 1996–97) is evidence of his learned discernment.

You won't see me: Beatles projects that never saw the light of day

The album titles that never were

Off The Beatle Track was George Martin's suggestion, duly rejected as the title of The Beatles' debut album. *Revolver* could at various points have been called any number of things: *The Beatles On Safari, Magic Circles*, *Freewheelin' Beatles*, *Bubble And Squeak*, *Four Sides To The Circle*, *After Geography* and *Abracadabra*. And, named after the Ibsen play, *A Doll's House* was the proposed title of the album that became *The Beatles* (aka *The White Album*). There was even striking cover artwork painted, showing miserable Beatles faces with a rabbit, bird, cat and hyena. The title and cover were abandoned after the rock group **Family** released *Music In A Doll's House* in mid-1968, and the artwork was eventually used for a Dutch *Love Songs* compilation in the 70s. **Everest** was the working title for *Abbey Road*. Inspired, according to McCartney, by engineer Geoff Emerick's favoured brand of cigarette, the title was scuppered because none of The Beatles could be bothered to go all the way to the

Beatles Island

In July 1967 Magic Alex and Alistair Taylor found a cluster of small Greek islands in the Aegean, totalling around 100 acres and covered in olive trees which, it was hoped, would provide a Tracey Island like HQ for all Beatles activities. The cost was to be £90,000 plus taxes, bribes etc. Lennon, out of his brain on LSD, insulted the ruling military junta when he arrived for a reconnaissance trip, but publicity pictures of the group having a nice time in Greece were published and the project looked possible. Unfortunately, accountants told The Beatles they only had £137,000 in the bank at the time and Chancellor James Callaghan refused to let more than £95,000 out of the country. "I wonder how you're going to furnish it?" he asked.

Himalayas for a cover shoot. The zebra crossing outside the studio seemed less bother.

The movies never made

Announced in February 1965, just before work began on *Help!*, ***A Talent For Loving*** was the movie to be developed by Pickfair, Brian Epstein's new film company, with former UA head honcho Bud Ornstein. It was a Western adapted from a novel by Richard Condon, the author of *The Manchurian Candidate*, in which The Beatles would appear as four settlers in the West fresh over from Liverpool. Lennon was heard to deny at an August 1965 press conference that *A Talent For Loving* was their next film because "Paul and I won't write anything with that name." It was abandoned when the final film in the UA deal couldn't be agreed upon. (***The Beatles Meet Elvis Presley*** was one proposed film vehicle turned down by producer Walter Shenson.)

With a script begun in late 1966 by Richard Lester associate Qwen Holder and with *Blowup* director Michelangelo Antonioni poised to direct, ***Shades Of A Personality*** was seriously considered as the follow-up to *Help!* in June 1967. To be shot in Malaga, Spain, the film would feature John as a man whose various personality traits would be played by the other Beatles. Trendy playwright **Joe Orton**'s proposed Beatles movie, delivered in February 1967, was entitled ***Up Against It***. The plot told the tale of one Ian McTurk and his friends, played by The Beatles, who after dressing as women, committing a murder and being imprisoned, end up in bed together with a Miss Drumgoole. The project was abandoned several months before Orton was murdered by his boyfriend.

John once even suggested they acquire the rights to ***Lord Of The Rings***. He intended to play Gollum and saw Paul as Frodo, George as Gandalf and Ringo as Sam Merryweather. The Tolkein estate killed the idea by refusing to sell the rights to The Beatles.

Bad Apple ideas

Almost the whole Apple venture, with the exception of Apple Records, was one huge abortive project that failed to happen. But here are a few notable things that were never completed.

Apple School was to be a progressive educational establishment where Beatle children and offspring of Apple employees would be educated in the "art of propaganda in the advertising field", among other more traditional disciplines. Old schoolfriend Ivan Vaughan was to head it and he received a £10,000 retainer, while poet **Ivor Cutler** was appointed advisor. Lennon was the keenest, though was persuaded to shelve the idea until Apple started showing profit elsewhere.

Apple Electronics was the branch of Apple that Lennon was most excited about and the one that failed most spectacularly. Alex Mardas (aka Magic Alex) had dazzled The Beatles with brooches that beeped and boxes that flashed, and he was duly given the funding to develop his brainwaves into inventions. Of one hundred patents applied for, none was accepted and nothing was ever produced. Among Magic Alex's non-inventions were: a giant artificial sun to light the Apple boutique; a 78-track recording studio in the basement of the Apple building (incorporating 78 speakers); **a solar-powered electric guitar**; hi-fi speakers built into wallpaper; paint that made things invisible; a flying saucer to fly over the West End of London; a generator the size of a dustbin lid (to spread the Maharishi's message via a giant radio station in his Rishikesh ashram, with enough juice left to bathe the entire area in light); **a hovering house** supported by an invisible beam; and a phone which, when spoken to, dialled the required number.

The music side of Apple didn't exactly go according to plan either, for The Beatles themselves or for the acts they signed. John signed **Contact**, a band who had a song about flying saucers. It never materialized. **Captain Beefheart** rang Apple and asked to be signed but was eventually turned down. And **Zapple**, Barry Miles' spoken-word label, was closed after two releases: John and Yoko's *Life With The Lions* and George's *Electronic Sounds*.

Among the mooted projects subsequently scrapped in the wake of Allen Klein's swingeing cuts were an album of readings by Beat poet **Allen Ginsberg**, an album of **Lord Buckley** (an eccentric raconteur and jazz hipster from the 1950s West Coast) routines, and children's stories read by actress **Hermione Gingold.** One of the rarest of all Apple releases is **Saturday Night Special**, a brilliant 1972 Cajun single by a rootsy New Orleans band called **The Sundown Playboys**, which appeared in the UK on 45rpm and 78rpm editions. It was a fabulous flop, and a proposed album of Cajun party music was quietly cancelled.

But their most famous non-event was ***Get Back***. This was to be their return-to-their-roots project, a new album written and rehearsed to be played live at an unusual venue – original suggestions included the Houses of Parliament, the pyramids and the **Taj Mahal** – with the whole shebang simultaneously filmed for a documentary. A 1969 update of the 1963 "Please Please Me" cover was shot by the original photographer, Angus McBean. When the project mutated into *Let It Be*, the pictures were later used for the *Red* and *Blue* albums.

Beatles rumours Gossip & conjecture

John killed Stuart Sutcliffe

At his autopsy, Stuart Sutcliffe was said to have died from "cerebral paralysis due to bleeding into the right ventricle of the brain". This was thought at the time to have been caused by Stuart banging his head after slipping on the stairs at the home of Astrid Kirchherr in Hamburg. It was after this incident that Stuart was seen to suffer from increasingly severe headaches and blackouts, culminating in his fatal brain haemorrhage on April 10, 1962.

However, there were some who believed Sutcliffe's injury originated in a violent beating. There was the gang of troublemakers who set about the group after a gig at Lathom Hall, Seaforth, Liverpool, in May 1960. This incident, though it did cause Lennon to break his little finger, was exaggerated by books such as Allan Williams' *The Man Who Gave The Beatles Away* to include ultimately fatal kicks to Sutcliffe's head.

In another twist, based on Lennon's alleged guilty confession of responsibility to Yoko (and personal assistant Fred Seaman) who then told Dakota employee Marnie Hair, who then told author **Albert Goldman**, a further dramatic scenario emerges. Arguing with Sutcliffe on the streets of Hamburg, Lennon flew at his friend in a drunken rage (perhaps similar to that which landed Lennon in trouble with Bob Wooler in mid-1963), only regaining control when he saw Sutcliffe at his feet having been kicked and punched into near-unconsciousness.

This picture is reinforced by the publication in 2001 of *The Beatles' Shadow: Stuart Sutcliffe's Lonely Heart's Club* by **Pauline Sutcliffe**, the sister who desisted from publicizing her beliefs until their mother, Millie, had passed away. She suggests that not only did Lennon administer a fatal beating, but that Stuart and John were erstwhile lovers. The matter remains unresolved.

Ringo wasn't on the early Beatles records

Most people know that session drummer Andy White and not Ringo drummed on the best-known recording of **Love Me Do**. However, in 1978 the renowned US session drummer **Bernard Purdie** was quoted in *Gig* magazine as saying that in summer 1963 he overdubbed the drumming on several early Beatles cuts at

Ringo, annoyed at being told to keep the noise down, on the set of *Help!*

the express wish of Brian Epstein. "I had never heard of The Beatles," said Purdie, "but their manager, Brian Epstein, called me and took me down to Capitol's 46th Street studio. I did all the overdubbing on the 21 songs in 9 days. Epstein called me into his office and gave me the additional [five figure] check. I thought they were paying me all that money because they liked what I played. Then he told me I was being paid to keep my mouth shut." Purdie also intimated that guitar parts were being overdubbed at other secret sessions.

Some maintain that Purdie's account is pure fantasy. Others suggest that the overdubbing sessions may have occurred, instigated by a manager keen to have his unknown group's sound accepted in the US market, but that they were not used in the end. Yet another suggestion is that Purdie was used on **Tony Sheridan** recordings to beef up the sound. Yet Purdie insists that on many early Beatles cuts, "Ringo never played on anything."

Ringo's response? "I've heard that rubbish before. Everyone was expecting me to come out and fight it. You don't bother fighting that shit."

Lennon and Epstein were lovers

Early on, John Lennon affected a typical roughneck response to Epstein's homosexuality in public: "If he lays a finger on me I'll punch his lights out," Pete Best remembers him saying. But gradually, realizing the hold he had over this gentle, helplessly besotted man who, after all, only wanted to make The Beatles bigger than Elvis, Lennon's response to his manager developed more nuance.

In the frequent visits John made to the Epsteins' house in late 1961 and early 62 to discuss the marketing of the group, John and Brian developed what Brian's brother **Clive** described as "a mental contact between them that was perfect". According to NEMS employee Peter Brown, Brian purchased the Falkner Street flat with the purpose of seducing John there, but Lennon never came alone. Brian made a standing offer to take John to Copenhagen for a weekend, which never occurred, but in April 1963, in the wake of the success of **Please Please Me**, John agreed to accompany Brian on a ten-day holiday to Barcelona.

In Spain, Brian and John watched bullfights, shopped, clubbed and sat in cafés frankly discussing Epstein's homosexuality, chatting about what he found attractive about the passing men. Lennon enjoyed it: "Thinking like a writer all the time," he said later, "'I am experiencing this'".

Given later anecdotal accounts, that the pair's relationship became physical at some point seems likely. Peter Brown relates that Epstein reported back that Lennon had allowed Epstein some physical intimacy. Lennon's friend **Pete Shotton** relates a similar account as reported to him by Lennon. Albert Goldman further speculates that Epstein and Lennon continued the affair until just before Epstein's death, citing an incident in 1967 where Brian's mother Queenie caught John and Brian in a rough-looking clinch and called the police. By the time they arrived, Lennon had scarpered and Brian was oozing about a misunderstanding.

Some commentators, such as Ray Coleman, play down the suggestion by pointing to Lennon's overt heterosexual behaviour, reasoning that any liaison with Epstein would have been untypical, therefore unlikely. Even McCartney sees the situation prosaically, and has called Lennon "a smart cookie ... he wanted Brian to know who he should listen to in this group, and that was the relationship."

Lennon, for his part, was unusually cryptic, characterizing his relationship with his manager as "intense" and "almost an affair" that was "never consummated". "It's interesting and will make a nice *Hollywood Babylon* someday about Brian Epstein's sex life," Lennon said in 1980, "but it's irrelevant, absolutely irrelevant."

Brian Epstein was murdered

Though the inquest judged Brian Epstein's death to be accidental, a view that most commentators seem to share, rumours concerning foul play have circulated from time to time.

One story involved Epstein's suffocation during sadomasochistic sex by a Coldstream Guard introduced to him by Brian Summerville, The Beatles' former press agent. Brian's lawyer David Jacobs – himself a part of London's gay scene – then purportedly removed the evidence soon after the discovery of the body in order to avoid a sex scandal.

Another story pointed the finger at figures in the entertainment underworld aggrieved by Epstein's protracted legal pursuance of merchandising royalties which, in the resulting confusion, led to millions of dollars in lost revenue for both The Beatles and the manufacturers. Nicky Byrne, the man appointed by David Jacobs to oversee Beatles merchandising, remembers the anger felt by US manufacturers at Epstein's action manifesting itself as heated threats to kill Epstein. "Wait until the courts have finished with him," Byrne is said to have suggested to the shadowy figures. Byrne recounts to Philip Norman that when the writs were finally settled in 1967 he received mysterious, anonymous phone calls hinting at Brian Epstein's imminent meeting "with an accident". Days later, Epstein was dead.

In a curious postscript David Jacobs, who had latterly suffered from drug abuse and mental fragility, was found hanged in the garage of his Brighton house in December 1968. Only days before, he had asked for police protection and telephoned a private detective, telling him, "I'm in terrible trouble, they're all after me," naming six prominent showbusiness figures. A verdict of suicide was reached.

Paul is dead

In the autumn of 1969, a phone call to Detroit radio station WKNR-FM suggested that if a portion of **Revolution 9** was played backwards, the words that seemed to appear –

Paul is dead: selected "evidence"

- On *Sgt Pepper*, the album Paul was making when he died, the whole cover depicts a funeral scene, with many of the mourners themselves being dead.
- The hand on *Pepper*'s cover seen hovering above Paul's head indicates the blessing of his soul.
- On *Pepper*'s back sleeve "Paul" is facing away because the plastic surgery was not yet convincing enough.
- At the end of *Strawberry Fields Forever*, John is heard saying "I buried Paul".
- Both "Within You Without You" and "A Day In The Life" are about Paul's death and William's acceptance into The Beatles.
- On *The White Album*, John can be heard muttering "Paul is dead man, miss him, miss him, miss him" just before "Blackbird" suggests to "William" he must "take these broken wings and learn to fly" – ie learn how to be Paul McCartney.
- On *The White Album* Ringo sings "you were in a car crash and you lost your hair" to Paul on **Don't Pass Me By**.
- During the "Your Mother Should Know" white-tails sequence in *Magical Mystery Tour*, each Beatle except Paul wears a red carnation; Paul's is black.
- The cover of *Abbey Road* depicts Ringo as a black-clad undertaker, George as a denim-clad gravedigger and John as the white-clad preacher; Paul is barefoot (and "therefore" is the corpse!).
- The Volkswagen car on *Abbey Road*'s sleeve has the number plate 28 IF; some pointed out that, at the time its release, Paul would have been 28 if he had lived. Erroneously, as it happens – he would actually have been 27.

"Turn me on, dead man" – surely proved that Paul McCartney was in fact dead.

This errant nonsense soon mushroomed into an international story with TV, radio and magazine articles examining the dozens of clues placed by The Beatles in their lyrics and album sleeves indicating that McCartney had in fact died in a car crash on November 9, 1966. Having suffered fatal head injuries (the crash was also supposed to have burnt off his hair), Paul was supposedly replaced by one **William Campbell** – the winner of a Scottish McCartney lookalike competition in 1965 – with the help of plastic surgery and an apparent talent transplant.

The Beatles could barely be bothered to deny it, but a persistent media, perhaps sensing the imminent demise of the group itself, forced Apple into almost comical rebuffs. McCartney, having successfully kidded artist **Peter Blake** for a few moments that he was actually a copy of the real Paul, later recounted that "I was rather pleased you know, because I knew I wasn't dead. So I just watched the play happen." The gossip eventually blew away in the wind, but Lennon referred to the incident in 1971 to make his own bitter point in his infamous **How Do You Sleep?** attack on his former partner, saying, sneeringly, that the rumour-mongers had been right all along. McCartney acknowledged the old rumour's resonance by calling his 1994 in-concert album *Paul Is Live*.

Klaatu are The Beatles

In 1976, a group called Klaatu released their mysterious, eponymous debut album in August on Capitol with no specific artist or production credit. With the music broadly *Pepper*-era Beatlesesque (but also Pink Floydian and ELO-like), a rumour grew that The Beatles had re-formed under an assumed name, fuelled by an article by one Steve Smith in the *Providence Journal* which listed 150 items of evidence that indicated Klaatu were indeed the Fabs. These included:

• A University of Miami voice-print test that proved that the lead vocalist on Klaatu and McCartney records were one and the same.

• If one of the tracks, "Sub Rosa Subway", is played backwards through oscillators and filters, "It's us, it's The Beatles!" can apparently be heard.

• Ringo is shown on his *Goodnight Vienna* album portraying the character called Klaatu from the movie *The Day The Earth Stood Still*. Apple promo for Ringo's album included the phrase "Don't Forget – Klaatu Barada Nikto".

Capitol refused to either confirm or confound the rumour, resulting in 300,000 sales in the space of eight weeks in mid-1977. Later identification of Klaatu as Canadians John Woloschuk, Dee Long and Terry Draper saw interest in the group wane over the course of their next few albums, and they finally disbanded in 1982.

Beatleosity: A diversion on four aspects of musicological fabness

Starr's feel

Playing 4/4 rock drums is not technically tricky. (The classic, archetypal technique consists of playing quavers on a hi-hat; playing the first and third beat on the kick drum, and playing the second and fourth on the snare.) But great rock drumming goes beyond technique into the microsecond realm of **feel**. A scurrilous rumour persists that Ringo couldn't drum. This is clearly nonsense.

Certainly he couldn't, by his own admission, play a "mummy-daddy roll" (neither could Keith Moon) and some of his most memorable parts (the emphatic, flammed off-beat quavers on **Ticket To Ride**; the virtuoso crash/hi-hat/triplet tom-roll figure of **Come Together**) may have been McCartney's suggestions, but everything Ringo played was executed with a sleepy, solid, deeply felt groove. Phil Collins once characterized this as Ringo's "drag". Just compare the feel of The Beatles' **Drive My Car** with the 1993 McCartney band version on *Paul Is Live*: the former has a luxurious, contained, heavy rubber elasticity, the latter a brittle excitability.

Ringo's trademarks – including the half-open hi-hat sizzle of most early tracks, the semiquaver tom-roll into the verse of **Help!** and the chorus of **Wait** – are characterized by the same don't-hurry-me authority, as are his fills. His celebrated work on **Rain** is almost in a different time frame and his booming toms on **A Day In The Life** conduct a thrilling, arcane dialogue with the vocal.

Then there's the massive, trance-inducing cymbals-and-tom soundscape of **Tomorrow Never Knows**. Being left-handed apparently contributed to his idiosyncratic approach to the order in which the drums were hit; that, in tandem with his sound, makes his superb "backward" fills on **She Said She Said** almost, one suspects, inimitable.

Harrison's harmonic gloom

Why does George's Beatles-era oeuvre have such a pervading dourness? It's partly his voice (the inexpressive second cousin to the versatile Lennon and McCartney), partly the tone of some of his lyrics (the scroogey whinge of **Taxman**, or the sweeping, condemnatory allegory **Piggies**) but mainly, perhaps, it's his musical choices. **If I Needed Someone, Love You To** and **Within You Without You** all have an Indian-inspired drone as a pedal point with a steadfast exploration of a single mode (usually the melancholy mixolydian) for the melody. However inventive within his self-imposed limitations Harrison is – the twisting, relentless bridge of **Within You Without You** is particularly ingenious and **The Inner Light** achieves a charming tuneful optimism – inevitably the general effect can lean toward the monotonous.

Surprisingly, of the 23 Harrison songs recorded by The Beatles, only three (**Don't Bother Me, While My Guitar Gently Weeps** and **I Me Mine**) take an obviously downbeat minor key. Elsewhere, his shadowy musical tastes are otherwise expressed. A favourite of his, the diminished chord (darker than a minor chord with a flat fifth and double flat seventh as well as a flat third) dominates **Blue Jay Way**. In this case, the static bleakness of the diminished sound perfectly conveys the languor of the narrator and the inert haze of the "fog upon LA". The disturbing flat-ninth dissonance of **I Want To**

George at The Cavern, late 1961

Lennon's timeplay

On the one hand an unreconstructed rocker, and on the other a restless experimenter, John's duality is sometimes expressed in his instinctive subversion of even metre. Beats are dropped and added with guileless design, the formalities of which he'd cheerfully claim ignorance, preferring to admit that his "rhythm sense has always been a bit wild". It is significant that he preferred **Carl Perkins**' original disorientating 6/4 intro to **Blue Suede Shoes** (using it for his Toronto 1969 gig) to Elvis's more straightforward 4/4 intro.

There's a thoughtful impatience to Lennon's timeplay, a keenness to draw in the slack: witness the dropping into 3/4 for one bar in **Strawberry Fields Forever** to sing the title with a tumbling emphasis. Elsewhere, his time-tricksiness is appropriately meaningful. The 7/4 (or 4/4 then 3/4) verses of **All You Need Is Love** suit the relaxed urgency of his sermon and in **Good Morning Good Morning**, the dizzying timings of the verse (1x10 beats, 1x12 beats, 1x9 beats, 1x6 beats then 1x8 beats) suitably reflect the haphazard chaos of his rage; he has "nothing to say" but "it's OK". The odd emphases in the moments before the chorus of **I'm Only Sleeping** sound like dropped beats

Tell You is also derived from diminished harmony. Interestingly, the warmth and sweetness of his later Beatles compositions (**Long Long Long**, **Something** and **Here Comes The Sun**) heralded a new phase of Harrisongs; they were never quite as saturnine again.

but are actually strong chord-changes at mid-bar points, suggestive of the purposeful directionlessness of a dozy lie-in.

The hallucinatory nostalgia of the bridge of **She Said She Said**, with its two bars of 4/4 and nine even-crotchet bars of 3/4, is fittingly confusing, but Lennon's perplexing peak is reached on **Happiness Is A Warm Gun**: bars of 6/4 drop the initial 4/4 themes, the "I need a fix ..." section has an unpredictable 3/8 sway, "Mother Superior jumps the gun" in 9/4, and the final strain hits 4/4 with a 6/8 interlude. Little wonder the rhythm track needed nearly a hundred takes.

McCartney's bass parts

Always a bouncingly competent country rocker, by 1965 McCartney's bass playing began to come into its own. His performances on *Rubber Soul*, especially the medium-tempo rhythm-section speciality grooves (locked in with Starr at his peak) like **The Word** and **Drive My Car**, display an idiosyncratic but effective black-soul inflexion. He later loosened and developed that approach for his *tour de force*, **Rain**, lolloping and swaggering between low root octaves, fourths, fifths and flat sevenths with a shrewd high-root-fifth/low-root triplet figure on the second chorus. This bass-heavy recording, along with another supple achievement on **Paperback Writer**, was his first with a Rickenbacker (rather than the Hofner violin bass) and its bold style exploiting the bottom-end was much imitated.

"He's an egomaniac about everything else, but his bass playing he'd always been a bit coy about," commented Lennon. In fact, by *Pepper*, McCartney was taking his bass designs seriously enough to take up a whole precious track to record his part separately. **Getting Better** has characteristic high/low pedal points in the verse, and exquisitely restrained, between-beat harmonic commentary in the chorus implying myriad inversions of the chopping chords above. This, and the refusal of the bass to resolve the implied II–V progression of the "where it will go" section of **Fixing A Hole**, displayed a new sophistication, undoubtedly informed by his study of Brian Wilson's advanced work on *Pet Sounds*.

McCartney's playing was often at its best on others' material (when he was interested, that is: witness his sullen work on **Across The Universe** – seen in the *Let It Be* film – or on **Yer Blues**). His lines on Harrison's **Savoy Truffle** and Lennon's **Everybody's Got Something To Hide** have a real rock-soul verve and his binding lines on **Come Together** are full of inventive spontaneity. His almost too flashy lines on Harrison's **Something** provoked complaints from its composer suggesting that, on occasion, McCartney's eagerness to dazzle could result in the misdirection of his unarguably refined musicality.

Press conference quips 1964–66

Press: "How did you find America?"
John: "Turned left at Greenland."

Press: "What do you call that hairstyle?"
George: "Arthur."

Press: "What about this campaign in Detroit to stamp out The Beatles?"
Paul: "We're starting a campaign to stamp out Detroit."

Press: "How do you feel about a nightclub, Arthur, named after your hairstyle?"
George: "I was proud – until I saw the nightclub."

Press: "Ringo, you've done a lot of that, let's say, slapstick work in *Hard Day's Night*."
Ringo: "Let's say slapstick. One two three..."
The Beatles: "SLAPSTICK!"
Press: "Are you going to have a leading lady for the film you're about to make?"
Paul: "We're trying to get the Queen. She sells."

Press: "Do you wear wigs?"
John: "If we do, they must be the only ones with real dandruff."

Press: "Do you speak French?"
Paul: "Non."

Press: "Girls rushed toward my car because it had press identification and they thought I met you. How do you explain this phenomenon?"
John: "You're lovely to look at."

Press: "Were you worried about the oversized roughnecks who tried to infiltrate the airport crowd on your arrival?"
Ringo: "That was us.'

Press: "How does it feel to be putting on the whole world?"
Ringo: "We enjoy it."
Paul: "We aren't really putting you on."
George: "Well, just a bit."
John: "How does it feel to be put on?"

Press: "What do you do when you're cooped up in a hotel room between shows?"
George: "We ice skate."

Press: "Are you afraid military service might break up your careers?"
John: "No. There's no draft in England now. We're going to let you do our fighting for us."

A pre-gig press conference, Metropolitan Stadium in Minneapolis, August 1965

Press: "What would you do if the fans got past the police lines?"
George: "We'd die laughing."

Classic Beatles cover versions

Peter Sellers **A Hard Day's Night**

(1965; from *Legends Of The 20th Century*; EMI)

The ex-Goon turned respected comic actor intoned **A Hard Day's Night** in the pinched, declamatory style of Laurence Olivier's performance as Richard III. Wringing much double-entendre fun from Lennon's faintly suggestive text, Sellers performed it on the *Music Of Lennon & McCartney* TV special and had a #14 hit single with it in December 1965. (Five further previously unreleased, offbeat Beatle readings can be found on the four-CD set A *Celebration Of Sellers*.)

Joe Cocker **With A Little Help From My Friends**

(1968; from *With A Little Help From My Friends*; A&M)

Not so much interpretation as reinvention, Ringo's amiable swing from *Sgt Pepper* is turned into a full-blooded heavy gospel number thanks to Leon Russell's inspired arrangement, Cocker's blowtorch bellow and croon, and some superb backing vocals.

José Feliciano **In My Life**

(1968; from *Feliciano!*; RCA)

A supreme interpreter of Beatles songs, the blind Puerto Rican singer and guitar player cut several excellent Fab covers in the late 60s and early 70s, including **Here There And Everywhere**, **Blackbird**, **And I Love Her** and **Norwegian Wood** (all present on the deleted compilation *Sings And Plays The Beatles*). His relaxed yet soulful performances, lilting Latin arrangements and yearning voice highlighted emotions occasionally underplayed in The Beatles' own pop readings, especially the early songs. His best was perhaps this version of Lennon's nostalgic reverie, a version which alerted many new listeners to the song's true depths.

Al Green **I Want To Hold Your Hand**

(1968; from *Unchained Melodies*; Hi Records)

An early cut for Hi Records, and a flop single which lay in the vaults for many years, Green's irreverent but joyful reading retains almost nothing of the original, apart from the little bent guitar note between the lines of the verses, which are turned into urgent, pleading things à la **Otis Redding**, while horns carry the hook in the choruses. With hand-holding not the only physical act on the singer's mind, it may not have been a suitable choice of song for the future Rev. Green, but the simultaneously pious and lascivious singer has the wherewithal, as ever, to carry it off.

Richie Havens **Here Comes The Sun**

(1971; from *Alarm Clock* LP; currently available on *Resumé;* Rykodisc)

George's gentle, literal song struck a chord with black singers at the height of the civil rights struggle, the perfect metaphor for better times arriving. (Other notable versions include **Nina Simone**'s sweet, lullaby-like reading on a 1972 album of the same name.) This elated, upbeat campfire arrangement for acoustic guitar, pedal steel and bongos captures the Woodstock vibe Havens was famous for. A frequent and distinguished visitor to The Beatles catalogue, he featured several similarly arresting covers on his 1969 double album *Richard P. Havens 1983* (Verve).

Earth, Wind & Fire **Got To Get You Into My Life**

(1978; from *Sgt Pepper's Lonely Hearts Club Band OST*; Reprise)

Perhaps the single good thing to come from Robert Stigwood's useless 1978 film based on *Sgt Pepper* (starring **The Bee Gees**) was this super-hip cover from the masters of cosmic jazzy soul, EW&F. The song is completely reworked into a new masterpiece, incorporating a dazzling vocal arrangement and snazzy horn licks.

Frank Sinatra **Something**

(1979; from *Trilogy*; Reprise)

Frank had been singing a soft-rock version of **Something** since the early 70s but for the "Present" section of his *Past, Present and Future* triple vinyl album, he asked old pal **Nelson Riddle** to score it in the impressionist orchestral style of his classic 1958 album *Only The Lonely*. The result was a dramatic Beatles cover and certainly among Sinatra's more graceful encounters with post-1960s pop.

Siouxsie & the Banshees **Dear Prudence**

(1983; from *Best Of Siouxsie And The Banshees*; Polydor)

In their early live shows in the late 70s, when they were a punk group, they would stumble their way through a chaotic cover of **Helter Skelter**, a version of which appeared on their 1978 debut album *The Scream*. By 1983, their mature art-pop sound had resulted in some arresting records but no really big hits. This nightmarish cover was a notably powerful adaptation of a Beatles song to the sound and attitude of a new generation and was the group's biggest hit ever, reaching #3 in the UK.

Bobby McFerrin **From Me To You**

(1985; from *Spontaneous Inventions*; Blue Note)

A brilliant a cappella performance by the elastic-voiced jazz wit McFerrin. Not only does he sing the melody, but the bass line and percussive groove are somehow in simultaneous evidence too. It has to be heard to be believed, and McFerrin has taken a similarly astonishing approach to **Drive My Car** and **Blackbird**.

Diana Krall **And I Love Her**

(1995; from *I Got No Kick Against Modern Jazz*; GRP)

Jazz singer and pianist Diana Krall tenderly applies her Shirley Horn influenced sultry approach to McCartney's first mature melody with gorgeous results. A rolling acoustic trio groove at a leisurely tempo and an unhurried piano solo stretches the performance to over seven luxurious minutes.

The Black Keys **She Said, She Said**

(2002; from *The Big Come Up*; Alive)

If The Beatles had grown up in Akron, Ohio, and gone on to jam with North Mississippi blues legends such as Junior Kimbrough and **RL Burnside**, they might have sounded something like this. Dan Auerbach's creamy, soulful vocals, the overdriven, self-confessedly "medium fidelity" recording technique, and the nonchalant slide guitar give the track a gentle intensity that marks it as a superior modern Beatles cover.

Bizarre Beatles covers

The Beatles catalogue has attracted more than its fair share of grotesque covers, most of which are actually preferable to most attempts at a straight version, whether or not the intention was sincere or sardonic. Lovers of this kind of nonsense are particularly directed to the excellent *Exotic Beatles* albums on Exotic Records, now running to three volumes. There now follows a list of some of the most outré Beatles interpretations that, for one reason or another, will drop the jaw.

Bill Cosby **Sgt Pepper's Lonely Hearts Club Band**

(1968; currently available on *Glass Onion*; Warner Jazz)

On which the famed US comedian bellows the lyric like a silly uncle who has wandered, unsure of his role, onto an otherwise cooking Atlantic soul session featuring The Watts 103rd Street Rhythm Band. Which is about right.

William Shatner **Lucy In The Sky With Diamonds**

(1968; from *The Transformed Man* LP; currently available on *Spaced Out – The Best Of Leonard Nimoy & William Shatner*; MCA)

A work of stupendous pomp, in which Captain James T. Kirk recites **Lucy**'s lyric with hilariously hammy fervour. From an album made after *Star Trek* was cancelled and featuring similar inappropriate readings of Dylan and Shakespeare, Shatner's overcooked oeuvre is either ahead of its time and knowingly camp or misguided schlock. Either way, it commands an inevitable cult following. Recently voted Worst Beatles Cover Ever by viewers of digital TV channel Music Choice.

Cathy Berberian Ticket To Ride

(1970; from *Revolution* LP; currently available on *Exotic Beatles 3*; Exotica)

Legendarily elaborate classical singer Berberian (1925–83) expanded her repertoire beyond opera mid-career to sing experimental **John Cage** pieces, subtle parodies of bad salon singers and an entire album of Beatles covers, the long out-of-print *Revolution*, from which this track is the only available on CD. Archly warbling her soprano over a jaunty cod-baroque arrangement of Lennon's 1965 slo-mo classic, it's horribly amusing. For a while.

Arthur Mullard Yesterday

(1973; currently available on the album *Exotic Beatles 1*; Exotica)

An ex-boxer with a London-accented voice as smashed in as his face, Mullard was a popular comic actor on British TV in the 70s who also made monstrous records humorously exploiting his clueless vocal style. Though clearly forced rubbish, his mauling of McCartney's overexposed standard is a happy antidote to the thousands of solemn readings.

Nina Baden-Semper Step Inside Love

(1973; currently available on the album *All You Need Is Covers*; Castle)

The glamorous actress who found UK fame as part of the *Love Thy Neighbour* TV cast released a cash-in album called *Songs For Neighbours*. Ms Baden-Semper screech-whispers her way through McCartney's subtle melody in a hopeful, excruciating come-hither style, with only marginal attempts at tuning, tone or sense.

The Residents Beyond The Valley Of A Day In The Life

(1977; from the single *The Beatles Play The Residents and The Residents Play The Beatles*; currently available on *Third Reich And Roll*; East Side)

Naturally, The Residents begin their **A Day In The Life** with the song's epochal final chord. The San Franciscan pranksters have deconstructed Elvis, **Hank Williams** and Aaron Copland in their long career at the avant-garde coal-face; but this cunning, splattery, sonic collage of over twenty Beatles tunes is perhaps their *pièce de résistance* – more a four-minute summation of the Fabs' entire career than a mere cover. The version of **Flying** on the B-side is probably even weirder.

Laibach **Let It Be**

(1988; *Let It Be* LP; Mute)

Slovenian art-guerrillas Laibach produced a startlingly effective *kunstwerk* when they re-recorded the entire *Let It Be* album, barring the title track (and replacing **Maggie Mae** with a folk song of their own country). Their Wagner-goes-punk-techno approach reaps surprising dividends: **Get Back** is delivered in a stentorian, quasi-Nazi bark; **I've Got A Feeling** becomes a mass political rally; yet **Across The Universe**, sung by a female chorale over a synth drone and harpsichord, is undeniably beautiful. Extraordinary.

Fred Lonberg-Holm **Taxman**

(1992; from *Downtown Does The Beatles Live At The Knitting Factory*; Knitting Factory Works)

New York based avant-garde cellist uses George's *Revolver* opener as a jumping-off point for five minutes of his own fiery improvisational work. Witty, intense, unsettling.

Arto Lindsay, Mark Ribot and friends **Don't Let Me Down**

(1992; from *Downtown Does The Beatles Live At The Knitting Factory*; Knitting Factory Works)

Avant-rock luminaries join forces for a ramshackle reading full of hesitation, false entries and extraneous noise and scribble. It's a brilliant pastiche of The Beatles' own sloppy *Let It Be* era rehearsals (as seen in the film) and one of the funniest Fabs covers ever.

Jim Carrey **I Am The Walrus**

(1998; from George Martin's *In My Life*; Echo)

A wonderfully demented delivery of Lennon's surreal masterpiece, full of surprise and fresh phrasing from comic film actor Carrey who, on this evidence, can really sing. Producer George Martin's glossy rearrangement is terrific, making Carrey's **virtuoso lunacy** all the more enjoyable.

The great Beatlesong giveaway

The songs they wrote for other people

I'll Be On My Way (Lennon/McCartney)

Billy J. Kramer and The Dakotas

A Buddy Holly like McCartney song that made it to the B-side of Billy J. Kramer's debut single in April 1963. "That's Paul, through and through," remembered Lennon later. Never commercially recorded by the group, a Beatles version from June 1963 made it to the *Live At The BBC* CD in 1994.

Tip Of My Tongue (Lennon/McCartney)

Tommy Quickly

Brian Epstein did everything he could to launch Liverpool telephone engineer Tommy Quickly's singing career, including letting him record The Beatles' **No Reply** (which the singer botched, so it was never released). He debuted in August 1963 with this perky, McCartney-penned left-over (offered as a Beatles original in November 1962 but rejected by George Martin), which failed to chart anywhere. By 1965, the hit-free Quickly had retired from the music scene.

Bad To Me (Lennon/McCartney)

Billy J. Kramer and The Dakotas

Originally Lennon was as keen as McCartney to exploit their burgeoning reputation as made-to-order songsmiths, especially as fellow Liverpudlians Billy J. Kramer and The Dakotas had their first chart hit with Lennon's **Do You Want To Know A Secret** in May 1963. For a follow-up, Lennon devised this perkily competent dry-run of **If I Fell** (complete with a plaintive "prologue" verse and sophisticated cadences) while on a Spanish holiday with Brian Epstein. It hit #1 in the UK in August 1963, made #9 in the US and sold over a million copies worldwide.

Love Of The Loved (Lennon/ McCartney)

Cilla Black

A pre-Beatles McCartney tune that the group did at the Decca audition but never recorded commercially. Brian Epstein chose it to launch the career of former Cavern hat-check girl Cilla Black: "The Girl With The Bright Red Hair And The Jet Black Voice", as he presented her. Despite a brassy, beaty production courtesy of George Martin and a spirited delivery from Cilla, the song itself is evidently callow and the record peaked at only #35 in autumn 1963.

Hello Little Girl (Lennon/McCartney)

The Fourmost

Faintly inspired by memories of his mother singing Cole Porter's **You're The Top**, Lennon remembered **Hello Little Girl** as the first song he ever finished. Performed by The Quarry Men/Beatles as early as 1958, it appears on the Decca audition tape (and the *Anthology 1* CD) though was never recorded for release by them. Donated to another Epstein-managed Liverpool group, The Fourmost, five years after it was written – and long since dropped from The Beatles' set – it became The Fourmost's first hit, reaching #9 in autumn 1963.

I'll Keep You Satisfied (Lennon/ McCartney)

Billy J. Kramer and The Dakotas

A melodic, cheerfully suggestive ode written by McCartney for Billy J. Kramer and The Dakotas' third single, it reached #4 in the UK in November 1963.

I'm In Love (Lennon/McCartney)

The Fourmost

An old Lennon song became The Fourmost's second single and was a much subtler recording than their debut. Featuring dramatic chords and surprising dynamics, it peaked at #20 in the UK in winter 1963. "It sounds like me," said Lennon when asked about it in 1980, "[but] I don't remember a hell of a thing about it."

World Without Love (Lennon/McCartney)

Peter and Gordon

In early 1964, folk duo Peter and Gordon – comprising Jane Asher's brother Peter in partnership with Westminster school chum Gordon Waller – were preparing to record their debut single. He persuaded his sister's boyfriend, Paul McCartney, to write them a song and **World Without Love** came their way, a song whose first line – "Please lock me away" – always caused John Lennon great amusement. Set as a quasi-rumba, it was the sort of exotic "square" pop The Beatles, especially McCartney, could still turn their hand to, but were on the verge of phasing out of their act. The song hit #1 in both the UK and US in spring 1964 and made "British Invasion" stars of Peter and Gordon.

One And One Is Two (Lennon/McCartney)

The Strangers with Mike Shannon

Written in January 1964 in Paris by Lennon and McCartney for Billy J. Kramer. Lennon was unhappy with their efforts, judging that "Billy J's career is over when he gets this song." Billy agreed and passed on it, recording **Little Children** instead, a massive UK and US hit for him. **One And One Is Two** was recorded instead by The Strangers with Mike Shannon and released in May 1964 on Phillips, but wasn't a hit. A terrific bootleg of McCartney enthusiastically demoing the song in a George V Hotel room exists.

Nobody I Know (Lennon/McCartney)

Peter and Gordon

Featuring cascading 12-string guitar lines along with clichéd lyrics that would have been laughed out of Studio Two and a corny upward change of key, the song has got "give it to Peter and Gordon" all over it. McCartney duly did so and it hit #10 for them in June 1964, and got to #12 in the US.

Like Dreamers Do (Lennon/McCartney)

The Applejacks

An adept teenage McCartney composition that The Beatles were still performing into 1962 (it appears on *Anthology 1* as part of the Decca audition tapes) though they never recorded it for commercial release. Midlands group The Applejacks hit #20 in the UK with a version of it (McCartney's "love her"s had become "love you"s) in July 1964.

From A Window (Lennon/McCartney)

Billy J. Kramer and The Dakotas

After their worldwide smash hit with **Little Children**, Billy J. Kramer and The Dakotas reprised that record's distinctive military snare-drum figure for the arrangement of McCartney's winningly modest song. Originally written for Peter and Gordon – Lennon remembered it being from McCartney's "artsy period with Jane Asher" – it made a UK #10 and a US #23 in August 1964.

It's For You (Lennon/McCartney)

Cilla Black

After the disappointment of her Lennon/McCartney debut **Love Of The Loved**, Cilla Black had achieved two consecutive UK #1s with moody, slightly camp art-pop waltzes: Bacharach's **Anyone Who Had A Heart** and the soaring Italian melody **You're My World**. Cilla's fourth single, **It's For You**, is a fascinating, undervalued effort by McCartney to write in a similar style, featuring ambitious minor-key harmonic choices and irregular phrase lengths. If the #7 placing in September 1964 was a slight

Paul and "Our Cilla" rehearse Step Inside Love in 1968

commercial dip for Cilla, the song itself represented a stride or two forward for its composer.

I Don't Want To See You Again (Lennon/McCartney)

Peter and Gordon

The third of McCartney's offerings to Peter and Gordon, this vacuously neat little ditty didn't make the UK charts at all in October 1964 but reached #16 in the US.

That Means A Lot (Lennon/McCartney)

P.J. Proby

Recorded, botched and shelved by The Beatles during the *Help!* sessions, it was donated to steroidal crooner P.J. Proby, who was looking to reverse the slide in his chart profile. Despite a suitably brooding George Martin arrangement – a distinct improvement on The Beatles' efforts, heard in their uninspired state on *Anthology 2* – **That Means A Lot** stalled at #30 in the UK in autumn 1965.

Woman (Lennon/McCartney)

Peter and Gordon

The fourth and last McCartney song to be appropriated by Peter and Gordon, **Woman** is by far the best of the songs the Beatle gave the duo and reflects his late-1965 melodic maturity. Treated to a lush orch-pop production for P&G's January 1966 single, it was credited as being written by "Bernard Webb" in the UK and "A. Smith" in the US, a ruse of McCartney's to see if the song would make an impact without the Lennon/McCartney tag. It peaked at only #28 in the UK despite Paul letting the cat out of the bag soon after release.

Love In The Open Air **(McCartney)**

George Martin Orchestra

Composed by McCartney as part of his *Family Way* soundtrack (and the first time his work was given a solo credit), this poignant George Martin arranged theme didn't chart in mid-1967 but did win an **Ivor Novello** award. Used upon the entrance of the bride at McCartney's marriage to Heather Mills, it was also more widely aired as the pre-show music for McCartney's 2002/2003 tour.

Catcall **(McCartney)**

Chris Barber

A jazzily minor-key Paul McCartney instrumental written during the Quarry Men days and performed under the name **Catswalk**. It was recorded by Chris Barber's Jazz Band in 1967 with McCartney and Jane Asher adding wordless vocals. Released in October 1967, it failed to chart, despite a pleasing fade as the tune grinds down into "The Stripper" tempo.

Step Inside Love **(Lennon/McCartney)**

Cilla Black

Perhaps McCartney's most successful effort at Bacharachesque adult pop, it was composed for Cilla Black's 1968 TV series and became a #8 hit in the UK in June of that year. McCartney can be heard messing around with it on a September 1968 session with The Beatles on *Anthology 3*.

Thingumybob **(McCartney)**

Black Dyke Mills Band

A proficiently idiomatic, jolly brass-band march composed for McCartney as the theme to an LWT TV series starring Stanley Holloway and recorded in Bradford in April 1968. With an arrangement of **Yellow Submarine** on the flip-side, it was the second Apple single ever, released simultaneously with **Hey Jude** in September 1968, though it did not chart.

Goodbye **(Lennon/McCartney)**

Mary Hopkin

The spring of 1969 follow-up to Hopkin's McCartney-produced autumn 1968 smash hit **Those Were The Days**, Paul's folky pop song featured a sumptuously rich acoustic guitar sound and a sweet vocal from 18-year-old Mary. Peaking at #2 in the UK, it was the only McCartney song the Apple-signed singer did.

Sour Milk Sea (Harrison)

Jackie Lomax

George Harrison's pet project, getting Ringo, McCartney, Eric Clapton and singer Lomax together and producing a rocking song he wrote in India, similar in feel to his **Savoy Truffle**. One of the first four Apple singles released in late August 1968, it failed to chart, and was one more in a series of career disappointments for Lomax.

Penina (McCartney)

Carlos Mendes

This attractive doo-wop-style song was given to Portuguese recording artist Carlos Mendes by McCartney while on holiday in Portugal. Released only in that country in July 1969, The Beatles can be heard jamming on something similar during the January 1969 *Get Back* sessions (named **Appanina** on some bootleg releases).

Come And Get It (McCartney)

Badfinger

Written by Paul for Ringo's *Magic Christian* movie, this expertly, obliquely catchy pop song was demoed by McCartney in an hour before an Abbey Road session in June 1969 and recorded by Apple signings Badfinger almost note-for-note. Peaking at #4 in early 1970, it is considered by many to be the best Beatles song never recorded by The Beatles.

The best Beatles websites

There are hundreds. You can spend your whole life surfing Beatles sites, finding things you didn't know, rereading things you did, just because you can. And most sites contain their own links, so the fun need never stop. Of course, some of them are rubbish, but the following are pretty good for one reason or another.

The Official Beatles Website

www.beatles.com

The "official" site was originally built around the 27 tracks that made up the *1* release in 2000 but it now incorporates substantial microsites relating to a decade's worth of Beatles business: the *Anthology* and *First US Visit* DVDs, the *Let It Be...Naked*, *Capitol Albums*, *Love*, the 2009 remasters, and the *Beatles Rock Band* game. A diverting, if a little corporate and over-designed, Beatles cyber-experience.

The Official Solo Websites

www.johnlennon.com
www.paulmccartney.com
www.georgeharrison.com
www.ringostarr.com

Massively developed since their early days, these handsome sites are the places to go for the best solo news and official merchandise. The Lennon site is generous with streaming video (mostly of the promo films) as is the Starr site, with Ringo filming video updates for the fans every few months. Among the UNICEF information and the discography, the Harrison site contains several useful microsites about *Brainwashed*, the Concert For Bangladesh and George's Material World Foundation. The McCartney site is light on history, concentrating instead on current plugs and activities, of which there are many.

Beatle Links

www.beatleslinks.net

Links to over 1000 wide-ranging Beatles sites, categorized and rated. A good place to start getting a feel for the range of Fab-related cyberspace.

Beatles Ultimate Experience

www.beatlesinterviews.org

An amazing database of over 100 full-length interviews from the 1960s. They are arranged in chronological order and searchable by keyword. One of the best Beatles resources on the web.

The Internet Beatles Album

www.beatlesagain.com

A multi-layered site, fun to explore and packed full of information including Beatle Myths, The Internet Beatles Reference Library (an impressive series of articles retrieved from the old rec. music.Beatles newsgroup) and Today In Beatles History, a searchable day-to-day diary of events.

Beatlemoney

www.beatlemoney.com

Good searchable site that extracts quotations from a range of printed sources covering the financial matters of Lenmac, Northern, Apple, etc. Ranging from legal affidavits to facsimiles of NEMS contracts to photocopies of cleaning bills, there's much of interest here.

Rockin' Beatles – unheard

In chronological order of original or influential artist release, early live-show covers played in Liverpool and Hamburg but which were never recorded, demoed, bootlegged or broadcast.

"How High The Moon" (Les Paul & Mary Ford, 1951)
"Beautiful Dreamer" (Slim Whitman, 1954)
"Moonglow" (McGuire Sisters, 1956)
"True Love" (Bing Crosby & Grace Kelly, 1956)
"Love Me Tender" (Elvis Presley, 1956)
"Begin The Beguine" (Pat Boone, 1957)
"Come Go With Me" (Del-Vikings, 1957)
"Peggy Sue" (Buddy Holly, 1957)
"Everyday" (Buddy Holly, 1957)
"Maybe Baby" (Buddy Holly, 1958)
"Good Golly Miss Molly" (Little Richard, 1958)
"Summertime" (Gene Vincent, 1958)
"Up A Lazy River" (Gene Vincent, 1958)
"Love Of My Life" (Everly Brothers, 1959)
"Over The Rainbow" (Gene Vincent, 1959)
"Raining In My Heart" (Buddy Holly, 1959)
"September Song" (Johnny Ray, 1959)
"Crackin' Up" (Bo Diddley, 1959)
"Apache" (The Shadows, 1960)
"Are You Lonesome Tonight" (Elvis Presley, 1960)
"I Wonder If I Care As Much" (Everly Brothers, 1960)
"Cathy's Clown" (Everly Brothers, 1960)
"Darktown Strutter's Ball" (Joe Brown & the Bruvvers, 1960)
"Don't Let The Sun Catch You Crying" (Ray Charles, 1960)
"Harry Lime Theme" (Chet Atkins, 1960)
"Shakin' All Over" (Johnny Kidd and the Pirates, 1960)
"It's Now Or Never" (Elvis Presley, 1960)
"Walk Don't Run" (The Ventures, 1960)
"Mama Said" (The Shirelles, 1961)
"More Than I Can Say" (Bobby Vee, 1961)
"Hit The Road Jack" (Ray Charles, 1961)
"If You Gotta Make A Fool Of Somebody" (James Ray, 1961)
"Runaway" (Del Shannon, 1961)
"Stand By Me" (Ben E. King, 1961)
"September In The Rain" (Dinah Washington, 1961)
"Will You Still Love Me Tomorrow" (The Shirelles, 1961)
"The Loco-Motion" (Little Eva, 1962)
"Sharing You" (Bobby Vee, 1962)
"A Picture Of You" (Joe Brown and the Bruvvers, 1962)

Mersey Beat

www.mersey-beat.com

An excellent searchable archive of the articles that originally appeared in Bill Harry's *Mersey Beat* music paper 1961–65, including Lennon's "Beatcomber" pieces, plus some new pieces by Harry.

The Beatles Help In The World

beatleshelp.topcities.com/help.htm

A remarkable site devoted almost exclusively to all international releases of the *Help!* album. Interesting not so much for the bizarrely comprehensive content (beware the accompanying synthesized versions of your *Help!* favourites as you admire the Chilean label scans) as evidence of what some people will do with their time.

From Abbey Road To Cyberspace

www.cyber-beatles.com

Useful source of up-to-date news and reviews of the solo and post-split Beatles projects.

Beatles Behind The Scenes

www.whizzo.ca/beatles/bts/bts.html

A diverting series of conversation transcriptions taken from tapes of Beatles sessions,

Fab memorabilia

Here are some examples of Beatles memorabilia recently sold at UK and US auction rooms and eBay – and what they went for:

Hand-painted bass drum-skin used on the *Sgt Pepper* cover: £541,250

Signed copy of the management deal The Beatles signed with Brian Epstein in 1962: £122,850.

John Lennon's leather necklace, worn in 1967/68 £117,250

Vox Kensington guitar, custom-made in 1966, played by Lennon on "Hello, Goodbye" and George Harrison on "I Am The Walrus": £117,250

John Lennon's 1953 Austin Princess hearse, driven in the *Imagine* video: $150,000

Four baseballs signed by John, Paul, George and Ringo: £49,000

John Lennon's white suit, worn on the cover of *Abbey Road*: $118,000

Letter, dated April 18, 1969, to John Eastman forbidding him to "hold [himself] out" as representative of The Beatles, signed by John, George and Ringo: £48,000

Concert poster of a show on April 27, 1963, at Memorial Hall, Northwich: £7,767

John Lennon's jacket worn in *Imagine*: $32,000

Rare NEMS Beatles Record Player from 1964: $4,125

Bazooka Bubble Gum Wax Box, 36 unopened packs in original box: $4050

Beatles Bar ice-cream box: $1230

Three original (used) Beatles tickets, from concerts in 1964 and 1966: $265

Set of four original Remco Beatles dolls with instruments: $270 often involving Lennon having trouble get-tingsomething right. As the group try to record "Think For Yourself" he says, "Bear with me or have me shot."

Beatles Beatles Beatles

members.tripod.com/~taz4158/beatles.html

A good selection of articles and rare recordings available as streaming audio.

Donald Sauter's Beatles Pages

www.geocities.com/donaldsauter/index.html#beatles

Several interesting articles (including a call for a Wikipedia-style Beatles resource), several very stupid ones (including a list of all Beatles mentions in *National Geographic* magazine) and a massive quiz called Beatle Significa.

YouTube

www.youtube.com

An astonishing treasure trove of easily accessible, previously very elusive video and audio clips. Start with "The Beatles extremely rare footage" and you'll still be sitting there two hours later.

Beatles Christmas records

Every Christmas, between 1963 and 1970, members of the Beatles UK fan club received a flexi-disc message specially recorded for them by their heroes. Friendly, unfettered and obliquely reflective of the mood of the band as years passed, they provide a fascinating glimpse of the group from another angle, one most Beatles fans won't have seen. Produced by George Martin (until 1968), the early discs featured giggly "happy crimble and a merry new year" wishes, out-of-tune carols with Lennonized words, a cheerfully slaughtered version of "Yesterday" (the pay-off line of which becomes "Bless you all on Christmas Day") and increasingly outlandish, Goons-ish voices.

In 1966 and 1967, The Beatles went to the trouble of creating very odd six-minute playlets, complete with narrator, dialogue, songs and sound effects. While the early discs had the Fabs cavorting around the microphone together, the 1968 and 1969 discs (unsurprisingly, in retrospect) feature contributions recorded separately, with Lennon's pieces being particularly barbed and edgy. Yoko appears more on the 1969 disc than Paul does. The final disc in 1970 compiled the previous seven discs, a collection released briefly in the US on vinyl as *The Beatles' Christmas Record*. Though most of the material is commercially unavailable, the 1967 song "Christmas Time Is Here Again" appeared as the B-side of the "Free As A Bird" single in 1994.

Index

A

B

C

D

J

K

L

T

U

V

W

X

Y

Z

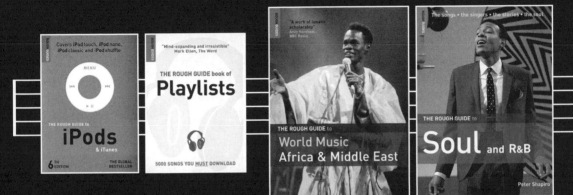

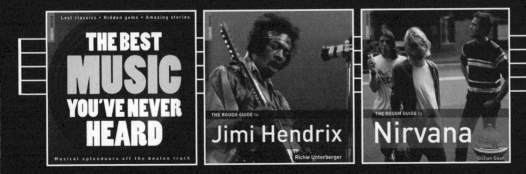

ROUGH GUIDES

Get Connected!

"Brilliant! ... the unmatched leader in its field"

Sunday Times, London, reviewing The Rough Guide to the Internet